VOID
Library of
Davidson College

BECOMING
A MIGHTY VOICE

BECOMING A MIGHTY VOICE

Conflict and Change in the United Furniture Workers of America

Daniel B. Cornfield

RUSSELL SAGE FOUNDATION / NEW YORK

The Russell Sage Foundation

The Russell Sage Foundation, one of the oldest of America's general purpose foundations, was established in 1907 by Mrs. Margaret Olivia Sage for "the improvement of social and living conditions in the United States." The foundation seeks to fulfill this mandate by fostering the development and dissemination of knowledge about the political, social, and economic problems of America. It conducts research in the social sciences and public policy, and publishes books and pamphlets that derive from this research.

The Board of Trustees is responsible for oversight and the general policies of the Foundation, while administrative direction of the program and staff is vested in the President, assisted by the officers and staff. The President bears final responsibility for the decision to publish a manuscript as a Russell Sage Foundation book. In reaching a judgment on the competence, accuracy, and objectivity of each study, the President is advised by the staff and selected expert readers. The conclusions and interpretations in Russell Sage Foundation publications are those of the authors and not of the Foundation, its Trustees, or its staff. Publication by the Foundation, therefore, does not imply endorsement of the contents of the study.

BOARD OF TRUSTEES
Gary MacDougal, Chair

Robert McCormick Adams	Peggy C. Davis	Howard Raiffa
Anne Pitts Carter	Patricia King	Harold Tanner
Joel E. Cohen	Gardner Lindzey	Eric Wanner
Philip E. Converse	James G. March	William Julius Wilson

Library of Congress Cataloging-in-Publication Data

Cornfield, Daniel B.
    Becoming a mighty voice : conflict and leadership change in the United Furniture Workers of America / Daniel B. Cornfield.
       p.   cm.
    Includes bibliographical references.
    ISBN 0-87154-200-5 (alk. paper)
    1. United Furniture Workers of America—History.   I. Title.
HD6515.F92U53 1989
331.88′184′0097309043—dc20
                                                                                                      89-70192
                                                                                                          CIP

Copyright © 1989 by Russell Sage Foundation. All rights reserved. Printed in the United States of America. No part of this publication may be reproduced, stored in a retrieval system, or transmitted, in any form or by any means, electronic, mechanical, photocopying, recording, or otherwise, without the prior written permission of the publisher.

The paper used in this publication meets the minimum requirements of American National Standard for Information Sciences—Permanence of Paper for Printed Library Materials, ANSI Z39.48-1984.

10 9 8 7 6 5 4 3 2 1

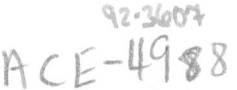

To Hedy

Contents

	Preface and Acknowledgments	*ix*
1	Union Leadership in Transition	*1*
2	Local Unions and National Leaders: Institutional Bases of Ethnic and Gender Leadership Succession	*29*
3	Building a Furniture Industrial Union: The UFWA's Formative Years, 1932–1950	*65*
4	Maintaining the Union: The UFWA's Period of Stability, 1950–1970	*121*
5	Revitalizing the Union: The Ascent of Minorities and Women During the UFWA's Period of Decline, 1970–1987	*155*
6	Status Conflict and Leadership Change	*243*
	Subject Index	*267*
	Name Index	*283*
	Index of Unions	*289*

Preface and Acknowledgments

The integration of ethnic minorities and women into the leadership of institutions endures as a prominent social issue in the United States. The political and legislative achievements of the civil rights and women's movements have contributed to the emergence of minorities and women as leaders during the post–World War II era. However, these achievements have conflicted with the interests of entrenched groups who have attempted continuously to undermine the inroads that minorities and women have made into leadership positions. Despite these inroads, persistent ethnic and gender conflict frustrates the realization of integration.

Labor unions are among the many institutions that have served as arenas of ethnic and gender conflict over access to leadership positions. As labor union memberships diversified during this century, ethnic and gender groups of workers have increasingly vied with one another for the leadership of their unions, especially since the civil rights era of the 1960s. The democratic structure of labor unions—unions may be seen as private representative democracies—is the context, complete with formally constituted convention and officer election procedures, within which ethnic and gender conflicts over leadership have occurred. Unlike corporations and other organizations whose internal deliberations are often not open to public scrutiny, labor unions, as formally democratic organizations, have sometimes been the scene of visible factionalism among caucuses of ethnic and gender groups. Moreover, civil rights organizations associated with the labor movement, such as the Coalition of Black Trade Unionists and the Coalition of Labor Union Women, founded in 1973 and 1974, respectively, actively foster the mobilization of minority and women union members in order to integrate labor union leadership. During the last quarter-century, minorities and women have made significant inroads into, but continue to be underrepresented in, union leadership positions.

The question of union leadership integration; that is, the conditions that promote and retard integration, arises with the longstanding concerns of two strains of sociological thought about the fate of worker self-organization in industrial society. First, the triumph of hierarchical bureaucracy over democracy is the longstanding concern of Robert Michels' "iron law of oligarchy." Formally democratic organization, according to the iron law, inevitably degenerates into de facto oligarchy as an organization increases in size. With growth, a democratic organization such as a labor union becomes more hierarchical and spawns an expert leadership which, monopolizing the means of communication within the organization, perpetuates its control of an inert membership. The second longstanding concern is over Werner Sombart's question, "Why is there no socialism in the United States?" Among the many answers given to Sombart's question is the status diversity of the United States working class. According to this perspective, workers fail to unify politically because they are hopelessly divided among themselves by ethnicity, gender, skill level, occupation, income, and other dimensions of social status.

Together, these two strains of thought suggest that the integration of new social groups into union leadership positions is unlikely to occur because entrenched leadership groups will not relinquish their control to other groups, much less to those whose social backgrounds differ from their own. The two traditions address the forces that perpetuate social segregation but neglect those that promote the integration of new social groups into union leadership positions.

Becoming a Mighty Voice is a sociological analysis of the forces that both promote and retard the integration of new social groups into union leadership positions. The analysis builds on a third tradition of sociological thought about the fate of worker self-organization in industrial society. This tradition, described in Chapter 1, has been developed by several scholars from diverse theoretical perspectives, who have portrayed internal union politics as a dynamic, variable process. In this approach, leadership stability is no more likely to occur than is leadership change. From this perspective, leadership stability and change depend on changing economic conditions, the availability of resources that are relevant to the mobilization of factions, inevitable membership frustration with and opposition toward dictatorial leaders, and the like. This tradition of viewing union politics dynamically is more helpful than the traditions that have evolved from Michels and Sombart for addressing the question of union leadership integration, if only because it treats leadership as a variable process oscillating between stability and change.

The dynamic approach to the internal union political process, however, has addressed neither the question of union leadership integration nor the impact of the relationship between unions and employers on union leadership change. Given that the chief mission of unions is to wrest improved employment and work conditions from employers by organizing workers into unions, and that employers, through their ongoing efforts to identify new, cheap, non-union sources of labor, affect the social composition of union memberships, it is essential to analyze how changes in the relationship between unions and employers generate union leadership integration or perpetuate segregation.

I induce a theory of union leadership change in Chapter 6 from the case of the United Furniture Workers of America (UFWA). No claim is made that the UFWA is a microcosm or representative of all labor unions in the United States. Indeed, the UFWA case is a deviant one because the UFWA has integrated its national leadership, both ethnically and by gender, in addition to experiencing a long period of leadership stability, as shown in Chapters 1 and 2. Moreover, UFWA leadership integration and factionalism between status groups occurred during the formative and decline periods of UFWA history, discussed in Chapters 3 and 5, respectively, while no integration occurred during a period of membership stabilization, as analyzed in Chapter 4. Furthermore, the UFWA history is a complete one. From its roots in the Communist party's Trade Union Unity League in the early 1930s, the UFWA was established by the Committee for Industrial Organization in 1937; grew through the late 1940s; stabilized during the 1950s and 1960s; and declined during the 1970s and 1980s, merging into the International Union of Electronic Workers (IUE) as a division of the IUE in 1987. The case of the UFWA, then, permits an analysis of the conditions that promote and retard union leadership integration over the diverse eras—growth, stability, and decline—of a union history.

I first encountered the UFWA while participating with the UFWA in a coalition of civil rights activists, feminists, trade unionists, and democratic socialists who were organizing a community speakout against the Reagan administration in 1981 in Nashville, the location of international UFWA headquarters. After the speakout and another anti-Reagan demonstration in 1982, I met later that year with UFWA President Carl Scarbrough who, desiring a written history of the union, granted me permission to conduct a study of the UFWA. I am deeply and gratefully indebted to Carl for granting me access not only to the union, but also to past issues of the *Furniture Workers Press,* UFWA convention proceedings, UFWA membership and financial data, and the union's photocopying facilities, all of which are housed in the UFWA archives in Nashville and which I relied on heavily in mustering the empirical evidence for this book. I am also indebted to Nilda Villar, assistant to Carl Scarbrough, who guided me patiently and generously through the archives and facilitated my retrieval of the data.

Carl and Nilda also helped me to arrange personal interviews with several current and retired UFWA leaders and members and four high-ranking IUE officials. The 85 interviews I conducted with 63 people, in their homes and union halls, are another important source of data in this study. Together, the people whom I interviewed represented the ethnic, gender, occupational, geographical, and ideological diversity of the UFWA leadership, as well as diverse leadership ranks and offices; and their age diversity allowed me to interview them about different eras of UFWA history. To all of the people whom I interviewed, and they are acknowledged in footnotes throughout the book, I am grateful for their sharing with me their insights, memories, feelings, and intense dedication to their union and to the labor movement. I am especially grateful to Max Perlow and Abraham Zide, founding members of the UFWA, for providing me with original documents about the origins and formation of the UFWA.

In the academic realm, Ivar Berg, Seymour Martin Lipset, and Ruth Milkman made thorough and thoughtful comments on the entire manuscript. Mayer Zald provided me with helpful comments on sociological theory. Several graduate students in the sociology department at Vanderbilt University performed superb research assistance. They are Diane Bates, Carolyn Breda, Deborah Carter, H. B. Cavalcanti, Kathleen Kitzmiller, Mark Leners, and Judy Maynard. Linda Willingham expertly typed the entire manuscript. I am grateful to all of these people for helping me to bring the work to publication.

Carl Barsky of the U.S. Bureau of Labor Statistics (BLS) kindly provided me with unpublished BLS data and rare BLS publications on the furniture manufacturing industry which supplemented the published BLS and U.S. Census data incorporated in this book.

For financial support, I am gratefully indebted to the Vanderbilt University Research Council, the Vanderbilt Institute for Public Policy Studies, and most of all, to the Russell Sage Foundation.

Finally, Hedy Weinberg, my wife, made rigorous editorial commentary on the whole manuscript and shared my excitement in writing this book.

DANIEL B. CORNFIELD

1
Union Leadership in Transition

United in the new movement for industrial unionism, workers would "develop a mighty voice" for eradicating "some of the injustices that exist under our present economic system."[1] These words of Morris Muster, president of the United Furniture Workers of America, rallied the delegates to the founding convention of the Furniture Workers in 1939. They also expressed the growing desire of factory workers in many mass production industries during the 1930s to unite, regardless of their craft, occupation, and skill level, in industrywide or industrial unions. The new movement for industrial unionism, reflected in the establishment of the Committee for Industrial Organization in 1935, had emerged in conflict with the prevailing craft unionism of the American Federation of Labor, which had emphasized the organization of skilled craft workers into separate craft unions. The birth of industrial unionism constituted an effort to unify workers of diverse skill levels in order to improve the livelihoods of all workers in an industry.

The movement for industrial unionism would not be the last effort to unify workers of diverse social statuses, being one phase in a cycle of

---

[1] *Proceedings of the First Constitutional Convention of the United Furniture Workers of America—CIO,* Rockford, IL, February 13–17, 1939, p. 26.

recurring division and reunification among workers. Since the late 1960s, black, Hispanic, and women workers, the new factory workforce, have contended with white male trade unionists for greater representation in the labor movement and have begun to ascend the hierarchy of union offices during the 1970s and 1980s. Occurring in the wake of the civil rights and women's movements, the mobilization of ethnic minorities and women in the labor movement has been expressed in the establishment of the Coalition of Black Trade Unionists in 1973 and the Coalition of Labor Union Women in 1974.

Social stratification and status conflict among workers is one answer that has been given to the question posed by Werner Sombart in 1906, "Why is there no socialism in the United States?"[2] Notwithstanding the absence of socialism in the United States, the labor movement has periodically wrestled with status conflict among workers by attempting to unify established and emerging worker groups within its ranks. Each of the worker insurgencies, both that of the emerging, non-skilled, factory workforce during the 1930s and that of the new factory workforce of minorities and women during the 1970s and 1980s, was a conflict between an established, higher-status group and an emerging, lower-status group in the labor movement. In both cases, the labor movement attempted to unify itself as the emerging group mobilized for greater representation and participation in the governance of labor unions. Union leadership change, that is, the entry of new social groups into elective union offices, is part of the recurring effort of a union to reunify a membership that has become diversified, stratified, and factionalized.

This book is a sociological analysis of union leadership change: why status conflict recurs in the labor movement and new leadership groups emerge as union officers. The half century of recurring status conflict, leadership change, and unity in the United Furniture Workers of America illustrates how status conflict develops inside unions and generates a change in the social composition of elected union leaders.

The recurrence of status conflict and union leadership change stems from the periodic entry of new, low-wage, non-union workers into an industry. The entry of new workers, in turn, results from the adversarial relationship between unions and employers. Unions and employers pursue divergent ends, the former attempting to improve worker livelihoods through unionization, and the latter attempting to minimize labor costs of production. As unions organize workers, employers search for new, non-

---

[2] Werner Sombart, *Why Is There No Socialism in the United States?* (1906; reprint, White Plains, NY: M. E. Sharpe, 1976); William Form, *Divided We Stand: Working-Class Stratification in America* (Urbana, IL: University of Illinois Press, 1985); Seymour Martin Lipset, "Why No Socialism in the United States?" in *Sources of Contemporary Radicalism*, eds., Seweryn Bialer and Sophia Sluzar (Boulder, CO: Westview Press, 1977), pp. 31–149.

union workers. The union, then, typically recruits members whose wages and social status are lower than that of the existing membership, generating status conflict in the union. Patterns of union leadership change have corresponded to changes made by employers in the social character of the workforce.

Leadership Change in Unions

Changes in the social characteristics of union leaders are partly associated with changing characteristics in the working class and the geographical extension of industrialization. According to Fink's survey of labor leaders, for example, the percentage of foreign-born leaders declined from approximately 36 percent to less than 4 percent between 1900 and 1976, especially with the reduction in immigration after World War I. As the course of industrialization and unionization shifted southward from the Middle Atlantic and midwestern regions, labor leaders who were born in southern and border states came to account for almost one-third of labor leaders between 1900 and 1976.[3]

Despite the rapid increase in women's labor force participation and the growing proportions of women and minority union members, women and minorities continue to be underrepresented in national union leadership positions. Between 1970 and 1987, the percentage of white women union members increased from 17.8 percent to 27.0 percent; the percentage of black women increased from 3.7 percent to 6.3 percent; the percentage of black male union members declined slightly from 8.7 percent to 8.2 percent; and the percentage of white male members declined from 69.9 percent to 55.6 percent.[4] Little information is available about the racial and gender traits of union leaders. The most comprehensive survey was taken by the U.S. Commission on Civil Rights in 1978–1979 of the twelve largest non-referral unions (unions that do not provide a job referral function for their members). White men accounted for over 90 percent of the national union officers. In local unions, 12.6 percent of the offices were filled by white women, 8.5 percent by black women, and 12.3 percent by black men.[5] The Coalition of Labor Union Women surveyed the gender traits of national union officers in the seventeen largest labor organizations in 1979. The number of women officers exceeded 50 percent in two

---

[3] Gary Fink, ed., *Biographical Dictionary of American Labor* (Westport, CT: Greenwood Press, 1984), p. 71; Form, *Divided We Stand*, p. 203.

[4] U.S. Department of Labor, Bureau of Labor Statistics, *Selected Earnings and Demographic Characteristics of Union Members, 1970,* Report 417 (Washington, DC: Government Printing Office, 1972), p. 6; idem, *Employment and Earnings* 35 (January 1988): 222.

[5] U.S. Commission on Civil Rights, *Nonreferral Unions and Equal Employment Opportunity* (Washington, DC: Government Printing Office, 1982), pp. 95, 97.

organizations with a majority of women in their memberships (American Nurses Association and National Education Association), ranged between 15 percent and 25 percent in three of the seventeen organizations, and was less than 8 percent in eleven of the labor organizations.[6] In a follow-up study of the same seventeen organizations, Baden found that the percentage of women officers had increased in eight of the organizations by 1985. The percentage of women officers in the fourteen organizations reporting 1985 data was less than 8 percent in five of the organizations, from 8 percent to 18 percent in seven of the organizations, and in excess of 32 percent in the rest. According to Hoyman and Stallworth, blacks occupy an increasing number of executive board seats in several large unions, including the Automobile Workers, the Teachers, the Steel Workers, and the State, County and Municipal Employees.[7]

Inroads made by women and minorities have been facilitated not only by their growing presence in the labor movement but also by the civil rights and women's movements. Both movements have generated organizations within the labor movement that have endeavored to open the doors of union offices to women and minorities, encouraged them to seek office, and created greater awareness in the labor movement about civil rights issues. These include the Coalition of Black Trade Unionists and the Coalition of Labor Union Women mentioned earlier.[8]

The few inroads made by minorities and women into union leadership constitute an instance of increased social integration within the organized working class. Given that most unions are affiliated with the American Federation of Labor–Congress of Industrial Organizations (AFL-CIO), increased social integration has begun to occur not only within unions but also within the larger labor movement, as minority and women representatives of national unions participate increasingly in AFL-CIO affairs.

However, theories of working class stratification tend to emphasize the persistence of stratification and occupational segregation within the working class, despite the beginnings of social integration in the leader-

---

[6] Coalition of Labor Union Women, *Absent from the Agenda* (Washington, DC: Coalition of Labor Union Women, 1980), Table 5.

[7] Naomi Baden, "Developing an Agenda: Expanding the Role of Women in Unions," *Labor Studies Journal* 10 (Winter 1986): 238; Michele Hoyman and Lamont Stallworth, "Participation in Local Unions: A Comparison of Black and White Members," *Industrial and Labor Relations Review* 40 (April 1987): 324. Also see Linda LeGrande, "Women in Labor Organizations: Their Ranks Are Increasing," *Monthly Labor Review* 101 (August 1978): 8–14.

[8] Philip Foner, *Organized Labor and the Black Worker 1619–1981* (New York: International Publishers, 1981), pp. 432–433; idem, *Women and the American Labor Movement: From World War I to the Present* (New York: Free Press, 1980), p. 509; Alice Cook, Val Lorwin, and Arlene Kaplan Daniels, eds., *Women and Trade Unions in Eleven Industrialized Countries* (Philadelphia: Temple University Press, 1984), pp. 299–300; Ruth Milkman, "Women Workers, Feminism and the Labor Movement since the 1960s," in *Women, Work and Protest*, ed., Ruth Milkman (Boston: Routledge & Kegan Paul, 1985), p. 301.

ship of the labor movement, slow and infrequent though this process might be. Sociologist William Form, countering the argument that technological change deskills and homogenizes the working class, maintained that industrialization has been accompanied by increased social differentiation of the working class. An increasingly complex occupational division of labor, he claimed, has tended to stratify workers by skill level and income. Unions contribute to this stratification by achieving higher wages than those of non-union workers, although Form also demonstrated that wage disparity among unionized workers is lower than that among non-union workers. Similarly, neo-Marxian and institutional economists argue that economic and labor market segmentation have stratified the working class. Unevenness in the emergence of the large corporation among industries and firms has bifurcated the economy into "core" and "periphery" segments and the labor market into corresponding "primary" and "secondary" segments. The large, unionized, capital-intensive, oligopolistic firms and industries of the core, claim these economists, maintain employment conditions such as wages, fringe benefits, and career opportunities that are superior to those of the small, non-union, labor-intensive firms of the competitive industries on the economic periphery. With little or no mobility between primary and secondary labor markets, the stratified and segmented working class is incapable of developing a unified political voice.[9]

For Marxist-feminists, male-dominated craft unions of skilled workers are one of several forces that have contributed to the maintenance of occupational sex segregation. According to Hartmann and others, the segregation of women and men in different, as well as differentially rewarded, occupations has resulted partially from cultural beliefs and stereotypes about men and women; from employer discrimination in hiring and making job assignments; from sex typing of occupations; from institutional barriers to job mobility, such as seniority rules for making job assignments; and from informal barriers to employment, including male co-worker hostility toward women who are employed in traditionally "male" jobs and other features of on-the-job interpersonal relations that inhibit women from seeking, as well as being recruited for, jobs that have been traditionally dominated by men. Craft unions, according to Hartmann, have reinforced occupational sex segregation by refusing to admit women

---

[9] Form, *Divided We Stand*; David Gordon, Richard Edwards, and Michael Reich, *Segmented Work, Divided Workers* (Cambridge: Cambridge University Press, 1982); Suzanne Berger and Michael Piore, *Dualism and Discontinuity in Industrial Societies* (Cambridge: Cambridge University Press, 1980); Daniel Cornfield, "Political Consequences of Economic Segmentation," *Contemporary Sociology* 16 (March 1987): 146–151; Richard Apostle, Don Clairmont, and Lars Osberg, "Economic Segmentation and Politics," *American Journal of Sociology* 91 (January 1986): 905–931.

as union members and, hence, into the male-dominated skilled trades, an expression of the long-standing tradition of patriarchy in capitalist society. Class conflict, claimed Hartmann, has provoked this expression of patriarchy in the labor market. As employers attempted to erode the bargaining strength of unionized craftsmen by hiring low-wage, non-union, women workers, the patriarchal craft unions responded by denying union membership to, rather than uniting with, women workers.[10]

Several writers have written about the role of unions, racism, and other factors that have perpetuated occupational race segregation and limited minority access to the labor movement, creating a castelike "split labor market," as Bonacich put it, and a "dual racial labor system," in Hill's terms. Despite the enactment of the Civil Rights Act of 1964, which banned employment discrimination by race, sex, and other criteria, employer racism has perpetuated occupational race segregation in much the same fashion that sexism and patriarchy have perpetuated occupational sex segregation. Also, craft unions of skilled, white, male workers have continued to deny union membership to blacks, and it was only after public protest during the late 1960s that blacks began to be admitted to these unions. Industrial unions of mass production factory workers have often been lax in sponsoring the promotion of minority members into the employer-operated apprenticeship-training programs for skilled journeyman factory jobs. Institutional barriers established through collective bargaining, such as seniority-based job assignment systems, have also prevented black factory workers from being promoted to higher-status jobs and have conflicted with the deployment of affirmative-action criteria for making job assignments. Furthermore, it was mainly after the protests of black union members during the late 1960s that blacks were elected to leadership positions in mass production labor unions.[11]

[10] Heidi Hartmann, "Capitalism, Patriarchy, and Job Segregation by Sex," in *Women and the Workplace,* eds., Martha Blaxall and Barbara Reagan (Chicago: University of Chicago Press, 1976), pp. 137–169; Heidi Hartmann and Barbara Reskin, eds., *Women's Work, Men's Work* (Washington, DC: National Academy Press, 1986); Alice Kessler-Harris, " 'Where Are the Organized Women Workers?' " *Feminist Studies* 3 (Fall 1975): 92–110; Julie Matthaei, *An Economic History of Women in America* (New York: Schocken, 1982).

[11] Edna Bonacich, "Advanced Capitalism and Black-White Relations in the United States: A Split Labor Market Interpretation," *American Sociological Review* 41 (February 1976): 34–51; Herbert Hill, *Black Labor and the American Legal System,* vol. I (Washington, DC: Bureau of National Affairs, 1977); Ray Marshall, *The Negro and Organized Labor* (New York: Wiley, 1965); Foner, *Organized Labor and the Black Worker;* Russell Schutt, "Craft Unions and Minorities: Determinants of Change in Admission Practices," *Social Problems* 34 (October 1987): 388–402; William Gould, *Black Workers in White Unions* (Ithaca: Cornell University Press, 1977); Philip Nyden, "Evolution of Black Political Influence in American Trade Unions," *Journal of Black Studies* 13 (June 1983): 379–398; Hoyman and Stallworth, "Participation in Local Unions"; Daniel Cornfield, "Ethnic Inequality in Layoff Chances: The Impact of Unionisation on Layoff Procedure," in *Redundancy, Layoffs and Plant Closures,* ed., Raymond Lee (London: Croom Helm, 1987), pp. 116–140; U.S. Commission on Civil Rights, *The Challenge Ahead: Equal Opportunity in Referral Unions* (Washington, DC: Government Printing Office, 1976).

Notwithstanding the persistence of stratification and segregation within the working class, minorities and women have come to comprise an increasingly large proportion of U.S. labor union membership, as previously shown. Although the Civil Rights Act of 1964 banned the formally discriminatory practices of both employers and labor unions, most unions had already abandoned such practices prior to the enactment of the act. By 1955, for example, fewer than 3 percent of all national U.S. unions formally barred blacks from membership, and less than 3 percent of U.S. union members belonged to unions with formally racially restrictive admissions criteria.[12] Comparable data on sexually restrictive union admission practices are unavailable, but Milkman claimed that most unions permanently lifted any formal bans on the admission of women during World War II, when many women temporarily filled the war-production factory jobs vacated by the mass exit of male factory workers into the armed services.[13] Minorities and women increasingly entered the ranks of the labor movement during the 1930s and 1940s. The sketchy available data on historical union membership trends suggest that blacks and women, prior to the 1930s, each accounted for less than 10 percent of U.S. union membership. With the labor shortages, the employment of blacks and women, and the spread of unionism in the war-production industries during World War II, blacks and women had come to comprise roughly 10 percent and 22 percent, respectively, of U.S. union membership by the end of the war. The returning GIs who reclaimed their jobs displaced some black and women workers during the immediate postwar period, generating a decline in women's share of union membership (comparable union membership data by race are unavailable). Women's share of union membership, however, remained higher than its prewar level, and since the mid-1950s the percentage of U.S. union membership accounted for by blacks and women has increased.[14]

Two forces have contributed to the entry of minorities and women into the ranks of the labor movement during the twentieth century. The first is the shift from craft unionism to industrial unionism that accom-

---

[12] James Bambrick and George Haas, *Handbook of Union Government Structure and Procedures* (New York: National Industrial Conference Board, 1955), p. 63.

[13] Ruth Milkman, *Gender at Work* (Urbana, IL: University of Illinois Press, 1987), p. 85.

[14] Kessler-Harris, " 'Where Are the Organized Women Workers?' "; Milkman, *Gender at Work*, p. 85; Marshall, *The Negro and Organized Labor*, p. 49; Barbara Wertheimer, "The United States of America," in *Women and Trade Unions in Eleven Industrialized Countries*, eds., Alice Cook, Val Lorwin, and Arlene Kaplan Daniels (Philadelphia: Temple University Press, 1984), p. 289; Ruth Needleman and Lucretia Tanner, "Women in Unions: Current Issues," in *Working Women*, eds., Karen Koziara, Michael Moskow, and Lucretia Tanner (Washington, DC: Bureau of National Affairs, 1987), p. 189; Foner, *Organized Labor and the Black Worker*, pp. 269–274; U.S. Department of Labor, Bureau of Labor Statistics, *Employment and Earnings* 35 (January 1988): 222; Leo Troy and Neil Sheflin, *Union Sourcebook*, first ed. (West Orange, NJ: Industrial Relations Data and Information Services, 1985), Appendix A, pp. 1–3.

panied the shift from entrepreneurial capitalism to corporate mass production manufacturing during the late nineteenth and early twentieth centuries. Craft unionism was the predominant type of unionism at the time of the founding of the AFL in 1886. Under the entrepreneurial capitalism and craft workplace social organization of this era, casual labor typified the employment relationship between skilled craftsmen and employers, that is, craftsmen often worked on temporary projects for multiple employers during a year, as in the construction industry, which comprised a substantial share of the AFL membership. The local craft union functioned partly as an employment exchange, referring unemployed workers for employment to prospective employers. The local craft union also dispensed to its membership various welfare benefits, including unemployment compensation and retirement pensions, which were financed by union membership dues.

The collective bargaining strength of the local craft union lay in its capacity to restrict the supply of craftsmen in a local labor market area. Local craft union membership was limited to the skilled workers of one craft in a local labor market area such as a city. Union strength rested not only on the scarcity of the craftsmen's high-level skills, but also on union control of journeyman training in the union apprenticeship program. Moreover, the craft union, whose membership typically consisted of native-born white men of Northern and Western European descent, often restricted the labor supply by refusing to admit workers into the union and apprenticeship program, including blacks, women, and immigrants, whose social backgrounds differed from those of the existing union membership, or by creating segregated black local unions. In addition to conducting these ethnocentric, racist, and sexist union practices, AFL craft unions supported federal and state legislation during the late nineteenth and early twentieth centuries that restricted the number of Asian and Eastern, Central, and Southern European immigrants and limited the work hours of women, children, and convict labor, in order to minimize wage competition with the union craftsman.[15]

Industrial unionism emerged by the 1930s, along with corporate mass production manufacturing, which employed many of the non-skilled workers who were excluded from craft union membership. Mass production manufacturing replaced casual labor with steady, regular employment in the "internal labor market" of a single employer over the course of a year. Indeed, the huge capital investment of the large corporation de-

---

[15] Herbert Northrup, *Organized Labor and the Negro* (New York: Harper, 1944); Charles Franklin, *The Negro Labor Unionist of New York* (New York: Columbia University Press, 1936); Sterling Spero and Abram Harris, *The Black Worker* (New York: Columbia University Press, 1931); Susan Lehrer, *Origins of Protective Labor Legislation for Women, 1905–1925* (Albany, NY: State University of New York Press, 1987); Vernon Briggs, *Immigration Policy and the American Labor Force* (Baltimore: Johns Hopkins University Press, 1984).

manded constant production with stable employment. Consequently, large corporations, partly at the urging of unions, which wanted to limit capricious managerial personnel decision making, instituted seniority rules for compensating workers and making job assignments. With the wage, retirement pension, job security, and promotion chances of an individual worker pegged to the amount of his/her seniority with the one employer, greater privileges accruing with more seniority, a worker was dissuaded from quitting and changing employers lest he jeopardize his economic livelihood, career chances, and retirement income.[16]

Industrial unionism differed from craft unionism in several important ways that facilitated the entry of minorities and women into the labor movement. The strength of the industrial union rested on its capacity to recruit all workers of an industry, regardless of their skill level, craft, and occupation, especially because the non-skilled factory worker was easily substitutable and commanded less market power than the craftsman. Consequently, local industrial union membership often consisted of the full-time production workforce of a specific mass production factory or employer (or factories and employers) as opposed to the geographical and occupational membership criteria of the local craft union. Unlike craft unions, industrial unions recruited membership from the ranks of an existing workforce and did not attempt to restrict labor supply, reserving for the employer alone the hiring and training of labor. Moreover, the inclusiveness of the recruitment strategy of industrial unionism led these unions to recruit all workers, regardless of their ethnicity, race, and gender.[17]

Industrial unionism grew during the early twentieth century in part because mass production technology had led to the dissolution of many skilled crafts and the creation of non-skilled factory jobs that differed little from one another in terms of type and level of skill requirements. Industrial unionism was also catalyzed by the passage of the Wagner Act of 1935 during the Roosevelt New Deal era. This pro-labor legislation limited employer interference in union organizing and established the National Labor Relations Board (NLRB), which regulated the industrial union recruitment process by conducting plant-specific union representation elections among the workers. Furthermore, wages had plummeted during the Great Depression and mass unemployment of the 1930s, motivating many workers to unionize in order to achieve higher wages and greater job security.[18]

[16] Sanford Jacoby, *Employing Bureaucracy* (New York: Columbia University Press, 1985); Daniel Cornfield, "Ethnic Inequality in Layoff Chances."
[17] Spero and Harris, *The Black Worker*; Northrup, *Organized Labor and the Negro*; Franklin, *The Negro Labor Unionist*; Marshall, *The Negro and Organized Labor*.
[18] Daniel Cornfield, ed., *Workers, Managers, and Technological Change: Emerging Patterns of Labor Relations* (New York: Plenum, 1987), pp. 3–24, 331–353.

Industrial unionism had been growing within the AFL and, in 1935, found its official expression in the AFL Committee for Industrial Organization (CIO). The core of CIO support consisted of the AFL industrial unions in mining, the needle trades, automobiles, rubber, glass, steel, and oil. Ideological and jurisdictional conflicts between craft and industrial unions led to the expulsion of ten CIO unions from the AFL in 1936. The CIO unions formed a rival labor federation, which was renamed the Congress of Industrial Organizations at the founding CIO convention in 1938.[19] The two federations merged, forming the AFL-CIO, in 1955.

Until the AFL-CIO merger, intense rivalry in membership recruitment between the two labor federations increased the number of minorities and women in the labor movement. The CIO not only spread industrial unionism among minority and women workers but also led the AFL to practice industrial unionism among these worker groups and, more generally, among the non-skilled. The CIO remained more receptive to organizing the non-skilled and minorities and women. Whereas the total 3.9 million CIO membership accounted for 36 percent of the combined AFL and CIO membership in 1945, the CIO accounted for roughly 60 percent of the black membership in the two labor federations (comparable data on union membership by gender are unavailable).[20] Moreover, total U.S. union membership grew rapidly during the late 1930s and the economic mobilization of the World War II years. Between 1930 and 1945, the percentage of the U.S. nonagricultural workforce that belonged to unions increased from 13 percent to 36 percent, the highest it would be in the twentieth century. Tremendous recruitment gains were made in the blue-collar sectors of the economy. Between 1930 and 1947, the number unionized increased from 7.8 percent to 40.5 percent in manufacturing, from 21.3 percent to 83.1 percent in mining, and from 22.6 percent to 67.0 percent in transportation. In construction, the traditional membership base of the AFL craft unions, the number unionized increased from 64.5 percent to 87.1 percent between 1930 and 1947. Only a minority of white-collar workers and employees in the service sector had entered the labor movement by the end of the war.[21]

The second force that increased the proportion of minorities and women in the ranks of the labor movement was the post–World War II growth of unionization among white-collar workers and workers in the public and private service sectors of the economy. The extension of

---

[19] Irving Bernstein, *Turbulent Years* (Boston: Houghton Mifflin, 1971), pp. 352–431.
[20] Marshall, *The Negro and Organized Labor,* p. 53; Troy and Sheflin, *Union Sourcebook,* Appendix A, p. 3.
[21] Daniel Cornfield, "Declining Union Membership in the Post–World War II Era: The United Furniture Workers of America, 1939–1982," *American Journal of Sociology* 91 (March 1986): 1112–1153; Troy and Sheflin, *Union Sourcebook,* chapter 3, p. 15.

unionization among these workers increased the presence of minorities and women in the labor movement not just because minorities and women were disproportionately employed in these occupations and industries, that is, not just because of the general pattern of occupational race and sex segregation. Given that many of the clerical and service workers, like the industrial union membership in manufacturing, were non-skilled workers who commanded less market power than the skilled craftsmen, the unions that recruited members from these occupational and industrial sectors have adopted an inclusive recruitment strategy, organizing all workers regardless of their ethnicity, race, gender, and occupation. Among the large unions in these sectors are the State, County and Municipal Employees; the Government Employees; the Postal Workers; the Letter Carriers; the Teachers; the Service Employees; the Food and Commercial Workers; the Communications Workers; and the Hotel Employees and Restaurant Employees. These unions resemble industrial unions more closely than craft unions in that they tend to recruit members from existing workforces through representation elections and perform no job referral and apprentice-training functions.

Union membership in the service sector has come to account for a substantial share of U.S. union membership during the post–World War II era. By 1987, almost 60 percent of U.S. union members were employed in government; communications and public utilities; wholesale and retail trade; finance, insurance, and real estate; and other service industries. Occupationally, union members employed in clerical, professional, and service jobs accounted for 42 percent of U.S. union membership in 1987.[22]

The post–World War II growth in unionization among service and white-collar workers is attributable to several factors. First, employment in these industries and occupations has grown generally as the U.S. economy has shifted from manufacturing to services. Second, increased bureaucratization and office automation have accompanied service-sector growth, often leading to blocked career mobility, inferior wages, and centralized managerial control of workers, issues that may motivate workers to unionize. Third, public-sector unionization, which is not covered by the Wagner Act and the National Labor Relations Board, was boosted by the enactment of federal and state public employee collective bargaining laws during the 1960s and 1970s, which facilitated public-sector unionism.[23]

Also, unions have adopted more aggressive recruitment campaigns

---

[22] U.S. Department of Labor, Bureau of Labor Statistics, *Employment and Earnings* 35 (January 1988): 223.
[23] Cornfield, *Workers, Managers, and Technological Change*; idem, "Women in the Automated Office: Computers, Work, and Prospects for Unionization," in *Advances in Industrial and Labor Relations*, vol. 4, eds., David Lewin, David Lipsky, and Donna Sockell (Greenwich, CT: JAI Press, 1987), pp. 177–198.

among service and white-collar workers, especially during the 1970s and 1980s, when blue-collar union membership rapidly declined. By 1987, only 17 percent of the U.S. workforce belonged to unions. Union decline is partly attributable to blue-collar union membership losses stemming from increased foreign imports to the United States, capital flight out of the industrialized North to the non-union South and Third World, and automation of production technology. Membership declines have also resulted from increased obstacles to union recruitment, especially increased employer aggression in countering union organizing drives.[24]

Finally, the civil rights and women's movements of the 1950s, 1960s, and 1970s motivated minority and women workers to unionize, as well as the labor movement to organize these workers, who tended to be employed in the service and white-collar economic sectors. Organizations within the labor movement, such as the Coalition of Labor Union Women and the Coalition of Black Trade Unionists, and outside the labor movement, including civil rights and working women's organizations, have encouraged minorities and women to unionize and unions to organize these workers.[25]

The distribution of black, women, and white male union members by occupation and industry of employment reflects the general pattern of occupational race and sex segregation in employment and the unevenness in the development of craft unionism, industrial unionism, and service white-collar unionism among industrial and occupational sectors. Whereas white men accounted for 61 percent of union members in 1980 (latest year of available data), blacks and women accounted for the majority of union members who were employed in professional, clerical, and cleaning, food, and health service occupations. Blacks and women were represented roughly in proportion to their percentage of all union members in the semi-skilled factory operative occupations. White men accounted for the majority of union members employed as skilled craftsmen, non-skilled operatives and laborers, and protective service workers. By industry, blacks and women comprised a majority of union members employed in the communications, finance, insurance and real estate, and professional and personal services industries; almost half of the union membership in retail trade; and almost 40 percent of union members in nondurable goods manufacturing, other services, and government. White men comprised a disproportionately large majority of the union membership in

---

[24] Cornfield, "Declining Union Membership"; U.S. Department of Labor, Bureau of Labor Statistics, *Employment and Earnings* 35 (January 1988): 222.

[25] Foner, *Organized Labor and the Black Worker*; idem, *Women and the American Labor Movement*.

mining, construction, durable goods manufacturing, transportation, utilities, and wholesale trade.[26]

The growing presence of minorities and women in the ranks of the labor movement has increased their political strength within unions, contributing to the beginning of social integration of elected union leadership. However, little research has addressed the process by which minorities, women, or any new social group emerges as leaders. Rather, research on union leadership change has emphasized the determinants of electoral competition for office. This emphasis, in turn, derives from a broader desire to examine the determinants of democratic governance within unions and has been inspired by Robert Michels's "iron law of oligarchy," presented in his 1911 work, *Political Parties*.[27]

Michels argued that formally democratic organizations, while maintaining their democratic structure, would inevitably degenerate into oligarchies as they increased in size. Growth would generate an increasingly complex and impersonal bureaucratic structure, in which expert administrators would perpetuate their control by monopolizing the means of communication with members, developing appointed staffs, and choosing their successors. Leadership stabilization, according to Michels, resulted not only from the technical requirements of bureaucracy and an inevitable differentiation of the elected from the electorate, but also from declining electoral competition for office. Michels reduced this declining competition to the "intellectual superiority" of leaders and to such psychological factors as "the gratitude felt by the crowd" toward their leaders, an "instinctive need for stability," and a "general sentiment of indifference," which "is natural to the crowd."[28] Although few writers have given credence to Michels's psychological reductionism, the Webbs put forth a similar thesis about the impact of growth on union bureaucratization some fifteen years before Michels, as have numerous writers since the appearance of *Political Parties*.[29]

---

[26] Courtney Gifford, ed., *Directory of U.S. Labor Organizations*, 1982–1983 ed. (Washington, DC: Bureau of National Affairs, 1982), pp. 50–51, 57–58.

[27] Robert Michels, *Political Parties* (1911; reprint, New York: Free Press, 1962).

[28] Ibid., pp. 92, 105, 107, 121.

[29] Sidney Webb and Beatrice Webb, *Industrial Democracy* (1897; reprint, London: Longmans, Green and Co., 1920); Sylvia Kopald, *Rebellion in Labor Unions* (New York: Boni and Liveright, 1924); Will Herberg, "Bureaucracy and Democracy in Labor Unions," *Antioch Review* 3 (September 1943): 405–417; Joel Seidman, "Democracy in Labor Unions," *Journal of Political Economy* 61 (June 1953): 221–231; Richard Lester, *As Unions Mature* (Princeton: Princeton University Press, 1958); Philip Marcus, "Union Conventions and Executive Boards: A Formal Analysis of Organizational Structure," *American Sociological Review* 31 (February 1966): 61–70; Frances Piven and Richard Cloward, *Poor People's Movements* (New York: Vintage, 1979), p. 101; Eva Etzioni-Halevy, *Bureaucracy and Democracy*, rev. ed. (Boston: Routledge & Kegan Paul, 1985).

Unwilling to accept the absolute and inexorable trend toward oligarchy posited in the iron law, other writers have endeavored to discern the features of formal organization that promote electoral competition. In their pioneering work on the unusual, two-party system in the International Typographical Union (ITU), Lipset, Trow, and Coleman argued that the institutionalization of parties promoted electoral competition and that the capacity of the ITU to maintain its party system derived from the high and homogeneous status of the printers. Oligarchy, for Lipset et al., was not inevitable, but likely, when the status of the union officers exceeded that of the occupations of the union members.[30]

Arguing that institutionalized opposition and parties were neither necessary nor sufficient for promoting electoral competition within unions, Edelstein, countering Lipset, held that autonomous suborganizations could be part of the formal union structure which, in turn, could promote electoral competition.[31] Using a sample of fifty-one national unions, Edelstein and Warner found that several dimensions of formal organizational structure, derived from union constitutions, were correlated with the closeness of the vote in officer elections. Closeness of vote varied directly with the number of hierarchical levels elected, whether the top officer was elected by referendum, the absence of automatic succession in event of a vacancy, or the percentage of the executive council elected by the convention; it varied inversely with the time between union conventions, the percentage of convention delegates required for a roll call vote, and the percentage of the executive council appointed by national officers.[32]

Although Edelstein and Warner demonstrated that oligarchical tendencies are a variable that depends on diverse organizational structures rather than an iron law, their analysis emphasized the static, structural arena that may facilitate electoral competition, neglecting the outcome. That is, the issues promoting leadership change, as well as the nature of the new groups that rise to positions of leadership, were omitted in their analysis. This omission, in turn, derives from the emphasis of this research tradition, namely, the focus on the determinants of electoral competition. The chances of leadership change, the characteristics of emerging leadership groups, and the dynamic conditions external to the union that may

---

[30] Seymour Lipset, Martin Trow, and James Coleman, *Union Democracy* (New York: Free Press, 1956); Seymour Lipset, "The Political Process in Trade Unions: A Theoretical Statement," in *Labor and Trade Unionism,* eds., Walter Galenson and Seymour Lipset (New York: Wiley, 1960), pp. 216–242.

[31] J. David Edelstein, "An Organizational Theory of Union Democracy," *American Sociological Review* 32 (February 1967): 19–31.

[32] J. David Edelstein and Malcolm Warner, *Comparative Union Democracy* (New Brunswick, NJ: Transaction, 1979), p. 126.

catapult new groups into leadership positions have been deemphasized in this "structuralist" critique of the iron law. Indeed, Cook has observed, for example, a "permeability of unions . . . to the ideas and goals of sex equality, largely germinated within the women's movement, taken up by international governmental agencies, and implanted in the unions mainly by outside liberal sources."[33]

Furthermore, the static, cross-sectional experimental design of the structuralist research is inconsistent with the formulation of the iron law of oligarchy. The iron law is a "developmental" or "life-cycle" thesis on organizational change, emphasizing the impact of growth, not size, and structural change, not governmental structure, on leadership stability.[34] Moreover, structure itself is often more dynamic than what is depicted or implied by the structuralist research. Edelstein and Warner studied the mean closeness of elections over the 1949–1966 period, but they used static measures of structure to predict closeness. However, not only might the size of a union change dramatically over a fifteen-year period, but also a union may alter its constitution at its constitutional conventions. For example, the United Furniture Workers of America (UFWA), which fell into Edelstein and Warner's sample, amended some of its constitutional provisions about officer qualifications during the period of their study. In 1958, union staff and administrative personnel were prohibited from serving in most executive board positions, and a union member now had to be employed for at least two years in one of the jurisdictional trades or in a UFWA shop (except for newly organized local unions) in order to serve on the executive board.

Another research tradition, also critical of the iron law, has emerged with a more fluid depiction of union structure and the dynamic process of leadership change. A. J. Muste's 1928 imagery of union structure alternating between being an "army" and being a "town meeting" is an early formulation of the continuous resolution of the ongoing tension between democracy and bureaucracy within unions, what Child et al. recently referred to as administrative and representative rationality.[35] For Muste, consensus and hierarchical obedience predominated in the union during growth periods of the business cycle, and factionalism prevailed under

---

[33] Alice Cook, "Introduction," in *Women and Trade Unions in Eleven Industrialized Countries,* eds., Alice Cook, Val Lorwin, and Arlene Daniels (Philadelphia: Temple University Press, 1984), p. 15.

[34] Philip Marcus, "Organizational Change: The Case of American Trade Unions," in *Explorations in Social Change,* eds., George Zollschan and Walter Hirsch (Boston: Houghton Mifflin, 1964), pp. 749–777.

[35] A. J. Muste, "Factional Fights in Trade Unions," in *American Labor Dynamics,* ed., J. B. S. Hardman (New York: Harcourt Brace and Co., 1928), pp. 332–348; John Child, Ray Loveridge, and Malcolm Warner, "Towards an Organizational Study of Trade Unions," *Sociology* 7 (January 1973): 71–91.

adverse macroeconomic conditions, when the union encountered difficulties in satisfying membership needs. In 1948, Pierson distinguished between forces "for" and "against" union democracy. The "curse of bigness" jeopardized democracy, whereas an "idealistic tradition in trade unions," along with competition between them, kept leadership accountable to members, prompting occasional internal rivalry.[36] Similarly, Howe and Widick, in their 1949 study of the United Automobile Workers, argued that the bureaucratic tendencies of the union were held in check by the persistence of factionalism, resulting from the union's "bottom-up," rather than "top-down," origins, its unharmonious relations with the large auto corporations, and the presence of small groups of dissident radicals.[37] Indeed, as Gouldner put it in 1954, referring to Michels, "if oligarchical waves repeatedly wash away the bridges of democracy, this eternal recurrence can happen only because men [sic] doggedly rebuild them after each inundation.... There cannot be an iron law of oligarchy... unless there is an iron law of democracy."[38] According to Zald and Ash, oligarchization was most likely to occur when the social movement organization was "becalmed" and its leadership complacent; and Zald and Berger claimed that bureaucratic insurgency was likely in organizations that depended on an ideologically committed professional staff who could serve as reference for evaluating the organization. Similarly, Herman Benson, executive director of the Association for Union Democracy, recently wrote that "even when unions appear thoroughly bureaucratized and the membership inert, the labor movement itself tends to regenerate the democratic spirit. When unions call for justice, equality, fair play, and human dignity in society, these stirring ideals are echoed in the ranks and demanded inside the unions."[39]

Several studies of factionalism, insurgency, and reform movements within unions have appeared in recent years, emphasizing the conditions conducive to effective opposition. Treating these movements for union democracy as social movements, many of these studies have taken a "re-

---

[36] Frank Pierson, "The Government of Trade Unions," *Industrial and Labor Relations Review* 1 (July 1948): 594–596.
[37] Irving Howe and B. J. Widick, *The UAW and Walter Reuther* (New York: Random House, 1949), pp. 259–266.
[38] Alvin Gouldner, "Metaphysical Pathos and the Theory of Bureaucracy," *American Political Science Review* 49 (June 1955): 506.
[39] Mayer Zald and Roberta Ash, "Social Movement Organizations: Growth, Decay and Change," *Social Forces* 44 (March 1966): 327–340; Mayer Zald and Michael Berger, "Social Movements in Organizations: Coup d'Etat, Bureaucratic Insurgency, and Mass Movement," *American Journal of Sociology* 83 (January 1978): 823–861; Herman Benson, "The Fight for Union Democracy," in *Unions in Transition,* ed., Seymour Martin Lipset (San Francisco: Institute for Contemporary Studies, 1986), p. 369. Also see Herman Benson, "Apathy and Other Axioms: Expelling the Union Dissenter from History," *Dissent* 19 (Winter 1972): 211–224.

source mobilization" approach to explaining the rise and effectiveness of competing groups within unions.[40] Resource mobilization theory, according to McCarthy and Zald, holds that aggrieved groups engage in collective action only when they gain the capacity for controlling relevant resources such as organization, leadership, money, and labor and when these resources become available. For example, Hemingway argued that horizontal and vertical divisions within the union generate tensions among groups who, consequently, deploy diverse resources in bargaining with the opposition. These resources include meetings, caucuses, and direct actions, among others.[41] According to Benson, federal law, especially the Landrum-Griffin Act of 1959, has established civil liberties for union members and stimulated activism within unions.[42] Other writers, such as Nyden, Schutt, and Friedman, have stressed the importance of strengthening the link between union leaders and members, maximizing direct membership participation in the movement, in order for effective opposition, whether through electoral victory or influence on incumbents, to emerge. In contrast, effective opposition to oligarchy is less likely when the insurgents rely on their institutional environment such as officials and activists in other parts of the union, non–trade unionists, and other organizations for support and resources.[43] The manner in which the movement procures its resources influences the effectiveness of its opposition to oligarchy and, hence, the development of oligarchy itself. As Nyden put it, criticizing the inevitability and unidirectionality of the iron law of oligarchy, such " 'natural laws' of organization may in fact be the products of the nature of the political economy at a particular time in history."[44]

The iron law of oligarchy, then, may be applicable only under specific conditions or during certain historical periods. Given that Michels's iron

---

[40] Roderick Martin, "Union Democracy: An Explanatory Framework," *Sociology* 2 (May 1968): 205–220; John Hemingway, *Conflict and Democracy* (Oxford: Clarendon Press, 1978); Paul Clark, *The Miners' Fight for Democracy* (Ithaca, NY: Cornell University, New York State School of Industrial and Labor Relations, 1981); Samuel Friedman, *Teamster Rank and File* (New York: Columbia University Press, 1982); Mary Dickenson, *Democracy in Trade Unions* (St. Lucia, Australia: University of Queensland Press, 1982); Jerry Lembke and William Tattam, *One Union in Wood* (New York: International Publishers, 1984); Philip Nyden, *Steelworkers Rank-and-File* (New York: Praeger, 1984); idem, "Democratizing Organizations: A Case Study of a Union Reform Movement," *American Journal of Sociology* 90 (May 1985): 1179–1203.
[41] John McCarthy and Mayer Zald, "Resource Mobilization and Social Movements: A Partial Theory," in *Social Movements in an Organizational Society: Collected Essays*, eds., Mayer Zald and John McCarthy (New Brunswick, NJ: Transaction, 1987), pp. 15–42; Hemingway, *Conflict and Democracy*, pp. 13–25.
[42] Benson, "The Fight for Union Democracy," pp. 347–352, 369.
[43] Nyden, "Democratizing Organizations," p. 1194; Russell Schutt, *Organization in a Changing Environment: Unionization of Welfare Employees* (Albany, NY: State University of New York Press, 1986), pp. 29–34; Friedman, *Teamster Rank and File*.
[44] Nyden, *Steelworkers*, p. 11. Also see Schutt, *Organization in a Changing Environment*, p. 32.

law was cast in terms of organizational growth, an analysis of the conditions promoting oligarchy, as well as of the emergence of new groups into leadership positions, ought to compare leadership trends during periods of union growth, stability, and decline. Yet, few studies of insurgency within unions have examined the frequency and patterns of leadership change and the emergence of new social groups, such as blacks and women, during diverse periods in the history of a union. The emphasis of these studies, like that of the structuralist research tradition, has been on the determinants of effective electoral competition and opposition, rather than on the outcomes of the electoral process within unions. The story of the United Furniture Workers is helpful in illuminating how political, economic, and social conditions external to the union, as well as union growth, stability, and decline, have led to leadership stability, status conflict among established and emerging membership groups, and shifts in the ethnic, racial, gender, and ideological characteristics of national, elected union leadership.

The United Furniture Workers

The United Furniture Workers of America was established in 1937 as an affiliate of the Committee for Industrial Organization. Founded by dissidents in the AFL-affiliated Upholsterers International Union (UIU), the UFWA was chartered as an industrial union to organize all furniture manufacturing production workers regardless of their craft.

The history of the UFWA, to be discussed in Chapters 3–5, reaches back to 1932, when a group of progressive trade unionists in New York City founded the Furniture Workers Industrial Union (FWIU). Affiliated with the Trade Union Unity League (TUUL) of the Communist party, the FWIU was dissolved in 1935 and merged into the UIU as the party entered its so-called Popular Front phase, dismantling the TUUL and cooperating with other progressive groups in the fight against fascism. The former FWIU activists and their local unions left the UIU in 1937 because the UIU refused to affiliate with the CIO and to embrace fully the principles of industrial unionism. The UFWA remained affiliated with the CIO and, with the 1955 merger of the two labor federations, has continued to be an affiliate of the AFL-CIO. Having faced heavy membership losses during the 1970s and 1980s, the UFWA merged with the International Union of Electronic, Electrical, Technical, Salaried and Machine Workers on January 1, 1987, forming the International Union of Electronic, Electrical, Salaried, Machine and Furniture Workers, in order to step up its organizing activities.

The UFWA, then, constitutes a "complete" organization history. More-

Table 1.1
UFWA Membership and Number of U.S. Furniture Manufacturing Workers, 1939–1985

Year	(1) UFWA Membership	(2) Furniture Production Workers (thousands)	Year	(3) UFWA Membership	(4) Furniture Production Workers (thousands)
1939	14,085	n.a.	1962	31,365	304.5
1940	n.a.	n.a.	1963	31,180	308.7
1941	19,628	n.a.	1964	32,244	320.9
1942	n.a.	n.a.	1965	31,732	340.3
1943	22,988	n.a.	1966	32,748	364.4
1944	26,616	n.a.	1967	33,557	357.6
1945	29,456	n.a.	1968	29,418	371.5
1946	34,662	n.a.	1969	34,369	382.9
1947	43,389	282.0	1970	30,690	362.4
1948	38,952	290.0	1971	29,799	364.5
1949	32,200	261.0	1972	30,156	400.4
1950	32,766	302.0	1973	30,031	420.0
1951	n.a.	292.6	1974	29,967	401.9
1952	35,373	291.2	1975	24,244	337.3
1953	35,017	300.8	1976	27,042	364.0
1954	33,754	274.2	1977	25,937	381.8
1955	36,947	292.6	1978	27,124	406.3
1956	38,552	300.6	1979	26,453	405.9
1957	38,527	298.2	1980	24,751	375.8
1958	33,387	284.4	1981	23,244	373.8
1959	35,790	305.7	1982	22,334	341.8
1960	32,671	303.5	1983	20,809	356.1
1961	31,369	289.5	1984	21,163	390.6
			1985	19,367	396.2

Sources: For number of furniture production workers, U.S. Department of Labor, Bureau of Labor Statistics, *Employment and Earnings, United States, 1909–1978*, Bulletin no. 1312–11 (Washington, DC: Government Printing Office, 1979), p. 80; *Supplement to Employment and Earnings* (Washington, DC: Government Printing Office, 1983), p. 27; *Employment and Earnings*, vol. 33, no. 1, January 1986, p. 218.

over, throughout the fifty years of growth and decline of the UFWA, its leadership stabilized in some periods and turned over in others, as changing political and economic conditions generated status conflict within the union and swept new social groups into union office. Trends in UFWA membership and leadership succession illustrate this dynamic process by which new social groups emerged as union officers.

Trends in UFWA Membership

Three periods are discernible in the trends in UFWA membership, shown in columns 1 and 3 of Table 1.1, which correspond to significant events in labor history, political and economic conditions, and developments in the furniture manufacturing industry. I summarize briefly each of these periods here and treat them in greater detail in subsequent chapters. First, in the formative, or growth, period of 1939–1950, UFWA membership rose sharply from 14,085 to a high of 43,389 in 1947 and then dropped abruptly to 32,200 by 1949. The sharp increase in membership through 1947, not unlike that of many other unions in the mass production industries, is attributable to several factors, including the encouragement of unionization by the enactment of the Wagner Act in 1935; the formation of the CIO in 1935 and, consequently, the greater availability of resources for organizing less skilled workers in furniture and other mass production industries; and the growth of mass production industries during World War II.

The sharp decline in UFWA membership between 1947 and 1949 was partly a consequence of Cold War political conditions. As a union with several of its leaders in the Communist party, the UFWA was red-baited intensively and lost almost five thousand members in raids by other unions, including the Upholsterers, United Automobile Workers, Carpenters, Woodworkers, and United Mine Workers. At issue was compliance with the non-Communist affidavit of the Taft-Hartley Act. Spearheaded by the National Association of Manufacturers and opposed by the labor movement, the Taft-Hartley Act of 1947 required all unions to sign affidavits verifying that their union officers were not members of the Communist party, lest they be denied support from the National Labor Relations Board. Although the UFWA officers signed the affidavit in 1949, it was one of a dozen unions slated that year for expulsion from the CIO on the grounds of Communist domination, if the UFWA failed to unseat its left-wing officers. The matter was resolved at the stormy 1950 UFWA convention in Chicago, when the left-wing officers were defeated in factionalized, contested elections and the UFWA convention delegates voted to stay in the CIO.

The 1947–1949 decline in membership is also attributable to adverse economic conditions in furniture manufacturing. In the period between its 1948 and 1950 conventions, the UFWA lost almost five thousand members due to unemployment.

The second period, lasting from 1951 to 1969, was the period of stability. The union's membership, which averaged about thirty-four thousand during this period, fluctuated in a cycle that corresponded roughly

Table 1.2
Growth and Decline Years for UFWA Membership and Employed
U.S. Furniture Manufacturing Production Workers, 1949–1969

Growth Years		Decline Years	
UFWA Membership	Furniture Production Workers	UFWA Membership	Furniture Production Workers
1949–1950	1949–1950		1950–1952
	1952–1953	1952–1954	1953–1954
1954–1956	1954–1956	1956–1958	1956–1958
1958–1959	1958–1959	1959–1963	1959–1961
1963–1964, 1965–1967	1961–1966	1964–1965	
1968–1969	1967–1969	1967–1968	1966–1967

Source: Derived from Table 1.1.

to the business cycle of the furniture manufacturing industry. This is indicated by the parallel trends in UFWA membership and the employment of furniture manufacturing production workers, shown in Table 1.1. Broadly, both UFWA membership and furniture production worker employment increased through the late 1950s, declined through the early 1960s, and increased through the late 1960s. A more detailed depiction of these parallel trends is presented in Table 1.2, which compares the growth and decline years of UFWA membership to those of furniture manufacturing and production worker employment.

Stability was achieved in part by the cessation of union raids on the UFWA following the 1950 convention. Moreover, in the spirit of the AFL-CIO merger of 1955, the UFWA teamed up briefly with the Upholsterers in a joint organizing venture during the late 1950s.

Despite the removal of these barriers to growth, the Taft-Hartley Act of 1947 imposed several constraints on union organizing that inhibited labor movement growth, generally, and that of the UFWA, specifically. Chief among these were the outlawing of closed shop contracts and a provision that allowed states to enact "right-to-work" laws, prohibiting union shop contracts. The latter constraint was especially damaging to the UFWA because the furniture manufacturing industry was growing more rapidly in the union-resistant southern states, which enacted right-to-work laws, than in other regions, where such laws were relatively uncommon. Therefore, as northern furniture manufacturers migrated southward, leaving the stronghold of UFWA membership, or opened southern branch operations, the UFWA was faced with an organizing task whose costliness derived not only from the increasing geographical decentralization of the industry but also from the growth of the industry in a region whose political climate reinforced its anti-union sentiment.[45]

Another barrier to growth that began during the period of stability was the proliferation of employer-provided welfare plans such as health insurance and retirement pension benefits, especially among large, nonunion employers. Many unions in the mass production industries, including the UFWA, gained these benefits through collective bargaining during or immediately after World War II. A 1948 NLRB interpretation of the Taft-Hartley Act encouraged this trend by classifying these benefits as items negotiable through collective bargaining. However, in light of tax law changes during the war that enabled employers to deduct fringe benefits as a business expense, large, non-union employers in furniture manufacturing and other mass production industries soon began providing these benefits to their employees, in part to preempt unionization efforts. Consequently, the UFWA and other unions were decreasingly successful in organizing large companies, gaining new members primarily from small companies that lacked employee fringe benefits and were often prone to bankruptcy.[46]

The third period, from 1970 to the present, is the period of decline. The correlation between UFWA membership and furniture manufacturing employment becomes more tenuous in this period, as UFWA membership declines in most years to about nineteen thousand in 1985, while the employment of furniture manufacturing production workers continues to fluctuate along a slightly inclined keel (see Table 1.1). Nonetheless, adverse macroeconomic conditions have contributed to UFWA decline. The deep, nationwide recession of 1975 led not only to the largest decline in the employment of furniture manufacturing production workers of the post–World War II era but also to the largest drop in UFWA membership since 1949.

The decline in UFWA membership, one which is replicated in many mass production unions, is partly attributable to an acceleration of those barriers to growth that began in the previous period of stability. Added to these barriers in the period of decline are an increase in furniture imports, which contributed to bankruptcies and UFWA membership losses; a predominantly Republican chain of U.S. presidents, which has made union organizing more difficult; and increased employer resistance to unionization campaigns, with the assistance of a burgeoning profession of anti-union management consultants.

Membership trends in the UFWA are similar to those of the percentage of unionized workers in furniture manufacturing and in the U.S.

---

[45] Cornfield, "Declining Union Membership."
[46] Ibid.

nonagricultural workforce. According to U.S. Bureau of Labor Statistics surveys of furniture manufacturing, the percentage of unionized workers declined from 46.0 percent to 35.0 percent between 1945 and 1954, fluctuated between 33.3 percent and 40.0 percent during the 1954–1968 period, and declined from 38.0 percent to 14.0 percent between 1968 and 1986 (among the other unions in furniture manufacturing are the Upholsterers and the Carpenters).[47] In the U.S. nonagricultural workforce, the percentage of unionized workers increased from 22.6 percent in 1937 to its all-time high of 35.5 percent in 1946, fluctuated between 31.1 percent and 34.5 percent during the 1947–1959 period, and declined from 32.1 percent in 1959 to 17.0 percent in 1987.[48]

In sum, changing political and economic conditions, events in labor history, and the geographical mobility of furniture manufacturing have fashioned the periods of growth, stability, and decline in the UFWA. In turn, changes in UFWA leadership are closely tied to these three periods.

Changes in UFWA Leadership

The general executive board (GEB) is the ruling body of the International UFWA during the period between constitutional conventions.[49] Since 1970, the GEB has consisted of a president, a secretary-treasurer, four regional vice presidents (East, Midwest, South, and West), eleven geographical district positions, ten positions representing different furni-

[47] U.S. Department of Labor, Bureau of Labor Statistics: *Wage Structure, Wood Furniture, 1945*, Series 2, no. 30 (Washington, DC: U.S. Department of Labor, Bureau of Labor Statistics, 1946); *Wage Structure, Household Furniture, 1954*, Report no. 76 (Washington, DC: U.S. Department of Labor, Bureau of Labor Statistics, 1954); *Wage Structure, Wood Household Furniture, Except Upholstered, April–May 1959*, Report no. 152 (Washington, DC: Government Printing Office, 1960); *Industry Wage Survey, Wood Household Furniture, Except Upholstered, July 1962*, Bulletin no. 1369 (Washington, DC: Government Printing Office, 1963); *Industry Wage Survey, Wood Household Furniture, Except Upholstered, May–June 1965*, Bulletin no. 1496 (Washington, DC: Government Printing Office, 1966); *Industry Wage Survey, Wood Household Furniture, Except Upholstered, October 1968*, Bulletin no. 1651 (Washington, DC: Government Printing Office, 1970); *Industry Wage Survey, Wood Household Furniture, Except Upholstered, October 1971*, Bulletin no. 1793 (Washington, DC: Government Printing Office, 1973); *Industry Wage Survey, Wood Household Furniture, Except Upholstered, November 1974*, Bulletin no. 1930 (Washington, DC: Government Printing Office, 1976); *Industry Wage Survey: Wood Household Furniture, June 1979*, Bulletin no. 2087 (Washington, DC: Government Printing Office, 1981); *Industry Wage Survey: Wood Household Furniture, June 1986*, Bulletin no. 2283 (Washington, DC: Government Printing Office, 1987).
[48] U.S. Department of Labor, Bureau of Labor Statistics, *Handbook of Labor Statistics*, Bulletin no. 2000 (Washington, DC: Government Printing Office, 1979), p. 507; idem, *Employment and Earnings* 35 (January 1988): 222; Troy and Sheflin, *Union Sourcebook*, chapter 3, p. 15.
[49] The term *International* typically refers to the national office of a U.S. labor union that has Canadian members.

ture product lines or "branches" (upholstered furniture, case goods, metal furniture, etc.), and the four regional representatives. The number of actual incumbents varied with formal changes before 1970 in the numbers of district, branch, and regional representative seats and because some seats remained unfilled, especially during the formative period. All of the GEB members are elected by and from the local union delegates at the International UFWA constitutional convention. Biennial conventions were held until 1976, when, for reasons of financial exigency, the UFWA shifted to holding quadrennial conventions (during World War II, the fourth UFWA convention, which would have met in 1945, was postponed to 1946). The term of office for all GEB positions is the period between conventions (i.e., two-year terms before 1976 and four-year terms beginning in 1976), and an incumbent may be reelected for an unlimited number of terms.

Continuity and change in UFWA leadership correspond closely to the periods of growth, stability, and decline. One indicator of leadership stability is the percentage of "new" GEB members, that is, incumbents who did not serve on the GEB during the previous term. The trend in the percentage of new GEB members, beginning with the second UFWA convention in 1941, is shown in Table 1.3. The percentage of new GEB members was higher during the periods of growth (1941–1950) and decline (1970–1984) than in the intervening period of stability (1952–1968). The percentage exceeded 42.3 percent in the formative period, remained below 25.0 percent in seven of the nine years of the period of stability, and exceeded 25.0 percent in four of the six years of the period of decline. This pattern suggests that leadership stabilized along with membership stabilization and that leadership turnover increased during periods of rapid membership change, whether growth or decline.

The succession of social groups on the GEB also corresponds closely to the periods of growth, stability, and decline. The percentage distribution of GEB members by ethnicity and race and by gender is shown in Table 1.4. During the formative period, the percentage of Jewish GEB members declined while Italian and Northern and Western European GEB members increased. The ethnic and racial distribution of GEB members changed little during the period of stability. A majority or near majority were Northern and Western European; roughly 25 percent to 39 percent were Jewish or Italian; and less than 18 percent were black or other European. In the period of decline, the percentages of Jewish and Italian GEB members declined, those for all European GEB members fluctuated at a level lower than those of the previous period, and the proportion of blacks and Hispanics increased to about one-third of GEB members. Men accounted for all GEB members through the periods of growth and stability. Since 1970, the percentage of women serving on the GEB has increased to almost 17 percent of GEB members.

Table 1.3
Percentage of UFWA GEB Members Who Did Not Serve on the GEB During the Previous Term, 1941–1984

Convention Year	%	Total Number GEB Incumbents
Formative Period		
1941	52.2	23
1943	42.3	26
1946	50.0	22
1948	51.7	29
1950	46.2	26
Period of Stability		
1952	29.6	27
1954	17.9	28
1956	22.2	27
1958	32.1	28
1960	11.5	26
1962	23.1	26
1964	14.8	27
1966	14.8	27
1968	11.1	27
Period of Decline		
1970	53.3	30
1972	20.0	30
1974	23.3	30
1976	36.7	30
1980	33.3	30
1984	40.0	30

These changes in the ethnic and racial and gender characteristics of GEB members are attributable mainly to two factors, both of which led to factionalized status conflict within the UFWA and which I will summarize here and treat in greater detail in subsequent chapters. The first is the changing geographical distribution of UFWA membership. As the UFWA extended its base of organizing operations out of New York City, where Jewish and Italian workers predominated through the 1950s, to small furniture towns in the Great Lakes and New England regions (e.g., Grand Rapids, Michigan, and Gardner, Massachusetts) and to the South, the UFWA came to incorporate a greater percentage of Northern and Western European members. The union's growth on the West Coast, especially in Los Angeles and San Francisco, increased the proportion of Hispanic UFWA members during the post–World War II era. Second, political con-

Table 1.4
Percentage Distribution of UFWA GEB Members, by Ethnicity and Race and by Gender, 1939–1984

Convention Year	Jewish	Italian	Northern and Western European	Other European	Black	Hispanic	Total[a]	N	% Women
Formative Period									
1939	52.6	5.3	42.1	0.0	0.0	0.0	100.0	19	0.0
1941	39.1	8.7	47.8	0.0	0.0	4.3	99.9	23	0.0
1943	26.9	19.2	50.0	0.0	0.0	3.8	99.9	26	0.0
1946	31.8	18.2	40.9	9.1	0.0	0.0	100.0	22	0.0
1048	24.1	13.8	48.3	10.3	3.4	0.0	99.9	29	0.0
1950	11.5	15.4	57.7	11.5	3.8	0.0	99.9	26	0.0
Period of Stability									
1952	11.1	14.8	55.5	7.4	7.4	3.7	99.9	27	0.0
1954	10.7	14.3	57.1	3.6	10.7	3.6	100.0	28	0.0
1956	11.1	18.5	51.9	7.4	11.1	0.0	100.0	27	0.0
1958	10.7	17.9	50.0	7.1	14.3	0.0	100.0	28	0.0
1960	11.5	19.2	53.8	7.7	7.7	0.0	99.9	26	0.0
1962	15.4	23.1	42.3	11.5	7.7	0.0	100.0	26	0.0
1964	14.8	22.2	44.4	11.1	7.4	0.0	99.9	27	0.0
1966	14.8	22.2	44.4	11.1	7.4	0.0	99.9	27	0.0
1968	14.8	14.8	48.1	11.1	11.1	0.0	99.9	27	0.0
Period of Decline									
1970	10.0	16.7	40.0	6.7	20.0	6.7	100.1	30	3.3
1972	6.7	20.0	43.3	6.7	16.7	6.7	100.1	30	3.3
1974	6.7	13.3	53.3	3.3	16.7	6.7	100.0	30	6.7
1976	0.0	13.3	43.3	3.3	33.3	6.7	99.9	30	10.0
1980	0.0	10.0	50.0	3.3	23.3	13.3	99.9	30	16.7
1984	0.0	6.7	50.0	10.0	20.0	13.3	100.0	30	16.7

[a]May not sum to 100% due to rounding.

ditions and social movements within and external to the entire labor movement contributed to ethnic and racial and gender changes in UFWA leadership. The defeat of the Communists, some of whom were Jewish, in 1950 accelerated the decline in the percentage of Jewish GEB members. The civil rights movement, coupled with UFWA organizing successes among southern blacks and the growing percentage of black workers in the Middle Atlantic states' furniture industry during the 1960s and 1970s, stimulated the mobilization and increasing presence of blacks on the GEB during the 1970s and 1980s. The women's movement of the 1970s, along with a growing proportion of women workers in the Great Lakes furniture industry beginning in the 1960s, contributed to the mobilization and increasing percentage of women GEB members during the 1970s and 1980s.

In sum, change in UFWA leadership, as well as in the succession of social groups in leadership positions, occurred most often during the periods of rapid change in UFWA membership, the periods of growth and decline. Few leadership changes occurred during the intervening period of membership stability. Moreover, leadership change often reflected external political conditions that impinged upon the UFWA. Leadership change in the UFWA, then, appears to be more dynamic, and more subject to the changing political and economic context within which the union attempts to grow, than is implied by the iron law of oligarchy and theories of social stratification and segregation within the working class.

Continuity and Change in Union Leadership

The dynamism of UFWA leadership, that it underwent eras of continuity and change, suggests that the iron law is not very ironclad and that social segregation may erode. Rather, the iron law of oligarchy seems to apply to union leadership during periods of membership stabilization and not during periods of rapid growth or decline, and social segregation seems to erode in periods of organizational flux. It was during these periods of organizational flux that new groups, distinguished by their political ideology, ethnicity, race, and/or gender, assumed positions of leadership in the union.

Furthermore, neither the iron law nor any theory of working class stratification and segregation is consistent with the periodic eruptions of status conflict into leadership change. These theories assume that opposition to incumbents will fail to materialize from a membership that is inherently passive, apathetic, and reverent. The great worker insurgencies in the United States during the 1930s and the late 1960s, however, suggest that new worker groups, demanding representation in the governance of labor unions, periodically enter the unions as a result of the ongoing employer search for non-union labor.

What forces promote continuity and change in the elected leadership and under which conditions do new groups emerge into leadership positions? The remaining chapters address these questions. Status conflict and leadership change are manifested in competition and cooperation among groups within the union whose identities and capacities for gaining access to leadership positions are shaped as much by the union governmental structure as they are by changing political and economic conditions and social movements external to the union. These external conditions also affect the capacity of the union to grow and, hence, to accomplish its mission of improving the standard of living of workers. New groups often emerge as leaders when this capacity is impaired by such opposing forces as employer and government resistance to unionization or when the union fulfills its purpose by organizing the unorganized and incorporating new groups of workers.

In the next chapter, I examine the forces that promote leadership continuity and change. This is followed by an analysis of leadership change during the periods of growth, stability, and decline in Chapters 3, 4, and 5, respectively. Finally, in the concluding chapter, I derive a sociological theory of status conflict and leadership change from the UFWA case.

2
Local Unions and National Leaders: Institutional Bases of Ethnic and Gender Leadership Succession

Local unions constitute the voting constituencies within national unions that elect the national leaders. Leadership change in the national union is as dynamic as the fates of local unions. New groups rise to national union office with the rise of new constituencies, based in large, stable, local unions, that can compete successfully with older constituencies for national union offices.

Local unions are also the training grounds for national union leaders. It is in the local union that the trade union activist learns to handle members' grievances, negotiate contracts, administer the union, and organize the unorganized.[1] Based on their capacities to endure marketplace adversity, local unions are more or less successful at remaining stable sites for national leadership development.

The fates of local unions during the twentieth century have become increasingly tied to those of the employers with whom they bargain.[2] As

---

[1] On the local union, see Leonard Sayles and George Strauss, *The Local Union,* rev. ed. (New York: Harcourt Brace & World, 1967).

[2] Daniel Cornfield, "Declining Union Membership in the Post-World War II Era: The United Furniture Workers of America, 1939–1982," *American Journal of Sociology* 91 (March 1986): 1112–1153.

discussed later, the advent of mass production not only transferred many union functions to the corporation, but it also defined increasingly the local union membership as the workforce of a specific employer, rather than as an at-large group of casual laborers of a craft in a local labor market area.

Consequently, employer resistance to unionization during the post–World War II era, expressed by geographical capital mobility out of the high-wage, unionized North to the low-wage, non-union South, jeopardized many local unions.[3] As unions followed the movements of capital in their efforts to organize the unorganized, new local unions emerged, bringing with them new voting constituencies whose ethnic and gender composition mirrored that of the regions into which unions extended their organizing drives. Such "local union dynamics," then, and union-management conflict have contributed to the succession of ethnic and gender groups in national union office, as I discuss in the case of the UFWA later in this chapter.

This emphasis, showing the impact of local union dynamics on continuity and change in national union leadership, is a dynamic institutional alternative to Michels's iron law of oligarchy and theories of working class stratification described in the previous chapter. Michels reduced the putative stability of leadership and the absence of electoral opposition in formally democratic organizations to crowd psychology and a conspiratorial desire of incumbents to perpetuate their power. Similarly, persistent racism, ethnocentrism, and sexism, according to theories of working class stratification, contribute to the stability in the pattern of stratification, economic segmentation, and occupational segregation among status groups within the working class. Missing from the iron law and theories of working class stratification is an account of leadership change, the formation and institutionalization of new voting blocs, and the emergence of new social groups as leaders.

After discussing the historical forces that tied local union and employer fates to one another, I examine the impact of local union dynamics on ethnic and gender leadership succession in the UFWA, from its first convention in 1939 to its final convention in 1984. I conclude this chapter with an institutional approach to the analysis of leadership change that addresses the impact of forces external to the union on the institutionalization of new voting constituencies and the emergence of new groups of leaders in the union.

---

[3] Ibid. Also see Barry Bluestone and Bennett Harrison, *The Deindustrialization of America* (New York: Basic Books, 1982).

Union Captivity:
Local Union Structure and the Marketplace

A national union (often referred to as an international union if it has Canadian members) is a federation of local unions. National union membership is distributed among the local unions, rather than on an at-large basis. In turn, a worker joins the local union that represents the workforce of the "shop"—factory or office, mine or outdoor site—in which he or she is employed.[4]

The degree of local union autonomy from the national union varies among national unions. Local unions have more or less authority, for example, to conduct strikes and negotiate contracts with employers. With the geographical extension of product and labor markets and the rise of the multilocational business enterprise, beginning in the second half of the nineteenth century, national unions were formed out of the mergers of geographically separate local unions of the same craft. The national union attempted to limit the geographical mobility of both workers and firms by standardizing wage rates across regions. In this respect, local union autonomy diminished with the geographical extension of capital and markets and the emergence of national unions.[5]

The functions of the local union changed with the advent of mass production and the shift from craft unionism to industrial unionism. Prior to the 1930s, workers often worked for more than one employer during the year, changing jobs seasonally or after the completion of a project. In this era of casual labor the local craft union comprised the at-large members of a single craft or occupation in a local labor market area. The local craft union performed several functions, chief of which was the job-referral function: serving as an employment exchange for unemployed union members and prospective employers. Other functions included worker training in a union apprenticeship program, bargaining with employers over the wage for the craft in the local labor market, and providing workers with union-controlled fringe benefits (retirement pensions, unemployment benefits, mortuary benefits, etc.) at cost and financed solely by union membership dues.[6] Casual labor all but disappeared with the advent of mass production by the 1930s, as large firms stabilized their

---

[4] On the structure of unions, see Jack Barbash, *American Unions: Structure, Government and Politics* (New York: Random House, 1967).

[5] See Theodore Glocker, *The Government of American Trade Unions,* Johns Hopkins University Studies in Historical and Political Science, series 31, no. 2 (Baltimore: Johns Hopkins University Press, 1913); Lloyd Ulman, *The Rise of the National Trade Union* (Cambridge, MA: Harvard University Press, 1955).

[6] Cornfield, "Declining Union Membership."

workforces in "internal labor markets" with seniority rules for allocating and compensating labor. Also, the labor movement argued for seniority rules in order to rationalize personnel decision making and limit capricious management. The membership of the new industrial unions of the 1930s, organized on an industrywide, rather than craft, basis, tended to comprise all occupational groups of the full-time, year-round workforces of single employers in the mass production industries. Whereas employment was often conditional on craft union membership in the earlier era of casual labor, mass production effectively rendered union membership in an industrial local union conditional on employment in a specific shop.[7]

Political forces also tied local union membership to specific shops. The Wagner Act of 1935 established an election system for union organizing in which the workers of a specific shop would decide to unionize or not in an election supervised by the National Labor Relations Board. The act itself was the culmination of a struggle between organized labor and management over workplace control, which began around the time of World War I. Throughout the 1920s, organized labor championed craft unionism, while the anti-union employers of the "open shop movement" espoused employer-controlled, shop-specific, employee representation plans or company unions, in which elected worker representatives negotiated wage and hour adjustments with the employer. The Wagner Act was pro-labor legislation that allowed workers to establish their own unions in the shop, free of employer control, and, in 1937, the Supreme Court outlawed company unions.[8]

With the tying of local union membership to specific shops, the role of the local union shifted from provider to advocate. Several union functions including job referral, training, and provision of fringe benefits were transferred effectively to the corporation. The job-referral and training functions were transferred to the corporate personnel department, which now hired and trained its workforce, with the advent of continuous employment under mass production. The transfer of the job-referral function to the corporation was hastened by the 1947 Taft-Hartley Act. Spearheaded by the anti-union National Association of Manufacturers, the act outlawed the closed shop contract, whereby an employer agreed to hire only union members, undermining the contractual basis of the union job-referral function. The union fringe benefit function was transferred to the employer during the Great Depression of the 1930s, when many union fringe benefit programs were jeopardized, and during the wage freezes of World

---

[7] Ibid.
[8] Daniel Cornfield, "Labor-Management Cooperation or Managerial Control? Emerging Patterns of Labor Relations in the United States," in *Workers, Managers, and Technological Change: Emerging Patterns of Labor Relations*, ed., Daniel Cornfield (New York: Plenum, 1987), pp. 331–353.

War II, when unions began to achieve employer-provided fringe benefits through collective bargaining. The transfer of the fringe benefit function was facilitated by tax law changes in 1942, which allowed employers to deduct fringe benefits as a business expense, and by the Taft-Hartley Act, which allowed fringe benefits to be considered negotiable items in collective bargaining. By the end of World War II, the local union was engaged primarily in negotiating contracts for its shop-specific membership and handling members' grievances against the employer. No longer serving as a provider of jobs, training, and benefits, the local union was transformed into an advocate for workers. The transformation from provider to advocate, however, has not been complete. In industries with casual labor, such as construction, longshoring, and entertainment, unions continue to serve as providers.[9]

The tying of local union membership to a specific shop led the union to become what Thompson called a "captive organization," one that is highly dependent on its task environment.[10] Union captivity, as I have called it elsewhere, and the shift from provider to advocate tie local union survival chances and membership livelihoods to that of the employer.[11] Plant shutdowns and employer relocation strategies for avoiding unions jeopardize the local union itself and the livelihoods of the members, what Burawoy called "hegemonic despotism."[12]

The main local union strategies for overcoming union captivity and increasing local union longevity are to organize the workers of large shops, which are least prone to bankruptcy, and to organize additional shops into the local union, becoming a multi-shop or "amalgamated" local union. Amalgamated locals are more likely to survive than single-shop locals, because the risk of union closure due to plant shutdowns is distributed across several shops and the simultaneous closure of all the shops is unlikely. Further, large locals, whether amalgamated or single-shop, are more likely than small locals to survive, because they have more resources for hiring full-time union personnel who can organize additional shops for the local union.[13]

Union captivity and local union strategies for overcoming captivity can strategically affect which groups arise as national union leaders. Given that amalgamated and large locals have the greatest survival chances, it is these local unions that often generate the majority of national union leaders, as shown in the case of the UFWA.

[9] Daniel Cornfield, "Workers, Managers, and Technological Change," in *Workers, Managers, and Technological Change*, pp. 3–24; idem, "Declining Union Membership."
[10] James Thompson, *Organizations in Action* (New York: McGraw-Hill, 1967), p. 30.
[11] Cornfield, "Declining Union Membership."
[12] Michael Burawoy, "Between the Labor Process and the State: Factory Regimes under Advanced Capitalism," *American Sociological Review* 48 (October 1983): 587–605.
[13] Cornfield, "Declining Union Membership."

Leadership Change in the United Furniture Workers of America

Ethnic and gender groups succeeded one another on the national UFWA general executive board, as described in the previous chapter (see Table 1.4). The succession of these groups in leadership positions was associated with UFWA local union dynamics, which were played out in diverse ways among the different regions of the United States. Moreover, who succeeded whom depended on which local unions could endure independent of the frequent plant shutdowns characterizing the competitively structured furniture manufacturing industry, that is, an industry with many small, labor-intensive, mobile and closure-prone, family-owned, single-plant companies.[14] After discussing the impact of local union structure on local union survival chances, I turn to the changing geographical distribution of voting constituencies and, then, to their effect on ethnic and gender leadership succession in the UFWA. I conclude this chapter with implications of the UFWA case for the iron law of oligarchy and a theory of leadership change.

Local Union Structure and Size and the Emergence of National Leaders

Most national leaders in the UFWA have come from large, amalgamated, local unions, as shown in Table 2.1. The percentages of national UFWA general executive board members from amalgamated locals and from locals with five hundred or more members are presented in columns 1 and 2, respectively. At the first UFWA convention in 1939, for example, 85 percent of the twenty GEB members were from amalgamated locals, and 50 percent were from locals with five hundred or more members. The percentage from amalgamated locals exceeded 85 percent through 1968 and 73 percent through 1984; the percentage from locals with five hundred or more members exceeded 66 percent between 1948 and 1976 and was 56.6 percent in 1984, reflecting the decline in local union size since 1968 (Table 2.1, column 3).

Compared with the size distribution of all locals attending the UFWA conventions, the numbers of GEB members from locals with five hundred or more members are disproportionately large. The number of all UFWA locals with five hundred or more members never exceeded 30 percent, as shown in column 3 of Table 2.1, and the percentage of GEB members from locals with five hundred or more members was, at a minimum, two and

[14] Ibid.

Table 2.1
*Percentage of GEB Members from Amalgamated Locals
and Locals with 500 or More Members,
Percentage of UFWA Locals with 500 or more Members,
and Percentage of UFWA Membership in Locals
with 500 or More Members, 1939–1984*

Year	(1) % GEB Members from: Amalgamated Locals[a]	(2) % GEB Members from: Locals with 500 or More Members	(3) % UFWA Locals with 500 or More Members[b]	(4) % UFWA Membership in Locals with 500 or More Members[c]
1939	85.0 (20)	50.0	14.3 (49)	61.0 (12.7)
1948	89.7 (29)	86.2	25.0 (88)	76.8 (39.7)
1958	92.9 (28)	75.0	20.9 (91)	74.0 (36.0)
1968	92.6 (27)	81.5	29.9 (67)	79.4 (28.9)
1976	76.7 (30)	66.6	17.9 (78)	64.5 (23.3)
1984	73.3 (30)	56.6	16.2 (68)	65.9 (20.1)

[a] Number of GEB members in parentheses.
[b] Number of locals in parentheses.
[c] UFWA membership in thousands in parentheses.

one-half times greater than the percentage for all locals. However, the number of GEB members from locals with five hundred or more members was not disproportionately large in comparison with the distribution of UFWA membership by local union size. The percentage of UFWA members in locals with five hundred or more members, shown in column 4 of Table 2.1, exceeded 61 percent in every year and was similar in magnitude to the percentage of GEB members from locals with five hundred or more members. Unfortunately, data on the total number of amalgamated locals for the convention years in Table 2.1 are unavailable. However, available data for 1967 and 1982 indicate that the percentage of amalgamated locals was 36 percent and 33 percent, respectively, in these years. In sum, although a majority of UFWA locals were single-shop locals with fewer than five hundred members, a majority of UFWA members and GEB members were from locals with at least five hundred members.

The tendency of the GEB to comprise members from large locals was partly reinforced by UFWA constitutional limitations on the number of

GEB seats allocated to local unions. Between 1939 and 1974, no local union could have more than two GEB seats, and locals with less than 1,000 members could have no more than one seat. To accommodate a few large locals that merged for reasons of financial exigency in the early 1970s, the UFWA amended its constitution in 1974, placing maximum limits of one GEB seat for locals with less than 1,000 members, two seats for locals with 1,000 to 1,999 members, three seats for locals in the 2,000–3,999 membership range, and four seats for locals with at least 4,000 members (see Chapter 5 for further discussion of this constitutional amendment).

Large locals accounted for the majority of GEB members in a given term because they tended to endure for longer periods of time than small locals. The greater durability or stability of large locals is shown in Table 2.2, where local unions are classified by cohort and size. I refer to a local union cohort as all local unions whose first national UFWA convention was attended in a given year. For example, the "1939 cohort" consists of only those local unions who first sent delegates to the convention of 1939. In other words, a local union cohort is a group of local unions which were "born politically," or entered national union politics for the first time, in the same convention year. The political birth of a local union often follows soon after its establishment. Each percentage in Table 2.2 is the percentage of the locals in a given cohort, classified by local union size and for the whole cohort, that sent delegates to the conventions held in the years indicated in the column headings. For example, of the forty-nine locals in the 1939 cohort, 36.7 percent sent delegates to the 1948 convention; 28.6 percent sent delegates to the 1958 convention, and so forth. Twenty-two of the forty-nine locals in the 1939 cohort were large locals, and twenty-seven were small locals. Of these twenty-two large locals, 54.5 percent sent delegates to the 1948 convention, and 50 percent sent delegates to the 1958 convention, and so on; of the twenty-two small locals, 22.2 percent attended the 1948 convention, and 11.1 percent attended the 1958 convention, and so on.

Four relevant patterns appear in Table 2.2. First, the percentage of locals in a given cohort attending a convention tends to decline progressively over time. This trend reflects mainly the disappearance of locals due to plant shutdowns. Although locals may cease to exist for a variety of reasons other than plant shutdowns, including local union mergers, secession, and decertification by the membership, most of the UFWA local union closures resulted from plant shutdowns, as I have shown elsewhere.[15] Nonetheless, the percentage of a local union cohort attending a subsequent convention is not a perfect indicator of local union survival chances, because not all existing unions send delegates to conventions.

[15] Ibid., p. 1138.

Table 2.2
Percentage of Local Unions with Delegations at the UFWA Convention for Local Union Cohorts, by Local Union Size, 1948–1984

Local Union Cohort and Size[a]	1948	1958	1968	1976	1984	N
1939 cohort	36.7	28.6	24.5	16.3	14.3	49
Large locals	54.5	50.0	45.5	27.3	22.7	22
Small locals	22.2	11.1	7.4	7.4	7.4	27
1941–1948 cohorts	—	42.7	30.2	33.3	22.9	96
Large locals	—	57.5	47.5	47.5	42.5	40
Small locals	—	32.1	17.9	23.2	9.8	56
1950–1958 cohorts	—	—	15.3	20.3	9.3	59
Large locals	—	—	27.8	27.8	8.3	18
Small locals	—	—	9.8	17.1	9.8	41
1960–1968 cohorts[b]	—	—	—	52.4	42.9	21
Small locals	—	—	—	60.0	40.0	15
1970–1976 cohorts	—	—	—	—	45.5	22
Large locals	—	—	—	—	55.6	9
Small locals	—	—	—	—	38.5	13

[a] Local union membership at the time of the first convention to which the local sent delegates. Large = 100 or more members; small = less than 100 members.
[b] Includes 6 large locals not shown separately.

Note, for example, that the percentages of small locals of the 1941–1948 and 1950–1958 cohorts that attended the 1976 convention exceeded those at the 1968 convention.

The second pattern in Table 2.2 shows that, for each local union cohort, the percentage of large locals in attendance at almost every subsequent convention exceeded that of small locals. This suggests, as discussed earlier, that large locals have greater survival chances than small locals.

The third pattern in Table 2.2 reveals that the size of the local union cohorts, that is, the number of locals in a cohort, declined progressively in the post–World War II era and stabilized in the 1970s. In other words, the UFWA chartered fewer and fewer new locals in each successive cohort after its formative period of the 1940s (see Chapter 1 for discussion of the UFWA's formative period and its subsequent periods of stability and decline). The declining rate at which the UFWA chartered new locals is indicative of the increasing obstacles to union organizing that I discussed in the previous chapter. To recapitulate, the southward redistribution of furniture factories into a traditionally union-resistant region and the rapid diffusion of employer-provided fringe benefits among the non-union furniture companies retarded the growth of unionization in the industry. Nor is the declining rate at which the UFWA chartered new locals the result of the saturation of furniture manufacturing with unionization. Recall, as discussed in Chapter 1, that the percentage of unionized production workers in furniture manufacturing declined during the post–World War II era as employment in the industry increased.

The fourth pattern in Table 2.2 demonstrates that the percentages of the 1950–1958 cohorts in attendance at subsequent conventions are smaller than those of the cohorts that preceded and succeeded them. This pattern is partly attributable to the relatively small sizes of the local unions in the 1950–1958 cohorts. Less than one-third of the locals in the 1950–1958 cohorts had at least a hundred members, but over 40 percent of the locals in the pre-1950 cohorts had at least a hundred members. The low attendance of the 1950–1958 cohorts is also attributable to the changing geographical characteristics of the post–World War II cohorts that I discuss in greater detail in the next section. Briefly, compared with the 1960–1976 cohorts, the 1950–1958 cohorts consisted of a larger share of locals located in the East and the Midwest, where the furniture industry prospered through the 1940s but declined with plant shutdowns and local union closures during the post–World War II era. In contrast, the 1960–1976 cohorts comprised a larger share of locals in the South, where, since 1945, furniture manufacturing establishments have flourished.[16]

In sum, the data in Table 2.2 suggest why most GEB members came from large locals and imply that the older locals generated a majority of the GEB members. The large locals had the greatest longevity and, consequently, were the most persistent participants at subsequent conventions. Further, the short-lived, 1950–1958 local union cohorts created little or no competition for GEB seats with the pre-1950 local union cohorts. Local union competition for GEB seats would resume between the pre-1950 and the relatively stable 1960–1976 cohorts, although the number of local unions in the latter cohorts was less than one-third of that in the pre-1950 cohorts.

The stability and greater numbers of locals in the cohorts of the pre-1950 formative era suggest that most changes in GEB membership were associated with personnel changes within locals that already had representatives on the GEB, rather than with the supplanting on the GEB of incumbent locals by succeeding locals. This is borne out by the data in Table 2.3. This table contains the percentage of "new" GEB members, that is, the percentage of GEB members elected in a given convention year who did not serve on the GEB in the previous term, as in Table 1.3. In Table 2.3, unlike Table 1.3, the percentage of new GEB members is calculated sepa-

[16] Ibid.

Table 2.3
Percentage of New GEB Members, by Presence of Their Locals on the GEB in the Previous Term, 1941–1984[a]

Convention Year	% From New Locals[b]	% From Old Locals	N
1941	26.1	26.1	23
1943	26.9	15.4	26
1946	18.2	31.8	22
1948	24.1	27.6	29
1950	15.4	30.8	26
1952	18.5	11.1	27
1954	14.3	3.6	28
1956	7.4	14.8	27
1958	10.7	21.4	28
1960	3.8	7.7	26
1962	7.7	15.4	26
1964	7.4	7.4	27
1966	0.0	14.8	27
1968	3.7	7.4	27
1970	20.0	33.3	30
1972	0.0	20.0	30
1974	13.3	10.0	30
1976	10.0	26.7	30
1980	3.3	30.0	30
1984	13.3	26.7	30

[a] A new GEB member is one who did not serve on the GEB in the previous term.
[b] A new local is a local union which had none of its members on the GEB in the previous term; an old local is one which had at least one of its members on the GEB in the previous term.

rately for new GEB members from "new" and "old" local unions. A "new local" is one which had no representatives on the GEB in the previous term, and an "old local" is one which had at least one representative on the GEB in the previous term. At the second UFWA convention in 1941, for example, 26.1 percent of all twenty-three GEB members were new members from new locals, and 26.1 percent of the twenty-three were new members from old locals. In most years, the majority of new GEB members came from locals that had already held at least one GEB seat in the previous term. In only four of the twenty convention years (1943, 1952, 1954, 1974) did the percentage of new GEB members from new locals exceed that from old locals. Three of these four years were in either the UFWA's growth period of the 1940s or the beginning of the period of stability in the early 1950s (see Chapter 1 for a discussion of the UFWA's periods of growth, stability, and decline). This suggests that the same local unions tended to furnish the GEB with leaders, especially during the post–World War II era. Moreover, this is not inconsistent with the Table 2.2 data on local union survival. The pre-1950 local union cohorts outlived the 1950–1958 cohorts, tended to comprise larger local unions than those of the 1950–1958 cohorts, and consisted of a greater number of local unions than the total number of locals in the 1950–1976 cohorts.

In sum, the preponderance of GEB representation from large locals and the tendency for the same locals to generate new GEB leadership derived from the inability of the UFWA to incorporate large numbers of large locals after its formative period of the 1940s. This inability, in turn, resulted from the progressive difficulty of union organizing, faced by both the UFWA and the larger labor movement, arising from increased government and employer resistance to unionization after World War II. The Taft-Hartley Act of 1947, the enactment of right-to-work laws in the South shortly thereafter, the redistribution of factories out of the unionized North to the union-resistant South, and the increasing efforts by large, non-union employers to preempt unions by providing "union-scale" wages and fringe benefits, aided by changes in federal tax and labor laws, all served to slow the progress of union organizing in furniture manufacturing and other industries. In this social and political environment, then, the large UFWA local unions that were chartered in the pre-1950 era tended to supply the UFWA with most of its national leaders during the post–World War II period. Nonetheless, the impact of local union dynamics on national leadership change in the UFWA took diverse forms in different regions of the United States.

Regional Differences in Local Union Dynamics and National Leadership Change

Given local union captivity, the geographical redistribution of furniture factories, along with national UFWA organizing strategy, led to a redistribution of local unions during the post–World War II era that affected the emergence of new groups on the GEB. In addition to the effect of regional differences in furniture manufacturing growth rates on the geographical redistribution of local unions, the declining density of furniture factories reduced the capacity of local unions to amalgamate and, thereby, overcome union captivity.

Two trends in the location of furniture factories have led to the geographical redistribution of local unions. The first is the southward and westward shift out of the Midwest and the Northeast. In an effort to employ cheap, non-union labor and to be located closer to raw materials and growing consumer markets, northern furniture manufacturers either migrated southward or opened southern branch operations. Southern population growth also contributed to the growth of the southern furniture manufacturing industry. In 1900, almost three-fourths of furniture manufacturing establishments were located in the New England, Middle Atlantic, and Great Lakes regions, while fewer than 13 percent were located in the South and on the West Coast. By 1947, the number of furniture factories had increased by 11 percent in the Great Lakes region, 115 percent in the Southwest, 224 percent in the Southeast, and 189 percent on the West Coast; in the New England and Middle Atlantic regions, the number of furniture factories declined absolutely by 33 percent and 15 percent, respectively. Similar changes occurred during the 1947–1981 period, except that the number of furniture factories in the Great Lakes region declined absolutely by 22 percent. By 1981, furniture factories were more geographically decentralized than they had been in 1900. In 1981, less than one-fourth of furniture factories were located in the New England and Middle Atlantic regions, approximately one-third were in the South, 20 percent were on the West Coast, and the rest were scattered in the mountain and plains states.[17]

The second trend is the "ruralization" of furniture manufacturing. According to a recent study, the number of furniture factories has increased in rural areas, that is, counties with fewer than ten thousand residents that are outside the boundaries of standard metropolitan statistical areas. Between 1959 and 1982 (years of available data), the number of furniture factories in rural areas increased by 96 percent in New England, 19 percent in the Middle Atlantic region, 60 percent in the Great Lakes region, and 163 percent in the South. The number of urban furniture factories declined absolutely in the New England, Middle Atlantic, and Great Lakes regions during the same period, and, in the South, the number of urban furniture factories increased at less than one-fourth of the growth rate for southern, rural factories.[18]

From its start, the UFWA was determined to extend its organizing campaigns southward out of the Northeast to standardize wage rates across regions. Indeed, according to Article XXIII, section 6, of the constitution that was adopted at the founding UFWA convention in 1939, one of the duties of the UFWA president is "to supervise contracts in every district and to work for the standardization of wages, hours and working conditions in the various branches of our industry."[19] Recognizing the impor-

---

[17] Ibid., p. 1131.
[18] Daniel Cornfield and Mark Leners, "Unionization in the Rural South: Regional Patterns of Industrialization and the Process of Union Organizing," in *Research in Rural Sociology and Development*, vol. 4, eds., William Falk and Thomas Lyson (Greenwich, CT: JAI Press, 1989), pp. 137–152.
[19] *Constitution of the United Furniture Workers of America,* adopted at the First Constitutional Convention of the United Furniture Workers of America, 1939, Rockford, IL, p. 19.

tance of organizing the low-wage South, the delegates to the 1939 convention resolved to concentrate the UFWA organizing effort in that region:

> WHEREAS, The Southern area constitutes the major economic problem existing in this country today, and
> WHEREAS, This condition particularly affects the livelihood of the furniture workers in all parts of the United States, and
> WHEREAS, The Northern and Eastern representatives, who represent the heaviest concentration of furniture workers at this Convention, agree that the conditions of the Southern worker constitute the greatest menace to the livelihood and security of the workers in their own areas, . . . Therefore be it RESOLVED, That this Convention go on record, authorizing the G.E.B. to recognize the Southern area as the natural concentration point for the greatest amount of activity in organizing the unorganized furniture worker.[20]

The geographical distribution of UFWA membership shifted in accordance with this organizing strategy and the redistribution of furniture factories. In 1939, 91 percent of UFWA members were located in the New England, Middle Atlantic, and Great Lakes regions. By 1982, the proportion in these regions had declined to 60 percent, while southern membership increased to almost one-third of the total and West Coast membership grew to about 10 percent of the membership.[21]

Also, the UFWA increasingly chartered local unions in rural areas during the post–World War II era, as a consequence of the ruralization of the industry and an organizing policy of branching out from its metropolitan origins to rural areas. As UFWA President Morris Muster put it in his report to the second UFWA convention in 1941,

> What concerns us now is that we must organize this decentralized industry. Our jurisdiction can be found in every State of the Union-bedding shops, upholstering shops, furniture shops . . . , etc., are to be found from the largest urban center to the smallest hamlets. . . . We must gear our organization to be able to encompass the most important points to be organized. Once we succeed in that, then the rest can be handled in what is commonly known as the mopping up process.[22]

These "most important points" for UFWA organizing activity were the areas with dense concentrations of furniture factories, that is, major met-

---

[20] *Proceedings of the First Constitutional Convention of the United Furniture Workers of America,* Rockford, IL, February 13–17, 1939, p. 181.
[21] Cornfield, "Declining Union Membership," p. 1133.
[22] *Proceedings of the Second Constitutional Convention of the United Furniture Workers of America—CIO,* Chicago, IL, May 19–23, 1941, p. 17.

ropolitan areas and furniture manufacturing towns such as Gardner, MA, Grand Rapids, MI, High Point, NC, and Fort Smith, AR. The UFWA organizing effort did branch out from these areas dense with furniture factories into rural areas, as shown in Table 2.4, which contains the percentage of the locals in a local union cohort and region that are located in metropolitan areas and furniture manufacturing towns (not shown in the table are the percentages of locals in other, typically rural, areas). For example, of the twenty-two eastern locals in the 1939 cohort, 54.5 percent were located in metropolitan areas, 4.5 percent were located in furniture towns, and the rest, not shown in the table, were located in rural areas; of the nine southern locals in the 1939 cohort, 88.9 percent were located in furniture towns; and so on. Two patterns appear in Table 2.4. First, for each region, the percentage of locals in metropolitan areas and furniture towns for the pre-1950 cohorts tends to exceed that of the 1950–1976 cohorts. This is consistent with President Muster's organizing strategy, outlined earlier. The locals of the pre-1950 cohorts were more likely than those of later cohorts to be located in areas with dense concentrations of furniture factories, that is, the "ruralization" of UFWA locals during the post–World War II era.

Second, the locations of the early cohorts varied among regions. A majority of the eastern and western locals of the 1939 cohort were located in metropolitan areas, mainly New York, Philadelphia, San Francisco, and Los Angeles. A majority of the southern locals of the 1939 cohort were located in Fort Smith, AR, a furniture town. Most of the midwestern locals of the 1939 cohort were located in rural Indiana and Michigan. Although a majority of the locals in the post-1939 cohorts in all regions were in rural areas, the likelihood of a local's being located in a factory-dense area (metropolitan area or furniture town) tended to be greater in the East than in the other regions.

Regional differences in the size of local unions are associated with the degree of local union ruralization in a region, as suggested by the data in Table 2.5, which shows the percentage of locals with at least 250 members by local union cohort and region. For example, 36.0 percent of the twenty-five eastern and western locals in the 1939 cohort had at least 250 members. Two patterns appear in Table 2.5. First, the percentages of locals with 250 or more members of the 1950–1976 cohorts in all regions, except the Midwest, are smaller than those of the 1941–1948 cohorts. Assuming that industry ruralization tended to isolate local unions in rural areas away from large urban markets, the post–World War II decline in local union size may reflect the influence of both industry and local union ruralization in these regions. In the Midwest, the percentage of locals with 250 or more members changed little between cohorts. This may be indicative of the consistently high percentage of rural locals in the Midwest (see Table 2.4).

Table 2.4
Percentage of Local Unions in Metropolitan Areas and Furniture Towns for Local Union Cohorts, by Region[a]

Local Union Cohort	East		Midwest		South		West		All Regions	
	Metro. Area	Furn. Town	Metro. Area	Furn. Town	Metro. Area	Furn. Town	Metro. Area	Furn. Town	Metro. Area	Furn. Town
1939	54.5	4.5	13.3	20.0	0.0	88.9	66.7	0.0	32.7	24.5
	(22)[b]		(15)		(9)		(3)		(49)	
1941–1948	15.6	3.1	8.1	5.4	8.3	12.5	0.0	0.0	10.4	6.3
	(32)		(37)		(24)		(3)		(96)	
1950–1958	7.4	22.2	0.0	0.0	0.0	5.9	—	—	3.4	11.9
	(27)		(15)		(17)		(0)		(59)	
1960–1968	0.0	14.3	0.0	0.0	11.1	0.0	—	—	4.8	4.8
	(7)		(5)		(9)		(0)		(21)	
1970–1976	12.5	12.5	0.0	0.0	0.0	11.1	—	—	4.5	9.1
	(8)		(5)		(9)		(0)		(22)	

[a] Metropolitan areas are the 20 largest U.S. cities in census years. Furniture towns are nonmetropolitan towns with large concentrations of furniture factories: Jamestown, NY, Gardner, MA, Rockford, IL, Grand Rapids, MI, Sheboygan, WI, Fort Smith, AR, Memphis, TN, High Point, NC, and Thomasville, NC. The percentage of locals in the residual location category within a region and cohort—"other location"—is not shown.
[b] Number of locals in parentheses.

Table 2.5
Percentage of Local Unions with 250 or More Members, by Local Union Cohort and Region[a]

Local Union Cohort	East and West[b]	Midwest	South	All Regions
1939	36.0	13.3	0.0	22.4
	(25)[c]	(15)	(9)	(49)
1941–1948	20.0	10.8	20.8	16.7
	(35)	(37)	(24)	(96)
1950–1976	7.1	12.0	11.4	9.8
	(42)	(25)	(35)	(102)

[a] Local union membership at the time of the first convention to which the local sent delegates.
[b] Includes 3 western locals in both the 1939 cohort and the 1941–1948 cohorts.
[c] Number of locals in parentheses.

Second, the eastern and western locals in the pre-1950 cohorts tended to have higher percentages of locals with 250 or more members than the midwestern and southern locals in these cohorts (with the exception of the southern locals in the 1941–1948 cohorts). This reflects the more urban origins of the founding UFWA locals in the East and West, compared with those in the other regions. Several of the eastern and western locals were located in factory-dense, major metropolitan areas. These locals had already become large and amalgamated when they were in the AFL-affiliated Upholsterers International Union (see Chapters 1 and 3 for a discussion of UFWA origins). Championing the cause of industrial unionism over AFL craft unionism, and wishing to affiliate with the Committee for Industrial Organization, these large, urban, amalgamated locals broke away from the UIU in 1937, forming the UFWA, CIO, and they were among the largest local unions at the founding UFWA convention in 1939. In contrast, most of the southern locals in the 1939 cohort were small, single-shop locals located in Fort Smith, AR, some of which had broken away from the AFL-affiliated Carpenters union to enter the CIO. Most of these locals had merged by 1941, constituting an amalgamated local. The early cohorts of midwestern locals tended to comprise small, single-shop locals in rural areas.

Regional differences in the development of unions led to regional differences in the distribution of convention votes among the local unions of a given region. Each local that sends delegates to the national UFWA convention is allocated a certain number of votes, which is its voting strength and is equal to local union membership. Furthermore, local union voting strength is not based on the number of delegates for the local, and the voting strength of the local is divided evenly among that local's delegates. Votes, then, are cast effectively by local unions or by delegates representing a proportion of their locals, rather than by individuals. Therefore, changes in the number and size of local unions during the period between conventions may redistribute the votes among local unions, both within and between regions.

Trends in the convention vote distribution among local unions varied between the more metropolitan eastern and western regions, on the one hand, and the largely rural Midwest and South, on the other. These trends are presented in Appendix Tables 2.A–2.C at the end of the chapter. The trends in the East and West are shown in Appendix Table 2.A, which presents the percentage distribution of convention votes by local union cohort within each of the eastern (left side of the table) and western (right side of the table) regions for every national UFWA convention, beginning with the second one in 1941. At the 1941 convention, for example, 77.7 percent of the total voting strength of the eastern region was accounted for by the locals of the 1939 cohort and the rest, 22.3 percent, by the 1941 local union cohort; in the West, the 1939 cohort accounted for 47.5 percent of the western voting strength at the 1941 convention, and the 1941 cohort accounted for the rest. The trends in both regions are similar. Throughout all of the conventions, the majority of the convention votes within each region were accounted for by the local unions of the 1939 and 1941 local union cohorts. In the East, the proportion of votes allocated among the post-1941 cohorts began to increase during the 1960s, exceeding one-third of the eastern vote by the last convention, in 1984.

The domination of votes in the East and West by the 1939–1941 cohorts is indicative of the greater size, structural complexity, and, hence, longevity of the locals in these cohorts, compared with those in later cohorts. The 1939–1941 cohorts in these regions consisted of the large, amalgamated locals, mainly located in the factory-dense areas of New York City and Baltimore; the furniture towns of Gardner, MA, and Jamestown, NY; and Los Angeles and San Francisco, which entered the UFWA as amalgamated locals. These locals tended to outlive the subsequent local union cohorts, which comprised a larger share of small, single-shop locals, owing to the ruralization of the industry and increased difficulty in organizing large shops during the post–World War II era.

In the Midwest, later local union cohorts were able to capture larger shares of the votes, compared with those in the East and West, as shown in Appendix Table 2.B. The percentage of midwestern votes accounted for by the 1939 cohort declined from 50.1 percent to 3.2 percent between 1941 and 1984; that accounted for by the 1941 cohort averaged about 50 percent during the 1940s and then fluctuated from 29.0 percent to 49.3 percent along a fairly even keel after 1950; the percentage accounted for by the 1943–1946 cohorts increased to 44.4 percent in 1958, decreased to 19.1 percent in 1970, and increased to 45.1 percent by 1984; and the share of later cohorts increased fairly steadily to almost one-third in the late 1970s and then declined to less than one-fourth by 1984.

The greater instability of the cohort shares of votes in the Midwest, compared with the East and West, is attributable to the low life expectancies of the small, rural, single-shop locals that characterized this region. These locals tended to turn over as new cohorts entered the union in this region. Nonetheless, the shares of the 1941 and the 1943–1946 cohorts were more stable than those of the other cohorts and, together, the 1941–1946 cohorts accounted for a majority of midwestern voting strength in every year after 1941. Compared with the 1939 and post-1946 cohorts, the 1941–1946 cohorts consisted of, or were able to spawn, more large, amalgamated locals in factory-dense areas. Among the locals of the 1941 cohort were the large, amalgamated UIU local in Chicago, which broke away to the UFWA in 1940; the large UFWA local in Cleveland, which began as a single-shop UFWA local in 1940 and became amalgamated soon thereafter; and the UFWA local in Grand Rapids, MI, a furniture town, which became a large, amalgamated local by the end of World War II. The 1943–1946 cohorts included a large, amalgamated local in Sheboygan, WI, a furniture town, and a local in Ionia, MI, a small town with a large furniture plant that was converted into a prosperous automobile parts plant by the 1950s. Those cohorts of midwestern local unions consisting of some large, stable, amalgamated locals, as in the East, were those which continued to account for the majority of convention votes in the region.

The trends in vote distribution in the South also exhibit an unstable pattern, shown in Appendix Table 2.C. The percentage of southern votes accounted for by the 1939–1941 cohorts declined to 24.4 percent by 1948, fluctuated between 20 percent and 30 percent in eleven of the thirteen conventions held between 1950 and 1976, and then declined to 4.6 percent by 1984; the percentage accounted for by the 1943–1948 cohorts increased to 75.6 percent by 1948, fell to 38.2 percent in 1958, and increased haltingly to 67.2 percent by 1984; the percentage accounted for by the 1950–1958 cohorts increased to 33.7 percent in 1958 and declined to zero by 1984; and the percentage accounted for by later cohorts increased to roughly 30 percent by the early 1980s. Note that the percentages accounted for by successive cohorts tended to complement one another in the South. As each successive cohort increased its share of the votes, the share of the previous cohort tended to decline. However, the shares of the 1939–1941 and 1943–1948 cohorts were more stable than those of later cohorts and, together, the 1939–1948 cohorts accounted for most of the southern voting strength in every year.

In the South, the overall instability in the trends of cohort vote shares resulted from the high rates of turnover among the small, rural, single-shop locals that prevailed in this region. As in the other regions, the cohorts with the most stable trends were those comprising large, amalgamated locals, typically located in factory-dense areas. Among the locals of the 1939 cohort were the amalgamated Fort Smith local and a large, single-shop Fort Smith local at Ward's Furniture Co. that had been organized by the CIO in 1936. In the 1943–1946 cohorts were a large, amalgamated local in Sumter, SC, a small factory town; a local in Memphis, TN, which amalgamated continuously, its membership surpassing that of the Fort Smith locals in the 1960s, when the Fort Smith furniture industry began to decline, and becoming one of the largest in the UFWA by 1970; and large, single-shop locals in Thomasville, NC, and Henderson, NC.

In sum, the trends in the distribution of convention votes among local unions differed in the four regions. In all of the regions, the local union cohorts comprising the greatest number of large, amalgamated locals were those with the most stable bloc of votes and which tended to command a majority of votes for the longest period of time. What differed in the regions was the prevalence and timing of the creation of the amalgamated locals. These regional differences, in turn, depended on the density of furniture factories in the area and the timing of the UFWA organizing drives in the region. In the factory-dense, metropolitan areas on the two coasts, where the several large, amalgamated locals broke from the UIU to form the UFWA in 1937, a stable voting bloc of local unions was set by the end of the second UFWA convention in 1941 and persisted as such until the last UFWA convention in 1984. As UFWA organizing drives shifted to the nonmetropolitan Midwest and South, where small, rural, single-shop locals prevailed and, consequently, local union turnover rates were high, amalgamated locals were spawned during the 1940s and constituted a stable voting bloc by the 1950s. After the establishment of these stable voting blocs in all of the regions, the post–World War II cohorts tended to comprise small, single-shop, and, hence, short-lived locals, owing to industry ruralization and increased obstacles to union organizing, and they commanded only a minority of the convention votes in each region.

Consequently, different local union cohorts supplied the GEB with leaders in the various regions, as shown in Table 2.6. The data in Table 2.6 are the percentage distribution of all GEB members who served in the specified era from a given region by the cohort of their local unions. For example, of the forty GEB members from the East and West who served for at least one of the terms between 1939 and 1948, 77.5 percent were from locals of the 1939 local union cohort, and 22.5 percent were from locals of the 1941 local union cohort. In the East and West, where the 1939–1941 cohorts comprised a majority of votes in every year, almost all of the GEB members from these regions were from locals of the 1939–1941 cohorts at every UFWA convention.

The complex leadership patterns in the Midwest and the South, as

Table 2.6
Percentage Distribution of GEB Members, by Local Union Cohort for Regions, 1939–1984

Local Union Cohort	1939–1948	1950–1958	1960–1968	1970–1984
East and West				
1939	77.5	58.3	65.0	60.5
1941	22.5	41.7	30.0	36.8
Later cohorts	0.0	0.0	5.0	2.6
Total	100.0	100.0	100.0	99.9[a]
N	40	24	20	38
Midwest				
1939	44.4	14.3	20.0	17.4
1941	55.6	50.0	53.3	30.4
1943	0.0	7.1	13.3	8.7
1946	0.0	21.4	13.3	17.4
Later cohorts	0.0	7.1	0.0	26.1
Total	100.0	99.9[a]	99.9[a]	100.0
N	18	14	15	23
South				
1939	71.4	40.0	33.3	7.1
1941	0.0	0.0	0.0	0.0
1943	14.3	0.0	16.7	21.4
1946	14.3	60.0	50.0	50.0
Later cohorts	0.0	0.0	0.0	21.4
Total	100.0	100.0	100.0	99.9[a]
N	7	10	6	14

[a] Does not sum to 100% due to rounding.

shown in Table 2.6, contrast with the stable patterns in the East and West. In the Midwest, an increasingly broad range of local union cohorts accounted for the GEB members from this region, beginning in the 1950s, as new cohorts continuously arose in the region. The 1941 cohort, which included the large, amalgamated locals in Chicago and Cleveland, accounted for a majority of the midwestern GEB members until 1970–1984, by which time no cohort accounted for a majority. In the South, a widening range of local union cohorts came to account for the southern GEB members, especially by the 1960s, when the Fort Smith locals (1939 cohort) had begun to decline and the Memphis, Henderson, and Sumter locals (1943–1946 cohorts) had risen.

The successive development of stable voting blocs based on amalgamated locals in the regions, first in the East and West, then in the Midwest, and later in the South, is reflected in the changing geographical distribution of convention votes and GEB members in the UFWA, shown in Table 2.7. These changing distributions also reflect the ruralization and southward shift of the furniture manufacturing industry. Table 2.7 shows the percentage distribution of GEB members and convention votes by location in selected years. For each year, the distribution of GEB members is shown in the upper row and that for convention votes is shown in the lower row. The heaviest concentrations of both GEB members and convention votes shifted from the metropolitan East in 1939 to the nonmetropolitan Midwest and South by 1984. The percentages of GEB members and votes accounted for by the nonmetropolitan East, metropolitan Midwest, and West remained low and stable. At the founding convention in 1939, the locals of the metropolitan East held 58.9 percent of the UFWA convention votes and elected 45 percent of the GEB members. By the time of the last UFWA convention in 1984, the nonmetropolitan Midwest and South together held 42.1 percent of the convention votes and elected half of the GEB members. The changing geographical distribution of convention votes, as well as the greater stability of the pre-1950 local union cohorts, contributed to the succession of ethnic and gender groups on the GEB.

Ethnic and Gender Succession on the GEB

Local union dynamics are relevant to ethnic and gender leadership succession because the ethnic and gender composition of the workforce and union membership may change within a local union, vary regionally, or both. Given the changes in the ethnic and gender composition of the furniture manufacturing workforce, as well as the geographical extension of furniture factories and UFWA organizing drives into a socially heterogeneous set of regions, the ethnic and gender composition of the UFWA GEB changed between 1939 and 1984, as described in the previous chapter (see Table 1.4).

Unfortunately, data on the ethnic and gender traits of local union members are unavailable for the UFWA and most unions. To discern the ethnic and gender traits of local union memberships, I conducted approximately fifty on-site, personal interviews with knowledgeable, current and retired, UFWA officials and activists in all regions of the United States and consulted photographs and articles in all available back issues of the *Fur-*

Table 2.7
Percentage Distribution of GEB Members and Convention Votes, by Location, 1939–1984

Convention Year	East, Metro.[a]	East, Nonmetro.	Midwest, Metro.	Midwest, Nonmetro.	South	West	Total[b]	N[c]
1939								
GEB	45.0	10.0	5.0	20.0	10.0	10.0	100.0	20
Votes	58.9	6.0	2.1	23.7	6.3	3.1	100.1	12.7
1948								
GEB	44.8	6.9	10.3	10.3	13.8	13.8	99.9	29
Votes	35.5	13.8	7.6	17.8	13.0	12.3	100.0	39.7
1958								
GEB	32.1	10.7	10.7	21.4	17.9	7.1	99.9	28
Votes	34.4	16.6	6.9	21.0	15.4	5.7	100.0	36.0
1968								
GEB	40.7	7.4	11.1	22.2	11.1	7.4	99.9	27
Votes	39.5	10.6	7.6	14.3	19.8	8.1	99.9	28.9
1976								
GEB	30.0	10.0	3.3	26.7	20.0	10.0	100.0	30
Votes	24.7	14.4	6.7	19.2	24.7	10.3	100.0	23.3
1984								
GEB	23.3	10.0	6.7	30.0	20.0	10.0	100.0	30
Votes	30.2	12.3	4.9	20.5	21.6	10.6	100.1	20.1

[a]Metropolitan areas are the 20 largest U.S. cities in census years.
[b]May not sum to 100% due to rounding.
[c]For convention votes, N is in thousands.

niture Workers Press, the monthly UFWA newspaper (see Chapter 5 for trends in the racial, ethnic, and gender composition of the furniture manufacturing workforce).

The degree of stability in the local union voting blocs within a region affected the process by which ethnic succession on the GEB occurred in the different regions. In the metropolitan areas with the oldest and most stable local union voting blocs, ethnic succession was mainly a function of ethnic change in the membership of the large, stable, amalgamated, local unions in these areas. In contrast, any succession of GEB members from nonmetropolitan areas, which tended to comprise ethnically homogeneous union memberships, resulted primarily from the succession of local union cohorts, given the relatively high rates of local union turnover in these areas.

These patterns are shown in Table 2.8, which gives the percentage distribution of all GEB members, classified simultaneously by ethnicity (derived from their surnames and from my personal interviews), the starting years of their first terms on the GEB, and the cohort of their local unions, in each of six locations. For example, 19.6 percent of all fifty-one GEB members from the metropolitan areas of the East who served at least one term between 1939 and 1984 were Jewish, began their first terms on the GEB in 1939 or 1941, and were members of local unions from the 1939 local union cohort; 13.7 percent were Italians who entered the GEB between 1941 and 1950 and were members of local unions in the 1939–1941 local union cohorts; and so forth.

Given the stability and dominance of the 1939–1941 local union cohorts in the metropolitan East, all of the ethnic succession on the GEB from this area resulted from the changing ethnic composition in the memberships of these locals. Most of the pre-1950 GEB members from this area were Jewish or Italian, reflecting the ethnic composition of New York City furniture workers, over 75 percent of whom during the late 1930s were foreign-born.[23] The Italian GEB members succeeded the Jewish members by just a few years. This is indicative of the fact that most of the activists who led the breakaway from the AFL into the CIO, forming the UFWA, were Jewish and among the first to serve on the GEB.

After 1952, no new groups entered the GEB from the metropolitan East until 1970, when several of the early activists retired and were succeeded by blacks and a second generation of Italians, which lasted through the early 1980s. That the early group of Jewish and Italian members served until the 1970s resulted in part from the stability and large size of their

---

[23] Abraham Zide, "Organization of Labor in the Furniture Industry in New York City," (bachelor's paper, College of the City of New York, 1939), p. 14. Zide is a founding member of the UFWA.

Table 2.8
*Percentage Distribution of GEB Members for Regions,
by Ethnicity, Year of First Term on GEB, and Local Union Cohort*

Ethnicity	Year of First Term	Local Union Cohort	%
East, Metropolitan[a] (N = 51)			
Jewish	1939–1941	1939	19.6
Italian	1941–1950	1939–1941	13.7
Northern and Western European	1941–1950	1939–1941	11.8
Jewish	1946–1952	1939–1941	11.8
Black	1970–1984	1939–1941	13.7
Italian	1970–1980	1939–1941	15.7
Other			13.7
Total			100.0
East, Nonmetropolitan (N = 14)			
Northern and Western European	1939–1950	1939–1941	50.0
Italian	1958–1960	1939–1941	14.3
Northern and Western European	1970–1980	1941 and later	35.7
Total			100.0
Midwest, Metropolitan (N = 14)			
Italian	1939–1946	—[b]	21.4
Northern and Western European	1941–1950	—	35.7
Eastern European	1958–1962	—	28.6
Other			14.3
Total			100.0
Midwest, Nonmetropolitan (N = 35)			
—[c]	1939–1943	1939	20.0
—	1943–1954	1941–1943	14.3
—	1950–1958	1946–1948	11.4
—	1964–1970	1943–1946	11.4
—	1970–1984	1946 and later	25.7
—	1974–1984	1939–1943	14.3
Other			2.9
Total			100.0

(*continued*)

Table 2.8 (continued)

Ethnicity	Year of First Term	Local Union Cohort	%
South (N = 31)			
Northern and Western European	1939–1943	1939	16.1
Mainly Northern and Western European[d]	1948–1954	1943–1946	22.6
Northern and Western European	1952–1958	1939	9.7
Mainly black[e]	1962–1964	1943–1946	9.7
Black	1970–1984	1943 and later	38.7
Other			3.2
Total			100.0
West (N = 20)			
Mainly Northern and Western European, in metropolitan areas[f]	1939–1952	1939	30.0
Northern and Western European, in nonmetropolitan areas	1941–1952	1941	20.0
Mainly Northern and Western European, in nonmetropolitan areas[g]	1970–1976	1941	15.0
Mainly Hispanic, in metropolitan areas[h]	1976–1984	1939	25.0
Other			10.0
Total			100.0

[a] Metropolitan areas are the 20 largest U.S. cities in a census year; nonmetropolitan areas are all other places.
[b] The local unions of 92.9% of GEB members from the metropolitan Midwest are from the 1941 local union cohort.
[c] 85.7% of GEB members from the nonmetropolitan Midwest are of Northern and Western European descent.
[d] 3 of these 7 GEB members are black.
[e] 1 of these 3 GEB members is of Northern and Western European descent.
[f] 2 of these 6 GEB members are Hispanic, and one is Eastern European.
[g] 1 of these 3 GEB members is black.
[h] 1 of these 5 GEB members is black and one is Northern and Western European.

local unions and the fact that the more transient local union cohorts that emerged after 1941 never captured a significant share of the votes. By the time of the retirement of the early activists, the proportion of Jewish and Italian union members in the metropolitan East had declined, while that of black and Hispanic union members had increased. In New York City, according to the estimates of UFWA trade union activists, blacks and Hispanics made up a majority of the membership in local 140, a large bedding workers local, by the 1960s and 95 percent of its membership in 1985. The upholsterers local 76 continued to comprise many Italian members in the early 1970s. In the large Baltimore local 75, the largely Jewish, Italian, German, and Irish membership of the 1940s and 1950s was succeeded by black members, who first constituted a majority of the 1960s and about 80 percent of the local membership in the early 1970s.

Little ethnic succession occurred in the nonmetropolitan East, as shown in Table 2.8. Of the fourteen GEB members from this area, mainly the furniture towns of Jamestown, NY, and Gardner, MA, 85.7 percent were of Northern and Western European descent. Local 154, the large, amalgamated local in Gardner, consisted mainly of English, Irish, Scandinavian, and French-Canadian members. In Jamestown, the locals comprised English and Scandinavian members and, later, Italians, who first began to arrive in the area during the 1930s. What succession occurred here was largely between local union cohorts, with later cohorts supplying the GEB with members by the 1970s.

In the metropolitan Midwest, as shown in Table 2.8, the large, amalgamated, Chicago and Cleveland locals of the 1941 local union cohort supplied most of the GEB members from this area. Italian and Northern and Western European GEB members predominated through 1950, while Eastern Europeans entered the GEB around 1960. In Cleveland local 450, the membership was predominantly Italian and Eastern European in the 1940s, approximately 25 percent black in the early 1960s, and about 40 percent black by the mid-1980s. In Chicago local 18B, the membership was approximately 40 percent foreign-born and largely Eastern European and Italian in 1940. By the late 1970s, a majority of the 18B membership was black and Hispanic. Despite these membership patterns, Eastern Europeans entered the GEB as late as 1958, perhaps because of the relatively high percentage of foreign-born workers in the membership of the 1940s.

Almost no ethnic succession occurred among the GEB members from the nonmetropolitan Midwest, as shown in Table 2.8, where 85.7 percent of the GEB members were of Northern and Western European descent. In local 800, the large, amalgamated local in Sheboygan, WI, where the membership was primarily of German and German-Russian descent, the percentage of native-born members increased from roughly 50 percent to 95 percent between the late 1940s and 1960. The large, single-shop local 420 in Ionia, MI, and amalgamated local 415 in Grand Rapids, MI, tended to consist of German, Dutch, Irish, English, and some Eastern and Southern European members. Given the emergence of successive local union cohorts, each new cohort tended to supply the GEB with members from this area, although the stable 1939–1946 local union cohorts generated GEB leaders in the late 1960s and from the mid-1970s onward.

In the South, blacks had succeeded Northern and Western Europeans on the GEB by the 1970s, as shown in Table 2.8. Northern and Western European GEB members from the South predominated through the early 1960s, reflecting mainly the ethnic composition of the Fort Smith union membership. In the 1930s, most of the Fort Smith union members were native-born and had been farmers in the Fort Smith area, and they continued to be primarily of English and Irish descent through the 1980s.

With the decline of the Fort Smith locals and the rise of amalgamated locals 282 in Memphis and 273 in Sumter, SC, in the early 1960s, blacks began to enter the GEB from the South and, beginning in 1970, all new southern GEB members were black. The entry of southern blacks on the GEB resulted not just from the fact that the membership of the 1943–1946 local union cohorts, centered mainly in Memphis and Sumter, surpassed that of the 1939 cohort, which was centered in Fort Smith. In addition, whereas the Fort Smith local union membership remained predominantly white, the Memphis local union membership had become approximately 65 percent black by the early 1960s. The Sumter local had been predominantly black since the 1940s.

In the West, as shown in Table 2.8, Hispanics began to succeed Northern and Western Europeans on the GEB from the locals in metropolitan areas during the late 1970s, while the local in the nonmetropolitan area, Portland, OR, local 1090, tended to supply the GEB with Northern and Western Europeans through the 1970s. The ethnic succession on the GEB from the West Coast metropolitan areas tended to reflect the changing ethnic characteristics of amalgamated locals 576 in Los Angeles (which became local 1010 in 1950) and 262 in San Francisco. About half of the Los Angeles local union membership in 1950 was of Mexican descent, the remainder comprising Northern and Western Europeans who had migrated to California from Oklahoma and Arkansas and a few black and Jewish members. By the late 1970s, roughly 80 percent of the Los Angeles local union membership was of Mexican descent. In San Francisco, immigrant Italians comprised much of the local union membership in the 1930s. By the late 1960s, the percentage of Italians in the local had declined to less than 25 percent, and, through the 1980s, the membership was roughly 25 percent Hispanic, 20 percent black, 10 percent Asian, and the rest of mixed European descent. From the 1940s onward, the local union membership in Portland, OR, was predominantly Northern and Western European.

Turning to gender succession on the GEB, women first entered the GEB in the 1970s, as described in the previous chapter (see Table 1.4). Seven of the ten women GEB members were from the nonmetropolitan Midwest or South, the regions which, together, came to account for the largest single bloc of votes in the UFWA during the 1970s (see Table 2.7). These regions were also those with the highest percentages of women workers in the wood furniture manufacturing industry at that time. According to U.S. Bureau of Labor Statistics surveys of this industry, the percentage of women workers declined after World War II, when many women had entered the industry, through the early 1960s, and then increased from the late 1960s into the 1980s. The surveys indicate that women made significant inroads between 1965 and 1974, especially in the southern and Great Lakes regions (see Chapter 5 for discussion of the growing proportion of women workers in the furniture manufacturing industry). During this time, the percentage of women workers increased from 7.5 percent to 31.6 percent in the Southeast, from 17.5 percent to 41.3 percent in the Southwest, and from 18.2 percent to 37.7 percent in the Great Lakes region. In contrast, the percentage of women workers did not exceed 29 percent in the other regions and was as low as 11.8 percent on the West Coast in 1974. By 1986, the percentage of women workers had increased to 31.6 percent in New England, to 22.1 percent in the Middle Atlantic states, to 38.4 percent in the Southeast, to 45.8 percent in the Great Lakes region, and to 13.8 percent on the West Coast.[24]

The ethnic characteristics of the ten women GEB members reflected more closely than their gender the social composition of their local unions. Half of the women GEB members were from locals whose mem-

---

[24] U.S. Department of Labor, Bureau of Labor Statistics, *Wage Structure, Wood Furniture, 1945*, Series 2, no. 30 (Washington, DC: U.S. Department of Labor, Bureau of Labor Statistics, 1946); *Wage Structure, Household Furniture, 1954*, Report no. 76 (Washington, DC: U.S. Department of Labor, Bureau of Labor Statistics, 1954); *Wage Structure, Wood Household Furniture, Except Upholstered, April–May 1959*, Report no. 152 (Washington, DC: Government Printing Office, 1960); *Industry Wage Survey, Wood Household Furniture, Except Upholstered, July 1962*, Bulletin no. 1369 (Washington, DC: Government Printing Office, 1963); *Industry Wage Survey, Wood Household Furniture, Except Upholstered, May–June 1965*, Bulletin no. 1496 (Washington, DC: Government Printing Office, 1966); *Industry Wage Survey, Wood Household Furniture, Except Upholstered, October 1968*, Bulletin no. 1651 (Washington, DC: Government Printing Office, 1970); *Industry Wage Survey, Wood Household Furniture, Except Upholstered, October 1971*, Bulletin no. 1793 (Washington, DC: Government Printing Office, 1973); *Industry Wage Survey, Wood Household Furniture, Except Upholstered, November 1974*, Bulletin no. 1930 (Washington, DC: Government Printing Office, 1976); *Industry Wage Survey: Wood Household Furniture, June 1979*, Bulletin no. 2087 (Washington, DC: Government Printing Office, 1981); *Industry Wage Survey: Wood Household Furniture, June 1986*, Bulletin no. 2283 (Washington, DC: Government Printing Office, 1987).

bers were mostly women. However, the five black women GEB members, four of whom were southerners, were from predominantly black locals. Three of the five white women GEB members were of Northern and Western European descent from nonmetropolitan midwestern locals whose memberships were comprised mainly of this ethnic group. The one Hispanic woman GEB member was from the predominantly Hispanic Los Angeles local.

Gender succession on the GEB was associated with the succession of local union cohorts, especially in the nonmetropolitan Midwest and South, where local union turnover rates were high. The seven women GEB members from the nonmetropolitan Midwest and South were from locals in the 1946 and later cohorts. In contrast, the three women GEB members from metropolitan areas were from locals in the 1939–1941 cohorts. Like ethnic succession, gender succession, then, occurred in two ways. First, in the metropolitan areas comprising the large, stable, amalgamated locals of the 1939–1941 cohorts, gender succession reflected change in the memberships of the locals. Second, in nonmetropolitan areas where local union cohorts tended to succeed one another, gender succession often resulted from the succession of local unions.

In sum, the emergence of new groups on the GEB was closely related to local union dynamics. Given that convention votes were allocated to delegates on the basis of local union size and that the local unions staffed the GEB, the rise and fall of local unions affected the distribution of votes within and between regions as well as who entered, exited, and remained on the GEB. The rise and fall of local unions, given local union captivity, resulted from both the geographical mobility of employers and variation among locals in their capacity to free themselves from captivity through amalgamation. The redistribution of furniture factories after World War II was toward the low-wage South and rural areas in all regions. Amalgamated locals tended to survive independently of employer mobility, or at least to outlive single-shop locals, which often closed due to plant shutdowns. Consequently, ethnic and gender succession on the GEB was generated by regional unevenness in the development of stable voting blocs based in amalgamated locals. The decline in the number of Jewish and Italian GEB members, followed by increases in Northern and Western Europeans and, later, blacks, Hispanics, and women, was associated with the rise of stable voting blocs, first in the East and West, then in the rural Midwest, and finally in the South. This succession reflected regional differences in furniture worker ethnicity, the changing ethnic makeup on the two coasts, and the entry of women into the industry during the late 1960s, especially in the South and rural Midwest. Succession on the GEB resulted as much from national UFWA organizing strategy and the incorporation of new membership groups in the union as it did from employer efforts to avoid the union by moving their factories to low-wage, non-union areas.

An Institutional Alternative to Static Theories of Working Class Organization

The rates at which new members entered the GEB were highest during the UFWA's periods of growth (1939–1950) and decline (1970–1984) and lowest in the intervening period of stability (1952–1968), as discussed in detail in the previous chapter (see Table 1.3). Recall, I suggested that this dynamism in UFWA leadership posed a challenge to Michels's iron law of oligarchy and to theories of working class stratification and segregation. The inevitable oligarchical degeneration of growing, formally democratic organizations, as posited in the iron law, was based partly in psychological reductionism: leadership stability resulted from crowd psychology, the unflinching reverence of the rank-and-file for their leaders, the intellectual superiority of leaders, and a conspiratorial desire and capacity of leaders to perpetuate their power.[25] Similarly, persistent racism, ethnocentrism, and sexism, according to theories of working class stratification, retard the upward social mobility of minorities and women and generate occupational race and sex segregation. No doubt, few leaders want to be unseated. However, the psychological reductionism of the iron law and persisting obstacles to the mobility of minorities and women are inconsistent with temporal variation in leadership turnover rates and the emergence of new ethnic and gender groups as elected leaders. Furthermore, this inconsistency stems from the omission in the iron law and theories of working class stratification of changing constituencies or voting blocs within formally democratic organizations and the institutional bases of constituency stability.

The analysis of ethnic and gender succession on the GEB in this chapter argues for a dynamic institutional alternative to Michels's iron law and theories of working class stratification. As pointed out in recent research by both Edelstein and Hemingway, the structure of the organization itself can carve out constituencies with competing interests who seek representation in leadership positions.[26] In the UFWA, the relevant structural features are local unions and the partly geographical structure of the GEB. Depending on their relative sizes and stability, local unions within a region were more or less successful in staffing the GEB with leaders.

However, missing in this recent research are the factors, both internal and external to the organization, that affect the relative strength of these competing constituencies carved out of the organizational structure. In the UFWA, as in many unions, the fates of local unions or voting constituencies

---

[25] Robert Michels, *Political Parties*, (1911; reprint, New York: Free Press, 1962), pp. 92, 105, 107, 121.
[26] J. David Edelstein, "An Organizational Theory of Union Democracy," *American Sociological Review* 32 (February 1967): 19–31; John Hemingway, *Conflict and Democracy* (Oxford: Clarendon Press, 1978).

are affected by their own size, their structural complexity (i.e., whether or not they are amalgamated), and, therefore, their capacities for overcoming captivity. Their fates are simultaneously affected by the degree of labor-management adversity, the movements of employers away from unions, and the degree of employer and government resistance to unions. Constituencies in the union, then, become entrenched or disappear, depending on their capacities for enduring independently of adverse relationships with employers. The long hiatus in leadership change during the UFWA's period of stability resulted from the inability of newly incorporated constituencies to form, grow, and compete with the older, more stable constituencies in the metropolitan areas, an inability that stemmed from increased employer and government resistance to unionization and the subsequent incorporation of small, short-lived, single-shop locals in isolated rural areas. Leadership change did occur during the 1970s in the period of decline, when the leadership that had emerged by the early 1950s retired and when newer, stable, and growing constituencies finally took root in regions other than the declining ones housing the old constituencies.

Therefore, it was in periods of organizational flux that new, stable constituencies emerged in formerly unorganized locations, new groups were incorporated into the union, and ethnic and gender succession occurred on the GEB. Ethnic succession was most pronounced during the UFWA's periods of growth and decline, and gender succession first occurred in the latter period, because new constituencies emerged and stabilized in these periods, rather than in the period of stability.

From this perspective, the iron law and theories of working class stratification are most applicable to periods in the history of an organization when it fails to incorporate new constituencies. In such periods of stability, the distribution of votes among institutionally created constituencies is stable, and incumbents can command the votes. Periods of stability, arguing from the UFWA case, appear likely when the organization encounters resistance to further growth from external forces, such as hostile adversaries. Hence, leadership stability is likely when a union encounters employer resistance or when it saturates its jurisdiction (which did not happen to the UFWA).

The changing distribution of votes among the constituencies in a formally democratic organization affects the emergence of new groups as leaders. Indeed, votes are a necessary prerequisite for attaining elective office. As such, an analysis of leadership continuity and change that examines the determinants of changes in the distribution of votes emphasizes forces that facilitate leadership change, but not the types of issues that motivate or compel leadership change. It is to these latter forces that I now turn in an examination of leadership change during the UFWA's periods of growth, stability, and decline in Chapters 3, 4, and 5, respectively.

Appendix Table 2.A

Percentage Distribution of UFWA Convention Votes in Eastern and Western Regions, by Local Union Cohort, 1941–1984

Convention Year[a]	East					West				
	1939 Cohort	1941 Cohort	Later Cohorts	Total	N (thousands)	1939 Cohort	1941 Cohort	Later Cohorts	Total	N (thousands)
1941	77.7	22.3	—	100.0	11.3	47.5	52.5	—	100.0	2.1
1943	75.8	24.2	0	100.0	13.1	65.0	35.0	0.0	100.0	1.7
1946	62.3	28.9	8.8	100.0	16.8	79.9	20.1	0.0	100.0	3.2
1948	64.7	26.6	8.7	100.0	19.5	80.1	19.9	0.0	100.0	4.9
1950	68.1	22.8	9.1	100.0	17.9	82.9	17.1	0.0	100.0	3.9
1952	65.9	24.5	9.6	100.0	18.8	76.1	23.9	0.0	100.0	2.9
1954	58.5	31.2	10.3	100.0	16.3	71.7	28.3	0.0	100.0	1.7
1956	53.2	30.8	16.0	100.0	18.5	96.2	3.8	0.0	100.0	2.1
1958	53.6	31.5	14.9	100.0	18.4	98.4	1.6	0.0	100.0	2.1
1960	55.9	33.4	10.7	100.0	16.4	98.2	1.8	0.0	100.0	2.1
1964	57.4	28.8	13.8	100.0	15.9	91.6	8.4	0.0	100.0	2.5
1966	56.0	31.8	12.2	100.0	15.9	100.0	0.0	0.0	100.0	2.3
1968	59.1	15.5	9.7	100.0	14.5	87.5	12.5	0.0	100.0	2.4
1970	56.7	29.0	14.3	100.0	15.1	84.3	15.7	0.0	100.0	2.6
1972	53.9	29.4	16.7	100.0	12.8	88.2	11.8	0.0	100.0	2.7
1974	50.7	21.9	27.4	100.0	12.7	86.6	13.4	0.0	100.0	2.9
1976	53.4	21.8	24.8	100.0	9.1	83.2	16.8	0.0	100.0	2.4
1980	48.8	19.7	31.5	100.0	9.3	100.0	0.0	0.0	100.0	2.3
1984	47.6	18.2	34.2	100.0	8.5	100.0	0.0	0.0	100.0	2.1

[a] 1962 data are unavailable.

Appendix Table 2.B
Percentage Distribution of UFWA Convention Votes in the Midwestern Region, by Local Union Cohort, 1941–1984

Convention Year[a]	1939	1941	1943–1946	Later Cohorts	Total[b]	N (thousands)
1941	50.1	49.9	—	—	100.0	5.3
1943	35.7	48.8	15.5	—	100.0	6.9
1946	20.2	53.7	26.1	—	100.0	10.5
1948	22.6	51.0	22.4	4.0	100.0	10.1
1950	25.4	39.2	30.3	5.1	100.0	6.9
1952	24.8	36.6	32.3	6.3	100.0	7.9
1954	17.5	42.8	33.5	6.3	100.1	8.7
1956	13.8	41.5	39.5	5.2	100.0	9.2
1958	12.8	34.8	44.4	8.0	100.0	10.1
1960	14.0	36.9	23.3	25.7	99.9	9.1
1964	16.0	46.9	29.1	8.1	100.1	6.8
1966	16.5	48.6	22.6	12.2	99.9	6.2
1968	13.9	49.3	21.0	15.9	100.1	6.3
1970	12.5	39.8	19.1	28.7	100.1	7.2
1972	13.8	37.5	21.0	27.7	100.0	6.5
1974	13.1	33.5	23.4	30.1	100.1	7.6
1976	4.8	36.1	27.9	31.1	99.9	6.0
1980	4.3	36.2	36.4	23.1	100.0	6.9
1984	3.2	29.0	45.1	22.6	99.9	5.1

[a] 1962 data are unavailable.
[b] May not sum to 100% due to rounding.

Appendix Table 2.C
Percentage Distribution of UFWA Convention Votes in the Southern Region, by Local Union Cohort, 1941–1984

Convention Year[a]	1939–1941	1943–1948	1950–1958	Later Cohorts	Total[b]	N (thousands)
1941	100.0	—	—	—	100.0	0.9
1943	75.6	24.4	—	—	100.0	1.3
1946	40.2	59.8	—	—	100.0	5.1
1948	24.4	75.6	—	—	100.0	5.2
1950	23.5	67.9	8.6	—	100.0	4.1
1952	21.1	58.2	20.7	—	100.0	5.1
1954	25.4	49.4	25.1	—	99.9	5.3
1956	25.2	42.0	32.8	—	100.0	5.8
1958	28.1	38.2	33.7	—	100.0	5.5
1960	35.6	40.1	24.2	0.0	99.9	5.0
1964	33.1	57.0	7.0	3.0	100.1	3.9
1966	29.8	53.0	7.6	9.5	99.9	4.9
1968	27.0	48.3	10.0	14.7	100.0	5.7
1970	24.1	44.3	11.0	20.6	100.0	6.7
1972	22.6	46.2	5.1	26.0	99.9	6.4
1974	22.7	47.2	5.2	24.8	99.9	6.5
1976	23.5	48.8	3.8	24.0	100.1	5.8
1980	7.4	59.5	2.8	30.2	99.9	6.1
1984	4.6	67.2	0.0	28.2	100.0	4.3

[a] 1962 data are unavailable.
[b] May not sum to 100% due to rounding.

3

Building a Furniture Industrial Union: The UFWA's Formative Years, 1932–1950

Building a national, industrial union of furniture workers did not just entail the establishment of a union constitution and the conducting of vigorous organizing drives. It also entailed the uniting of workers who had a common purpose but who differed in terms of ethnicity, region of origin, skill level and craft, and products manufactured.

The effort to realize industrial unionism in the furniture industry, beginning in the early 1930s, persevered through tensions external to and within the union. The chief external tension was with craft unionism, the older form of unionism that organized unions along craft or occupational lines, often under the banner of the American Federation of Labor. The major AFL unions in the furniture industry had been the Upholsterers and the Carpenters, each of which practiced traditional craft unionism by organizing mainly the skilled workers in their respective trades.

As mass production technology entered furniture manufacturing during the 1920s, generating many non-skilled production jobs, the sentiment for industrial unionism, whereby workers of all occupations, regardless of skill level, would belong to the same union, increased accordingly.[1] The Furniture Workers Industrial Union, which was founded in the early 1930s and affiliated with the Trade Union Unity League, collided with the AFL and was dissolved in the mid-1930s, several of its members entering the Upholsterers union. With the founding of the Committee for Industrial Organization in 1935 and the chartering of the United Furniture Workers of America as a CIO affiliate in 1937, several former FWIU activists left the Upholsterers and, along with other CIO activists, helped to build the UFWA and industrial unionism in furniture.

The major internal tensions faced by the furniture industrial unionists derived from the increasingly heterogeneous membership accompanying the UFWA organizing drives in several regions of the United States during the late 1930s and 1940s. The membership became more diverse in terms of ethnicity, craft, product, region, and political attitude, with each group seeking representation on the UFWA general executive board. The UFWA developed a constitution that attempted to maximize regional, craft, and product-line representation on the GEB.

The succession of ethnic groups on the GEB during the UFWA's formative period resulted from both external and internal pressures on the UFWA. Beginning with a majority of Jewish GEB members from the urban East in the late 1930s, the GEB came to comprise a majority of Northern and Western European members from the small towns of the East, Midwest, and South by 1950, the end of the formative period. The main internal pressure effecting this shift was the emergence in the UFWA of these latter groups, who tended to harbor more conservative political beliefs than the UFWA founders from the urban East. The Cold War anti-unionism and anti-Communism, as reactions to labor movement growth and to the deterioration of U.S.-USSR relations, were the major external pressures contributing to the shift in the ethnic composition of the UFWA GEB. These national political conditions severely jeopardized the membership and growth of the UFWA, which held a left-wing political stance. Consequently, in 1950, the UFWA ousted its left-wing officers, who were largely Jewish members from the urban East, and the more conservative Northern and Western Europeans from the nonmetropolitan Midwest and East came onto the GEB. The succession of ethnic groups on the GEB, then, reflects the UFWA's struggles to grow and unionize the furniture industry, from the conflict between craft and industrial unionism, beginning in the early 1930s, to the Cold War conflict of the late 1940s and early 1950s.

[1] *Proceedings of the Third Constitutional Convention of the United Furniture Workers of America—CIO,* Cleveland, May 17–21, 1943, p. 150. David Hounshell, *From the American System to Mass Production 1800–1932* (Baltimore: Johns Hopkins University Press, 1984), pp. 125–151.

Furniture Workers Industrial Union, 1932–1935

The Furniture Workers Industrial Union, founded in 1932 as an affiliate of the Trade Union Unity League, was the first explicit effort to bring industrial unionism to the furniture manufacturing industry.[2] The TUUL, a labor federation established by the Communist party in 1929 as an alternative to the AFL and craft unionism, promoted industrial unionism. It espoused, among other things, the seven-hour day, the five-day week, social insurance, racial equality, and socialism and had made organizational inroads in mining, the needle trades, and textiles by the time of the formation of the FWIU. The establishment of the TUUL was as much the outcome of a perceived inadequacy of the AFL, which had neglected less skilled workers, as it was a response to a shift in party strategy. Rather than attempting to infuse the AFL with socialist trade unionism, as it had endeavored to do with the Trade Union Educational League (TUEL) between 1920 and 1929, the Communist party attempted to compete with the AFL when it formed the TUUL. As party leader William Z. Foster put it, "The major difference between the T.U.U.L. and T.U.E.L. was that whereas the old T.U.E.L. placed the main stress upon the work within the conservative trade unions, the new Trade Union Unity League put its main emphasis upon the organization of the unorganized into industrial unions." This shift in party strategy, in turn, not only resulted from the expulsion of TUEL militants from the AFL, which had condemned the TUEL as dual unionism, but followed the inauguration of the Communist party's so-called "Third Period," a "sharpening of working class struggle on every front," at the Sixth World Congress of the Communist International held in Moscow in 1928.[3] From its start, then, industrial unionism in the furniture industry was partly enmeshed in developments in world socialism.

Nonetheless, furniture trade unionism in New York City, where the FWIU was founded, had been moving toward industrial unionism before the establishment of the FWIU. This movement took the form of increased amalgamation and joint activity among local unions representing different crafts mainly in the AFL-affiliated Carpenters and Upholsterers unions. In 1913, the Carpenters chartered three local unions in New York for three

---

[2] Abraham Zide, "Organization of Labor in the Furniture Industry in New York City" (bachelor's paper, College of the City of New York, 1939).

[3] William Z. Foster, *History of the Communist Party of the United States* (New York: International Publishers, 1952), pp. 202, 248, 257, 258, 265, 266. Quotations from Foster, pp. 257–258 and pp. 265–266, respectively. Also see Walter Galenson, *Rival Unionism in the United States* (New York: American Council on Public Affairs, 1940); Max Kampelman, *The Communist Party vs. the CIO* (New York: Praeger, 1957); David Saposs, *Communism in American Unions* (New York: McGraw-Hill, 1959); Bert Cochran, *Labor and Communism: The Conflict that Shaped American Unions* (Princeton: Princeton University Press, 1977); Harvey Klehr, *The Heyday of American Communism* (New York: Basic Books, 1984).

crafts engaged primarily in the dining room chair and parlor frame industry. Local 2035 comprised cabinetmakers, local 1057 consisted of machine hands, and local 569 was composed of woodturners. Although each of these locals was autonomous, they formed the Furniture Council in 1913 to conduct strikes and to bargain with employers. The council succeeded in raising wages, establishing a wage scale, and reducing hours to a maximum of fifty-four per week. Wages increased during World War I, but, during the 1920–1921 depression, employers attempted to cut wages and increased the work week from forty-four to fifty-two hours. In 1930, the three locals of the council were amalgamated into one local, Carpenters local 1204, whose membership comprised some five hundred or six hundred workers in the dining room chair and living room furniture industries.[4]

The Upholsterers International Union had been present in New York City since the nineteenth century. In 1918, the UIU amalgamated several small upholsterers locals into two locals. Local 76 of the UIU was composed of wholesale upholsterers in shops and UIU local 44 consisted of retail upholsterers in furniture and department stores. In 1922, the UIU chartered a mattress makers local, local 108, which had a negligible membership. By 1927, local 76 had recruited over two thousand members and had established a forty-hour work week.[5]

Despite the movement toward industrial unionism, coordinated striking and bargaining activity was hampered by the craft organization of the New York City furniture unions. In addition to the Carpenters and UIU locals, the wood carvers belonged to the New York Woodcarvers Association, which was established in 1866. Given that multiple craft unions represented the workforce in a single shop, it was often the case that some crafts continued to work while another was out on strike at the same shop. Furthermore, the craft union leaders, who "were satisfied to maintain a small bureaucratic organization," had left unorganized thousands of New York City furniture workers, especially the unskilled workers in the juvenile, reed, breakfast set, and other woodworking furniture industries, by the early 1930s. With the onset of the Great Depression and mass layoffs, craft union membership in the New York City furniture industry declined. Between 1929 and 1932, UIU local 76 membership declined from one thousand eight hundred to two hundred; UIU local 108 membership remained under one hundred; and the membership of Carpenters local 1204 declined from eight hundred to eighty during this period. Employers cut wages, and militant workers, who complained about the

---

[4] Zide, "Organization of Labor," pp. 28–32; Max Perlow, *A Story of 76B, Seven Years Progress* (New York: UFWA Local 76B, circa 1941), p. 130.
[5] Zide, "Organization of Labor," pp. 31–32.

deteriorating work conditions to unresponsive union officials, often "found themselves jobless and blacklisted in other factories," sometimes "with the obvious approval of union officials."[6]

Amidst these conditions, the TUUL formed the FWIU in 1932 in order "to unite all workers in the furniture industry irrespective of craft, skill, or color, nationality, age, sex, religion, or political affiliation into an industrial union," according to the Preamble of the FWIU Constitution. Given the attacks on the FWIU by employers, who condemned it as being Communist-led, and by union officials, who charged it with dual unionism, the FWIU's "existence was kept as secret as possible since no worker dared to admit openly to membership through fear of losing his job." The FWIU was divided into four sections: Cabinet, Upholstery, Metal Bed, and Mattress, each with its own executive board. The FWIU was governed by a joint council consisting of representatives from the four sections. Joe Kiss served as FWIU national secretary and Morris Pizer was national organizer.[7]

Most of the founders of the FWIU were Eastern European Jewish immigrants, several of whom were Communist party members or fellow travelers. They fled from persecution and arrived in the United States during the latter part of the great Eastern, Central, and Southern European immigration wave that had begun in the 1880s, filled the expanding factories in the northern metropolitan areas with workers, and came to an abrupt halt in 1924, an era of growing nativistic sentiment, with the enactment of restrictive federal immigration legislation. The minutes of FWIU meetings were written in Yiddish, in light of the predominance of Jewish FWIU members.[8]

Among the founders of the FWIU were Morris Pizer, Max Perlow, Alex Sirota, and Abraham Zide. Pizer, born in Russian Poland in 1904 and the son of a Jewish tailor, arrived in the United States in 1921 and began working in an upholstery shop in Boston. Three years later he moved to New York City and sought out the union, which suggested that he take a non-union job. He found a non-union job and helped to organize his fellow workers within three months. By the late 1920s, Pizer had become active in the TUEL. He became a full-time union organizer in 1931 and was the primary founder of the FWIU.[9]

[6] Ibid., pp. 28–36, 42; Perlow, *A Story of 76B*, p. 131. Quotations from Zide, pp. 33 and 35–36, respectively.

[7] Zide, "Organization of Labor," pp. 36, 41—quotations from p. 36; personal interviews with Max Perlow in New York City, November 23, 1984, and June 11, 1985.

[8] Personal interview with Solly Silverman in West Palm Beach, FL, September 22, 1986.

[9] "Tribute to an Outstanding Trade Union Leader, Morris Pizer, Our International President, 1946–1970," pamphlet issued by the UFWA, circa 1970; *Who's Who in Labor* (New York: Dryden Press, 1946), p. 282; Gary Fink, ed., *Biographical Dictionary of American Labor* (Westport, CT: Greenwood Press, 1984), pp. 465–466; personal interview with Max Perlow, November 23, 1984; *Furniture Workers Press*, March 1984, pp. 1–2.

Max Perlow, the son of a tailor who was a local union secretary in the Amalgamated Clothing Workers, was born in the Ukraine in 1902 and arrived in the United States in 1922. He took a job at the Eagle Chair Co. in New York, which employed Jewish and Italian immigrants, and joined the Carpenters in 1923. Already an activist in Jewish worker organizations in Europe, Perlow became active in the TUEL during the late 1920s, by which time he had been elected president of Carpenters local 1057 and a delegate to the Furniture Council. At a union meeting in 1930, having exposed corruption among the local union business agents who were selling jobs, "Perlow was dragged from the platform. . . , beaten up by the exposed leaders and their stooges, thrown out of the hall and immediately expelled from the union." Those who protested the action were treated in a similar fashion. After three years of unsuccessful attempts to become reinstated in the AFL, Perlow was notified in 1933 by William Hutcheson, national president of the Carpenters, that the local could readmit him. Perlow was prohibited from attending union meetings and denied other membership privileges. By this time, he had become involved in organizing for the FWIU and served on the FWIU board.[10]

Alex Sirota, born in Bessarabia in 1903, arrived in the United States in 1920. A mattress worker, he helped to organize an independent mattress workers union in 1923 that was affiliated with the United Hebrew Trades and was elected recording secretary. By the late 1920s, Sirota was active in the TUEL and, later, participating in the founding of the FWIU, served on the FWIU board.[11]

Abraham Zide was born in Lithuania in 1905 and immigrated to the United States in 1920. In 1924, he began working in a furniture frame shop in Brooklyn and joined the Carpenters. Zide actively participated in the 1933 strike at the Newport Parlor Frame Corp. where he was employed, which opened up a successful, industrywide FWIU organizing drive, discussed later. He served as financial secretary of the FWIU from its inception.[12]

By the fall of 1932, FWIU membership in New York City had increased to about 850, with some 250 woodworkers, 200 upholsterers, 300 mattress makers, and over 100 metal bed workers. Subsequent recruitment drives, especially among woodworkers, increased membership to 1,200 by the end of 1932.[13]

The 1933 strike at the Newport Parlor Frame Corp., the largest shop in

[10] Personal interviews with Max Perlow; Perlow, *A Story of 76B,* pp. 130–131.
[11] Personal interview with Alex Sirota in New York City, November 23, 1984.
[12] Personal interview with Abraham Zide in New York City, November 16, 1984; Perlow, *A Story of 76B,* pp. 131, 132, 134.
[13] Zide, "Organization of Labor," pp. 42–43.

its trade in New York, led to increased organization of furniture workers and to the establishment of trade- and citywide working conditions for the FWIU shops. The first shop in the parlor frame trade to be organized by the FWIU was Junius Parlor Frame, where Max Perlow had become employed after his reinstatement in the Carpenters. In February 1933, the Junius workers gained wage increases, a work week reduction from forty-nine to forty-four hours, and recognition of the shop committee. In March, the Newport Corporation instituted the third wage cut of the year and received no opposition from the officials of the Carpenters union that represented the shop. On the day the wage cut took effect, the Newport workers met at the FWIU office with Morris Pizer and Jack Hochstadt, an upholsterer who was the FWIU Cabinet Section organizer, and decided to call a strike the following day. The Newport workers struck on March 22, with roughly half of the sixty-person workforce participating. Perlow was pulled out of the Junius shop and assigned with Hochstadt to carry out the strike. The strikers were resisted by both the employer and the Carpenters union. "Gangsters beat up pickets, who were given inadequate police protection. The homes of strikers were visited, and their families intimidated and threatened." In early April, gangsters attacked three of the strike leaders including Perlow, who received injuries requiring seven stitches in his head, while they were eating in a restaurant, and the employer's son was charged with the assault. News of the strike spread citywide among furniture workers, who sent funds and shop committees to lend moral support to the strikers. An oral settlement was reached on May 2, providing for shop committee recognition, access to the shop by an organizer, rehiring of all strikers, firing of all scabs, withdrawal of the wage cut, six weeks' worth of back pay in wages, abolition of the piece work system, and a work week reduction from forty-nine to forty-four hours. After the strike, the FWIU organized several shops, signing up members of the Carpenters and UIU locals 76 and 108 and metal bed and mattress workers who had not been unionized, and "encountered as much opposition from the locals of the American Federation of Labor as it did from employers." On July 24, the FWIU called a general strike in the trade that resulted in a forty-hour work week during the season, a thirty-five-hour week in the slack season, wage increases of 25 percent or more, a closed union shop, time and one-half for overtime, and 1 percent of the payroll paid by the employers into a union-controlled unemployment fund.[14]

Beginning in 1934, employers reacted vigorously to the FWIU, demanding wage reductions and increases in hours, as illustrated by the

---

[14] Ibid., pp. 38–43—quotations from pp. 38 and 43, respectively; Perlow, *A Story of 76B*, pp. 131–132.

cases of the Miller Parlor Frame Co. and, again, the Newport Corporation. In an effort to avoid the union, the Maujer Parlor Frame Co. changed its name to Miller Parlor Frame and moved its shop from New York City to Jersey City, where anti-union Mayor Frank Hague supported the open shop. A few months later, the Junius Co. moved to Jersey City and merged with Miller. The FWIU decided to extend its organizing drives to Jersey City and, testing Mayor Hague's denial of permission to picket, began picketing the Miller Co. in June 1934. Picketers were arrested, and the American Civil Liberties Union came to the support of the union, protesting the unconstitutionality of the ban on picketing. Mass meetings were held in New York and New Jersey to protest the ban, and several dignitaries, including Alfred Bingham, Corliss Lamont, and Justine Wise Tulin, as well as Goldie Perlow, wife of Max Perlow, were arrested for picketing or observing the picket line. The AFL-affiliated Woodcarvers Association rallied behind the FWIU and "even William Green [national AFL president] made statements condemning the actions of the Jersey Mayor." The FWIU won the test of the right to picket and "was subsequently victorious in bringing the Miller Parlor Frame shop back into the organized ranks."[15]

The FWIU also fought the Newport Corp., which began pressing for wage reductions and longer hours. After locking out the workers for four months, the company opened a shop in February 1935 some thirty-five miles from New York City in Ford, NJ. The FWIU picketed the Ford plant, and the company, which had returned to Brooklyn in May, locked out the workers in June. Given the low level of unionization in the New York furniture industry at the time, the FWIU made concessions to the employers, including a forty-hour work week, instead of the thirty-five-hour week that had been established for the slack season. Consequently, contracts were renewed not only with Newport but also with other FWIU shops that had been lost. Nonetheless, the concessions lowered the prestige of the FWIU, and some shops did not renew contracts.[16]

The FWIU, using its contacts in the Communist party, had attempted to organize other furniture centers in the United States including Boston, Gardner, MA, Lancaster, PA, Jamestown, NY, Grand Rapids, MI, Los Angeles, and the South, but it made few inroads. Having faced employer opposition, intensive red-baiting, and attacks condemning it as a dual union, especially by the UIU, the FWIU was dissolved in July 1935.[17]

Moreover, the FWIU was dissolved shortly after the Communist party had disbanded the TUUL. The party began advocating labor unity, and in early 1935 the TUUL unions in steel, autos, and the needle trades affiliated

---

[15] Perlow, *A Story of 76B*, pp. 132–133.

[16] Ibid., pp. 133–134; Zide, "Organization of Labor," p. 45.

[17] Personal interviews with Max Perlow; Perlow, *A Story of 76B*, p. 134; Zide, "Organization of Labor," p. 44.

with the AFL. In March 1935, the TUUL transformed itself into the Committee for the Unification of the Trade Unions and disbanded altogether four months later. By August 1935, with the declaration of anti-fascism at the Seventh Congress of the Communist International in Moscow, the party moved from its "Third Period" into its "Popular Front" era, "a great antifascist people's front of workers, farmers, intellectuals, and all other toiling, democratic sections of the population." Unable to function independently, the FWIU sought to affiliate with the AFL.[18]

In the AFL, 1935–1937

The UIU had already been practicing industrial unionism, by organizing several furniture trades, when the FWIU entered it in the summer of 1935. Since 1911, the UIU and the Carpenters had battled one another about which union was to have jurisdiction over furniture woodworkers, typically in plants in which the upholsterers were already organized. The UIU had similar jurisdictional conflicts with the AFL-affiliated painters union.[19]

With the entry of the FWIU into the UIU, the UIU admitted some of the FWIU shops into existing UIU locals and also chartered some new locals. The 90 members of the FWIU Upholstery Section joined UIU upholsterers local 76 in New York City, increasing local 76 membership to about 225. In July 1935, the UIU chartered a new furniture woodworkers local 76B in New York for the 113 members of the FWIU Cabinet Section. The Mattress and Metal Bed sections of the FWIU, which initially received separate local union charters from the UIU, were amalgamated a few weeks later as a new UIU bedding workers local 140, consisting of 276 wholesale mattress workers in New York.[20]

With the passage of the Wagner Act and the opening of a major UIU organizing drive in the fall of 1935, "announcing the new unity and strength of the affiliated locals," the UIU embarked successfully along a path of industrial unionism, despite the reservations held by the UIU International leadership, which adhered to a traditional, AFL, craft unionism philosophy. Between 1935 and 1937, membership soared in the UIU

---

[18] Foster, *History of the Communist Party*, pp. 304, 321—quotation from p. 321; personal interview with Max Perlow, November 23, 1984.

[19] Personal interview with Max Perlow, November 23, 1984; testimony of Arthur McDowell at hearings before the Subcommittee to Investigate the Administration of the Internal Security Act and other Internal Security Laws, U.S. Senate Committee of the Judiciary, 83rd Congress, first and second sessions, December 21, 1953, *Subversive Influence in Certain Labor Organizations*, p. 23; *Minutes of the Meeting of Unity Conference of Workers in the Furniture, Bedding and Allied Trades*, Lee House, Washington, DC, November 27–29, 1937, p. 7.

[20] Zide, "Organization of Labor," pp. 49, 52; Perlow, *A Story of 76B*, p. 134.

Table 3.1
*Membership and Percentage of Change in Membership
of UIU Local Unions in New York City, 1935–1937*

Local Union	1935 Membership	1937 Membership	1935–1937 % Change in Membership
Retail upholsterers Local 44	390	526	34.9
Wholesale upholsterers Local 76	225	1209	437.3
Furniture woodworking Local 76B	113	964	753.1
Retail mattress Local 108	139	276	98.6
Wholesale mattress Local 140	276	1056	282.6

Source: Abraham Zide, "Organization of Labor in the Furniture Industry in New York City" (bachelor's paper, College of the City of New York, 1939), Table 1, p. 52.

local unions of New York City, as shown in Table 3.1, especially those comprising former FWIU members, locals 76, 76B, and 140. Nationally, UIU membership increased by more than 70 percent from approximately twenty-one thousand to thirty-six thousand members between 1935 and 1937.[21]

Working conditions improved in the New York furniture industry. After two strikes in the juvenile furniture trade, local 76B had, by 1937, succeeded in signing closed shop agreements with all of the shops in the trade, raising the minimum weekly wage for unskilled workers from $10 to $16, eliminating piece work, reducing hours, and gaining a one-week paid vacation. In the breakfast set trade, local 76B conducted a general strike and signed a closed shop agreement with the Breakfast Room Furniture Manufacturers' and Assemblers' Association in 1937.[22]

The UIU International moved closer to industrial unionism at its June 1937 convention in Cleveland. The CIO was making significant organizational inroads in the steel, auto, rubber, glass, and other mass production industries, bringing to the fore the question of UIU affiliation with the CIO. Fearing a split in the UIU over the question of CIO affiliation, the pro-CIO

[21] Quotation from Zide, "Organization of Labor," p. 49; *Unity Conference Minutes*, pp. 11, 14; Perlow, *A Story of 76B*, p. 134.
[22] Perlow, *A Story of 76B*, p. 135.

delegates to the Cleveland convention did not raise the question and focused, instead, on "defeating the old cumbersome regime" in the UIU. Sal Hoffmann, the business manager of UIU local 77 in Philadelphia and supporter of industrial unionism, succeeded UIU International President Hatch in this office, and Pizer, Perlow, and Sirota were elected to the UIU International executive board. Moreover, the former FWIU activists supported Hoffmann, with the understanding that Hoffmann would bring the UIU into the CIO. Furthermore, the Cleveland convention moved the UIU formally into industrial unionism by amending its constitutional jurisdiction to include all crafts in the furniture industry, encroaching on the Carpenters jurisdiction and in violation of AFL policies.[23]

Entering the CIO, November 27–December 9, 1937

The tension between craft unionism and industrial unionism within the AFL led to the exit of the CIO unions from the federation in 1938. On September 5, 1936, the AFL executive council suspended the CIO unions, and, in November 1936, the AFL convention, held in Tampa, affirmed the action of the executive council. The CIO continued its organizing campaigns and, during the first six months of 1937, made significant inroads in the steel, automobile, maritime, rubber, electrical, textile, and lumber industries. In March 1937, the CIO began issuing certificates of affiliation to international, national, and local unions and, by October, had effectively chartered thirty-two national and international unions, six hundred local industrial unions, and eighty state and city central bodies. Taking up the CIO challenge, the AFL began organizing on an industrial basis in the mass production industries. On October 11, 1937, the AFL Convention, held in Denver, authorized the executive council to expel the CIO unions from the federation. The AFL and CIO entered into unity negotiations, lasting from October 25 to December 21, 1937, which ended in failure. By May 1938, the AFL had expelled ten CIO unions from the federation. No longer a committee within the AFL, the Committee for Industrial Organization renamed itself the Congress of Industrial Organizations in November 1938. The two labor federations would not unite until 1955.[24]

The tension between craft and industrial unionism continued to brew in the furniture industry. At its Denver convention in 1937, the AFL prohibited the UIU from expanding its jurisdiction to all furniture crafts, and the CIO, at its October 11–16, 1937, national conference in Atlantic City,

[23] Personal interview with Max Perlow, November 23, 1984; quotation from Zide, "Organization of Labor," pp. 54–55; *Unity Conference Minutes*, p. 7.
[24] *Report of Proceedings of the Fifty-Seventh Annual Convention of the American Federation of Labor,* Denver, October 4–15, 1937, pp. 110, 377–417; Irving Bernstein, *Turbulent Years* (Boston: Houghton Mifflin, 1971), pp. 683–684, 690, 696–697.

resolved to call a unity conference for creating an international industrial union in furniture manufacturing. The CIO issued a call, signed by CIO Chairman John L. Lewis and CIO Director John Brophy, for a "National Unity Conference of all Unions in the Furniture, Bedding and Allied Trades," to be held on November 27–29, 1937, at Lee House in Washington, DC. Invited to the unity conference were CIO local unions in furniture, the UIU and its locals, all AFL federal locals in furniture, and all other furniture local unions, whether independent or affiliated with the AFL or CIO. The furniture unity conference, which met at the designated time and place, occurred while the AFL-CIO unity negotiations were taking place. The 105 delegates to the furniture conference came mainly from twenty-seven UIU locals and twenty-seven CIO furniture locals. Less than 10 percent of the delegates were from independent and federal local unions.[25]

The UIU delegates to the furniture unity conference lacked consensus about affiliating with the CIO. Among the UIU's pro-CIO delegates were the former FWIU activists, Perlow, Pizer, and Sirota, and Morris Muster, a UIU vice president and business manager of UIU upholsterers local 76 in New York. However, UIU President Hoffmann hesitated about affiliating with the CIO. At the Denver AFL convention in October 1937, Hoffmann, along with Muster and UIU Vice President Alfred Rota, who constituted the UIU delegation to the convention, voted in favor of authorizing the executive council to expel the CIO unions. Hoffmann had been lobbied by pro-AFL and pro-CIO forces prior to the furniture unity conference. AFL "officers asked Hoffmann . . . to go to this conference and to do anything that was necessary to prevent a new union being formed." The pro-CIO forces in the UIU and Hoffmann met with CIO leader Sidney Hillman, who attempted to persuade Hoffmann to bring the UIU into the CIO. Moreover, Hoffmann was concerned that some two or three thousand linoleum layers, who were UIU members and held building-trades cards, would lose their jobs if the UIU broke from the AFL. Also, others have argued that Hoffmann hesitated about affiliating with the CIO because he feared losing his position and was anti-Communist.[26]

Dissensus in the UIU contributed to the course of events at the furniture unity conference. The resolutions committee consisted of Hoffmann,

[25] "Call for a National Unity Conference of all Unions in the Furniture, Bedding and Allied Trades," issued by the Committee for Industrial Organization and signed by John L. Lewis and John Brophy, circa October, 1937; memo from the Committee of Industrial Organization "to all organizations represented at the National Unity Conference of Unions in the Furniture, Bedding and Allied Trades, and to all other unions in the furniture industry," signed by Morris Muster, Emil Costello, Max Perlow, Joseph Persily, George Bucher, Joseph Proudman, and John Brophy, December 9, 1937; *Unity Conference Minutes*, pp. 3–6.

[26] *Proceedings*, 1937 AFL Convention, p. 416; quotation from McDowell testimony, pp. 25–26; personal interview with Max Perlow, November 23, 1984; Zide, "Organization of Labor," p. 61.

Perlow, and Muster from the UIU, three others representing the CIO, and one representative of the independent unions. The resolutions committee presented to the conference delegates a majority report, which was adopted 6 to 1 by the committee, and Hoffmann's minority report. Each report included a resolution on the establishment of an industrial union in furniture. The resolutions differed with respect to the method of establishing the union, safeguards for UIU autonomy, and CIO affiliation. Resolution 1 of the majority acknowledged the low level of unionization in the industry; attributed this to a lack of unity among the unions in the industry; claimed that the AFL hampered furniture industrial unionism by permitting several craft unions and federal local unions to organize furniture workers and by denying the UIU jurisdiction over all furniture crafts; maintained that furniture workers desired unity in one industrial union; held up the successful CIO organizing drives in steel, auto, rubber, and other mass production industries as indicators of the correctness of CIO policies; and called for the immediate establishment of a CIO-affiliated, international furniture industrial union and the commencement of "an aggressive organizing campaign throughout the furniture industry."[27]

In contrast, Hoffmann's resolution reflected his concerns about UIU autonomy and CIO affiliation. Resolution 2 of the minority noted the demoralization of furniture workers stemming from inferior employment conditions; argued for the desirability of industrial unionism, especially in light of the confusion caused by the competing unions in the industry; claimed that the UIU was the largest single unit of furniture union members and would continue to successfully organize the industry on an industrial basis "under its new progressive leadership"; stated that the UIU had always maintained the best employment conditions and was presently mobilizing an organizing drive to continue doing so; called upon the present furniture unity conference to recognize the UIU "as the central organization, having full and complete jurisdiction of all branches of the furniture and bedding industry," and urged all existing furniture unions to affiliate with the UIU; sought designation by the furniture unity conference of the furniture industry as a mass production industry to be organized on an industrial basis; requested both AFL and CIO recognition of the UIU as having complete and autonomous jurisdiction over the furniture industry and AFL and CIO transfer of all furniture unions to the UIU; asked for AFL and CIO cooperation with the UIU in organizing and improving conditions in the industry; requested that the question of affiliation be delayed so as not to jeopardize the AFL-CIO unity negotiations; and concluded that, should the AFL-CIO unity negotiations fail, "the question of affiliation of the [UIU] be submitted to and decided by a referendum of the general

[27] *Unity Conference Minutes,* pp. 7–8.

membership of the [UIU]" within forty-five days after the AFL-CIO unity negotiations.[28]

The resolutions were introduced at the evening session of the furniture conference on November 27. The UIU delegates dominated the debate for the remainder of the evening session, with Hoffmann advocating his resolution, and Perlow, Muster, and Pizer accounting for most of the statements favoring the majority resolution. Claiming that the UIU's sole purpose in attending the conference was to discern the possibilities for uniting with the CIO, and that the affiliation question required a UIU membership referendum, Hoffmann said that "we are not going to be stampeded by the C.I.O. right now because it can't be done." He went on to state that the UIU had come to the conference "with no love for the A.F. of L." and espoused industrial unionism, arguing that the UIU would be willing to leave the AFL because "under the present setup under the A.F. of L., we do not think it is possible to organize the furniture industry on an industrial basis." Referring to the AFL's denial of the UIU's expanded jurisdiction, he added that "I don't know what would be the case if the A.F. of L. in the Denver convention, had decided to grant us industrial organization. Maybe this meeting wouldn't have taken place." Hoffmann claimed that the AFL had promised to hand over all of its furniture federal locals if the UIU remained in the AFL, and he wanted similar assurance from the CIO, were the UIU to affiliate with the CIO, given the UIU's jurisdictional battles with the Carpenters and other AFL organizations. Fearing a split within the UIU, Hoffmann estimated that 70 percent of the UIU membership would vote to remain in the AFL if the majority resolution were adopted. If the furniture unity conference adopted his resolution, Hoffmann said the UIU leadership would "recommend to our general membership that they vote for C.I.O. affiliation."[29]

Speaking for the majority resolution, and differing with Hoffmann on why the UIU was attending the furniture conference, Perlow said that "we did not come to fish around and see how much and how many. We came here to meet the organized force of the furniture workers who are members of the C.I.O. in order to combine our forces . . . and organize the hundreds of thousands of unorganized furniture workers." Espousing industrial unionism and lambasting the AFL for denying the UIU its expanded jurisdiction, he claimed that the AFL was "sending scabs to break our strikes because they don't approve our policy of industrial unionism. We know when we sent delegates to the Denver [1937 AFL] convention that no matter how honest Brother Hoffmann and his fellow delegates were, they did not give us jurisdiction. Why? Because Bill Hutcheson

---

[28] Ibid., pp. 8–9.
[29] Ibid., pp. 9–17—quotations from pp. 11–12.

[Carpenters national president] is the boss over there, and he will never give away jurisdiction to any other organization except to Bill Hutcheson." Further, he rebuked Hoffmann for having voted in favor of authorizing the AFL expulsion of the CIO unions at the October 1937 AFL convention, claiming that the UIU, at its June 1937 convention, had decided not to fight the CIO. Perlow attributed the success of the UIU organizing drives of 1935–1937 to the impetus brought by the CIO policies "to the workers and to the working classes here in the United States for organization. We came with the swing of the C.I.O. This is how we organized the workers." Noting that some UIU leaders disapproved of CIO affiliation because employers sought to avoid fights with the CIO and preferred to deal with the AFL, Perlow argued that "we don't recognize that kind of approach," and later, that "we want to combine with these progressive forces who make organization possible, to stimulate the desire of the American workers to develop their militancy, to organize the mass production industries. . . . We came here to form an international union, an industrial union affiliated with the C.I.O." Speaking to Hoffmann, Perlow concluded by saying that "if you want to go with us, . . . you are welcome to go with us. If you do not want to go with us, we cannot help it. We will accomplish our goal and that is one international union affiliated with the C.I.O."[30]

The evening session was adjourned shortly thereafter, and the delegates continued the debate during the morning session of November 28. Toward the end of the morning session, John Brophy, who was chairing the conference, called for a vote on the report of the resolutions committee. At this point, however, UIU executive board member Sam Raevsky from local 77 in Philadelphia, the first UIU local union to have adopted an industrial form of organization some six years earlier, was given the floor, and he proposed a compromise resolution to be taken up by the resolutions committee. The delegates passed a motion to refer the resolution to the resolutions committee, and the convention adjourned until 3:00 P.M. At 3:00 P.M., the meeting was recessed until 7:00 P.M. at the request of the resolutions committee.[31]

The evening session began with the presentation of a compromise resolution that consisted of the following eight points:

1. All delegates to the furniture unity conference decide at the conference to form one furniture workers industrial union affiliated with the CIO;
2. The functioning of the union should go into effect 45 days after the adjournment of the furniture unity conference;

[30] Ibid., pp. 15–17.
[31] Ibid., pp. 25–26.

3. The UIU shall retain its autonomy and be recognized as the international union having jurisdiction over the furniture and bedding industry;

4. A referendum vote of all AFL and independent furniture unions on the question of CIO affiliation shall be taken within 45 days of the adjournment of the furniture unity conference;

5. Upon the completion of the referendum, all non-UIU locals shall transfer their membership to the UIU, which will waive initiation fees;

6. A committee representing the UIU, CIO and independent unions will be established in order to canvass these three groups and bring them into the CIO international union;

7. After 45 days, the CIO international union shall be an accomplished fact with those of the groups who have voted for CIO affiliation;

8. The CIO international union shall call on the CIO to help initiate immediately an aggressive organizing campaign in the furniture industry.[32]

The resolutions committee voted 6 to 1 for the resolution, with the committee representative of the independent unions casting the dissenting vote. Statements in support of the resolution were made by Hoffmann; Muster; Pizer; Perlow; Sirota; Rota, who had spoken in favor of Hoffmann's minority resolution the previous day; Brophy; and others. After a few points in the resolution had been clarified, the delegates, in a standing vote, adopted the resolution unanimously. It was decided that the canvassing committee, as provided for by the sixth point of the resolution, would consist of seven members, with each of the three groups choosing its representatives. The meeting was adjourned until 10:00 A.M. the next day.[33]

At the morning session of November 29, each of the three groups who were represented at the conference reported their choices for the members of the canvassing committee, the Committee of 7. Hoffmann, Muster, and Perlow were chosen as the UIU representatives; Emil Costello, George Bucher, and Joseph Persily were to represent the CIO; and Joseph Proudman was selected to represent the independent unions. The conference delegates then proceeded to pass eighteen resolutions on positions ranging from favoring the formation of a labor party, calling for continued support of New Deal social welfare programs, demanding the immediate release from prison of labor organizers Tom Mooney and Warren Billings,

---

[32] Ibid., pp. 26–28; resolution is paraphrased.
[33] Ibid., pp. 17, 28–31.

cooperating with employers in carrying out collective bargaining agreements, to supporting the striking workers at the Comfort Springs Co. in Baltimore.[34]

The furniture unity conference concluded on November 29 with a speech by CIO Chairman John L. Lewis. Encouraging the delegates in their newly instituted organizational effort, Lewis stated:

> There is just one thing to be done in this country—that is for American workers to organize themselves and become articulate and express themselves with respect to their working conditions—their industrial problems and their own degree of participation in their industries' income and profits and express themselves on these broad social, economic, and political questions which today confront every American with increasing gravity.
>
> It is time to organize now in your industry as in other industries. It is time to organize when the country is going through another economic tailspin which has been perfectly obvious for months. It is time to organize when employers of this country begin to shut up their mills, plants and factories, and turn Americans into the streets. It is time to organize when the government of the United States suddenly comes to have a passion for economy and restricts and limits the amount of aid and relief and help that will be given Americans when the employers turn them into the streets.
>
> Individually you are helpless. Collectively you can make yourselves heard and your collective voice penetrates not only the councils of industry, but it penetrates also the legislative halls of the country and the conference rooms where our statesmen sit and talk and sometimes think. So organize.[35]

The United Furniture Workers of America, CIO, was born on December 8, 1937, but not according to the plan that had been laid out at the furniture unity conference in November. The Committee of 7 was convened on December 8 in Washington, DC by John Brophy. Hoffmann did not attend the meeting and was expelled from the committee. The new Committee of 6 established immediately a furniture international union affiliated with the CIO and became its provisional executive board, with Muster as president and Costello as secretary-treasurer, both appointed by John L. Lewis on December 9. This board would serve until permanent officers were elected at a constitutional convention of the new union called by Lewis. The Committee of 6 was to notify all AFL and CIO locals of the creation of the UFWA, to call meetings of all AFL locals to authorize

---

[34] Ibid., pp. 32–41.
[35] Address of John L. Lewis, Chairman of the CIO, before furniture workers unity conference, Lee House, Washington, DC, November 29, 1937, pp. 1–2.

their affiliation with the UFWA, and to conduct mass meetings in principal cities to publicize the UFWA and begin organizational work.[36]

Each side blamed the other for the breakdown in the agreement that had been established at the furniture unity conference. On December 7, 1937, Hoffmann suspended Perlow, Pizer, and Sirota from the UIU executive board on the grounds of dual unionism, one day before the meeting of the Committee of 7 called by Brophy. Hoffmann's letter to Perlow informing him of his suspension charged him with aiding dual unionism, encouraging membership secession from the UIU, openly condemning the UIU, violating the membership pledge, threatening UIU officers, and engaging in "conduct unbecoming an officer of the" UIU. Perlow was given the right to a trial, which was held on January 3, 1938, in Washington, DC. After "reviewing the trial proceedings and testimony taken before the trial committee appointed by the Board," the UIU General Executive Board concluded that Perlow's suspension was "hereby affirmed" and "in compliance with the constitution" and ordered that Perlow "be expelled from the" UIU.[37]

In a memo of December 9, 1937, sent to "All Organizations Represented at the National Unity Conference of Unions in the Furniture, Bedding and Allied Trades, and to All Other Unions in the Furniture Industry," the Committee of 6 blamed Hoffmann for embarking on "a course of procedure in direct opposition to the conference decisions." "On November 30," claimed the committee, Hoffmann "issued a statement to the press declaring that no decision had been made to affiliate with the C.I.O., and began a campaign in the locals of the Upholsterers' International to influence the membership against affiliation with the C.I.O." The committee condemned Hoffmann for attempting "to eliminate pro-C.I.O. forces from the" UIU by suspending "the advisory board and secretary of the North Atlantic states council" and "pro-C.I.O. locals—starting with Local 45-B, which he has suspended on the pretext of non-payment of dues." Moreover, Hoffmann, according to the memo, had only advised the UIU executive board of a referendum "without any recommendation for C.I.O. affiliation," "failed to call any meeting of the Committee of Seven," and provided no explanation for his absence at the December 8 meeting convened by Brophy. The Committee of 6, therefore, "voted unanimously to remove" Hoffmann from the committee and "voted unanimously to estab-

---

[36] *Proceedings of the First Constitutional Convention of the United Furniture Workers of America—CIO*, Rockford, IL, February 13–17, 1939, p. 17; December 9, 1937, memo from CIO, signed by Muster, et al.; "Proceedings of the Furniture Unity Committee Called by Chairman John Brophy, December 8, 1937 at Washington, D.C."

[37] Personal interview with Max Perlow, November 23, 1984; letter to Max Perlow from Sal Hoffmann, December 7, 1937, and letter to Max Perlow from Sal Hoffmann and George Fay, April 1, 1938.

lish at once a furniture workers international union affiliated with the C.I.O." The former FWIU activists had entered the CIO. The Committee of 6 began building the UFWA in time for the founding UFWA convention in 1939. By February 1938, the UFWA had chartered thirty-seven locals.[38]

Building a Furniture Industrial Union: The Founding UFWA Convention, 1939

The founding UFWA convention established the structure and policies by which the UFWA would grow and bring industrial unionism to the furniture industry. As a national, industrial union composed of local unions of different sizes from different regions, which represented diverse product lines and crafts, the UFWA had to reconcile a centralized, national growth strategy with the desire for autonomy and representation in national UFWA governance among its local constituencies. The convention served to reconcile these divergent issues by endeavoring to formulate a constitution and growth strategy that were mutually compatible. The constitution and growth strategy, in turn, would lead not only to the incorporation of an increasingly diverse membership, but also to new constituencies who would compete with the older constituencies for offices on the national UFWA executive board.

On February 13–17, 1939, sixty delegates from forty-nine furniture locals convened at the Faust Hotel in Rockford, IL, to create the UFWA constitution, to determine policies, and to elect officers. The locals, whose total voting strength at the convention was 12,683 votes, accounted for 90 percent of all 14,085 UFWA members who had been recruited after the chartering of the UFWA in December 1937. Twenty-nine locals not present at the convention accounted for the remaining 10 percent of the membership.[39]

The delegates came from major metropolitan areas in the East, the Midwest, and the West; the small furniture towns of Rockford, IL, and Fort Smith, AR; and other small towns in the Midwest and South, as shown in Table 3.2. The eight large New York City locals accounted for almost half of the convention votes. Locals 76B, 76, and 140, represented by former FWIU activists and New Yorkers Perlow, Pizer, and Sirota, respectively, alone accounted for 35 percent of the convention votes. The large, amalgamated locals of the metropolitan East accounted for almost 60 percent of the convention votes, and the next largest constituency, the small locals of the nonmetropolitan Midwest, accounted for almost one-fourth of the votes.

---

[38] December 9, 1937, memo from CIO, signed by Muster, et al.; *Furniture Workers Press,* November, 1967, p. 1.

[39] *Proceedings,* 1939 UFWA Convention, p. 75.

Table 3.2
Number of Locals and Percentage Distribution of Convention Votes, by Location, First UFWA Convention, 1939

Location	Number of Locals	% Convention Votes
New York City	8	49.0
Boston, Philadelphia, and Pittsburgh	4	9.9
Nonmetropolitan[a] Middle Atlantic, and New England	10	6.0
East, subtotal	22	64.9
Rockford, IL	2	12.8
Other nonmetropolitan Great Lakes region	11	10.9
Chicago and Milwaukee	2	2.1
Midwest, subtotal	15	25.8
Fort Smith, AR	8	5.6
South, subtotal[b]	9	6.3
Los Angeles and San Francisco	2	2.7
West, subtotal[c]	3	3.1
Total	49	100.1[d]

Source: *Proceedings of the First Constitutional Convention of the United Furniture Workers of America,* Rockford, IL, February 13–17, 1939, pp. 74–75.
[a] Nonmetropolitan areas are places with smaller populations than those of the 20 largest U.S. cities in 1940.
[b] Includes one local from Roanoke, VA, with 84 members.
[c] Includes one local from Denver with 50 members.
[d] Does not sum to 100% due to rounding.

President Morris Muster of the UFWA presided over the convention, announcing that its purpose was "to create a Constitution for the United Furniture Workers of America; to create an instrument which will be democratic; to create an instrument which will deal specifically with the advance of our organization in our industry; to create an instrument which will give all of us the feeling of security, the feeling which a proper Constitution engenders in the hearts and minds of all of us in labor unions, rank and file and officials." Muster presented his report to the convention delegates, about one-third of whom, predominantly easterners, had been delegates to the furniture unity conference in December 1937. In describing the rationale for establishing the UFWA, he argued that the furniture industry had been neglected by the AFL-affiliated Carpenters and Upholsterers craft unions, that changing furniture production methods had rendered the organization of separate crafts infeasible, and that the CIO, which he praised for being the impetus to mass production unionization and for lending the UFWA organizing campaign funds, freed unionization from the jurisdictional disputes among craft unions. Muster mentioned that efforts taken since December 1937 to reach an understanding with the UIU had failed, and he described the UFWA's relationship with the Carpenters as one of "rivalry and complete indifference." Within the CIO, claimed Muster, the UFWA was ironing out jurisdictional disputes with the Steel Workers Organizing Committee and the United Automobile Workers, and he encouraged the locals to become active in state and local CIO bodies.

He called on the convention to establish a strong international union for the purposes of planning and supervising the unionization of the industry; researching and monitoring local employment conditions and local union contracts to aid local unions in collective bargaining; assisting small locals in contract negotiations; maintaining membership educational programs on employment conditions, trade unionism, and political awareness; issuing union labels; continuing to serve in an advisory role in such federal government agencies as the Wage and Hour Administration Board; and informing locals of developments at the National Labor Relations Board. Muster concluded with a cry for unity and the creation of an executive board representative of the various geographical areas and product lines comprised by the membership. The morning session of the convention on February 13 was capped off with speeches by CIO Director John Brophy and Adolph Germer, president of the Michigan CIO, both of whom attended the furniture unity conference in December 1937 and now encouraged the convention in its endeavors. Convention committees were appointed that afternoon.[40]

The Committee on Constitution was composed of former FWIU activists Perlow, committee chair, Pizer, and Sirota; George Bucher of Philadelphia local 37, who had been a CIO delegate to the furniture unity conference and a member of the Committee of 6; Ernest Marsh, originally from Arkansas, who had moved to Los Angeles and helped found CIO local 576, which he represented at the convention; Joseph Persily, a New Yorker who was a CIO delegate from Indiana to the furniture unity conference, a member of the Committee of 6, and a representative of local 496 in Bloomington, IN; Paul Green, a UIU delegate to the furniture unity conference, representing formerly UIU local 45B in New York City; Victor Anderson from the large Rockford local 707, which had been organized by the CIO; and Bert Emerson from Fort Smith local 280.[41]

During the remainder of the convention, the delegates adopted thirty-

[40] Ibid., pp. 9–34, 74–75—quotations from pp. 6–7 and 13, respectively; *Unity Conference Minutes,* pp. 3–6.
[41] *Proceedings,* 1939 UFWA Convention, p. 41; *Unity Conference Minutes,* pp. 4–5; personal interviews with William Gilbert in Manhattan Beach, CA, on July 17, 1985, Sam Sloan in Cicero, IL, on December 23, 1985, and Solly Silverman in West Palm Beach, FL, on September 22, 1986.

seven of the forty-three articles of the UFWA constitution with little or no debate. The delegates were united with respect to the purpose of the UFWA. The preamble to the UFWA constitution, which was broadcast live on radio station WROK from the convention floor as it was read to the delegates for their consideration,[42] stated:

> Realizing that we must adopt a form of organization that will most effectively serve to protect and defend our interests and improve our conditions as wage earners, we . . . have adopted the industrial form of organization. This organization will endeavor to unite all workers in our industry regardless of craft, age, sex, nationality, race, creed or political belief. We will at all times observe a policy of rank and file control, and will at all times pursue a policy of progressive struggle to improve our conditions.[43]

The objects of the organization, according to Article II, were to unite all workers in the jurisdiction; establish adequate industry wage standards; shorten the hours of labor and improve working conditions; make closed shop agreements with employers; advance furniture workers' economic, political, social, and cultural interests; aid in the adoption of laws for the economic and social welfare of all workers; and protect and extend democratic institutions and the civil rights and liberties of all workers.[44]

Administrative structure and procedure also raised few issues for the delegates. The delegates agreed on the procedures for conducting the biennial convention, the procedures for nominating and electing officers; the terms of office; the system of officer charges and trials; the duties of the officers, who consisted of the president, the secretary-treasurer, and one vice president each from the East, Midwest, South, and West; the duties of the general executive board; and several other administrative and procedural provisions.

However, the delegates debated two principles of democratic government, each of which was pitted against a concern for maintaining the union as a viable organization. Debate on the first principle, board representativeness, arose with discussion of Article XII on the composition of the general executive board. As an industrial union whose jurisdiction covered over thirty furniture product lines, the UFWA comprised members of diverse crafts or occupations, many of whom wanted representation in the form of seats on the GEB. The Committee on Constitution proposed to the delegates that the GEB consist of the six officers, one

---

[42] *Proceedings,* 1939 UFWA Convention, pp. 57–61.
[43] *Constitution of the United Furniture Workers of America,* adopted at the first constitutional convention, February 13–17, 1939, p. 2.
[44] Ibid., p. 3.

representative from each of ten geographical districts, and five industry branch representatives, one from each of the upholstery, case goods, miscellaneous, bedding and spring, and curtain industries. The proposal for these five industry branch seats led some delegates to question why their craft or product had been excluded. Louis Cohen from New York City local 91, which represented workers in spring manufacturing plants, felt that "an injustice is being done to us" because his industry lacked GEB representation. Similarly, Charles Kaslly, from local 155 in South Bend, IN, argued that "we in the Juvenile Furniture industry also feel slighted." Both delegates argued that their industries employed thousands of workers nationwide and, therefore, that they merited board representation. Arguing against the addition of more industry branch seats on the GEB, Bucher stated, noting that the UFWA was an industrial rather than craft union, "if we were to name . . . each one of the crafts we would have '57 varieties' at this convention," and "we would be here for twenty months." The article was referred back to the committee, which presented an alternative proposal with additional GEB seats for juvenile furniture and spring accessories. At this point, Fredric Teunis of New York City local 101, which represented piano workers, argued for a GEB seat for piano workers, emphasizing the "craft consciousness of these workers, the difficulty in trying to bring them into the . . . U.F.W.A.," and that "there is no man in this hall who knows the basic principles . . . of piano manufacturing." Perlow, among others, countered by stating that "we cannot have an Executive Board which shall be a mass meeting." The delegates adopted the committee's second proposal, which included the seven industry seats.[45]

Debate on the principle of board representativeness was also aroused by the discussion of Article XIII on the number of members from a given local union who could serve on the GEB. The constitution committee failed to achieve consensus and presented reports of the majority and the minority. The majority proposed that no more than one member of a local union could serve on the GEB, excepting the locals of the president and the secretary-treasurer, from each of which no more than two members could serve, including the president or secretary–treasurer. The minority proposed that no more than one member of a local with less than one thousand members could serve on the GEB, with the exceptions of the locals of the president and the secretary-treasurer, and that no local could have more than two members on the GEB. Green, supporting the majority proposal and challenging the possibility of large locals each having two GEB seats as in the minority report, argued that "in order to give every section of the country representation," in light of UFWA national organizing drives, "and in order to give every branch and every craft of our

[45] *Proceedings,* 1939 UFWA Convention, pp. 98–103, 126–130.

industry representation on the highest body of our International Union, we should not limit ourselves . . . to the position where some local unions precisely because of their size shall be given that added distinction." For the minority, Pizer argued not only that the UIU constitution had given greater representation to larger locals, but also that a large local is often a source of several qualified national leaders. After much debate, discussion of the article was postponed.[46]

With the resumption of discussion, the committee reversed its opinion, with a majority now supporting what had been the committee's minority proposal. The ensuing debate brought to the convention floor tension between the small locals of the nonmetropolitan South and Midwest, on the one hand, and the large, amalgamated locals of New York City, three of which had memberships in excess of one thousand, on the other. Fearing the domination of New York City locals on the board, A. L. Markham from Fort Smith local 281 asked, challenging the committee's proposal, "What in the devil are the small locals in the Eastern part or the Southern part or in the West going to do? They are not going to be familiar with the things which are going on in other places." Victor Anderson, the committee member from Rockford, explained his support of the committee proposal, revealing that he "was one of them who came to the Convention with the idea in mind to battle the brothers from the eastern states. I thought they had something up their sleeves when they came to Rockford. I must say they are the most willing and the hardest workers I have ever worked with. There is nothing you have to fear from those brothers." The delegates adopted the provision for allowing two GEB seats to locals with one thousand or more members.[47]

The second principle of democratic government the delegates debated concerned the amount of centralized control of the International union over the local unions, what is referred to obversely as local union autonomy. The issue of local union autonomy surfaced in the discussion of Article XXVIII on membership initiation fees and dues. The majority report of the constitution committee called for a minimum initiation fee of $2 per member, $1 of which was to be passed on from the local union to the International. The committee minority report proposed only that an initiation fee of $1 per member be paid to the International, with no restriction on the amount of the initiation fee charged by the local to the member. Supporting the majority proposal, Perlow argued that "we cannot be too loose and set no initiation fee for the local unions . . . because in many cases it will do harm to those local unions." Arguing for the minority, Pizer stated that "there shall be no interference with local autonomy on

---

[46] Ibid., pp. 85–90.
[47] Ibid., pp. 85–90, 134–139.

that point." A few delegates indicated a desire for local flexibility in setting initiation fees because of their practice of lowering initiation fees during organizing drives and for open shops, as opposed to closed shops. The article was referred back to the committee, which returned unanimously with a compromise proposal. The new proposal called for a minimum initiation fee of $2, $1 of which was to be paid by the local to the International, and, during strikes and organizing drives, locals could reduce the initiation fee to a minimum of $1 with the approval of the International president. This was adopted by the delegates.[48]

A similar debate about local union autonomy occurred with respect to the provision in Article XXVIII on monthly membership dues. The committee proposed that locals assess a minimum of $1 from the members, unless otherwise authorized by the International president. Persily argued that the $1 minimum would jeopardize organizing drives in the low-wage South, where workers could not afford the $1 and locals often required lower dues. Pizer argued that each local should have the right to set its own dues. Sirota, arguing for the committee's proposal, felt that local unions could not exist on dues less than $1. The delegates adopted the committee proposal.[49]

In addition to debating principles of government, the delegates differed with respect to the appropriate amount of the per capita tax, the monthly tax per member paid by the local to the International, in light of differences in the abilities of local unions to afford to pay a given amount. Debate arose in the discussions of Article XXIX on the per capita tax and article XXX on per capita tax for unemployed members. The delegates agreed to a per capita tax of $.30 for each member whose weekly wage rate was $20 or less, $.50 for each member with higher wages, and $.30 per unemployed member.[50]

The delegates also debated Article I, on the name of the organization. The majority of the constitution committee favored changing the name to the "United Furniture Workers International Union," and the minority wanted to retain the "United Furniture Workers of America." Pizer, favoring the majority proposal, argued that the word *international* had "historically and traditionally" been adopted in the labor movement to distinguish the national union from local unions and that including this word would add "prestige and authority to the organization as a whole." Some delegates countered Pizer by noting that the CIO was breaking with tradition and CIO leader John L. Lewis's union, the United Mine Workers of America, did not include the word *international* in its name. Speaking for

---

[48] Ibid., pp. 142–146, 194–195.
[49] Ibid., pp. 146–150.
[50] Ibid., pp. 150–152, 284–289.

the minority, Perlow argued that workers were already familiar with the name, "United Furniture Workers of America," which was similar to the "United Mine Workers of America," "one of the strongest unions in the United States." After much debate, the delegates opted for retaining the "United Furniture Workers of America."[51]

As they enacted the various provisions of the UFWA constitution, the delegates also developed policy to strengthen the UFWA and bring industrial unionism to the furniture industry. As an industrial union consisting of diverse membership constituencies, the UFWA attempted to reconcile both local union autonomy and craft consciousness, on the one hand, and national, industrywide growth policies, on the other, as it did in its deliberations about constitutional provisions. One of the chief policies for establishing a foundation for further growth was the merger or amalgamation of local unions in close proximity to one another. Amalgamation stabilizes local unions, as discussed in Chapter 2.

The issue of local union amalgamation cropped up twice at the convention. The first instance concerned the amalgamation of the nine local unions in Fort Smith. The CIO had organized several Fort Smith furniture shops in the late 1930s, but the employers, who were organized in an association, refused to bargain with the unions, each of which was a single-shop local union. At the UFWA convention, the Committee on Local Unions, chaired by Sirota, presented a resolution for the amalgamation of the Fort Smith locals. Sirota explained that "it would be to the best interests of these local unions and also to the interest of the workers that are not organized as yet, and to lay the basis for organization in the South, to amalgamate these local unions into one strong, powerful union." Also, most of the shops manufactured similar products in the kitchen, living room, and dining room lines. However, local 281 at Ward's Furniture Co., the largest of the Fort Smith locals, refused to amalgamate because it enjoyed a relatively fruitful bargaining relationship with the employer. The convention resolved to have the GEB amalgamate eight of the nine locals. The employers association first recognized the unions in 1940 after a ninety-day strike at one of the shops in the summer, but it played one local off against another during contract negotiations. By 1941, the Fort Smith locals were amalgamated as local 270, while local 281 continued as a single-shop local.[52]

The second instance of debate about local union amalgamation concerned the upholsterers local 76 and the woodworkers local 76B, both in New York City. The chief participants in this debate were former FWIU

[51] Ibid., pp. 61–69.
[52] Ibid., pp. 207–208—quotation from p. 207; personal interviews with Elmer "Mule" Sutton and Austin Moran in Fort Smith, AR, on July 22, 1985.

activists Pizer from local 76, Perlow from 76B, and Sirota, chair of the Committee on Local Unions. At issue was whether some 500 frame makers for upholstered furniture from local 76B, whose total membership was 1,839, should merge with local 76, whose total membership was 1,510. The debate centered around a resolution submitted by local 76 and a committee report, each of which was cast in general terms, omitting specific reference to locals 76 and 76B. The resolution called on the International to aid in the reorganization of upholsterers and frame makers of separate local unions in the same community into one local union. In contrast, the committee report called for the amalgamation of upholsterers and frame makers local unions in the same community, if neither local union was a multi-craft union, that is, consisting of several other crafts; and for the GEB to assist the amalgamation of multi-craft locals, if it was their desire to amalgamate. Speaking for the local 76 resolution, Richard Bandler of that local argued that an increasing number of upholstered furniture factories were performing both upholstering and frame making under one roof and that it was inappropriate to have two locals, 76 and 76B, represent the workers in one factory, especially as this resulted in different employment conditions for the upholsterers and the frame makers. Upholsterers had a thirty-five-hour work week, while frame makers had a forty-hour work week, and each group had different holidays and pay schedules. In supporting the committee report, Perlow argued that his local 76B, which consisted not only of frame makers but also of woodworkers in nonupholstered furniture trades, had gone on record about a year before as favoring the complete amalgamation of locals 76 and 76B, but that the upholsterers did not want to include the nonupholstered furniture woodworkers in the amalgamation. He added that the frame makers had been organized for the longest time in 76B, that the frame makers were training the more recently organized nonupholstered furniture woodworkers in 76B, and that to remove the frame makers from 76B would demoralize the remaining groups in 76B. Further, he doubted that the frame makers would benefit from being in local 76, which was "still based on very craft lines." Countering Perlow's accusation of local 76's being "craftist," Pizer argued that the upholsterers wanted "to get closer to the frame makers." Sirota, supporting his committee's report, argued that the local 76 resolution was premature because 76B was still organizing and that removing the frame makers, "the live wires, the builders of an organization," would "be an injustice to" 76B. He also doubted the necessity of the resolution, given that the locals cooperated with each other by refusing to work with another's products when one local was on strike. The delegates turned down local 76's resolution and approved the committee report.[53]

[53] *Proceedings,* 1939 UFWA Convention, pp. 74, 208–215.

In sum, the convention deliberations on constitutional provisions and local union amalgamation constituted an effort to reconcile the board representativeness and local union autonomy issues with the establishment of a viable national industrial union whose membership varied with respect to the size and wealth of local unions, geographical area, product line, and craft. Board representativeness of geographical areas, product lines, and craft was reconciled with limiting the size of the board to manageable proportions. Local union autonomy was reconciled with the necessity of funding the International, an issue generated in part by cost-of-living and wealth differences among locals in different regions, and with a national growth strategy partly based on local union amalgamation. With its structure in place, the UFWA resolved to standardize wages across the nation by extending its organizing drives into the low-wage South, as discussed in Chapter 2; New England and the Midwest, especially the furniture towns of Gardner, MA, Keene, NH, and Grand Rapids, MI; the West Coast; centers of piano manufacturing in New York City, Cincinnati, and Indiana; and among the diverse crafts of the industry. On broader fronts, the UFWA resolved, among other things, to support the New Deal, to condemn race discrimination, to "prevent any American fascists from exterminating the labor movement in this country," and to support U.S. embargoes against "fascist Germany and Italy."[54]

Most of the individuals who were elected to serve on the GEB had participated in the building of the UFWA in the period since the December 1937 furniture unity conference and in the break from the AFL into the CIO. Twelve of the 19 people elected to the 23-seat GEB (4 seats were left vacant) had attended the unity conference, 8 as UIU delegates, 3 as CIO delegates, and 1 as an independent delegate. Of the 7 GEB members who were not at the unity conference, at least 4 had been engaged actively in union organizing prior to the founding UFWA convention.[55]

All of the GEB members were elected unanimously. Muster became president, and former FWIU activist Jack Hochstadt, now representing Boston local 136B, formerly a UIU local, was elected secretary-treasurer. Perlow was elected vice president of the East, and George Stewart, from Rockford local 707 and chairman of UFWA district 7 (Illinois), was elected vice president of the Midwest. Both Davis Spears from Fort Smith and Ernest Marsh from Los Angeles had been members of the Carpenters, had participated in CIO organizing in their regions, and were elected vice presidents of the South and West, respectively. Seven district seats were filled by Louis Gilbert, a UFWA organizer in New England who had been a UIU delegate to the unity conference, for district 1 (New England); Joseph

---

[54] Ibid., pp. 108–110, 113–114, 122–123, 157, 174–176, 181–186, 229–230.
[55] Ibid., pp. 239–273; *Unity Conference Minutes,* pp. 3–6.

Proudman, district 2 (upstate New York) chairman, an independent delegate to the unity conference from the furniture town, Jamestown, NY, and a former member of the Committee of 6, for district 2; Pizer for district 3 (greater metropolitan New York City); Persily, a CIO delegate to the furniture unity conference and a former Committee of 6 member, for district 6 (Indiana); Victor Failla of Chicago local 1608, a CIO delegate to the unity conference who brought his local from the Carpenters into the UFWA, for district 7 (Illinois); A. L. Markham of Fort Smith local 281 for district 9 (Arkansas and Oklahoma); and Howard Custer of San Francisco local 262 for district 10 (West Coast). Of the six industry branch seats filled, Richard Bandler of New York City local 76, chairman of UFWA district 3 and a UIU delegate to the unity conference, filled the upholsterers seat; Herbert Johnson of Rockford local 707 was elected to the case goods seat; George Bucher, a CIO delegate to the furniture unity conference and a former Committee of 6 member, represented miscellaneous industries; Sirota filled the bedding and springs seat; Paul Green from New York City local 45B, a UIU delegate to the furniture unity conference, was elected to represent curtains, venetian blinds, furniture covers, and the like; and Fred Fulford, who participated in the break from the AFL by helping to organize CIO local 155 in South Bend, IN, was elected to the juvenile furniture seat.[56]

New constituencies, defined by the structure created at the founding convention, would emerge in the UFWA as it extended its organizing drives to new locations. Moreover, the constituencies would compete with one another for leadership positions in the union, especially during the late 1940s and 1950, when the effort to realize industrial unionism, not only in furniture manufacturing but also in U.S. mass production industries generally, would encounter major political opposition. For now, the founding UFWA convention ended with President Muster proclaiming "to a better day in furniture!" and the delegates singing the old labor song, "Solidarity Forever."[57]

Organizing the Unorganized and Improving Employment Conditions, 1940–1947

With its structure and growth policy set at the founding convention, the UFWA grew rapidly during the 1940s until 1947, when the Taft-Hartley Act and Cold War politics served to limit labor movement growth, as discussed in Chapter 1. Throughout the 1940s, the UFWA gained members

---

[56] *Proceedings,* 1939 UFWA Convention, pp. 16–17, 239–273; *Unity Conference Minutes,* pp. 3–6; personal interview with Sam Sloan, December 23, 1985.
[57] *Proceedings,* 1939 UFWA Convention, p. 293.

in most regions of the United States and improved the employment conditions of furniture workers.

Organizing the Unorganized

Following its growth strategy through local union amalgamation, which it had laid out at the founding convention, the UFWA assembled at its second convention in May 1941 with 106 affiliated locals, 31 more than the number in 1939. Several small locals, including the Fort Smith locals, were merged into larger locals, and large, amalgamated locals were established in the furniture centers of Chicago, Cleveland, and Gardner, MA.[58]

Chicago local 18B, which entered the UFWA in February 1940, had been affiliated with the UIU as the woodworkers and finishers local union counterpart to the UIU upholsterers local 18. Local 18B of the UIU, whose members had been affiliated with local 18 at least since a 1933 citywide general furniture strike, was organized in September 1936 when the UIU had begun to increase its industrial unionism activities. Some shops had contracts with locals 18 and 18B, as in the case of UIU locals 76 and 76B in New York City, but the two locals often failed to cooperate during strikes and organizing campaigns, hampering the effort to realize industrial unionism in the Chicago furniture industry.[59]

Local 18B of the UIU was under the leadership of Financial Secretary Sam Sloan and Business Agents Nicholas Blattner and George Leach when it entered the UFWA. Blattner, a German immigrant and a cabinetmaker who arrived in the United States in 1912 and became an FWIU activist in 1933, and George Leach were leftists who had been expelled from the Carpenters in the early 1930s because they campaigned to waive the union membership dues of unemployed carpenters. Sloan, the son of a union railroad fireman and the nephew of a railroading uncle who had been in the Boilermakers union and the Industrial Workers of the World, was born in Kansas in 1911 and arrived in Chicago via Texas in 1924. In 1933, he began working as a machine hand in the American Furniture Co., which manufactured occasional and novelty furniture, and in 1937 he was elected financial secretary of 18B. Sloan and Blattner attended the furniture unity conference in December 1937 as UIU delegates. Waiting for the expiration of some contracts, they conducted a membership vote and brought 18B, consisting of about seven shops, into the UFWA in 1940. Chicago Local 1608 of the UFWA, which was represented by Victor Failla at the founding UFWA convention in 1939, had two shops (Harris Hub and Great Northern

---

[58] *Proceedings of the Second Constitutional Convention of the United Furniture Workers of America—CIO*, Chicago, May 19–23, 1941, pp. 13–15.
[59] Personal interview with Sam Sloan in Cicero, IL, on July 3, 1985.

Chair Co.) that were taken over by 18B in 1940. Failla had been defeated for business agent of UIU local 18B by Blattner in 1936 and received a charter from the Carpenters for local 1608 later that year. He attended the furniture unity conference in December 1937, and in 1938, after his local was placed under trusteeship by the Carpenters, he received a charter from the UFWA. Failla failed to pay the UFWA per capita tax, and Jack Hochstadt was made trustee of the local. Failla received a UIU charter for local 1608, and local 18B became the Chicago UFWA local.[60]

Cleveland local 450 entered the UFWA in 1940. The local began at the E. F. Hauserman Co., a manufacturer of steel partitions and doors, and had grown to represent about eight other shops by the late 1940s. The Hauserman workers, who had been represented by an AFL union, were divided on the issue of CIO affiliation when Vince Favorito, a left-wing CIO organizer, and Charley Baxter, a left-wing Hauserman employee, initiated a CIO organizing drive. The skilled workers wanted to remain in the AFL, and the other workers, who were dissatisfied with the AFL because they had no raises or job security, were pro-CIO. The company fired a group of pro-CIO workers led by Frank McCafferty, and the workers struck the plant to have the activists reinstated on the job. The UFWA won a representation election, and the workers gained a contract with a $.10 raise, dues check-off, weekly pay by check, and improved bonuses and holidays. Favorito became business representative for the local, and Baxter served as chief steward.[61]

In the furniture town of Gardner, MA, local 154 was chartered by the UFWA in July 1939. In 1933, the independent United Furniture and Allied Trade Workers' Union was established to unionize the Gardner area. The union was founded by Thomas Binnall, a staunch Democrat and Irish Catholic who was born on a farm near Gardner; Toivo Hannula; Louis Glad; William Leonard; Edward Sundin; and Leon Brown. The union organized the O. W. Siebert Co., a family-owned manufacturer of bicycles and tricycles, in 1934 and the L. B. Ramsdell Co. in 1935, and later gained its first closed shop agreement with the Gardner Upholstered Furniture Co. To extend its organizing activities further, the union affiliated with the UIU in 1935. Unable to organize the furniture plants on the craft basis of the AFL, the union became a CIO supporter, sent Axel Backman and Toivo Hannula as UIU delegates to the furniture unity conference in December 1937, and affiliated with the UFWA in 1939. Backman was local union president, Hannula was secretary-treasurer, and, in August 1940, Binnall, who had been working in Hedstrom Union, a baby carriage manufacturer,

---

[60] Ibid., *Unity Conference Minutes,* p. 3; *Furniture Workers Press,* May 1966, p. 7.
[61] Personal interviews with Robert Manista, Eugene Wysocki, John Kobyleski, and Julius Zahl in Cleveland on January 4, 1986.

was elected the first full-time business agent of the local. Local 154 subsequently grew, and in 1944 it hired another business agent, Lubert Taylor, a local cabinetmaker who was born in New Hampshire and shared Binnall's political views.[62]

On the West Coast, the membership of the Los Angeles local had almost tripled by the second UFWA convention, and that of San Francisco local 262 had almost quintupled. Local 262, which was present at the founding UFWA convention, began at the Simmons Co., a bed manufacturer. Fred Stefan, the son of a forester, was a German Catholic immigrant who arrived in San Francisco in 1923 at the age of twenty-four and, shortly thereafter, began working in the Simmons plant as an automatic drill press operator. A member of the Social Democrats in Germany, Stefan discussed the possibility of organizing the Simmons plant with his fellow workers, in light of the sweatshop conditions in the plant and managerial arbitrariness in making job assignments and discharges. During the mid-1920s, however, the Simmons workers, many of whom were immigrants from agricultural backgrounds and had little organizing experience, thought that unionism was infeasible because it was reserved for skilled workers. Stefan encountered much resistance to organizing and was red-baited by the workers. In the 1930s, after a major strike in longshoring, the bay area furniture workers, many of whom lived in the same neighborhoods as the longshoremen and frequented the same bars, began to unionize. The CIO Steel Workers conducted an organizing drive at the Simmons plant, which included Stefan as an organizer, and gained recognition in 1938. The union entered the UFWA and, subsequently, Stefan assumed a leadership role in the local. In Portland, OR, the UFWA chartered local 1090 at the Dornbecker Co., a manufacturer of residential furniture, which was among the largest UFWA locals by the time of the second UFWA convention.[63]

The UFWA penetrated further into the piano industry after chartering New York City local 102 at the Steinway Co. in January 1939. Several months before the second UFWA convention, the UFWA established the Piano Workers Organizing Committee and, by the second convention, had gained contracts with Story & Clark and Pratt & Reed. James Cerofeci, who was born in Italy in 1906 and arrived in the United States in 1909, began working in the Steinway plant in 1926 as a sander. After a three-year layoff that began in 1932, Cerofeci returned to work at Steinway and helped organize the 300 workers in the plant. Among the organizing issues was

---

[62] Personal interviews with Grace Perry and Rosie St. Jean in Gardner, MA, on January 8, 1986; *Unity Conference Minutes,* p. 4; "A Brief History of Our Union Local 154," photocopy of an article from an unidentified source, 1956.

[63] Personal interview with Fred Stefan in San Francisco on September 6, 1982; *Proceedings,* 1939 UFWA Convention, pp. 74–75; *Proceedings,* 1941 UFWA Convention, p. 147.

the favoritism shown by the company to the largely immigrant German workforce and discrimination against the Italian workers in instituting layoffs. Cerofeci became the business manager of local 102. By the time of the second UFWA convention, local 102 membership had increased to 630.[64]

The UFWA also made some inroads into the South and Indiana, whose membership had doubled by the second convention. In the South, locals were chartered in New Orleans, Austell, GA, and Hickory, NC.[65]

The membership of the UFWA continued to rise during World War II, despite the induction of some four thousand UFWA members into the armed services. The chief problems facing the furniture industry and other war-production industries were government limitations on the use of metal products, such as furniture hardware, steel springs for upholstered furniture, and metal furniture, in furniture manufacturing and the conversion of plants into war-related production. The UFWA addressed each of these problems and adhered to the wartime no-strike policy. In April 1942, the UFWA GEB directed President Muster to facilitate the conversion of the industry to war production, and Muster, Pizer, and Perlow served on the Furniture Industry Advisory Panel of the War Production Board. In its lobbying effort with the federal government, the UFWA urged the government to use wooden gliders and airplane parts and wooden truck cargo bodies. A November 1942 survey of UFWA locals, accounting for only 30 percent of UFWA membership, indicated that almost two-thirds of UFWA shops were engaged in war-production work. War products included mattresses, desks, kitchen equipment, shell boxes, flare boxes, and locker boxes. The UFWA had only limited success with labor-management productivity committees, having established only twenty such committees.[66]

The UFWA's organizing efforts during the war, financed largely by income from the large, amalgamated locals in New York City, New England, and the Pacific Coast, led to great membership gains, especially in the Southeast and Michigan, as shown in Table 3.3. Between 1943 and 1945, about half of the UFWA International income was generated by the locals in districts 1 (New England), 3 (greater metropolitan New York City area), and 10 (Pacific Coast). During the same period, roughly one-third of the UFWA International field organizational expenses (organizers' salaries, per diems, travel expenses, etc.) were deployed in districts 5 (Southeast) and 7 (Michigan). The 1943–1946 membership growth rates in

---

[64] Personal interview with James Cerofeci in New York City on November 19, 1984; *Proceedings,* 1941 UFWA Convention, pp. 14, 146.

[65] *Proceedings,* 1941 UFWA Convention, pp. 13–14.

[66] *Proceedings of the Third Constitutional Convention of the United Furniture Workers of America—CIO,* Cleveland, May 17–21, 1943, pp. 29–33, 42, 46–47.

Table 3.3

International UFWA Income, Field Organizational Expenses, Membership, and Membership Change, by District, 1943–1946

District	% International UFWA Income from Local Unions			% International UFWA Field Organizational Expenses			% UFWA Members		% Change in Number of UFWA Members
	1943	1944	1945	1943	1944	1945	1943	1946	
1. New England	13	14	13	13	10	9	12	12	46.6
2. Upstate New York	2	3	2	4	2	4	2	3	109.7
3. Greater metropolitan New York City	33	27	24	9	10	10	30	25	18.5
4. Pennsylvania, Maryland, and southern New Jersey	6	7	7	8	13	23	8	8	53.9
5. Southeast	3	5	9	14	22	22	4	8	176.7
6. Indiana	8	8	8	9	11	9	10	8	11.5
7. Michigan	7	7	9	17	15	13	5	9	130.0
8. Illinois and Wisconsin	9	9	9	10	7	3	10	9	19.3
9. Arkansas, Western Tennessee, Oklahoma, and Louisiana	5	7	6	7	8	7	5	6	61.0
10. Pacific Coast	10	10	10	6	2	0	10	10	36.5
11. Ohio	4	3	3	3	0	0	5	3	−14.5
All districts	100	100	100	100	100	100	101[a]	101[a]	40.4
N							22,393	31,429	

Source: *Proceedings of the Fourth Constitutional Convention of the United Furniture Workers of America—CIO*, Detroit, June 3–7, 1946, pp. 28–49, 52.
[a]Does not sum to 100% due to rounding.

districts 5 and 7, 176.7 percent and 130 percent, respectively, were the highest of the eleven UFWA districts.

Membership expansion between 1943 and 1946 occurred through the increased amalgamation of local unions in the factory-dense areas in most districts. District 1 (New England) membership increased largely from the continuous amalgamation of Gardner local 154. In district 2 (upstate New York), the increased amalgamation of Jamestown local 34 led to membership gains. The modest gains in district 3 (New York City) were largely attributable to the increasing amalgamation of piano local 102. In district 4 (Pennsylvania, Maryland, and Southern New Jersey), seven new locals were chartered, while Gettysburg, PA, local 466 and Hagerstown, MD, local 472 each expanded by amalgamation. The tremendous growth in district 5 (Southeast) resulted from the chartering of sixteen new locals, including Martinsville, VA, local 284, which grew through amalgamation, and from the continuous amalgamation of local 273 in Sumter, SC. What membership gains occurred in district 6 (Indiana) were attributable to the expansion of amalgamated locals 331 and 305 in Jasper and Batesville and to the chartering of amalgamated local 335 in Tell City, all in southern Indiana. The large membership gains in district 7 (Michigan) resulted from the continuous amalgamation of Grand Rapids local 415, which followed in the wake of the organizing efforts of the United Automobile Workers that had been aborted by the Manufacturers Association of Grand Rapids in the late 1930s and subsequent UFWA rivalry with the Carpenters. In district 8 (Illinois and Wisconsin), the chartering of Sheboygan, WI, local 800 in 1943 and its continuous amalgamation led to membership gains. District 9 (Arkansas, Tennessee, Oklahoma, Louisiana) membership increases stemmed from the rapid amalgamation of local 282 in Memphis, TN. In district 10 (Pacific Coast), the existing shops of locals 576 and 262 in Los Angeles and San Francisco had membership gains, but no representation elections were conducted, due to rivalries with the AFL. District 11 (Ohio) was the only district to experience a membership loss, which resulted in part from factionalism in Cleveland local 450, culminating in the trusteeship of the local by the International.[67]

The UFWA grew in most districts through the late 1940s.[68] By 1947, UFWA annual membership had reached its all-time high of 43,389, as discussed in Chapter 1.

[67] *Proceedings,* 1943 UFWA Convention, pp. 41–42; *Proceedings of the Fourth Constitutional Convention of the United Furniture Workers of America CIO,* Detroit, June 3–7, 1946, pp. 28–49; personal interview with Eugene Wysocki, January 4, 1986.

[68] *Proceedings of the Fifth Constitutional Convention of the United Furniture Workers of America CIO,* Chicago, June 7–11, 1948, p. 25.

Improving Employment Conditions

The UFWA's effort at improving employment conditions during the 1940s centered on gaining new fringe benefits, closing the North–South wage gap, and raising wages. Gains in fringe benefits were achieved primarily during World War II, when wages were frozen, along with union security clauses in contracts. By April 1943, almost three-fourths of UFWA contracts contained provisions for a closed shop, and almost one-third of the members were covered by a dues check-off arrangement. Over half of the UFWA members had gained paid vacations, and paid holidays were becoming more common. In May 1944 the UFWA established an industry-wide health-accident-life-insurance plan, which was employer financed through payments of 3 percent of the payroll. By June 1946, over 8,000 UFWA members and their families had achieved coverage under the plan through collective bargaining, and various benefits had been expanded. The number of UFWA members covered under the plan increased to 14,280 by June 1948. According to a national survey of wood furniture factories taken by the U.S. Bureau of Labor Statistics (BLS) in October 1945, these fringe benefits were relatively uncommon in the industry. Of the sampled establishments, about three-fourths lacked a life insurance or health insurance plan. Retirement pensions were uncommon in UFWA shops and in the industry generally.[69]

The UFWA effort to close the North–South wage gap occurred mainly through its involvement in furniture industry committees of the Wage and Hour Division of the U.S. Department of Labor. Muster, Pizer, and Marsh, now UFWA secretary-treasurer, along with AFL representatives, served on the industry committee when the Southern Furniture Manufacturers Association fought the establishment of a $.40 per hour minimum wage for case goods workers. The $.40 minimum was achieved in October 1941, leading to $.02–$.10 per hour raises for some 63 percent of southern workers and 37 percent of northern workers. Little headway was made in the bedding industry. The geographical wage differential persisted to the end of the war. According to the October 1945 BLS survey mentioned, the average hourly wage rate of furniture production workers varied from $1.04 on the West Coast and $.89 in the Middle Atlantic states to $.60 in the Southeast.[70]

---

[69] *Proceedings*, 1943 UFWA Convention, pp. 37, 40; *Proceedings*, 1946 UFWA Convention, p. 19; *Proceedings*, 1948 UFWA Convention, p. 31; U.S. Department of Labor, Bureau of Labor Statistics, *Wage Structure, Wood Furniture, 1945*, Series 2, no. 30 (Washington, DC: U.S. Department of Labor, Bureau of Labor Statistics, 1946), p. 48.

[70] *Proceedings*, 1943 UFWA Convention, pp. 42–43; U.S. Department of Labor, *Wage Structure, Wood Furniture, 1945*, p. 15.

The seventeen-week strike at the large Thomasville Chair Co. in North Carolina during the latter part of 1946 was a significant step toward closing the North–South wage gap. The company, one of the largest southern furniture manufacturers, paid its twelve-hundred-person workforce, on the average, $.45 per hour. Company owner Doak Finch controlled the two banks and the merchants in town and managed the factories with what the UFWA termed "a paternalistic approach that amounted to 'thought control.'" Finch operated a check-off system whereby the company deducted from workers' salaries the amount they owed local merchants for previous purchases and on their home mortgages, often overcharging them. He also checked off an annual $2 fee from workers' salaries for swimming privileges at the nearby lake, which he owned, regardless of whether the workers availed themselves of their privileges. On April 4, 1946, the men and women workers, one-third of whom were black, in nine Thomasville Chair Co. plants voted 817 to 335 in favor of affiliating with the UFWA, establishing UFWA local 286. The company refused to bargain with the union, and in July the workers struck the plants. By the ninth week of the strike, police had thrown tear gas bombs at the picketers, an attempt to break up the picketers with a truck had failed, the strikers had set up soup kitchens and other strike relief measures, a minister was conducting daily religious services on the picket line, and a racially integrated group of three thousand workers had paraded through the town. Moreover, the strike drew national attention and support from the labor movement. Over fifteen thousand dollars was donated to the Thomasville Strikers' Relief Committee by the International UFWA, UFWA locals, and other CIO and AFL unions, including the National Maritime Union; the United Electrical Workers; the Amalgamated Clothing Workers; the Chefs, Cooks, and Pastry Cooks; the Lithographers; the Shoe Workers; the Marine Cooks and Stewards; the Cigar Workers; and the Barbers and Beauty Culturists. By the twelfth week of the strike, Finch offered no more than a $.05 per hour wage increase, which the workers turned down, and he obtained a temporary court injunction to limit the picketing. In the seventeenth week, on November 22, company and union signed an agreement providing for a 15 percent general wage increase, a minimum $.10 per hour wage increase, paid vacations up to two weeks, union recognition, and checkoff for union dues. President Philip Murray of the CIO announced the union victory at Thomasville to the national CIO convention, which had coincided with the signing of the Thomasville pact.

Throughout the Thomasville strike, the UFWA underscored the significance of the racial unity that was maintained among the workers, despite efforts to divide them along racial lines, and the importance of the strike for future southern organizing drives. Following the strike, the

UFWA and the CIO proceeded to map out a southern furniture organizing drive, especially among the forty thousand largely non-union furniture workers in North Carolina.[71]

Wage raises were achieved primarily after the war. During the war, wages in the furniture and other industries were regulated and stabilized by the National War Labor Board according to the July 1942 "Little Steel" formula, allowing wages to rise no higher than 15 percent of January 1941 wages. After the war, strikes increased tremendously, as workers wanted to maintain their take-home pay at a level commensurate with their wartime pay, which had increased due to sizable payments for overtime at time and one half. By June 1948, some ten thousand UFWA members in all districts had participated in strikes, especially in New England and New York City. Between October 1945 and May 1946 the average hourly wage rate for wood furniture production workers increased by 15 percent.[72]

In sum, the UFWA spread industrial unionism in the furniture industry during the 1940s, incorporating members from diverse regions, crafts, and product lines and raising the standard of living of furniture production workers. Leadership changes in the UFWA reflected in part the growth and diversification of its membership.

The Growing Divide: Leadership Change During the Cold War, 1946–1950

Throughout the UFWA's formative period, the ethnic composition on the general executive board shifted as the UFWA incorporated an increasingly heterogeneous membership through its organizing drives out of New York City into the small towns of the Midwest, East, and South. The composition shifted from a majority of Jewish GEB members from the metropolitan East in 1939 to a majority of Northern and Western European members, largely from the nonmetropolitan areas of the East, Midwest, and South, in 1950.

Along with the geographical-ethnic shift in the GEB came a shift in GEB political attitudes. The originally left-leaning GEB, and the UFWA conventions, became increasingly polarized between leftist and non-leftist members.

The shift in the ethnic composition of the GEB was accelerated during

---

[71] *Furniture Workers Press,* March 1946, p. 1; April 1946, p. 1; July 1946, p. 7; August 1946, p. 1; September 1946, pp. 1, 3, 6; October 1946, pp. 1, 8, 12; November 1946, p. 1; December 1946, pp. 1, 3, 8; January 1947, pp. 1–2; February 1947, p. 1.

[72] Nelson Lichtenstein, *Labor's War at Home* (Cambridge: Cambridge University Press, 1982), p. 72; *Proceedings,* 1943 UFWA Convention, p. 40; *Proceedings,* 1946 UFWA Convention, pp. 96, 98; *Proceedings,* 1948 UFWA Convention, pp. 25, 33–34; U.S. Department of Labor, *Wage Structure, Wood Furniture, 1945,* p. 1.

the Cold War period, especially at the dramatic 1950 UFWA convention, when UFWA growth was jeopardized by national political conditions. The federal government and the National Labor Relations Board, particularly, with the enactment of the Taft-Hartley Act in 1947, became increasingly intolerant of Communist involvement in the labor movement, interrupting the growth of the UFWA, which maintained a left-wing political stance. When the CIO also became intolerant of Communists in the late 1940s, and raids on the membership by hostile AFL and CIO unions further jeopardized the UFWA, the UFWA shifted its political stance to liberalism and ousted its left-wing leaders in 1950. The defeat of the Left, many of whom were Jewish and from the metropolitan East, and their replacement with non-left officers from the nonmetropolitan areas of the Midwest and East, accelerated the increase in the proportion of Northern and Western Europeans on the GEB.

The Cold War, Taft-Hartley, the CIO, and Raiding

The Cold War with the USSR, increased anti-Communist fervor in the United States, and an effort by conservatives to restrain the labor movement, which had grown tremendously during World War II, occurred simultaneously during the late 1940s. These developments were partly reflected in the Taft-Hartley Act. Spearheaded by the National Association of Manufacturers and opposed vehemently by organized labor, the act prohibited major union security arrangements by outlawing closed shop agreements and allowing states to enact right-to-work laws, which prohibited union shop agreements. Also, section 9h of the act denied the services of the National Labor Relations Board to unions whose officials failed to sign affidavits verifying that they were not Communist party members.[73]

Between 1946 and 1949, the CIO became increasingly intolerant of communism and of Communists in the labor movement. At its 1946 convention, the CIO passed a resolution opposing the efforts of the Communist party or other political parties to interfere in CIO affairs. Secretary of State George Marshall addressed the October 1947 CIO convention, which supported the Marshall Plan. By this time, many unions had complied with section 9h of the Taft-Hartley Act. Through 1948, the CIO assisted several of its affiliated unions and state industrial councils in removing Communist leaders. In the wake of the Truman victory over Dewey and Progressive Party candidate Henry Wallace, who had received the support of the Left within the CIO, the CIO passed a resolution at its 1948 convention

---

[73] Christopher Tomlins, *The State and the Unions* (Cambridge: Cambridge University Press, 1985), pp. 293–300.

against proposals for a third party. At the 1949 CIO convention, both the United Electrical Workers and the United Farm Equipment Workers were expelled from the CIO on the grounds of Communist domination. The 1949 convention also amended the CIO constitution, authorizing the CIO executive board to expel, by a two-thirds vote, any union "the policies and activities of which are consistently directed toward the achievement of the program or the purposes of the Communist Party, any Fascist organization, or other totalitarian movement, rather than the objectives and policies set forth in the constitution of the CIO." Immediately after the 1949 CIO convention, ten unions, including the UFWA, were charged with following Communist objectives rather than CIO objectives and were slated for expulsion from the CIO. Nine of these unions were expelled by 1950. The UFWA remained in the CIO.[74]

Between 1946 and 1949, disagreement over U.S. foreign policy issues and Wallace's third-party candidacy mounted between the CIO and the UFWA, several of whose leaders were Communist party members or fellow travelers. On June 30–July 1, 1947, the UFWA general executive board endorsed the idea of a third party and condemned the Truman Doctrine, calling for an amicable settlement of international problems. At its January 22–24, 1948, meeting, the GEB approved Pizer's opposition to an anti-third-party resolution at a recent CIO board meeting. The 1948 UFWA convention, held in June, passed resolutions endorsing Wallace for president; condemning the Truman Doctrine and the Marshall Plan and calling for unity between the United States, Britain, and the USSR; and supporting the World Federation of Trade Unions, from which the CIO would withdraw in January 1949 because of tension over the Marshall Plan with the Russian trade unions. In August 1948, the CIO executive board endorsed Truman for president. Pizer was one of the pro-Wallace minority votes at this CIO board meeting.[75]

The relationship between the UFWA and the CIO had soured by November 1948, when national CIO officials informed the UFWA that its Wallace endorsement and opposition to the Marshall Plan were contrary to CIO policy. The UFWA retorted that "it was wholly inconsistent with traditional CIO policy to attack those unions which disagreed" and chastised the CIO convention, which had met in November, for engaging in red-

[74] Saposs, *Communism in American Unions,* pp. 153, 157–158; Cochran, *Labor and Communism,* pp. 267, 270–271, 305–306; Kampelman, *Communist Party vs. the CIO,* pp. 47–49, 159–160; *Proceedings,* 1948 UFWA Convention, p. 95; testimony of Allan Haywood before the U.S. Senate Subcommittee of the Committee on Labor and Public Welfare, 82nd Congress, second session, June 17, 1952, *Communist Domination of Unions and National Security,* pp. 265–269.
[75] *Furniture Workers Press,* July 1947, pp. 1, 6; February 1948, p. 1; September 1948, p. 4; *Proceedings,* 1948 UFWA Convention, pp. 227–228, 244–245; Kampelman, *Communist Party vs. the CIO,* p. 239; Cochran, *Labor and Communism,* pp. 297–298.

baiting. Further deterioration of the relationship between the UFWA and the CIO occurred in May 1949. The CIO executive board passed an ultimatum calling "for the resignation of any CIO board member whose union did not conform to the political line of the board's majority." Shortly thereafter, the UFWA GEB lambasted the CIO board: "It is indeed alarming when the CIO Board majority arrogates to itself the extraordinary power to ban the precious right of autonomy from Internationals and instead imposes a system of regimentation and control. This cannot but create a feeling of deep resentment and distrust among the rank and file of the CIO."[76]

Throughout the 1946–1950 period, the UFWA was raided by other unions critical of the UFWA's left-leaning political stance. After an abortive effort to establish a no-raiding agreement between the UFWA and the UIU in March 1946, the UIU raided the UFWA through 1949, especially in Michigan, Indiana, and various southern locations. By the summer of 1948, CIO unions such as the Woodworkers had begun to raid the UFWA and, at the November 1948 CIO executive board meeting, Pizer denounced the raiding, "calling upon the CIO to end fratricidal raiding within the ranks of the CIO." By June 1949, the UFWA had been raided by the CIO-affiliated United Automobile Workers (UAW), the Woodworkers, and the Paper Workers. Especially damaging to the UFWA was the loss in August 1949 of almost thirteen hundred members at the American Seating Co. in Grand Rapids to the UAW.[77]

Membership of the UFWA declined in the period between its 1948 and 1950 conventions, as discussed in Chapter 1. This resulted in part from the raids and in part from lack of support from the NLRB, which stemmed from the UFWA's noncompliance with section 9h of the Taft-Hartley Act, requiring union officers to sign the non-Communist affidavits. Although the GEB voted in favor of compliance in January 1948, it also voted to refer the decision to the UFWA convention, held in June, which voted against compliance. Faced with heavy membership losses from raids, the GEB resolved in favor of compliance in May 1949 and condemned the Taft-Hartley Act as "a long step in the direction of fascism."[78] Explaining its decision to comply, the GEB stated:

---

[76] *Furniture Workers Press,* December 1948, p. 7; August 1949, p. 3.

[77] Ibid., August 1946, pp. 1, 2, 7; September 1946, pp. 1, 3, 7; October 1946, pp. 4, 6, 12; November 1946, pp. 1, 7; December 1946, pp. 1, 2, 4, 8, 9; January 1947, p. 8; February 1947, pp. 1, 4; July 1948, p. 12; August 1948, p. 5; September 1948, pp. 1, 4, 6; October 1948, p. 6; November 1948, p. 5; June 1949, pp. 1, 2, 5, 12; August 1949, pp. 1, 3; September 1949, pp. 1–2; October 1949, pp. 5–6; March 1950, p. 1.

[78] Ibid., February 1948, p. 1; July 1948, p. 1; June 1949, p. 1; *Proceedings,* 1948 UFWA Convention, pp. 97–98.

We still believe that 9 (h) is an un-American and unconstitutional requirement.... We stand four-square for the repeal of the Taft-Hartley Act.

We find ourselves, however, constrained because of increased severity of the attacks upon us from employers, and also from certain unprincipled AFL and CIO unions, who seek our dismemberment, to take measures to preserve our organization. The welfare of our membership requires these measures.[79]

During the period between its 1948 and 1950 conventions, the UFWA lost almost five thousand members, roughly 13 percent of its membership, in raids by other unions. The distribution of the loss by raider and location is shown in Table 3.4. Approximately 60 percent of the membership loss from raids was attributable to UIU and UAW raids in the Great Lakes region.

In sum, as the Cold War crystallized during the 1946–1950 period, the UFWA's relations with the CIO and several unions deteriorated, placing UFWA membership in jeopardy. These developments, in turn, accelerated regional tensions that had been present in the UFWA since its founding convention in 1939.

Regional Division in the UFWA

As the UFWA extended its organizing drives out of New York City during the 1940s, it incorporated an increasingly heterogeneous membership with respect to ethnicity, as discussed in Chapter 2; political beliefs; and region. Liberal and left-wing immigrant Jewish members and Italian members tended to reside in the metropolitan areas of the Northeast, especially in New York City. Moderate-to-conservative, native-born, Northern and Western Europeans tended to reside in the small-town and rural areas of the Midwest, in New England, and in the South, west of the Mississippi River, including Fort Smith. Many black UFWA members resided in the south, east of the Mississippi River, especially in Memphis and the Carolinas (see Chapter 2).

Tension between the metropolitan East and the nonmetropolitan Midwest was already evident at the founding UFWA convention in 1939, as discussed earlier. The midwesterners were suspicious of the easterners, who had decided to hold the convention in Rockford. The midwesterners and the southerners feared the domination of New York City in UFWA governance, as shown in the debate between the small and large locals over the formula for allocating GEB seats to locals of different sizes.

[79] *Furniture Workers Press,* June 1949, p. 4.

Table 3.4
Percentage Distribution of UFWA Membership Loss Due to Raids,
by Raider and Location, 1948–1950

Raider	Location	%
UIU	Indiana and Illinois	30.2
UAW	Indiana, Michigan, and Illinois	29.9
UIU	New England	16.1
UBC	New York, Pennsylvania, and West Coast	9.9
UIU	South	5.7
IWA	West Coast	2.6
UAW	New England	2.1
UIU	West Coast	1.9
UMW	Ohio	1.7
Total		100.1[a]
N		4,826

Source: *Proceedings of the Sixth Constitutional Convention, United Furniture Workers of America—CIO*, Chicago, June 5–9, 1950, p. 28.
UIU = Upholsterers International Union (AFL); UAW = United Automobile Workers (CIO); UBC = United Brotherhood of Carpenters (AFL); IWA = International Woodworkers Association (CIO); UMW = United Mine Workers (Ind.).
[a] Does not sum to 100% due to rounding.

Regional division in the UFWA is reflected in regional differences in the results of four roll call votes at the 1943, 1946, 1948, and 1950 UFWA conventions, shown in Table 3.5. First, at the third UFWA convention in 1943, several midwestern delegates and others submitted a resolution to move the International UFWA headquarters from New York City to Chicago. Sentiment for such a move had been expressed at previous conventions. The proponents of the resolution argued that the Midwest was largely unorganized and lacked trained leadership and that organizing and servicing of locals in the Midwest, as well as organizing in all regions, would be enhanced by moving the International office to a more central location. The opponents held that, by virtue of wartime conditions, a move at that time would have been too disruptive and that headquarters should be near Washington, DC, to facilitate the UFWA's lobbying efforts on wartime production with government agencies.[80]

The resolution, which was defeated, received its strongest support in the nonmetropolitan Midwest, as shown in column 1 of Table 3.5. All of the nonmetropolitan midwestern delegates voted for the resolution. The greatest sentiment against the resolution was in the largely metropolitan

[80] *Proceedings*, 1943 UFWA Convention, pp. 97–122.

Table 3.5
Roll Call Vote Results on Selected Issues at UFWA Conventions, 1943–1950

Region[a]	(1) % Voting against Moving UFWA Headquarters to Chicago, 1943	(2) % Voting for Perlow for Secretary- Treasurer, 1946	(3) % Voting against Compliance with Taft-Hartley, 1948	(4) % Voting in Support of CIO Policy, 1950
Metropolitan East	76.7 (10,020)[b]	93.3 (8440)	68.4 (13,032)	78.5 (12,493)
Nonmetropolitan East	56.9 (2371)	61.7 (6026)	49.4 (6493)	99.1 (4890)
Metropolitan Midwest	33.0 (2281)	85.5 (2642)	100.0 (2831)	100.0 (2125)
Nonmetropolitan Midwest	0.0 (4211)	18.6 (7719)	26.6 (7196½)[c]	100.0 (4756)
South	72.4 (1020)	1.0 (4527)	56.8 (5047½)[c]	71.2 (3626)
West	100.0 (1656)	100.0 (2358)	56.6 (4865)	43.6 (3928)
All Regions	56.5 (21,559)	55.8 (31,712)	57.0 (39,465)	81.2 (31,818)

Sources: *Proceedings of the Third Constitutional Convention of the United Furniture Workers of America—CIO*, Cleveland, May 17–21, 1943, pp. 120–121; *Proceedings of the Fourth Constitutional Convention of the United Furniture Workers of America—CIO*, Detroit, June 3–7, 1946, pp. 223–226; *Proceedings of the Fifth Constitutional Convention of the United Furniture Workers of America—CIO*, Chicago, June 7–11, 1948, pp. 183–184; *Proceedings of the Sixth Constitutional Convention of the United Furniture Workers of America—CIO*, Chicago, June 5–9, 1950, pp. 159–160.

[a]Metropolitan areas are the 20 largest U.S. cities in census years; nonmetropolitan areas are all other places.
[b]Total number of votes in parentheses.
[c]The "½" indicates a split vote.

West and the metropolitan East. Within the East and Midwest, the nonmetropolitan areas were more likely than the metropolitan areas to support the resolution.

The second issue that reflected regional division in the UFWA was the officer elections at the fourth UFWA convention in 1946. I discuss these elections in greater detail later but will summarize them briefly here. With the Cold War, red-baiting, and the deterioration of UFWA-UIU relations, factionalism between the left-wing and the non-Left intensified within the UFWA. The 1946 elections were an abortive effort led by UFWA President Muster and others to reduce the influence of the Left on the GEB. The contest between Perlow, of the Left, and Frank Douthitt, of the non-Left, for the office of secretary-treasurer exemplifies the factionalism. Perlow was the incumbent and had first been elected to the position at the previous convention, in 1943. Frank "Toots" Douthitt, who had been president of UFWA district 6 in Indiana for five years, was a furniture worker from Bloomington, IN, and had been actively engaged in organizing in Indiana. His nominator lauded him for owning "one of the nicest little homes in Bloomington, which is made and saved out of largely unorganized labor's wages." Commenting further on his character, Douthitt's nominator used a baseball metaphor, stating "I have seen this fellow [Douthitt] play baseball. . . . He plays as hard when the score is nine to nothing in his favor as he does when it is nine to nothing against him." Douthitt's nomination was also justified in terms of bringing "geographical representation" to the GEB (both President Muster and Secretary Treasurer Perlow were from New York City).[81]

Perlow won the election with 55.8 percent of the votes, shown in column 2 of Table 3.5. Perlow carried the East, metropolitan Midwest, and West. Douthitt held strong majorities in the nonmetropolitan Midwest and South. Within the East and Midwest, the metropolitan areas were more likely than the nonmetropolitan areas to have voted for Perlow.

The third issue indicating regional division in the UFWA was the question of UFWA compliance with section 9h and other parts of the Taft-Hartley Act debated at the fifth UFWA convention in 1948. The GEB had been divided on the issue when, in January 1948, it voted 14 to 13 in favor of compliance but also unanimously referred the question to the fifth convention in June. The delegates to the fifth convention were united in their opposition to the Taft-Hartley Act, but they debated the question of compliance for two days. Proponents of compliance argued that the UFWA effort at organizing and fending off raiders would be easier if the UFWA complied with section 9h. Opponents of compliance argued that complying would contradict the progressive principles for which the UFWA stood

---

[81] *Proceedings*, 1946 UFWA Convention, pp. 221–226.

and would constitute submission "to the vicious Taft-Hartley Law and . . . the wishes and desires of the enemies of labor."[82]

The convention voted against compliance by a slim majority of 57 percent, shown in column 3 of Table 3.5. Strong majorities opposed compliance in the metropolitan areas of both the East and Midwest, and weaker majorities opposed compliance in the South and West. A majority favored compliance in the nonmetropolitan areas of both the East and Midwest, the latter being the region that subsequently suffered the greatest membership losses from raids (see Table 3.4).

The fourth issue that reflected regional division in the UFWA was the issue of supporting CIO policy at the sixth UFWA convention in 1950. Shortly after the November 1949 CIO convention, the CIO charged the UFWA with pursuing Communist rather than CIO goals, a topic I will treat later in greater detail. Threatened with expulsion from the CIO, the UFWA experienced subsequent factionalism between the Left and the non-Left over supporting CIO policy and, hence, effectively remaining in the CIO. In December 1949, the UFWA GEB voted 14 to 10 in favor of the left-wing resolution, submitted by Secretary-Treasurer Perlow, condemning CIO policy. The resolution stated that the UFWA had "always cherished . . . the right of our rank and file to decide all matters of policy and who its leaders should be"; that the constitutional changes adopted at the 1949 CIO convention constituted an attempt to remove rank-and-file control of the UFWA; that the CIO should return to its 1946 policies, pursuing wage increases, shorter hours, and elimination of Jim Crow and discrimination; and that the UFWA "will fight to remain in the CIO with honor and autonomy."[83]

Pizer, who had been serving as UFWA president since 1946, submitted a pro-CIO resolution supporting the CIO policies adopted at the November 1949 CIO convention. This resolution stated that the CIO had charged the UFWA with pursuing Communist goals; that the CIO had adopted programs for organizing the South, meeting workers' economic needs, attaining civil rights, and repealing the Taft-Hartley Act; and that "expulsion from the CIO would be a serious threat to our [UFWA's] contracts and working conditions." At the December 1949 GEB meeting, Pizer's resolution was defeated by a vote of 14 to 10. The GEB also voted 15 to 10 to refer both resolutions to the sixth UFWA convention, to be held in June 1950.[84]

The delegates to the sixth convention debated the two resolutions for

---

[82] *Proceedings*, 1948 UFWA Convention, pp. 95–185—quotation from p. 100; *Furniture Workers Press*, February 1948, p. 1.

[83] Quotations from *Furniture Workers Press*, December 1949, p. 5; Kampelman, *Communist Party vs. the CIO*, p. 160; Haywood testimony, pp. 267–269.

[84] *Furniture Workers Press*, December 1949, pp. 1–5.

one and a half days and voted to support CIO policy, with 81.2 percent of the votes favoring Pizer's resolution, shown in column 4 of Table 3.5. Given that pro-CIO sentiment prevailed in most regions, the regional differences in these results were less pronounced than those of the three other votes at previous conventions, discussed earlier. The strongest support for Pizer's resolution was in the nonmetropolitan East and in all areas of the Midwest. In the West, where the large Los Angeles local retained its left-wing leadership, a majority voted for Perlow's resolution.[85]

Pizer's resolution received strong support in the metropolitan East. Two of the large New York City locals, Pizer's local 76 and local 76B, which had ousted its left-wing leaders in March 1950, backed Pizer's resolution. New York City local 140, Boston local 136B, and Baltimore local 75, all of which retained their left-wing leaders, voted for Perlow's resolution.[86]

The South, which strongly supported Pizer's resolution, was nonetheless divided regionally on the issue. This regional division seemed to occur partly along racial lines. Some blacks, who criticized the CIO for neglecting civil rights issues, sided with the Left in the debate over CIO policy. The predominantly white district 9, which covered Arkansas and other western parts of the South and a majority of whose votes were centered in Fort Smith, cast all of its votes in favor of Pizer's resolution.[87]

District 5, which covered the eastern part of the South, voted in favor of Perlow's resolution by a slim majority of 55.3 percent of the votes. The predominantly white locals in Thomasville, Roanoke, VA, and Huntington, WV, accounted for over 80 percent of the district 5 votes cast in favor of Pizer's resolution. The predominantly black locals in Henderson, NC, and Sumter, SC, accounted for over 85 percent of the district 5 votes cast in favor of Perlow's resolution.[88]

Several black UFWA members had become disaffected from the CIO, which, they argued, neglected racial inequality and civil rights issues and, in some cases, promoted Jim Crow discrimination. Prior to the sixth convention, Rudolph Johnson, a black and president of Memphis local 282, which had a high proportion of black members, condemned the CIO for having segregated toilets in the Memphis CIO office and for supporting Jim Crow politicians in the South. However, Johnson, a sympathizer with the Left, subsequently lost the local presidency to Robert Brown, a black, and local 282, which was part of district 9, voted for Pizer's resolution at the 1950 convention. At the 1950 convention, Orlandis Hicks, a black delegate from Henderson, NC, stated that some black CIO union members

---

[85] *Proceedings of the Sixth Constitutional Convention of the United Furniture Workers of America CIO,* Chicago, June 5–9, 1950, p. 160.
[86] Ibid., p. 159; *Furniture Workers Press,* April 1950, p. 10.
[87] *Proceedings,* 1950 UFWA Convention, pp. 159–160.
[88] Ibid.

in Tennessee paid their dues but had nothing to do with the union. "Certainly Local 265," he said, "wants no such policy as that . . . we don't want any dictator to come in and tell us what to do."[89] Mildred McAdory, a black woman delegate and ex-southerner who was now a member of New York City local 140, criticized CIO policy and the convention, arguing:

> It is the sort of atmosphere . . . which my people describe as a lynch atmosphere . . . there are certain . . . locals in the South, with the consent of national policy, that operate Jim-Crow, lily-white locals and they have auxiliaries of the Negro people . . . if you brothers here think that you can build a local union . . . without putting up a fight for Negroes and Negro women especially, then you are wrong . . . you are never going to be able to organize the unorganized . . . until you understand that the Negro people are part . . . of the working class and of the labor movement . . . I want to stay in the CIO . . . , but . . . the CIO today is not . . . the same CIO it was then.[90]

In sum, as the UFWA incorporated an increasingly heterogeneous membership during its organizing drives of the 1940s, a regional division of attitudes emerged in the union. Along with the tremendous external pressures to conform to CIO policy and the jeopardization of UFWA membership by the Taft-Hartley Act and hostile union raids during the Cold War, this regional division would play a part in determining which groups would emerge into leadership positions in the UFWA.

Leadership Change

During the Cold War period of 1946–1950, Communist involvement in the labor movement was the chief issue associated with leadership change in the UFWA. The issue surfaced at the fourth UFWA convention in 1946, when an effort to unseat the Left from the GEB failed, and at the sixth UFWA convention in 1950, when such an effort succeeded. The resolution of the issue in the UFWA accelerated changes in the social composition of the GEB in addition to the shift in GEB political beliefs. With the UFWA organizing drives extending into the nonmetropolitan Midwest, the percentage of Jewish and immigrant GEB members had already begun to decline, while that of GEB members of Northern and Western European descent from the Midwest had increased (see Chapter 1, Table 1.4, and Chapter 2, Table 2.7). Given that several of the left-wing GEB members were Jewish, some of whom were immigrants, and that they tended to be

---

[89] Ibid., p. 160—quotation from pp. 140–141; personal interview with Leroy Clark in Memphis, TN, on May 31, 1985; *Furniture Workers Press*, April 1950, p. 7.
[90] *Proceedings*, 1950 UFWA Convention, pp. 132–133.

centered primarily in the urban areas on the two coasts, these trends in the social composition of the GEB were accelerated greatly by the defeat of the Left in 1950.

The 1946 Convention

The officer elections at the 1946 convention included an effort to reduce the influence of the Left on the UFWA GEB, led by UFWA President Muster; George Bucher from Philadelphia local 37; Frank Douthitt; Morris Miller, a midwestern regional director; and others. The effort failed with Perlow's victory over Douthitt for secretary-treasurer and Nicholas Blattner's victory over Miller for the midwestern vice presidency. The regional results of the vote for midwestern vice president were almost identical to those of the Perlow-Douthitt contest, described earlier. Although Muster was reelected president in an uncontested election, the Left succeeded in retaining a majority on the Officers Advisory Council, the seven highest GEB offices, and several other GEB seats.[91]

Condemning the UFWA for being a Communist-controlled organization, Muster resigned the UFWA presidency on June 29, 1946, twenty-two days after the close of the 1946 convention, and became the head of a furniture manufacturing business. George Bucher left the UFWA, helping UFWA local 37 secede to the UIU, but he remained secretary of the CIO Industrial Council in Philadelphia in order "to fight Commie domination on the home grounds—from within the CIO," as a Philadelphia newspaper put it. Nick Allegretti of local 18B, who had been elected midwestern vice president at the previous UFWA convention in 1943 but had subsequently entered and returned from the army, exited from the UFWA, joining the UIU staff and assisting in its raids on the UFWA in the Midwest. Douthitt was removed from his district 6 office and affiliated his local with the UIU. In an editorial in the September 1946 issue of the UIU newspaper, Miller and others who had worked with UFWA local 415 in Grand Rapids explained their departure from the UFWA by charging it with Communist domination and vicious red-baiting of the UFWA officers.[92]

After Muster's resignation, Pizer, who had been serving as eastern vice president since 1943, was elected acting president by a unanimous vote of the GEB on July 20 and was elected president by a membership referendum in December 1946. Pizer was an acceptable candidate to both the Left and the non-Left in the UFWA. Perhaps in anticipation of Muster's

[91] *Proceedings*, 1946 UFWA Convention, pp. 41, 212–232; *Furniture Workers Press*, October 1946, p. 7.
[92] *UIU Journal*, July 1946, p. 8—quotation from September 1946, pp. 2, 4; *Furniture Workers Press*, July 1946, pp. 1, 3; August 1946, pp. 2, 7; October 1946, p. 7; December 1946, p. 4; October 1949, p. 6; *Proceedings*, 1943 UFWA Convention, pp. 217–218; *Proceedings*, 1946 UFWA Convention, p. 43; personal interview with Sam Sloan, December 23, 1985.

exit (the *Proceedings* of the 1946 convention vaguely suggested that, during the convention, Muster was aware of the possibility that he would not continue as president), the 1946 convention unanimously passed with a standing vote an unusual resolution that acknowledged that Pizer's "words of wisdom have contributed a great deal of unity" to the UFWA and that lauded Pizer for "his foresight and stability and great leadership." The resolution was passed just before Pizer was reelected eastern vice president. Further evidence of Pizer's acceptability to both factions was that speeches seconding his nomination to the eastern vice presidency were made by Perlow and Sirota from the Left and Allegretti and Miller from the non-Left, among others.[93]

At the fifth UFWA convention in 1948, the Left retained a majority on the Officers Advisory Council, several other GEB members were left-leaning in their attitudes, and Pizer was reelected president. The big showdown between the Left and the non-Left would occur at the sixth UFWA convention in 1950.[94]

The 1950 Convention

In November 1949, when the UFWA was charged with Communist domination at the CIO convention and placed on trial for possible expulsion from the CIO, the issue of supporting CIO policy and, hence, of remaining in the CIO generated factionalism in the UFWA. President Pizer, who had already begun to distance himself from the Communist party in 1939 over the Nazi-Soviet non-aggression pact,[95] returned from the November 1949 CIO convention as an ardent CIO supporter, stating in his delegate report to the UFWA that

> my position is to remain in the CIO and support the policies and program of the CIO. We cannot allow our Union to be . . . broken up. . . . It will mean another union in the furniture industry, it will mean a civil war among our members. . . . Who can gain from such a fight? . . . It takes very few words to outline my program. . . . End a policy of continued defiance of CIO which can lead to nothing but expulsion from CIO and the destruction of our international union.[96]

At the CIO convention, Pizer met with Jacob Potofsky, president of the Amalgamated Clothing Workers, whom the CIO had assigned as chair

---

[93] *Proceedings*, 1946 UFWA Convention, p. 176—quotation from p. 216; *Furniture Workers Press*, July 1946, pp. 1–2; personal interviews with Abraham Zide and Solly Silverman; telephone interview with William Gilbert, October 31, 1986; personal interview with Joseph Magliacano in New York City on November 16, 1984.
[94] *Proceedings*, 1948 UFWA Convention, pp. 250–270.
[95] Personal interview with Solly Silverman.
[96] *Furniture Workers Press*, November 1949, p. 1.

of the committee that would hear the charges against the UFWA, and told him that the UFWA would support CIO policy at the forthcoming, sixth, UFWA convention in June 1950. At the sixth convention, Pizer, drawing on his experience with the FWIU and the TUUL, argued that a left-wing federation of labor unions would fail and called on the left-wingers to join the CIO and AFL in the fight against "reaction."[97]

The other UFWA delegates to the CIO convention, all of whom were left-wing GEB members including Secretary-Treasurer Perlow and Director of Organization Ernest Marsh, argued strongly for union autonomy within the CIO in their delegate report to the UFWA:

> In their frenzy to stamp out every vestige of minority viewpoint in the CIO, the national officers got this convention to adopt constitutional amendments which are even more outrageously undemocratic than anything in the Taft-Hartley law.... The United Furniture Workers will never surrender its militant fight to improve the economic conditions of the working people in the furniture industry [and] its democratic traditions. ... We shall use every available means to maintain our militant, democratic union within the ranks of the CIO. But if the national CIO leadership decides to expel us, we shall not turn over and die.[98]

During the next six months, before the sixth UFWA convention, the Left and non-Left factions in the UFWA campaigned among the UFWA members of all regions, each side arguing its position on CIO policy and often denouncing the other side. The pro-CIO forces organized the UFWA Rank and File Committee for CIO, with Thomas Binnall of Gardner local 154 chair, Jack Hochstadt of New York local 76 secretary, and Sam Sloan of Chicago local 18B treasurer, which carried the pro-CIO campaign to the UFWA members. The left-wing faction organized in a similar fashion. Several issues of *The Furniture Workers Press* carried impassioned editorials from both sides. By the time of the 1950 convention, the left-wing and non-left officers were sufficiently divided that they deviated from custom by submitting separate officers' reports to the convention.[99]

The pro-CIO forces defeated the Left at the sixth convention. With contested elections for seven of the twenty-eight GEB seats, the officer elections at the sixth convention were more factionalized than those at any previous or succeeding UFWA convention. Several left-wing GEB incumbents from the previous term did not seek reelection in 1950, and two left-wing candidates ran unopposed but were defeated.

[97] Kampelman, *Communist Party vs. the CIO*, p. 161; personal interview with Sam Sloan, December 23, 1985; *Proceedings,* 1950 UFWA Convention, p. 115.
[98] *Furniture Workers Press,* November 1949, pp. 1, 3.
[99] Ibid., June 1950, p. 3; *Proceedings,* 1950 UFWA Convention, pp. 13–42.

The major contests, and the only ones with roll call votes, were for the offices of president and secretary-treasurer. Pizer defeated Marsh for the presidency with 76.9 percent of the votes. Almost 70 percent of the votes cast for Marsh were from his home local, Los Angeles local 576, and New York City local 140, both of which retained their left-wing leadership, and from the predominantly black locals 265, in Henderson, NC, and 273, in Sumter, SC.

Fred Fulford, from South Bend, IN, defeated Perlow for secretary-treasurer with 73.3 percent of the votes. The regional results of the Fulford-Perlow contest were similar to those of the Pizer-Marsh election. The son of a Grand Rapids furniture worker who had been a labor movement activist, Fulford was born in 1912 and began working in a furniture factory at the age of sixteen. By 1932, he had become employed at the South Bend Toy Manufacturing Co., where he led a successful organizing effort that established an AFL federal charter for the local in 1935. Dissatisfied with the AFL, Fulford and others brought the local into the CIO, affiliating with the UFWA as local 155 in 1937. He participated in the subsequent amalgamation of the local, became an International UFWA organizer in the early 1940s working the Midwest, was associated with the Left in the UFWA, and served on the UFWA GEB in almost every term, beginning with the founding UFWA convention in 1939.[100]

On June 15, 1950, six days after the close of the sixth UFWA convention, the CIO executive board cleared the UFWA of all charges.[101]

Notwithstanding the defeat of the Left and the passage of the resolution in support of CIO policy, the sixth convention of the UFWA maintained a politically liberal stance. During the Cold-War period of witch-hunts and loyalty oaths, several UFWA positions on civil rights, civil liberties, political parties, and international relations were liberal. The convention resolved to call on organized labor to help repeal the Taft-Hartley Act, branding it "a naked and vicious weapon in the hands of the corporations and reactionary interests in their present attempt to weaken and destroy the labor movement." The convention also passed a resolution on human freedoms. This resolution called for the abolition of Jim Crow and discrimination against minority groups; condemned the "subversion of the freedoms guaranteed in the Bill of Rights," various types of government "thought control," the Un-American Activities Committee, and the abuse of loyalty oaths; and called for a broadening of the fight to

---

[100] *Proceedings,* 1950 UFWA Convention, pp. 230, 239; *Proceedings,* 1958 UFWA Convention, pp. 290–291; *Furniture Workers Press,* March 1974, pp. 1, 4, 5; personal interviews with Sam Sloan in Cicero, IL, on December 23, 1985, and Abraham Zide in New York City on November 16, 1984.

[101] *Proceedings,* 1950 UFWA Convention, pp. 225–239; *Furniture Workers Press,* June 1950, p. 8.

remove restrictions on the right to vote. Mildred McAdory of New York City local 140 introduced a resolution, passed by the convention, that the UFWA telegraph Mississippi Governor Fielding Wright, CIO President Philip Murray, and President Harry Truman, urging them to commute the death sentence of Willie McGee, a black man who had been convicted of rape by a white jury with no witness and insufficient evidence. In his presidential report to the convention, Pizer approved in principle of a third, pro-labor, political party, but he stated that, instead, the UFWA should work with the CIO political action committee because a third party was politically infeasible at the time. On the international situation, Pizer "called for the major powers to get together and settle their differences, to outlaw all war-making atomic weapons, to adopt a program for universal disarmament, and write a peace treaty which will give peace and security against war to the peoples of the world."[102]

After the convention, the only major expression of dissatisfaction with the sixth UFWA convention was the secession of Los Angeles local 576, which had retained its left-wing leadership. The UFWA established Los Angeles local 1010 in August 1950, which competed with local 576 for the membership. By November 1951, some seventeen hundred of the two thousand local 576 members had joined local 1010, according to the *Furniture Workers Press*. In addition, the UFWA sued independent local 576, seeking an injunction to prevent it from spending and concealing funds. After appeals, California courts ruled that the seceding local could not take the funds, which belonged to the UFWA, and this was upheld by the U.S. Supreme Court in June 1956.[103]

The defeat of the Left, given the membership growth that had occurred, especially in the nonmetropolitan areas of the East and Midwest, and the regional division of attitudes, altered the geographical and ethnic composition of the GEB. Between the 1948 and 1950 conventions, the number of Jewish GEB members from the metropolitan East declined from seven to three while the number of GEB members from the nonmetropolitan areas of the Midwest and East, almost all of whom were of Northern and Western European descent, increased from five to eight. At the 1950 convention, the office of secretary-treasurer, which had been filled by Jewish members from New York City in four of the five previous terms and once by Ernest Marsh from Los Angeles, was now filled by Fred Fulford of South Bend, IN. The proportions of each of the other geographical-ethnic groups on the GEB, including Italians and others from the metropolitan East; Northern, Western, and Eastern Europeans from the

---

[102] *Proceedings,* 1950 UFWA Convention, pp. 20–21, 215, 252–254.
[103] *Furniture Workers Press,* September 1950, p. 8; October 1950, p. 8; November 1950, p. 8; November 1951, p. 1; April 1953, p. 5; June 1956, p. 3.

metropolitan Midwest and West; and southerners, remained relatively constant between the 1948 and 1950 conventions. Over half of the GEB members who were elected at the founding UFWA convention in 1939 were Jewish. By 1950, the percentage of Jewish GEB members had declined to 11.5 percent, while the percentage of those of Northern and Western European descent on the GEB had increased from 42.1 percent in 1939 to 57.7 percent in 1950 and that of Italians from 5.3 percent to 15.4 percent (see Chapter 1, Table 1.4).[104] The defeat of the Left and the resolution of the issue over supporting CIO policy in 1950, then, hastened the succession of ethnic groups on the GEB that had already been accompanying the extension of UFWA organizing drives and membership growth in the small towns of the East and Midwest during the 1940s.

Leadership Succession During the Formative Period

The succession of ethnic groups on the GEB during the UFWA's formative period resulted from a set of tensions associated with the building of a national, industrial union in the furniture industry. In light of the prevailing craft unionism and the absence of unionization among many non-skilled furniture workers, the unprecedented effort to build an industrial union not only broke with traditional unionism, but also brought together workers from diverse backgrounds who were unknown to one another. Immigrant Jewish and Italian workers of the upholstered furniture industry of the urban East, black spring workers in the urban East, wood furniture workers of Northern and Western European descent from the small towns of the East, Midwest, and South, Southern blacks and West Coast Hispanics, ex-southerners, and immigrant Italians joined together to establish industrial unionism in the furniture industry. The tensions centered around the membership representativeness of the governing body of the union, and the founders devised a governmental structure that would simultaneously represent the diverse interests and facilitate the unionization of the industry.

Three interrelated forces led to ethnic succession on the GEB. First, UFWA membership became increasingly heterogeneous as the union extended its organizing drives out of New York City into the small towns of the East, Midwest, and South. Second, the political attitudes of the delegates to UFWA conventions diversified, as left-wing and liberal easterners mixed with a growing number of more conservative midwesterners and southerners. Third, anti-union and anti-Communist national political conditions and reactions to the tremendous growth of the labor movement

---

[104]*Proceedings,* 1948 UFWA Convention, pp. 250–270; *Proceedings,* 1950 UFWA Convention, pp. 225–251.

through World War II and the deterioration of U.S.-USSR relations after the war, severely jeopardized the growth of the labor movement including the UFWA, prompting the UFWA to shift its political stance and remove its left-wing leaders, who were mainly from the urban East. The increased social and political heterogeneity of the UFWA, which resulted from growth, combined with the subsequent jeopardization of UFWA growth, then, generated ethnic succession on the GEB.

The UFWA's formative period ended in 1950. Its membership had peaked, its place in the labor movement was secured, and its political orientation was defined. Leadership stabilized during the next twenty years. Five of the six executive committee (formerly the Officers Advisory Council) members who were elected to the GEB in 1950 served almost continuously until 1970, when Pizer retired from the presidency.

4
Maintaining the Union: The UFWA's Period of Stability, 1950–1970

The UFWA leadership on the general executive board stabilized between 1950 and 1970. With the ousting of the Left in 1950, the UFWA's formative period, characterized by factionalism and contested elections for the highest union offices, ended. Contested elections and factionalism all but disappeared, and GEB members were often reelected unanimously. The UFWA had entered a period of stability.

Five of the six UFWA officers who were elected in 1950 served almost continuously between 1950 and 1970. Morris Pizer and Fred Fulford served as president and secretary-treasurer, respectively; Fred Stefan served as vice president of the West; and Sam Sloan and Michael DeCicco were vice presidents of the Midwest and East, respectively, for almost the entire period of stability. The biographical backgrounds of Pizer, Fulford, Stefan, and Sloan, all of whom had helped to build the UFWA during the 1930s and early 1940s, are described in the previous chapter. DeCicco, born in Italy in 1909, arrived in the United States in 1920, joined Carpenters local 1057 in New York City in 1926, and worked as a shaper in several parlor frame shops. In 1933, he joined the Furniture Workers Industrial Union and, two years later, affiliated with Upholsterers local 76B when the FWIU merged into the Upholsterers (see Chapter 3). In 1938, after local

76B entered the UFWA-CIO, DeCicco was elected local president, then full-time business agent, and, in 1944, business manager, the highest local union office. He was first elected to the UFWA GEB in 1943 and became vice president of the East in 1948.[1]

Turnover occurred in the office of vice president of the South. Walter Carson was first elected to this office in 1946, serving until 1954, when he became ill. A worker at the Fort Smith Table Co. in Arkansas, Carson joined UFWA local 270 in 1938 and later served as local union business agent. He became an International UFWA representative in 1944 and continued to serve the Arkansas-Oklahoma area as a representative after 1954.[2] He was succeeded in the office by Floyd Buckner, Louis Campbell, and Carl Scarbrough.

Leadership turnover on the GEB declined between 1950 and 1970. During the 1939–1950 formative period, the median number of terms served by GEB members during this five-term period was one; during the 1950–1970 period of stability, which consisted of ten terms, the median number of terms served was three (see also Chapters 1 and 2).

Membership of the UFWA also stabilized during this period, averaging about thirty-four thousand and fluctuating with the business cycle (see Chapter 1). Few new membership groups entered the union who could challenge the incumbent officers.

If any period of UFWA history resembled Robert Michels's iron law of oligarchy (see Chapters 1 and 2), it was the 1950–1970 period of stability. Yet, UFWA conventions amended the UFWA constitution in order to *increase* rank-and-file access to elective GEB positions, rather than attempting to perpetuate an oligarchical regime. In 1954, the UFWA reduced the maximum number of paid, professional, International UFWA organizers who could serve on the GEB. In 1958, the UFWA constitution was amended further to restrict GEB positions to only workers who had worked for a minimum of two years in a trade covered by the UFWA jurisdiction or in a shop under a UFWA contract. Although the UFWA prohibited members "of the Communist Party, any Fascist organization, or any other totalitarian movement" from serving on the GEB in 1954, this amendment would have had only minimal impact on rank-and-file access to the GEB because most of the Communist party members in the UFWA had left the party by that time.[3]

---

[1] *Furniture Workers Press,* March 1967, p. 1.
[2] Ibid., July–August 1962, pp. 1, 5.
[3] *Proceedings of the Eighth Constitutional Convention of the United Furniture Workers of America—CIO,* Cleveland, June 14–18, 1954, pp. 147–160, 207–222, 234–235; *Proceedings of the Tenth Constitutional Convention of the United Furniture Workers of America—AFL-CIO,* New York, May 12–16, 1958, pp. 208–212, 262–271, 280; personal interview with Solly Silverman in West Palm Beach, FL, September 22, 1986.

Despite appearances, the UFWA period of stability was not an instance of the iron law of oligarchy. Rather, beneath the thin veneer of leadership and membership stability, the UFWA was engaged continuously in a dynamic struggle to remove itself from a vicious cycle of local union turnover that resulted mainly from increased employer resistance to unionization in furniture manufacturing. Several historical forces, not the least of which were the increasing concentration of furniture manufacturing capital and the geographical decentralization of the industry into nonunion regions, obstructed UFWA organizing drives and led to plant shutdowns and local union closures. As shown in Chapter 2, the UFWA locals chartered during the 1950s and 1960s in the South and Midwest tended to be small, single-shop locals in nonmetropolitan areas that were vulnerable to closure due to plant shutdowns. It was the cohort of amalgamated locals that were chartered before 1950 in the urban areas and small, but factory-dense, furniture towns that tended to outlive the locals chartered after 1950.

In an effort to stop the vicious cycle, the UFWA conducted vigorous organizing drives, an effort facilitated by declining rivalry with other international unions, and centralized and consolidated its structure and activities. However, plant shutdowns and local union closures offset organizing gains, and UFWA membership stabilized.

Although leadership stabilization coincided with organizational centralization, these processes, in contrast with the iron law of oligarchy, were not causally related. Instead, leadership stabilization and organizational centralization had a common cause: membership stabilization. Membership stabilization, including the vicious cycle of local union turnover, led the UFWA to centralize its operations. It also led to the virtual absence of new, emerging, membership groups who could challenge the incumbents, thereby contributing to leadership stabilization.

Moreover, the membership did not slip into apathy, a trend posited as inevitable by Michels's iron law. The UFWA effort to stop the vicious cycle of local union turnover created issues, especially financing organizing drives, that led to lively debates on the floor at several UFWA conventions between 1950 and 1970. United in their beliefs about the broad UFWA mission, the convention delegates squabbled over the affordability of various policy initiatives offered during this era. Consequently, alliances among local unions were transient, shifting along with changes in the relative wealth of local unions, and stable voting blocs or factions failed to emerge. No membership groups self-consciously seeking representation on the GEB challenged the incumbents.

Notwithstanding the appearance of oligarchical tendencies, the UFWA period of stability was characterized by a united, dynamic effort at confronting forces hostile to the union. Leadership stabilized not because a conspiratorial regime controlled an apathetic membership with a centralized structure, as Michels would have it, but because forces external to the union, especially employer resistance, stabilized the membership and prevented new, self-conscious membership groups from emerging in the union and challenging the incumbents.

Membership Stabilization

Membership of the UFWA stabilized between 1950 and 1970, as employers resisted the unionization of furniture manufacturing and UFWA local unions turned over. Employer resistance took several forms. The 1947 Taft-Hartley Act, a Cold-War product of the lobbying efforts of the National Association of Manufacturers, weakened union security arrangements, especially in the southern states with right-to-work laws. Non-union employers resisted UFWA organizing drives by improving employment conditions and intimidating workers in "captive audience" meetings. And, in an effort to avoid unions, employ cheap labor, and approach new, high-growth, consumer markets, employers relocated away from the unionized, high-wage midwestern, northeastern and metropolitan areas into the non-union, low-wage, right-to-work South, other nonmetropolitan areas, and the West. The geographical decentralization of the industry was facilitated further by the increasing concentration of furniture manufacturing capital, as the multi-unit corporation replaced the single-unit, family-owned enterprise. Consequently, the UFWA succeeded in organizing small shops and chartering small locals, those which were unstable and most likely to close due to plant shutdowns, as discussed in Chapter 2.

UFWA membership stabilized as the UFWA endeavored to replenish its membership losses. In addition to conducting vigorous organizing drives throughout the period of stability, the UFWA centralized and consolidated its structure and activities in order to conserve resources and maximize the effectiveness of its organizing effort.

Along with membership stabilization came stability in the geographical distribution of UFWA membership. Compared with the changing geographical redistribution of UFWA membership during the eleven-year formative period of the UFWA (1939–1950), that which occurred during the twenty-year period of stability (1950–1970) was relatively small, as shown in Table 4.1. Between 1939 and 1970, the percentage of eastern members declined while the percentage of southern members increased (Table 4.1, columns 1–3), reflecting the redistribution of the furniture manufacturing industry and the concentration of UFWA organizing drives in the South. However, the absolute values of the changes in each of the regional membership shares during the formative period tended to exceed those of the period of stability (Table 4.1, columns 4 and 5). In other

Table 4.1
Percentage Distribution of UFWA Membership at the 1939, 1950, and 1970 UFWA Conventions and Percentage Differences, by Location

	(1)	(2)	(3)	(4)	(5)
	% Distribution			% Difference	
Location	1939	1950	1970	1939–1950	1950–1970
East	64.9	54.5	47.7	−10.4	−6.8
Metropolitan	58.9	41.1	35.9	−17.8	−5.2
Nonmetropolitan	6.0	13.4	11.8	7.4	−1.6
Midwest	25.8	21.0	22.9	−4.8	1.9
Metropolitan	2.1	6.6	6.3	4.5	−0.3
Nonmetropolitan	23.7	14.4	16.6	−9.3	2.2
South	6.3	12.5	21.1	6.2	8.6
West	3.1	12.0	8.2	8.9	−3.8
Total	100.1[a]	100.0	99.9[a]		
N	12,683	32,766	31,594		

Sources: *Proceedings of the First Constitutional Convention of the United Furniture Workers of America—CIO*, Rockford, Illinois, February 13–17, 1939, pp. 74–75; *Proceedings of the Sixth Constitutional Convention of the United Furniture Workers of America—CIO*, Chicago, June 5–9, 1950, pp. 210–212; *Proceedings of the Sixteenth Constitutional Convention of the United Furniture Workers of America—AFL-CIO*, New York, NY, May 18–22, 1970, pp. 131–135.
Metropolitan areas are the 20 largest U.S. cities in census years; nonmetropolitan areas are all other places.
[a] Does not sum to 100% due to rounding.

words, the geographical shifts in UFWA membership occurred more rapidly during the formative period than during the period of stability.

Organizing and Declining Inter-Union Rivalry

Membership stabilization did not result from the absence of organizing activity. The UFWA conducted eleven hundred representation elections (elections in which the workers voted to unionize or not) between 1950 and 1970 and won almost two-thirds of them, as shown in Table 4.2.

However, four patterns in Table 4.2 suggest that the UFWA encountered increased obstacles to organizing, especially in the larger furniture factories. First, the number of representation elections conducted in each region declined between the 1950s and 1960s, and the declines in the number of elections conducted in large shops (those with one hundred or more workers) generally exceeded those in small shops. Second, the number of elections conducted in small shops exceeded the number in

Table 4.2
Percentage of UFWA Representation Elections Won by the UFWA,
by Region and Establishment Size, 1950–1970

Region and Establishment Size[a]	1950–1960[b]	1960–1970[b]
East	70.5	71.7
	(261)[c]	(233)
Less than 100 workers	75.7	77.9
	(206)	(195)
100 or more workers	50.9	39.5
	(55)	(38)
Midwest	54.0	50.0
	(124)	(112)
Less than 100 workers	61.4	62.1
	(70)	(66)
100 or more workers	44.4	32.6
	(54)	(46)
South	61.5	58.1
	(135)	(124)
Less than 100 workers	69.2	60.5
	(65)	(76)
100 or more workers	54.3	54.2
	(70)	(48)
West	63.6	71.1
	(66)	(45)
Less than 100 workers	65.4	69.8
	(52)	(43)
100 or more workers	57.1	—[d]
	(14)	
All regions	64.2	63.6
	(586)	(514)

Source: *Proceedings* of 1950–1970 UFWA conventions.
[a] Number of workers eligible to vote.
[b] Time periods begin and end in May or June of the stated year.
[c] Number of elections in parentheses.
[d] Two elections won by the UFWA.

large shops. Third, the percentage of elections won by the UFWA among the small shops exceeded that in large shops in all regions. Fourth, the UFWA's victory rate in small-shop elections remained fairly constant between the 1950s and 1960s; but, the UFWA's victory rate in large-shop elections, which all but disappeared in the West, declined in the East and Midwest and remained stable in the South.

Table 4.3
Percentage of UFWA Representation Elections
with at Least One Other Union on the Ballot, 1950–1970

Period[a]	%	N[b]
1950–1952	20.5	151
1952–1954	30.3	119
1954–1956	21.6	125
1956–1958	13.1	153
1958–1960	15.8	38
1960–1962	14.4	104
1962–1964	13.3	83
1964–1966	5.9	101
1966–1968	5.1	99
1968–1970	8.7	127

Source: *Proceedings* of 1950–1970 UFWA conventions.
[a] Time periods are between UFWA conventions and begin and end in May or June of the stated year.
[b] Total number of representation elections.

The declining capacity of the UFWA to win representation in large shops was unrelated to rivalry with other international unions, rivalry that had hampered the UFWA organizing efforts in the formative period before 1950 (see Chapter 3). Inter-union rivalry in representation elections, although more common in large shops than small shops,[4] declined between 1950 and 1970. The percentage of UFWA representation elections in which the UFWA was rivaled on the ballot by another union declined during this period, as shown in Table 4.3.

The decline of inter-union rivalry was associated with the improvement in the relationship between the AFL and CIO during the early 1950s and the merger of the two federations in December 1955. The AFL and CIO signed a No-Raiding Pact in December 1953, and the UFWA became a signatory when the 1954 UFWA convention endorsed the pact in June. The Upholsterers signed the pact in October 1954. The percentage of rivaled UFWA representation elections declined precipitously after the 1954 UFWA convention and again after the 1956 UFWA convention, by which time the two labor federations had merged (see Table 4.3). The merger reduced inter-union rivalry, especially among the unions representing furniture workers, shown in Table 4.4. During the 1950s, the UFWA was rivaled by the Carpenters and Upholsterers in half of the 120 multi-union representation elections in which the UFWA participated. During the

[4] Daniel Cornfield, "Declining Union Membership in the Post–World War II Era: The United Furniture Workers of America, 1939–1982," *American Journal of Sociology* 91 (March 1986): 1139.

Table 4.4
Percentage Distribution of Rivaled UFWA Representation Elections, by Rival and Period, 1950–1970

Rival	1950–1960[a]	1960–1970[a]
Carpenters	25.8	16.7
Upholsterers	24.2	10.4
Other AFL or formerly AFL union	19.2	41.7
Other	30.8	31.3
Total	100.0	100.1[b]
N	120	48

Source: *Proceedings* of 1950–1970 UFWA conventions.
[a] Time periods begin and end in May or June of the stated year.
[b] Does not sum to 100% due to rounding.

1960s, these unions competed with the UFWA in about one-fourth of the UFWA's multi-union elections, while non-furniture unions, especially former AFL affiliates, competed with the UFWA in the majority of the multi-union elections.[5]

Improved relations between the UFWA and the Upholsterers International Union also contributed to the decline in inter-union rivalry after 1956. In May–June, 1956, each of the UFWA and UIU conventions approved a joint organizing venture between the two unions. On October 1, the UFWA and UIU GEBs voted unanimously to approve the joint venture, the Confederated Upholsterers and Furniture Workers of America (CUF), and, on October 2, the agreement was signed, ending "a nineteen-year period of strife and separation" between these unions. Among the UIU representatives involved in the preparation of the CUF agreement were UIU President Sal Hoffmann, who headed the UIU in 1937 when portions of it split off to the CIO to form the UFWA, and UIU Vice President George Bucher, a CIO delegate to the furniture unity conference in 1937 and former UFWA member who resigned after having participated in the abortive effort led by Morris Muster to weaken the Left at the 1946 UFWA convention (see Chapter 3).[6]

Governed by a twelve-member joint board with equal representation from both unions, CUF's purpose was to promote "maximum cooperation between" the two unions, "eliminate organizational conflict and prevent jurisdictional controversies" and "establish a firm foundation for future organic unity." Specifically, its purpose was to conduct cooperative organizing drives. In a given organizing drive, the union with the most

[5] *Furniture Workers Press,* January 1954, p. 8; June 1954, p. 8; October 1954, p. 8.
[6] Ibid., June 1956, p. 5; October 1956, pp. 1–2.

members, plants, or both already under contract in the industry of which the target plant was a part received "predominant status" for the purposes of collective bargaining. When the target plant was a "runaway shop," the shop would "be allocated to the Union with which the offending employer was in contractual relationship, so as to restore the organizational status quo." The CUF Articles of Confederation also required arbitration for disputes between the unions over "predominant status."[7]

By October 26, 1957, when CUF was dissolved, the UFWA had participated in fifteen CUF organizing drives, receiving predominant status in over half of them, especially in the South. However, the two unions were unable to cooperate, and CUF was dissolved. The UFWA was raided briefly by the UIU after the CUF dissolution, but by the early 1960s hostilities had ceased. At a December 1960 meeting called by AFL-CIO President George Meany, the UFWA and the UIU agreed to cease raiding and to settle disputes amicably. At its December 1961 convention, the AFL-CIO amended its internal disputes procedure, establishing arbitration procedures and penalties for noncompliance. Consequently, the UFWA's relations with other unions in the furniture industry were "better now than at any time in the recent past," claimed Pizer in January 1962. The International UFWA officers could report to the 1962 UFWA convention in May that they were "currently considering undertaking joint organizing campaigns with the" UIU. In March 1964, the *Furniture Workers Press* announced that the UFWA and the UIU had reestablished a reciprocal agreement for inter-union transfers that had been discontinued in 1958, allowing members of either union to transfer to the other without paying initiation fees. The percentage of rivaled UFWA representation elections dropped again after the 1964 UFWA convention (see Table 4.3).[8]

Inter-union rivalry, then, had declined by the early 1960s. Other factors hindered UFWA organizing drives at large shops.

Employer Resistance in Union Organizing Drives

Increased employer resistance to UFWA organizing drives contributed to the declines in UFWA organizing activity and in the UFWA victory

---

[7] *Articles of Confederation, Confederated Upholsterers and Furniture Workers of America*, pp. 3–4, 19–23.

[8] *Proceedings,* 1958 UFWA Convention, pp. 38–39, 43–46; *Furniture Workers Press,* June 1956, p. 5; July-August 1956, p. 1; September 1956, pp. 1–8; October 1956, pp. 1–2; December 1956, p. 3; January 1957, pp. 1–2; February 1957, p. 3; March 1957, p. 1; May 1957, pp. 1, 3; June 1957, p. 1; July-August 1957, p. 1; October 1957, p. 1; November 1957, p. 1; January 1958, p. 3; April 1958, p. 8; May 1959, p. 1; June 1959, p. 3; July-August 1959, p. 8; November 1959, p. 1; May 1960, p. 12; June 1960, p. 8; April 1961, p. 1; May 1961, pp. 1, 3; first quotation from January 1962, pp. 1–2; January 1963, p. 3; March 1964, p. 4; second quotation from *Proceedings of the Twelfth Constitutional Convention of the United Furniture Workers of America—AFL-CIO,* Louisville, May 14–18, 1962, pp. 38–39.

rate at large-shop representation elections between 1950 and 1970. Employer resistance had already been expressed in the Taft-Hartley Act, passed as conservative, employer opposition to the advancing labor movement (see Chapters 2 and 3), which drained UFWA organizing resources during the 1950s and 1960s.[9] Section 14b of the act allowed states to enact right-to-work laws that outlawed union-shop contracts, whereby employees were required to join the existing union in the shop after a probationary employment period. Consequently, union organizing efforts in the right-to-work states, which were predominantly in the South, were often directed at the non-union workers in shops that already had union contracts, so-called "free riders," rather than at the non-union shops. Pizer explained the problem to the 1960 UFWA convention thusly:

> These free riders are leeches who not only drink the blood of the Union, but who leech upon their own. They, in the last analysis also pay for this. But this kind of people does exist. They are a menace and weaken our organizational activities. And that is why Congress included 14-B in the Taft-Hartley Law. They did it to enable state legislatures, wherever controlled by reactionaries, to put such laws into effect, to give the leeches a weapon to weaken the organization and themselves as workingmen.[10]

Although data on why workers decided to unionize or not are unavailable, existing data suggest that employers attempted to obstruct UFWA organizing drives. Employer resistance was expressed in at least three ways. First, employers located in highly unionized areas relocated or opened branch operations in non-union areas, a topic I address in a later section.

The second form of employer resistance was a union preemption strategy whereby non-union employers raised wages and improved fringe benefits to discourage unionization. The UFWA officers noted in 1955 that some large, southern, non-union furniture manufacturers raised worker wages to inhibit unionization. By 1968, this practice had become commonplace in the furniture industry, according to the UFWA officers. Similarly, the UFWA officers observed in 1960 that large, corporate furniture manufacturers often provided workers with their own welfare plans rather than the UFWA life and health insurance plan that had been established in 1944 (see Chapter 3). Indeed, this union preemption strategy also had become widespread among the large, non-union corporations in many industries after 1950 (see Chapters 1 and 2).[11]

[9] *Proceedings of the Eleventh Constitutional Convention of the United Furniture Workers of America—AFL-CIO,* Chicago, May 2–6, 1960, p. 185.
[10] Ibid., p. 140.
[11] Ibid., p. 48; Cornfield, "Declining Union Membership"; *Proceedings of the Fifteenth Constitutional Convention of the United Furniture Workers of America—AFL-CIO,* Memphis, May 27–31, 1968, p. 49; *Furniture Workers Press,* June 1955, p. 1.

In furniture manufacturing, the differential in wages between union and non-union production workers declined by the late 1960s, as shown in Table 4.5. In most regions, the ratio of non-union to union worker hourly wages, expressed as a percentage, increased between 1959 and 1968. On the average, non-union furniture worker wages were 77.6 percent of the magnitude of unionized furniture worker wages in 1959 and 85.9 percent in 1968.

The pattern of fringe benefit coverage among furniture workers was similar to the wage pattern. The UFWA established a national, multi-employer, noncontributory retirement pension plan in 1953. In 1954, some fourteen thousand UFWA members, over 40 percent of UFWA membership, had achieved pension coverage in their contracts. By 1968, over three-fourths of UFWA members had achieved such coverage. In addition, the percentage of UFWA members working under contracts that provided group insurance coverage increased from almost 60 percent in 1954 to approximately 80 percent in 1968.[12] However, fringe benefit coverage also spread to non-union furniture workers. The percentage of all furniture workers with selected fringe benefits, shown in Table 4.6, increased for most fringe benefits in most regions between 1954 and 1968. Furthermore, these percentages generally exceeded the percentage of unionized furniture workers in most regions, at least by 1968 if not earlier, as shown in Table 4.7. For example, the percentage of New England furniture workers with paid vacations increased from 88 percent to 100 percent between 1954 and 1968 (Table 4.6), but the percentage of New England furniture workers who were unionized was 48.5% in 1959 and 51.8 percent in 1968 (Table 4.7). This is not to suggest that the quality of non-union fringe benefits equaled that achieved in union contracts. However, the data suggest that fringe benefit coverage increased greatly among non-union furniture workers during the 1950s and 1960s, as it did for UFWA members.

In light of the absence of data on why furniture workers chose to unionize or not, it is difficult to know whether the union preemption strategy of the employers inhibited workers from unionizing. Nonetheless, the declining differential in the wages and fringe benefit coverage between non-union and unionized furniture workers suggests that at least one common reason for why workers unionize, to gain wage and benefit improvement,[13] was eroding in the furniture industry. Assuming that the large employers were most likely to practice the union preemption strategy, as implied earlier by the observations of the UFWA officers, these wage and fringe benefit trends may have contributed to the decline in both

---

[12] *Furniture Workers Press,* May 1952, p. 6; March 1953, p. 1; June 1953, p. 1; *Proceedings,* 1954 UFWA Convention, pp. 24–25; *Proceedings,* 1968 UFWA Convention, pp. 57–58.

[13] Thomas Kochan, "How American Workers View Labor Unions," *Monthly Labor Review* 102 (April 1979): 23–31.

Table 4.5
Ratio of Non-Union to Union Hourly Wages, Expressed as a Percentage, by Region for Production Workers in Wood Household Furniture Manufacturing (Nonupholstered), 1959 and 1968

Year	New England	Middle Atlantic	Border States	Southeast	Southwest	Great Lakes	Pacific	All Regions[a]
1959	78.0	91.1	82.4	92.4	98.4	84.7	91.7	77.6
1968	91.7	95.0	90.5	100.0	107.3	91.9	82.9	85.9

Sources: U.S. Department of Labor, Bureau of Labor Statistics, *Wage Structure, Wood Household Furniture, Except Upholstered, April–May 1959*, Report no. 152 (Washington, DC: Government Printing Office, 1960), Table 1, p. 8; *Industry Wage Survey, Wood Household Furniture, Except Upholstered, October 1968*, Bulletin no. 1651 (Washington, DC: Government Printing Office, 1970), Table 1, p. 5.
[a]Includes the Midwest and Mountain regions, not shown separately.

UFWA organizing activity and the UFWA victory rate in representation elections held at large shops.[14]

A third method of employer resistance to UFWA organizing drives, according to the 1966 report of the UFWA officers, was "the intimidating tactics unleashed by the manufacturers whenever the Union [opened] an organizing drive . . . Reduced to a science" by the late 1960s, these intimidating tactics entailed "the creation of an atmosphere of fear in the plant—fear of being picked on, fear of transfer to undesirable work, fear of disciplinary action, fear of layoffs and, above all, fear of discharge . . . On the day before the [representation election] is to take place, the 'captive audience' meeting is held. The workers are called together on company time and property, and the Big Wheel or his lawyer harangues them about the evils of organized labor for as long as he pleases." In the event of a union victory in the representation election, the intransigent employer would attempt to prevent the negotiation of a first contract with the union by deploying "delay-and-frustrate tactics." These tactics had become widespread by the late 1960s, especially among low-wage employers. The employer would "go through the motions of bargaining for a first contract but carefully refrain from offering even reasonably minimum terms. The union is then faced with the alternatives of calling a strike or carrying on a long protracted campaign of legal and consumer harassment." According to the UFWA officers, then, employer resistance to organizing drives contributed to the declining organizing activity of the UFWA.[15]

Employer Resistance and Membership Losses

Notwithstanding any gains in UFWA membership from the organizing drives, losses of existing UFWA members offset the organizing gains, leading to membership stabilization between 1950 and 1970. Membership losses derived partly from an employer resistance strategy of plant relocation away from the union. The relocation strategy entailed either the closing of the unionized plant, followed by relocation of the plant in a low-wage, non-union geographical area, the so-called "runaway" plant, or the transfer of work in "chain" companies from the unionized plant to a recently opened branch plant in a non-union, low-wage geographical area. Although geographical differences in furniture worker wages declined, southern wages continued to be lower than those of furniture workers in other regions, as shown in Table 4.8. Also, furniture production worker

---

[14] Cornfield, "Declining Union Membership."
[15] *Proceedings of the Fourteenth Constitutional Convention of the United Furniture Workers of America—AFL-CIO,* Milwaukee, May 9–13, 1966, pp. 45–48.

Table 4.6
Percentage of Wood Household Furniture (Except Upholstered) Production Workers in Establishments with Selected Fringe Benefits, by Region, 1954 and 1968

Fringe Benefit	New England 1954	New England 1968	Middle Atlantic 1954	Middle Atlantic 1968	Border States 1954	Border States 1968	Southeast 1954	Southeast 1968
Paid vacations	88	100	98	100	96	96	58	95
Paid holidays	80	100	86	100	43	56	29	69
Retirement pension	6	57	26	59	15	70	15	55
Employer financed[b]	—	57	—	56	—	69	—	52
Life insurance	62	90	86	90	64	98	71	93
Employer financed[b]	—	51	—	62	—	31	—	47
Hospitalization insurance	72	96	88	93	71	96	73	91
Employer financed[b]	—	38	—	66	—	21	—	31
Medical insurance	39	95	39	50	28	67	21	66
Employer financed[b]	—	36	—	42	—	17	—	21
Accidental death and dismemberment insurance	32	85	62	63	51	35	32	67
Employer financed[b]	—	51	—	47	—	10	—	39

Sources: Department of Labor, Bureau of Labor Statistics, *Wage Structure, Household Furniture, 1954*, Report no. 76 (Washington, DC: Department of Labor, Bureau of Labor Statistics 1954), Tables 13–15, pp. 16–19; *Industry Wage Survey, Wood Household Furniture, Except Upholstered, October 1968*, Bulletin no. 1651 (Washington, DC: Government Printing Office, 1970), Tables 27–29, pp. 40–43.
[a] Includes the Midwest and Mountain regions, not shown separately.
[b] Employer financing data are unavailable for 1954.

wages tended to be lower in the nonmetropolitan areas than in the metropolitan areas of most regions.[16]

Unionized plant closures also resulted from the desire of employers to relocate near raw materials and growing consumer markets, especially in the non-union, right-to-work South and West. It is difficult to separate the effects of the different employer motivations for plant relocation on UFWA membership losses. However, the UFWA officers decried the ad-

---

[16] U.S. Department of Labor, Bureau of Labor Statistics, *Wage Structure, Wood Household Furniture, Except Upholstered, April–May 1959*, Report no. 152 (Washington, DC: Government Printing Office, 1960), p. 8; *Industry Wage Survey, Wood Household Furniture, Except Upholstered, October 1968*, Bulletin no. 1651 (Washington, DC: Government Printing Office, 1970), p. 5.

Table 4.6 (continued)

	Southwest		Great Lakes		Pacific		All Regions[a]	
Fringe Benefit	1954	1968	1954	1968	1954	1968	1954	1968
Paid vacations	90	100	92	98	100	100	82	97
Paid holidays	64	90	82	98	100	100	60	81
Retirement pension	33	37	9	36	7	65	15	54
Employer financed[b]	—	37	—	30	—	0	—	51
Life insurance	78	74	82	91	73	78	75	91
Employer financed[b]	—	35	—	68	—	72	—	51
Hospitalization insurance	65	68	86	95	51	88	76	91
Employer financed[b]	—	33	—	74	—	72	—	44
Medical insurance	42	53	55	75	51	88	37	68
Employer financed[b]	—	19	—	58	—	72	—	34
Accidental death and dismemberment insurance	12	29	61	76	45	69	44	62
Employer financed[b]	—	18	—	59	—	63	—	40

verse impact of runaways and chains on UFWA membership at every UFWA convention between 1954 and 1968.[17]

The southward and westward redistribution of furniture manufacturing and industry ruralization, described in Chapter 2, were facilitated partly by the increased capital concentration of the industry during the post–World War II era. As furniture manufacturers diversified their product lines and corporate conglomerates purchased furniture manufacturers, the multi-unit corporation increasingly replaced the single-unit, often family-owned, enterprise as the dominant type of employer and producer

---

[17] Daniel Cornfield and Mark Leners, "Unionization in the Rural South: Regional Patterns of Industrialization and the Process of Union Organizing," in *Research in Rural Sociology and Development,* vol. 4, eds. William Falk and Thomas Lyson (Greenwich, CT: JAI Press, 1989), pp. 137–152; *Proceedings,* 1954 UFWA Convention, pp. 30, 32; *Proceedings,* 1958 UFWA Convention, pp. 39–40; *Proceedings,* 1960 UFWA Convention, pp. 42, 44; *Proceedings,* 1962 UFWA Convention, pp. 35, 45; *Proceedings,* 1966 UFWA Convention, p. 42; *Proceedings,* 1968 UFWA Convention, pp. 36–38, 53; *Proceedings of the Ninth Constitutional Convention of the United Furniture Workers of America—AFL-CIO,* South Bend, IN, May 14–18, 1956, p. 38; *Proceedings of the Thirteenth Constitutional Convention of the United Furniture Workers of America—AFL-CIO,* New York, May 11–15, 1964, pp. 46, 50, 54.

Table 4.7
Percentage of Unionized Wood Household Furniture Manufacturing (Nonupholstered) Production Workers, by Region, 1959 and 1968

Year	New England	Middle Atlantic	Border States	Southeast	Southwest	Great Lakes	Pacific	All Regions[a]
1959	48.5	58.2	27.8	8.1	54.6	49.6	80.2	35.3
1968	51.8	67.7	16.1	20.6	53.5	50.3	71.9	38.0

Sources: U.S. Department of Labor, Bureau of Labor Statistics, *Wage Structure, Wood Household Furniture, Except Upholstered, April–May 1959*, Report no. 152 (Washington, DC: Government Printing Office, 1960), Table 1, p. 8; *Industry Wage Survey, Wood Household Furniture, Except Upholstered, October 1968*, Bulletin no. 1651 (Washington, DC: Government Printing Office, 1970), Table 1, p. 5.
[a] Includes the Midwest and Mountain regions, not shown separately.

Table 4.8
Hourly Wood Household Furniture (Nonupholstered) Production Worker Wage and Wage Index,
by Region, 1954 and 1968
(Southeast = 100)

Year	New England	Middle Atlantic	Border States	Great Lakes	Pacific	Southwest	Southeast	All Regions[a]
1954								
Wage	$1.35	$1.48	$1.15	$1.43	$1.69	$.98	$1.02	$1.25
Wage index[b]	132	145	113	140	166	96	100	123
1968								
Wage	$2.20	$2.37	$1.85	$2.24	$2.84	$1.83	$1.87	$2.07
Wage index[b]	118	127	99	120	152	98	100	111

Sources: U.S. Department of Labor, Bureau of Labor Statistics, *Wage Structure, Household Furniture 1954*, Report no. 76 (Washington, DC: U.S. Department of Labor, Bureau of Labor Statistics, 1954), Table 1, p. 7; *Industry Wage Survey, Wood Household Furniture, Except Upholstered, October 1968*, Bulletin no. 1651 (Washington, DC: Government Printing Office, 1970), Table 1, p. 5.

[a]Includes the Midwest and Mountain regions, not shown separately.

[b]Wage index = regional or all-region wage, divided by the Southeast wage of the stated year, multiplied by 100.

Table 4.9
Percentage of Employment and Value Added by Manufacture Accounted for by Multi-unit Corporations, Furniture Manufacturing, 1954–1972

Year	% Employment Accounted for by Multi-unit Corporations	% Value Added by Manufacture Accounted for by Multi-unit Corporations
1954	30.4	34.7
1963	41.8	44.8
1972	56.8	59.4

Sources: U.S. Bureau of the Census, *Census of Manufactures 1954*, vol. 1, Summary Statistics (Washington, DC: Government Printing Office, 1957), p. 204–7; *1963 Census of Manufactures*, vol. 1, Summary and Subject Statistics (Washington, DC: Government Printing Office, 1966), p. 3–18; *1972 Census of Manufactures*, vol. 1, Subject and Special Statistics (Washington, DC: Government Printing Office, 1976), p. SR3–31.

in furniture manufacturing.[18] Between 1954 and 1972, the share of furniture manufacturing employment and value added by manufacture accounted for by multi-unit corporations increased from roughly one-third to almost 60 percent, as shown in Table 4.9.

Given the geographical redistribution and capital concentration of furniture manufacturing, UFWA locals often represented the workers in shops owned by chain companies. According to a 1962 UFWA survey of its locals, 56 locals, over half of all UFWA locals, had 83 contracts with 67 different chain companies. Two-thirds of these locals were located in the East and Midwest, roughly one-third were in the South, and almost none were located in the West. Moreover, the survey showed that the chain companies with whom the UFWA had contracts often operated non-union branch plants simultaneously, typically in the South and other nonmetropolitan places. The UFWA represented workers in 44 chain companies that also operated at least one non-union branch plant. Of these 44 companies, 41 percent operated at least one UFWA plant in the East or Midwest and at least one non-union southern plant; another 16 percent operated one or more UFWA plants in the South or West and at least one non-union southern plant; 30 percent operated at least one UFWA plant in any region and one or more non-union plants in the nonmetropolitan areas of the East or Midwest; and 13 percent operated at least one UFWA plant in any region and one or more non-union plants in nonsouthern, metropolitan areas.[19]

The geographical redistribution of furniture manufacturing, partly

---
[18] Ibid.
[19] *Proceedings*, 1962 UFWA Convention, pp. 48–52.

generated by runaways and the branching out of chain companies, led to plant shutdowns and, consequently, to UFWA local union turnover. The average annual UFWA local union charter and closure rates during 1963 and 1971 (years of available data) demonstrate this turnover. The local union charter rate is the average annual number of new UFWA locals chartered, expressed as a percentage of the number of existing UFWA locals; the local union closure rate is the average annual number of UFWA locals that closed *due to plant shutdowns,* expressed as a percentage of the number of existing UFWA locals. Between 1963 and 1971, the UFWA local union charter rate of 2.3 percent was exceeded slightly by the 2.5 percent UFWA local union closure rate. The UFWA, then, chartered almost as many locals as the number that closed due to plant shutdowns in a year. Local union turnover was especially common among small locals (less than 105 members). The charter and closure rates for large locals were negligible, but the 3.5 percent charter rate for small locals was exceeded by the 4.7 percent closure rate for small locals. Turnover was highest for small, new (less than twenty years old) locals. On the average, almost 6 percent of these locals closed annually due to plant shutdowns.[20] The size differential in local union turnover rates was attributable not only to the greater difficulty in organizing large shops and, hence, in chartering large locals, but also to the greater stability of the large locals, which derived from their amalgamated structures and the relatively low likelihood of bankruptcy among large employers, as discussed in Chapter 2. Moreover, new locals suffered an additional "liability of newness," owing to the scarcity of resources to facilitate amalgamation and, thereby, protect themselves from closure due to plant shutdowns.[21]

In sum, UFWA membership stabilized with increased employer resistance to unionization, capital concentration, and geographical decentralization of the industry into low-wage, non-union locations between 1950 and 1970. The UFWA encountered growing employer resistance to its organizing drives, especially among the large employers, as the industry relocated away from the union. The union was caught in a vicious cycle of organizing small shops and chartering small locals, those locals which were most likely to fold.

UFWA Efforts to Replenish Membership

In light of the geographical redistribution of the industry and the turnover of UFWA local unions, the UFWA instituted several strategies for centralizing and consolidating its structure and activities, in order to

[20] Cornfield, "Declining Union Membership," p. 1141.
[21] Ibid.; Daniel Cornfield, "Plant Shutdowns and Union Decline: The United Furniture Workers of America, 1963–1981," *Work and Occupations* 14 (August 1987): 434–451.

conserve resources and replenish its membership during the 1950s and 1960s. As early as the founding UFWA convention in 1939, the union had adopted a policy of pursuing geographical uniformity in wages, to limit employer mobility to low-wage, non-union regions, and a policy of local union amalgamation, to stabilize existing locals and protect them from plant shutdowns (see Chapters 2 and 3). Few locals had merged with one another by the time of the 1970 UFWA convention, when the UFWA's period of stability ended. Columbus, OH, local 451 and Springfield, OH, local 453 merged into Cleveland local 450. New York City local 76B and Newark, NJ, local 92 merged in 1970.[22]

However, the forces that generated UFWA local union turnover and membership stabilization, especially employer resistance and the geographical decentralization of the industry, compelled the UFWA to centralize and consolidate its structure and activities in three additional ways after 1950. First, in 1952, the UFWA centralized and rationalized its administrative structure in order to conduct effective organizing drives. Prior to 1952, the UFWA president was required by the constitution to have the approval of the whole International UFWA general executive board in the appointment and release of organizers. Also, the president, the secretary–treasurer, and four regional representatives constituted an advisory committee to the GEB. At the 1952 UFWA convention, the advisory committee was transformed into an executive committee, with the four regional representatives now serving as regional vice presidents, consisting of the six International UFWA officers (since 1948, the four regional representatives had not been designated as International officers). The UFWA president could now appoint, direct, suspend, or remove organizers with the approval of only the executive committee, rather than of the full GEB. The GEB became empowered to review and remove any personnel who were appointed by the International. The vice presidents, who, as regional representatives, had assisted the International officers, were given the new responsibilities of supervising the activities of the salaried regional director and coordinating regional organizing drives. The vice presidents were now required to make periodic reports to the president, the executive committee, and the GEB.[23]

These reforms, which remained intact for the duration of the UFWA's period of stability, were controversial in that they sparked a debate at the 1952 convention about the desirability of increased centralization in the International UFWA administrative structure. Proponents of the reforms

---

[22] *Proceedings of the Sixteenth Constitutional Convention of the United Furniture Workers of America—AFL-CIO*, New York, May 18–22, 1970, p. 35.

[23] *Constitution of the United Furniture Workers of America—CIO*, 1948 revision, p. 11; 1950 revision, pp. 12, 16, 20; 1952 revision, pp. 12, 16, 18–20.

wanted to decrease the decision-making time for appointing organizers. Opponents argued that limiting the approval of presidential appointments of organizers to the executive committee, rather than the full GEB, was too undemocratic. The reforms passed with a voice vote on the convention floor.[24]

The second policy adopted after 1950, establishing joint councils of local unions, was an effort to free up the International organizers from servicing local unions and, thereby, enable them to devote more time to organizing. As the industry decentralized geographically into isolated, nonmetropolitan areas, the UFWA increasingly chartered small, single-shop locals. Lacking the resources to hire their own full-time personnel, and sufficiently removed geographically from other locals not to amalgamate, these small, single-shop locals depended on the International UFWA organizers for servicing, that is, for negotiating and administering contracts with employers.[25]

Pizer and Fulford, who had learned of joint councils from the Textile Workers, proposed the establishment of joint councils at the 1958 UFWA convention. The proposal called for the establishment of joint councils among geographically proximate locals. The function of the joint councils was to organize and service the participating locals. Each participating local was to contribute funds to cover the salaries of the organizers and service people whom the joint council would hire. Local unions that hired their own organizers and service people were not required to affiliate with a joint council.[26]

Arguing for the proposal, Fulford claimed that the twenty-three International organizers spent half of their time servicing locals instead of organizing. For Pizer, the increased geographical decentralization of the furniture industry out of the metropolitan areas necessitated the establishment of joint councils, especially because many locals had failed to amalgamate according to the amalgamation strategy devised during the UFWA's formative period.[27] Geographical decentralization of the industry resulted in the establishment of small, single-shop, local unions in remote areas, making amalgamation difficult and rendering them dependent on the International for servicing, claimed Pizer.

> Most people do not wish to amalgamate . . . because they don't want to give up their local identity. . . . We have made various efforts to amalgamate; we have not succeeded because of this reason. . . . What we propose now is to band a number of local unions in each area. . . . They will still

[24] *Proceedings,* 1952 UFWA Convention, pp. 186–192.
[25] *Proceedings,* 1958 UFWA Convention, p. 219.
[26] Ibid.
[27] Ibid., pp. 223–225.

have their own union. . . . The geographic situation is such that if the plants are spread out thirty miles or forty miles or fifty miles, people are not eager to run around; but there will be the Joint Council that will act as representatives of those people.[28]

The main argument made in opposition to the proposal for joint councils was that the small locals could not afford to finance the joint councils. Nonetheless, the convention passed the proposal for joint councils after much debate that culminated in a roll call vote, which I analyze later in greater detail.[29]

By April 1959, almost one year after the 1958 UFWA convention, the UFWA had established seven joint councils, all located in nonmetropolitan areas dense with furniture factories: (1) southern Illinois, Indiana, northern Kentucky/western West Virginia; (2) Jamestown-Buffalo, New York; (3) Tennessee, Alabama, Georgia; (4) Virginia, North and South Carolina; (5) Pennsylvania, Maryland; (6) Arkansas, Oklahoma; and (7) New England. At its May 1959 meeting, the UFWA GEB approved the constitutions of the seven joint councils. Approximately fifty-eight locals, roughly half of all UFWA locals, participated in the joint councils.[30]

However, the joint council "program was slow in getting under way because of opposition in some areas," claimed the UFWA officers at the 1960 UFWA convention in May, and the convention voted unanimously to dissolve the joint councils. According to Pizer, who continued to approve of the joint councils, several participating locals complained that other locals were not financing the joint councils.[31]

In place of the joint councils, the 1960 convention reestablished the district councils, one for each of the eleven geographical districts, that had been discontinued in 1954. The purpose of the district councils, with which all locals were required to affiliate, was "to strengthen organization in their respective areas and to promote the objectives of the International Union by coordinating the activities of the Local Unions and assisting in the servicing and organizational activities of the Local Unions within the district." The district councils were empowered to tax the participating locals. Unlike the district councils that existed before 1954, which required a district membership referendum and GEB approval to institute a tax, those established in 1960 required no referendum or GEB approval for instituting a tax. In addition, the pre-1954 practice of International rebates to the district councils was not established in 1960. Unlike the joint councils,

---

[28] Ibid., p. 225.
[29] Ibid., pp. 218–237; *Furniture Workers Press,* May 1958, p. 1.
[30] *Furniture Workers Press,* July-August 1958, p. 1; September 1958, p. 5; November 1958, p. 3; April 1959, p. 3; March 1959, p. 4; June 1959, p. 4.
[31] Quotation from *Proceedings,* 1960 UFWA Convention, p. 40; idem, pp. 109, 139, 207.

which hired their own full-time personnel, the district councils worked with the International staff assigned to the area.[32]

With the dissolution of the joint councils, the 1960 convention also resolved to promote local union amalgamations, reiterating the strategy that had been formulated at the founding UFWA convention in 1939. The resolution proclaimed that the efficiency of the International was reduced by the prevalence of small locals in the UFWA and that amalgamation would improve local and International union efficiency without sacrificing democracy and local autonomy.[33]

However, the servicing activities of the International organizers continued to conflict with their organizing responsibilities and, at the 1966 UFWA convention, the UFWA amended its constitution, allowing geographically adjacent locals to form joint boards. Unlike the joint councils that had been discontinued in 1960, the joint boards were not mandatory, and those that hired full-time organizers or service people received a monthly rebate of $.25 per member from the International union. The district councils remained intact. Moreover, the UFWA convention passed unanimously the joint board provision.[34]

Few locals availed themselves of the opportunity to form joint boards by the time of the 1970 UFWA convention, when the UFWA's period of stability ended. In June 1966, Granville, NY, local 36 and four Vermont locals formed the Vermont-Granville Joint Board.[35]

The third policy implemented after 1950 was coordinated bargaining among geographically distinct UFWA locals representing workers of the same chain company and with the locals of other International unions representing workers of chains with whom UFWA locals had contracts. Based on an organizing strategy that made unorganized chain plants the primary target of UFWA organizing drives, coordinated bargaining served to establish geographically uniform employment conditions among the plants owned by a given chain company. The rationale of such geographical uniformity, as it had been since the 1939 founding UFWA convention before the advent of furniture manufacturing chains, was to inhibit geographical capital mobility and the transfer of work to non-union, low-wage plants, which had jeopardized collective bargaining gains made by the unionized workers and the existence of their locals.[36]

The UFWA had become determined to organize chain plants by the

---

[32] Quotation from *Constitution of the United Furniture Workers of America AFL-CIO,* 1960 revision, pp. 27–28; idem., 1952 revision, pp. 25–26; *Proceedings,* 1960 UFWA Convention, p. 139.
[33] *Furniture Workers Press,* May 1960, p. 9.
[34] *Proceedings,* 1966 UFWA Convention, pp. 237–241.
[35] *Furniture Workers Press,* June 1967, p. 3.
[36] Ibid., December 1967, p. 4; *Proceedings,* 1960 UFWA Convention, pp. 42, 249.

early 1950s. For example, at a May 1953 UFWA Eastern Regional convention, the delegates resolved to organize the plants of the Englander Co., a bedding chain. At its May 1959 meeting, the UFWA GEB decided to concentrate UFWA organizing efforts among chain plants, and the 1960 UFWA convention resolved unanimously to affirm the GEB chain plant organizing strategy.[37]

Coordinated bargaining among locals representing shops in the same chain was instituted when the 1958 UFWA convention amended the constitution, authorizing the UFWA president to establish chain plant councils. All locals having contracts with a given chain company were required to join that chain plant's council. These councils were to work for the standardization of employment conditions among the plants of the chain. The first chain plant council was established in November 1958 for the locals representing Kay Manufacturing Corp. workers. Representatives from UFWA locals 76 of New York, 136B of Chelsea, MA, and 262 of San Francisco met to establish the Kay Council and reported on first-contract negotiations at a Kay plant in High Point, NC, and an organizing campaign at a Houston, TX, Kay plant. By the 1960 UFWA convention in May, the UFWA had established a chain plant council for the Huttig Sash and Door Co. locals, and several other locals were engaged in coordinated bargaining without chain plant councils. The UFWA officers reported to the 1960 UFWA convention that the following UFWA locals were engaged in coordinated bargaining with the same chain: Cleveland local 450 with Fostoria, OH, local 452; local 450 with Marion, SC, local 386; Rockford, IL, local 707 with Logan, OH, local 290; New York local 102 with Memphis, TN, local 282; and, Columbus, OH, local 451 with Birmingham, AL, local 384.[38]

In addition, the UFWA officers reported that several UFWA locals were engaged in coordinated bargaining with other International unions at the same chain company: Gardner, MA, local 154 with the Papermakers and Paperworkers, the Woodworkers, and the Retail, Wholesale Department Store Employees Union at the General Box Co.; Buffalo, NY, local 103 with Machinists at the Wood & Brooks Co.; New York local 102 with the Machinists and the Independent Piano Workers at several piano manufacturers; Los Angeles local 1010 with the Steelworkers at the Adams Eng. Corp.; and Gardner local 154 with the Automobile Workers at the Heywood Wakefield Co.[39]

The UFWA established a few chain plant councils and coordinated bargaining efforts, which thrived during the 1960s. In May 1960, the UFWA

[37] *Proceedings*, 1954 UFWA Convention, p. 32; *Proceedings*, 1960 UFWA Convention, pp. 249–254; *Furniture Workers Press*, June 1953, pp. 1–2; June 1959, pp. 1, 4.
[38] *Proceedings*, 1958 UFWA Convention, pp. 214–215; *Proceedings*, 1960 UFWA Convention, pp. 42–44; *Furniture Workers Press*, November 1958, p. 1; May 1960, p. 1.
[39] *Proceedings*, 1960 UFWA Convention, p. 43.

convened a piano workers conference and established the National Piano, Organ and Musical Instruments Council with representatives from an independent local at the Aeolian Co. and the Allied Industrial Workers. The UFWA issued a call to all Winter Piano Co. unions to attend a conference in March 1961. The conference delegates, including representatives from the UFWA, the Machinists, and the Independent Union of Piano Workers, agreed to coordinated bargaining, organizing campaigns, and establishment of the National Winter Piano Council. By October 1963, the UFWA had completed the organization of the three-unit Curtis Mathes chain, a manufacturer of TV, radio, and record player cabinets with plants in Benton, AR, and Dallas and Athens, TX. In February 1965, the UFWA established a Curtis Mathes Council.[40]

In sum, the UFWA adopted several strategies for centralizing and consolidating its operations, in order to improve its organizing drives and reduce local union turnover resulting from employer resistance to unionization, increasing concentration of furniture manufacturing capital, and geographical decentralization of the industry to non-union, nonmetropolitan areas. Despite the successful UFWA effort at stabilizing its membership and preventing its own decline, the UFWA's strategies of centralization and consolidation were not foolproof. For example, by December 1969, the Curtis Mathes Co. was threatening to relocate its woodworking operations in Mexico. Moreover, financing of the International UFWA drives generated controversy within the UFWA, as well as new and shifting political alliances among UFWA local unions.

Shifting Alliances

Despite the relative stability of the geographical distribution of UFWA membership during the 1950s and 1960s, the geographical-ethnic voting blocs that had been forged in the formative era became less salient between 1950 and 1970. Instead, locals entered into shifting alliances that endured for shorter periods of time than the geographical-ethnic voting blocs of the formative period. Moreover, the bases of any alliances, such as local union size and geographical location, failed to remain constant.

The instability of voting blocs during the 1950s and 1960s was largely attributable to the type of issue that emerged and the income stratification among local unions. In light of the membership turnover described previ-

[40] *Furniture Workers Press,* May 1960, pp. 1, 3; November 1960, p. 1; February 1961, pp. 1, 5; March 1961, pp. 1, 3; March 1962, p. 1; April 1962, p. 2; May 1962, p. 3; May 1963, pp. 1, 4; June 1963, p. 8; July-August 1963, p. 1; October 1963, p. 1; November 1963, p. 3; June 1964, p. 1; October 1964, p. 1; February 1965, p. 1; March 1965, p. 8; May 1965, pp. 1, 4; June 1965, p. 1; September 1965, pp. 5, 8; October 1966, p. 5; May 1967, p. 2; June 1967, p. 4; July-August 1967, pp. 3, 5; November 1967, p. 3; December 1967, p. 4; July-August 1968, p. 5; September 1969, p. 8.

ously, the chief issue was the financing of the International's organizing drives. Locals differed on this issue, depending on their ability to support the International financially. Moreover, not only did the pattern of income stratification cut across the geographical-ethnic voting blocs, but it also shifted along with geographical unevenness in local union membership growth trends. Therefore, the instability of the local union voting blocs derived from the shifting capacities of local unions to finance the International's organizing drives. Changes in the relative wealth of local unions, in turn, partly resulted from the mobility of the furniture manufacturing industry, which moved southward out of the unionized North and from the metropolitan to the small-town areas in most regions (see Chapter 2). The mobility of the furniture industry, then, contributed to the shifts in local union membership growth trends, the changes in the pattern of income stratification among locals and, consequently, the instability in local union voting blocs.

The results of five roll call votes taken at UFWA conventions during the 1950s and 1960s, shown in Table 4.10, illustrate the virtual absence of persistent constituencies or factions in this era. First, at the 1954 convention, the delegates debated a proposal for reducing the maximum number of paid, International UFWA organizers who could be elected to the GEB. The proposal called for changing the maximum from one per each of the eleven districts to one per each of the four regions, excluding the four vice presidents.

The argument for the proposal, made by delegates from the large, metropolitan locals of the East and Midwest, was that the change would increase rank-and-file presence on the GEB, thereby reducing the ability of the president, who was authorized to hire and fire organizers, to control the GEB with threats of discharging the organizers who opposed him. The argument of the opposition, voiced mainly by midwesterners including Secretary-Treasurer Fulford, was that organizers, who were often rank-and-filers, made good leaders and should not be treated as "second-class citizens" by limiting their opportunity to serve on the GEB. Furthermore, the midwesterners wanted to avoid pitting two International staff members in the Midwest, William Gilbert in Chicago and Neil McCormick in Michigan, against one another for GEB positions. Underlying the argument of the opposition, then, appeared to be a concern about board representativeness: that reducing the number of organizers on the GEB would reduce midwestern representation on the board. This concern, in turn, may have rested on the small midwestern locals' greater dependence on, and familiarity with, the International organizers, compared with the large, metropolitan locals of the East and Midwest. The relatively small locals in the nonmetropolitan Midwest often could not afford to hire full-time local business agents for servicing the local and, therefore, depended on the

International staff for servicing. In contrast, the large, urban, amalgamated locals hired their own full-time personnel, who tended to be the local union members who served on the GEB and consequently were less dependent on the International for servicing and for generating potential leaders. For the small locals of the nonmetropolitan Midwest, then, the International organizer was a familiar person who had sufficient time and expertise to serve on the GEB.[41]

The delegates passed the proposal for limiting the number of paid International organizers on the GEB by a slim majority of 56.4 percent, shown in column one of Table 4.10. The results are classified by the location and size of the local unions casting the votes. Within all locations except the South, the large locals were more likely than the small locals to vote for the proposal. Among the large locals, those in the East, West, and metropolitan Midwest were more likely to support the proposal than those in the South and nonmetropolitan Midwest. These results suggest that the locals that were least dependent on the International for servicing, the large, amalgamated locals, were more likely to support the proposal than the more dependent locals, the newer and smaller locals in the nonmetropolitan Midwest and South. This geographical division among the locals is a continuation of the one that had persisted on many issues during the UFWA's formative period, before 1950 (see Chapter 3).

The second roll call vote, which occurred at the 1958 convention, concerned the proposal for establishing joint councils of local unions, as discussed earlier. Proponents argued that joint councils would improve the effectiveness of the International UFWA organizing drives by relieving the International organizers of their local union servicing responsibilities. Opponents argued that the small locals could not afford to finance the joint councils.

The proposal passed by a slim majority of 54.9 percent of the votes, shown in column 2 of Table 4.10. Within each location except the nonmetropolitan Midwest and West, the large locals were more likely than the small locals to vote for the proposal. Among the large locals, those in the East, metropolitan Midwest, and West were more likely than those in the nonmetropolitan Midwest and South to favor the proposal. These results are similar to the results of the 1954 roll call vote on limiting the number of organizers on the GEB.

The remaining three roll call votes were taken at the 1960, 1964, and 1968 conventions, and each concerned a proposal for increasing the monthly per capita tax paid by the local union to the International. The arguments for and against the increase made at all three conventions were

---

[41] *Proceedings,* 1954 UFWA Convention, pp. 208–217; telephone interview with William Gilbert, February 6, 1987.

Table 4.10
Roll Call Vote Results at UFWA Conventions, by Location and Local Union Size, 1954–1968

Location and Local Union Size[a]	% Voting for Limiting Number of Paid International Representatives on GEB, 1954	% Voting for Establishing Joint Councils, 1958	% Voting for Per Capita Tax Increase 1960	% Voting for Per Capita Tax Increase 1964	% Voting for Per Capita Tax Increase 1968
East	76.7	69.5	91.1	76.7	53.5
	(16,320)[b]	(18,263)	(16,661)	(15,623)	(14,394)
Metropolitan	79.4	80.1	92.9	90.2	49.7
	(11,319)	(12,129)	(12,009)	(11,791)	(11,101)
Small	47.6	26.7	100.0	67.3	100.0
	(1520)	(815)	(770)	(743)	(485)
Large	84.3	84.0	92.4	91.8	47.4
	(9799)	(11,314)	(11,239)	(11,048)	(10,616)
Nonmetropolitan	70.8	48.3	86.6	34.9	66.5
	(5001)	(6134)	(4652)	(3832)	(3293)
Small	27.1	13.4	73.4	71.4	72.1
	(2001)	(3074)	(2341)	(1872)	(1774)
Large	100.0	83.4	100.0	0.0	60.0
	(3000)	(3060)	(2311)	(2455)	(1519)
Midwest	37.8	37.7	87.7	60.1	15.4
	(8779)	(10,003)	(8923)	(6154)	(6350)
Metropolitan	63.0	99.4	68.8	66.0	0.0
	(2377)	(2493)	(2450)	(2400)	(2202)
Small	0.0	0.0	100.0	100.0	—
	(32)	(15)	(11)	(116)	—
Large	63.8	100.0	68.7	64.2	—
	(2345)	(2478)	(2439)	(2284)	(2202)

Nonmetropolitan	28.4	17.3	94.9	56.4	23.6
	(6402)	(7510)	(6473)	(3754)	(4148)
Small	7.2	22.1	87.2	68.0	52.5
	(2607)	(2610)	(2587)	(1451)	(1863)
Large	43.0	14.7	100.0	49.0	0.0
	(3795)	(4900)	(3886)	(2303)	(2285)
South	14.1	16.4	0.0	35.8	100.0
	(4713)	(4847)	(4712)	(3792)	(5178)
Small	26.5	5.2	—	37.6	—
	(2513)	(2249)	(1468)	(768)	(915)
Large	0.0	26.1	—	35.3	—
	(2200)	(2598)	(3244)	(3024)	(4263)
West	74.7	100.0	100.0	44.9	85.6
	(1683)	(2063)	(2106)	(2486)	(2352)
Small	10.7	—	—	0.0	100.0
	(476)	(34)	(38)	(182)	(295)
Large	100.0	—	—	48.4	83.5
	(1207)	(2029)	(2068)	(2304)	(2057)
Total	56.4	54.9	77.5	64.7	56.1
	(31,495)	(35,176)	(32,402)	(28,055)	(28,274)

Sources: *Proceedings of the Eighth Constitutional Convention of the United Furniture Workers of America—CIO*, Cleveland, June 14–18, 1954, pp. 219–221; *Proceedings of the Tenth Constitutional Convention of the United Furniture Workers of America—AFL-CIO*, New York, May 12–16, 1958, pp. 242–247; *Proceedings of the Eleventh Constitutional Convention of the United Furniture Workers of America—AFL-CIO*, Chicago, May 2–6, 1960, pp. 187–191; *Proceedings of the Thirteenth Constitutional Convention of the United Furniture Workers of America—AFL-CIO*, New York, May 11–15, 1964, pp. 260–261; *Proceedings of the Fifteenth Constitutional Convention of the United Furniture Workers of America—AFL-CIO*, Memphis, May 27–31, 1968, pp. 265–266.

[a]Metropolitan areas are the 20 largest U.S. cities in census years; nonmetropolitan areas are all other places. Small local unions = less than 500 members; large local unions = 500 or more members.

[b]Total number of votes in parentheses.

similar. Proponents argued that the International needed more money to cover organizing costs, which had escalated with the membership losses resulting from the shift of furniture factories out of the unionized areas and into the less unionized South. Opponents of the increases often argued that their locals could not afford the increase. At the 1960 convention, delegates from the low-wage South opposed the increase on the grounds that the southern locals could not as easily afford the increase as the locals in higher-wage areas.[42]

The results of the three roll call votes are shown in columns 3 through 5 of Table 4.10. Three patterns are discernible from these results. First, although the conventions passed each of the per capita tax increases, they did so with a declining majority during the eight-year period. The percentage voting for the increase declined from 77.5 percent in 1960 to 64.7 percent in 1964 and to 56.1 percent in 1968. Second, the relationship between local union size and the percentage voting for the increase was either nil within locations, inconsistent across locations, or both for the three roll call votes (although small locals tended to be more likely than large locals to favor the increase in 1968). Third, the percentage voting for the increase in each of the locations shifted in a nonuniform manner between 1960 and 1968. In the metropolitan East and the Midwest, the percentage favoring the increase declined between 1960 and 1968; in the nonmetropolitan East and the West, the percentage favoring the increase declined between 1960 and 1964 and increased between 1964 and 1968; and in the South, the percentage increased between 1960 and 1968.

These shifts in geographical vote results are partly associated with geographical differences in local union membership growth trends, as shown in Table 4.11. This table consists of growth rate and voting behavior data for the nineteen UFWA locals that were "large" (500 or more members) in at least two of the three conventions at which the roll call votes on per capita tax increases were taken. These nineteen locals accounted for roughly 80 percent of the votes at each of the three conventions. The growth rates for the nineteen locals are shown by local union location on the left side of the table. For example, the total membership of the large locals in the East declined by 4.0 percent between 1960 and 1964, by 6.7 percent between 1964 and 1968, and by 10.4 percent over the eight-year period. The voting behavior of the nineteen locals on the question of raising the per capita tax at the three conventions is shown on the right side of the table. The seven large eastern locals, for example, voted 6 to 1, 5 to 2, and 4 to 3 for the per capita tax increases at the 1960, 1964, and 1968 conventions, respectively.

---

[42] *Proceedings,* 1960 UFWA Convention, pp. 166–186; *Proceedings,* 1964 UFWA Convention, pp. 215–261; *Proceedings,* 1968 UFWA convention, pp. 218–254.

Table 4.11
Percentage of Change in Membership and Roll Call Vote Results on Per Capita Tax Increases for 19 Large UFWA Locals, by Local Union Location, 1960–1968[a]

Location	% Change in Membership			Locals Voting for and against Per Capita Tax Increase[b]		
	1960–1964	1964–1968	1960–1968	1960	1964	1968
East	−4.0	−6.7	−10.4	6–1	5–2	4–3
Metropolitan[c]	−1.7	−3.9	−5.5	5–1	5–1	3–3
Midwest	−5.0	−13.9	−18.2	5–1	3–3	0–6
Nonmetropolitan	−3.9	−22.2	−25.3	4–0	2–2	0–4
South	−6.8	23.8	15.4	0–4	1–3	4–0
West	11.4	−10.7	−0.5	2–0	1–1	2–0

Sources: *Proceedings of the Eighth Constitutional Convention of the United Furniture Workers of America—CIO*, Cleveland, June 14–18, 1954, pp. 219–221; *Proceedings of the Tenth Constitutional Convention of the United Furniture Workers of America—AFL-CIO*, New York, May 12–16, 1958, pp. 242–247; *Proceedings of the Eleventh Constitutional Convention of the United Furniture Workers of America—AFL-CIO*, Chicago, May 2–6, 1960, pp. 187–191; *Proceedings of the Thirteenth Constitutional Convention of the United Furniture Workers of America—AFL-CIO*, New York, May 11–15, 1964, pp. 260–261; *Proceedings of the Fifteenth Constitutional Convention of the United Furniture Workers of America—AFL-CIO*, Memphis, May 27–31, 1968, pp. 265–266.
[a] Large unions are all UFWA locals whose membership was 500 or more in at least 2 of the years 1960, 1964, and 1968.
[b] Number of locals voting *for* the per capita tax increase is to the *left* of each dash; number of locals voting *against* the increase is to the *right* of each dash.
[c] Metropolitan areas are the 20 largest U.S. cities in census years; nonmetropolitan areas are all other places.

The shifts in geographical voting behavior in Table 4.11 are associated with differences in geographical membership growth rates. The higher the growth rate of the locals in a given location, the more favorable they became toward per capita tax increases between 1960 and 1968. The southern locals, which sustained the highest rates of growth between 1960 and 1968, shifted from complete opposition to complete support for the per capita tax increases; the western locals exhibited stability in both their growth rates and voting behavior, tending to support the increases; the eastern locals, especially in the metropolitan areas, experienced an accelerated but moderate membership decline and shifted from strong support to a split vote on the per capita tax increases; and the midwestern locals, especially the nonmetropolitan ones, which experienced accelerated and large membership declines, shifted from strong support to strong opposition to the per capita tax increases between 1960 and 1968. Although an analysis of the relationship between the growth rates and voting behavior of individual local unions (not reported here) failed to demonstrate a consistent relationship, the results of the analysis in Table 4.11 suggest that changes in the membership strength of *blocs* of local unions in a common geographical area affected their voting behavior. Other factors that may have influenced the revenues and votes of individual unions are the recency and magnitude of wage increases gained through collective bargaining and local union dues increases, both of which vary among local unions.

In sum, the analysis of the roll call vote results suggests the absence of persistent constituencies or factions during the 1950s and 1960s. Rather, local unions shifted their alignments, differentiating themselves by size, location, or both. During the 1950s, the locals were divided by size and location. In the 1960s, the locals distinguished themselves more by their location than by their size, and the locational differences shifted. By the end of the 1960s, the divide between the metropolitan areas of the East, Midwest, and West, on the one hand, and the nonmetropolitan areas of the Midwest, South, and East, on the other, which had been forged during the formative era before 1950 (see Chapter 3), had become less salient. The voting behavior of the metropolitan areas of the East and Midwest increasingly, but incompletely, concurred with that of the nonmetropolitan Midwest; the voting behavior of the West diverged somewhat from that of the metropolitan East and Midwest; and southern voting behavior, which diverged from that of the nonmetropolitan Midwest, converged increasingly with western voting behavior.

The instability of voting alliances among locals during the 1950s and 1960s is related partly to the nature of the issues about which the convention delegates deliberated. Unlike the issues of the formative era, which concerned board representativeness, the UFWA's stance in national politics, and its relationship to the labor movement, most of the issues of the 1950s and 1960s pertained to the internal administration of the UFWA, especially financing the organizing drives conducted by the International. Whereas the broad political issues of the formative era effectively reinforced the geographic-ethnic voting blocs in the UFWA, the administrative issues of the 1950s and 1960s divided locals in terms of their financial abilities to support the International. This income stratification of the locals cut across the geographical-ethnic voting blocs of the formative era and shifted in accordance with the geographical unevenness in local union growth rates. In the case of the one roll call vote that pertained to board representativeness, the 1954 vote on reducing the number of paid, International organizers on the GEB, the small locals were more likely than the large locals to oppose the reduction, suggesting that, by virtue of their limited resources, the small locals depended on the International organizers for local support and representation of their interests on the GEB.

Shifting patterns of income stratification among the local unions, combined with recurring administrative financial issues, then, prevented the emergence of stable factions or voting constituencies during the 1950s and 1960s.

Leadership Stabilization

The UFWA leadership on the GEB stabilized during the 1950–1970 period along with membership stabilization. Membership stabilization resulted from the inability of the UFWA to remove itself from the vicious cycle of local union turnover, as well as from its successful effort to prevent its decline. Several historical forces generated this cycle of local union turnover. The increasing concentration of furniture manufacturing capital, geographical decentralization of the industry into non-union regions, and various employer resistance strategies, all of which occurred within the context of the Taft-Hartley Act and the weakening of union security arrangements, created obstacles to UFWA organizing drives, plant shutdowns, and, consequently, local union closures. The UFWA prevented membership losses by centralizing and consolidating its structure and activities and conducting vigorous organizing drives, especially in the South and among the unorganized plants of chain companies. This was facilitated by the decline of inter-union rivalry.

Membership stabilization and the UFWA's effort to unleash itself from the vicious cycle of local union turnover generated leadership stability and little or no ethnic succession on the GEB during the 1950s and 1960s. Three interrelated features of the UFWA's period of stability, in contrast with those of the UFWA formative period (1939–1950), promoted leadership stability. First, membership stabilization led to few changes in the configuration of political constituencies at UFWA conventions. The geographical distribution of UFWA membership changed little during the period of stability, in comparison with the dramatic changes that had occurred during the UFWA's formative period. Therefore, few new social groups, at least defined by their geographical location, entered the union between 1950 and 1970.

Second, the issues generated by the UFWA effort to stop the cycle of local union turnover, especially financing the UFWA organizing drives, led to new and transient alliances among locals whose relative wealth and, hence, ability to finance the drives shifted with industry conditions. These shifting alliances cut across the geographical-ethnic voting blocs that had been forged during the formative period. Moreover, the issue of financing the organizing drives divided the locals, not in terms of their beliefs about the appropriateness of the UFWA's broader mission, but only with respect to the affordability of various initiatives. Consequently, no stable, self-conscious voting blocs or factions seeking representation on the GEB emerged in the union. In contrast, the national, Cold-War, political conditions of the formative period exacerbated the geographical-ethnic tensions among voting blocs whose divergent political views contributed to their desire for representation on the GEB.

Third, UFWA membership only stabilized during this era; it did not decline. Therefore, the union was not in jeopardy, and no crisis prevailed that the UFWA conventions could associate with the behavior of UFWA leaders. During the UFWA's formative period, in comparison, it was jeopardized severely by union raids and attacks on its left-wing political stance that the UFWA conventions, especially in 1950, partly attributed to its leaders.

In sum, the absence of emerging social groups seeking access to leadership positions served to stabilize the incumbent leadership during the 1950s and 1960s. The seemingly "oligarchical" tendencies of UFWA leadership during this period derived from a unified, concerted effort by the UFWA to remove itself from a vicious cycle of local union turnover, a cycle brought on in large part by employer resistance to unionization. In contrast with the psychological reductionism of Michels's iron law of oligarchy, which posited an inevitable membership apathy toward a conspiratorial leadership and subsequent oligarchical union regime, the UFWA conducted lively debates about union policy during most of its ten conventions between 1950 and 1970. Leadership stabilized because external resistance to union growth stabilized UFWA membership, limiting the emergence of self-conscious social groups in the union.

5
Revitalizing the Union: The Ascent of Minorities and Women During the UFWA's Period of Decline, 1970–1987

Minorities and women emerged on the GEB during the 1970s and 1980s. The civil rights movement of the late 1960s played an important part in inspiring both minorities and women to mobilize for increased participation in UFWA governance. Black and Hispanic UFWA activists had participated in the civil rights movement and brought its momentum into the UFWA during the late 1960s. Likewise, the initial mobilization of women in the early 1970s was led by black women UFWA activists who were also inspired by the civil rights movement.

Minority and women's activism was also inspired by an ideology of working class unity, a desire for workers of all ethnic and gender backgrounds to unite, lest the employer divide them and undermine their wages, which was first formulated by the founding, left-wing, UFWA activists in the 1930s and was passed down to later generations of UFWA leaders through mentoring by their predecessors. The ideology not only legitimized the ethnic and gender integration of the GEB but also directly stimulated minority and women's activism in the UFWA.

The emergence of minorities and women on the GEB was occasioned by their entry into the furniture manufacturing industry, beginning in the mid-1960s. Prior to that time, the industry workforce comprised few

Table 5.1
Percentage of Unionized Wood Household Furniture (Nonupholstered) Production Workers, by Region, 1968 and 1986

Year	New England	Middle Atlantic	Border States	Southeast
1968	51.8	67.7	16.1	20.6
1986	14.3	32.0	n.a.	6.8

Sources: U.S. Department of Labor, Bureau of Labor Statistics, *Industry Wage Survey, Wood Household Furniture, Except Upholstered, October 1968,* Bulletin no. 1651 (Washington, DC: Government Printing Office, 1970), Table 1, p. 5; *Industry Wage Survey: Wood Household Furniture, June 1986,* Bulletin no. 2283 (Washington, DC: Government Printing Office, 1987), Table 1, p. 3.

minority and women workers. By the mid-1960s, technological changes in furniture production had created a growing proportion of semi-skilled factory operative occupations and had reduced relative employment in the skilled upholstery and cabinetmaking trades, making this growing, low-wage industry the recipient of many socially disadvantaged minority and women workers. At the same time, the urbanization of southern blacks and southwestern Hispanics that resulted from the mechanization of agriculture in these areas led many of these workers to seek employment in such low-wage industries as furniture manufacturing; and, as the one-earner household became decreasingly feasible under inflationary, macroeconomic conditions, women workers also found jobs in furniture manufacturing. These broad social forces are clearly evident in the biographical sketches I present of several of the minority and women UFWA leaders. Many entered the furniture factory and, later, union offices from farming backgrounds in which their parents had had little or no involvement in the labor movement. Therefore, the involvement of top-ranking UFWA leaders in the mentoring and development of minority and women leaders was essential to the ethnic and gender integration of the GEB during the 1970s and 1980s.

The geographical redistribution of the furniture manufacturing industry, and of UFWA membership, generated a realignment of political strength in the UFWA that facilitated the ethnic and gender integration of the GEB. In search of low wages and growing markets, furniture manufacturers moved out of the Northeast and urban Midwest into the South, nonmetropolitan Midwest, and West. Black and Hispanic furniture workers were disproportionately located in the South and West, respectively, and women furniture workers tended to be located in the South and nonmetropolitan Midwest. Industry geographical redistribution, along with growing furniture imports and employer resistance to unions, led to a decline in UFWA membership, rendering the incorporation of the new minority

Table 5.1 (continued)

Year	Southwest	Great Lakes	Pacific	All Regions[a]
1968	53.5	50.3	71.9	38.0
1986	0.0	35.0	30.9	13.9

[a] Includes the Middle West and Mountain regions, not shown separately.

and women workers from the growing regions of strategic importance to UFWA revitalization. Furthermore, the political strength of the old, large, urban, amalgamated UFWA locals in the Northeast and Midwest increasingly gave way to that of the newer locals in the South and nonmetropolitan Midwest. Consequently, minorities and women acquired political strength, which they seized as they mobilized for greater participation in UFWA governance.

Minorities and women had made inroads on the GEB by 1987, when the UFWA merged into the larger International Union of Electronic, Electrical, Technical, Salaried and Machine Workers (IUE), becoming the Furniture Workers Division of the IUE. A gesture of mutual survival, the merger of these two declining unions occurred in order to step up the organizing efforts of both. The ethnic and gender integration of the UFWA was one of the attractive features of the UFWA for the IUE, which saw in the UFWA the potential for making the IUE a more politically progressive International union. The ideology of working class unity, then, was exercised by both unions to strengthen them in a common venture.

Declining Membership

Membership of the UFWA declined from 30,690 to 19,367 between 1970 and 1985. Recessionary macroeconomic conditions, increasing foreign furniture imports to the United States, conservative national political conditions, and growing employer resistance to unionization not only jeopardized existing union membership but also led to a deceleration in UFWA organizing activity. Similarly, the percentage unionized of the wood household furniture production workforce dropped from 38.0 percent to 13.9 percent between 1968 and 1986, shown in Table 5.1. Consequently, the UFWA continued several of the growth policies it had previously adopted, including local union consolidation, membership diversification, and chain plant organizing, and undertook new steps to reduce the operating expenses of the International.

These new cost-reduction efforts, which took the form of amendments to the UFWA constitution, were addressed to those facets of governance that pertained to the accessibility of general executive board positions to aspirants to elective office. In contrast with the expectations of the "structuralist" research on union officer turnover (see Chapters 1 and 2), these constitutional amendments had little impact on the turnover rate of GEB members. Rather, these amendments, which, in theory, might have lowered the turnover rate had they been enacted earlier or endured longer, were made during an era when social and political forces beyond the UFWA organizational structure generated relatively high rates of turnover on the general executive board.

Jeopardization of Existing Membership

Several factors threatened existing UFWA membership during the 1970s and 1980s. Among them were plant shutdowns resulting from industry concentration, geographical capital mobility into non-union areas, and increasing foreign furniture imports to the United States. The nationwide recessions in 1974–1975 and 1979–1983 engendered layoffs in furniture manufacturing and UFWA membership losses (see Chapter 1, Table 1.1).

Membership losses were partly attributable to plant shutdowns and acceleration of the vicious cycle of local union turnover that had begun in the previous period of stability (1950–1970). Between 1963 and 1971, 2.5 percent of UFWA locals, on the average, closed annually due to plant shutdowns; between 1972 and 1981, 3.4 percent closed annually. The closure rate was particularly high for the small local union (less than 105 members). For small, new (less than twenty years old) locals, the closure rate increased from 5.8 percent to 7.0 percent, and that for small, old locals jumped from 0.7 percent to 5.0 percent between 1963–1971 and 1972–1981. The rate at which the UFWA chartered new locals, in an effort to recoup its losses, was lower than the local union closure rate. Between 1963–1971 and 1972–1981, the average annual percentage of newly chartered locals declined slightly from 2.3 percent to 2.1 percent; for large locals (105 or more members), the charter rate declined from 1.2 percent to 0.8 percent.[1]

Some of the forces that generated local union closures during the previous period of stability continued to operate during the period of decline. The furniture manufacturing industry became increasingly concentrated in all regions, with larger firms and establishments supplanting

---

[1] Daniel Cornfield, "Declining Union Membership in the Post–World War II Era: The United Furniture Workers of America, 1939–1982," *American Journal of Sociology* 91 (March 1986): 1141; idem, "Plant Shutdowns and Union Decline: The United Furniture Workers of America, 1963–1981," *Work and Occupations* 14 (August 1987): 434–451.

smaller ones.[2] Between 1951 and 1981, the number of furniture manufacturing establishments with one hundred or more employees increased by 29 percent, and that for smaller establishments declined by 14 percent.[3] The rate of concentration during the 1970s, however, was lower than that during the 1960s. The percentage of furniture manufacturing employment and value added accounted for by multi-unit corporations had increased by some fifteen percentage points between 1963 and 1972 (see Chapter 4, Table 4.9). Between 1972 and 1982, the percentage of furniture manufacturing employment accounted for by multi-unit corporations increased from 56.8 percent to 58.6 percent; that for value added increased from 59.4 percent to 62.7 percent.[4] Also, the furniture industry continued to decentralize geographically into the non-union, rural areas of most regions, the right-to-work South and West (see Chapter 2).[5] Production worker wages continued to be among the lowest in the southeast region in 1968 and 1986, as shown in Table 5.2.

Membership of the UFWA underwent a parallel geographical redistribution, shown in Table 5.3. Between 1970 and 1984, membership in the West and the nonmetropolitan areas of the East and Midwest declined at slower rates than in the corresponding metropolitan areas. In the South, particularly east of the Mississippi River, membership increased.

In addition to these forces, furniture imports to the United States from low-wage nations increased during the 1970s and 1980s, leading to plant shutdowns and local union closures in the United States. The value of domestic U.S. furniture industry shipments in 1984 was roughly three and one half times greater than the 1970 value; however, for furniture imports to the United States, the 1984 value was over eleven times greater than the 1970 value. By 1984, the value of furniture imports was almost 9 percent the size of domestic industry shipments.[6]

---

[2] Cornfield, "Declining Union Membership," pp. 1129–1130; Daniel Cornfield and Mark Leners, "Unionization in the Rural South: Regional Patterns of Industrialization and the Process of Union Organizing," in *Research in Rural Sociology and Development,* vol. 4, eds., William Falk and Thomas Lyson (Greenwich, CT: JAI Press, 1989), pp. 137–152.

[3] Daniel Cornfield, "Decline and Diversification: Causes and Consequences for Organizational Governance," in *Research in the Sociology of Organizations,* vol. 5, eds., Samuel Bacharach and Nancy DiTomaso (Greenwich, CT: JAI Press, 1987).

[4] See Table 4.9 and U.S. Bureau of the Census, *1982 Census of Manufactures,* Subject Series, *Type of Organization,* MC82-S-5 (Washington, DC: Government Printing Office, 1985), p. 5–27.

[5] Cornfield, "Declining Union Membership"; Cornfield and Leners, "Unionization in the Rural South." According to the June 1986 U.S. Bureau of Labor Statistics wage survey of wood household furniture (nonupholstered) workers, production worker hourly wages in metropolitan areas exceeded those in nonmetropolitan areas by 10 percent. The source of these data is *Industry Wage Survey: Wood Household Furniture, June 1986,* Bulletin no. 2283 (Washington, DC: Government Printing Office, 1987), Table 1, p. 3.

[6] U.S. Bureau of the Census, *Annual Survey of Manufactures: 1970 and 1971* (Washington, DC: Government Printing Office, 1973), p. 60; *U.S. General Imports, Commodity by*

Table 5.2
Average Hourly Wood Household Furniture (Nonupholstered)
Production Worker Wages and Wage Index, by Region, 1968 and 1986
(Southeast = 100)

Year	New England	Middle Atlantic	Great Lakes	Pacific
1968				
Wage	$2.20	2.37	2.24	2.84
Wage index	117.6	126.7	119.8	151.9
1986				
Wage	6.55	6.47	6.94	5.73
Wage index	113.5	112.1	120.3	99.3

Sources: U.S. Department of Labor, Bureau of Labor Statistics, *Industry Wage Survey, Wood Household Furniture, Except Upholstered, October 1968,* Bulletin no. 1651 (Washington, DC: Government Printing Office, 1970), Table 1, p. 5; *Industry Wage Survey: Wood Household Furniture, June 1986,* Bulletin no. 2283 (Washington, DC: Government Printing Office, 1987), Table 1, p. 3.
[a] Includes the Middle West and Mountain regions, not shown separately.

Of the various product lines represented by the UFWA, pianos and musical instruments suffered the most from imports. In 1960, the UFWA established the National Piano, Organ and Musical Instruments Council (NPOMI), a lobbying and information-sharing organization to which several international unions, in addition to the UFWA, belong. Throughout the 1970s and 1980s, NPOMI testified before the U.S. Tariff Commission, seeking protective tariffs to prevent domestic layoffs caused by imports, and it succeeded in gaining such tariffs and jobless pay for the unemployed. Other product lines represented by the UFWA that were jeopardized by imports include television cabinets and folding chairs. The UFWA actively participated in the Committee to Preserve American Color Television, a lobbying organization that includes industry and union members.[7]

Data are unavailable to determine the extent to which furniture imports to the United States originated from foreign operations owned by U.S. manufacturers who had sought cheaper labor outside the country. The UFWA identified some of these cases. For example, in 1971 Thomas-

---

World Area, FT 150/Annual 1970 (Washington, DC: Government Printing Office, 1971), p. 16; *1985 Annual Survey of Manufactures,* Statistics for Industry Groups and Industries, M85(AS)-1 (Washington, DC: Government Printing Office, 1987), p. 13; *U.S. General Imports/ Schedule A Commodity Groupings by World Areas and Country* (microfiche), Report FT 150, Annual 1984 (Washington, DC: Government Printing Office, 1985), p. 33.

[7] *Furniture Workers Press,* December 1970, p. 2; March 1971, p. 5; November 1972, p. 6; April 1975, p. 2; December 1976, p. 3; April 1977, p. 2; October 1978, pp. 5, 8; November 1978, p. 2; April 1983, p. 3; June 1986, p. 8; December 1986, p. 5.

Table 5.2 (continued)

Year	Border States	Southwest	Southeast	All Regions[a]
1968				
Wage	1.85	1.83	1.87	2.07
Wage index	98.9	97.9	100.0	110.7
1986				
Wage	n.a.	5.53	5.77	5.85
Wage index	—	95.8	100.0	101.4

Table 5.3
Percentage Distribution of UFWA Membership at 1970 and 1984 UFWA Conventions and Percentage Change, by Location

	% Distribution		1970–1984
Location[a]	1970	1984	% Change
East	47.7	42.5	−43.3
Metropolitan	35.9	30.2	−46.4
Nonmetropolitan	11.8	12.3	−34.0
Midwest	22.9	25.3	−29.6
Metropolitan	6.3	4.9	−50.8
Nonmetropolitan	16.6	20.4	−21.5
South	21.1	21.6	−34.9
Arkansas	8.5	1.4	−89.2
East of Mississippi River and Texas	12.6	20.2	1.6
West	8.2	10.6	−18.1
Total	99.9[b]	100.0	−36.3
N	31,594	20,115	

Sources: *Proceedings of the Sixteenth Constitutional Convention of the United Furniture Workers of America—AFL-CIO,* New York, May 18–22, 1970, pp. 131–135; *Proceedings of the Twenty-Second Constitutional Convention of the United Furniture Workers of America—AFL-CIO,* Chicago, June 25–29, 1984, pp. 102–104.
[a] Metropolitan areas are the 20 largest U.S. cities in census years; nonmetropolitan areas are all other places.
[b] Does not sum to 100% due to rounding.

ville Furniture Industries introduced a new import division at the Southern Furniture Show.[8] Also, the nineteen-month strike at the Memphis-based Trojan-Dante Luggage Co., with whom the UFWA had had contracts for twenty years, illustrates the effort taken by the employer to cut labor costs through importation and other means. Members of UFWA local 282 walked off the job in April 1985 when contract negotiations reached an impasse. The company was asking for a three-year wage freeze and wanted to revoke the twenty-year-old, company-provided, health insurance plan by requiring the workers to pay $45–$65 per month. Over the previous few years, the company had cut its workforce from six hundred to seventy, as it relocated roughly 85 percent of its plant production in Taiwan and South Korea, where workers were paid about $1.50 an hour. The company replaced the striking Memphis workers, whose average hourly wage was $4.96, with strikebreakers whom they paid $3.35 an hour. After a national boycott of Trojan-Dante products, a five-hundred-person rally in Memphis with participation by the labor and civil rights movements, and the awarding to the company of a place on the AFL-CIO Dishonor Roll, the workers and the company settled in October 1986. The workers won a $.30 per hour wage increase and over $100,000 in back pay.[9]

Increased union-busting efforts taken by employers in the form of union decertification campaigns also jeopardized existing UFWA membership. Between 1950 and 1970, the UFWA experienced five decertification elections and won two of them. Between 1970 and 1984, the UFWA participated in thirty-three decertification elections and won seventeen, or 52 percent, of them. From the sixteen decertification elections in which it was defeated during 1970–1984, the UFWA lost a total of 1,554 members, roughly 14 percent of the 1970–1985 UFWA membership loss.[10]

Employer resistance to the UFWA is illustrated by the decertification of the UFWA bargaining unit at the Indiana Desk Co. in Jasper, IN, a small, southern Indiana furniture manufacturing town known as "America's Woodworking Capital." In March 1982, 170 members of UFWA local 334, which had been in place for some forty years, struck the company during an impasse in contract negotiations. The company wanted to cut wages, substitute its own pension and insurance plans for the UFWA plans, and determine unilaterally the incentive pay rates for piece work (i.e., with no worker right to negotiate and arbitrate these pay rates). To mobilize the largely Catholic workforce, the UFWA brought in a Catholic priest, who cited various papal encyclicals to encourage worker support of the union.

---

[8] Ibid., May 1971, p. 7.
[9] Ibid., May 1985, pp. 1, 5; September 1985, p. 1; October 1985, pp. 1, 4; December 1985, p. 1; January 1986, pp. 1, 4; March 1986, p. 2; September–October 1986, p. 2.
[10] *Proceedings,* 1950–1984 UFWA conventions.

The UFWA called on the AFL-CIO to declare a national boycott of the company and conducted mass rallies, attended by several thousand representatives of UFWA locals and other international unions, in June and September 1982.

The company hired strikebreakers to work in the plant and the Indianapolis-based firm, Command Investigations Bureau (CIB), which employed armed guards and attack dogs. The plant was blocked from view with twenty-foot-high stacks of lumber, and dogs were allowed to prowl in the plant yard. The company engendered protest from labor groups and the American Civil Liberties Union when, in November 1982, it successfully persuaded the Jasper City Council to enact an ordinance prohibiting picketing in residential areas, in order to stop the picketing in front of the owner's home. However, a federal judge issued a temporary restraining order in February 1983, barring Jasper officials from enforcing the ordinance. Also, the city council denied the company a zoning variance for setting up a trailer to house the CIB guards, whom the UFWA accused of spying on workers in their homes and wiretapping their phones.

In September 1983, Indiana Desk was placed among the top five companies on the AFL-CIO's Dishonor Roll of Labor Law Violators. By January 1983, the National Labor Relations Board had issued four complaints against the company and, in some cases, against the CIB, for committing unfair labor practices including prolonging the strike by refusing to bargain in good faith and for assaulting, threatening, and carrying out surveillance of the strikers. In addition, the company was cited for violating the Indiana Occupational Safety and Health Act by padlocking thirteen exits, creating serious fire hazards. After hearing worker testimony, which began in December 1983, the NLRB, in April 1985, found the company guilty of numerous acts of violence. These acts included "threatening employees by a display of weapons, attack dogs and a martial arts performance by the CIB guards"; "menacing employee Oscar Warman and trying to force his vehicle off the road while pointing a pistol and camera out of the window of their vehicle toward Warman"; "threatening to kill employee Dedrick"; and shoving "striking employee Hawkins into the street and threatening to tear his head off."[11]

Despite these infractions, or perhaps because of them, the company mounted a successful union decertification campaign by mobilizing antiunion workers to file for decertification. By the time of the decertification election in April 1986, roughly two-thirds of the plant workforce consisted of non-union employees who had been hired after the beginning of the strike as strikebreakers. The UFWA was decertified by a vote of 85 to 63. The new hires tended to vote for decertification, while the union gained

[11] *Furniture Workers Press*, April 1985, p. 1.

most of its support from the workers who had been hired before the strike.[12]

Employer resistance to unionization was buttressed by the conservative national political conditions prevailing during the 1970s and 1980s. The predominantly Republican chain of presidents often staffed the NLRB with pro-management appointees whom the UFWA officers accused of thwarting union organizing efforts. The UFWA condemned Presidents Nixon, Ford, and Reagan for sympathizing with business interests, providing insufficient tariff protection for domestic industry from foreign imports, fostering an anti-union political climate, and encouraging employer union-busting, as in the case of Reagan's dismantling of PATCO, the air traffic controllers union, in 1981.[13]

Consistent with its liberal-left political stance, the UFWA supported liberal Democratic presidential candidates, and other Democrats in the absence of liberal ones, during this period. In 1972, the UFWA supported McGovern over Nixon, claiming that the former was a "friend of working people" and that the latter was a "principal author of the anti-labor Taft-Hartley Act."[14] Nixon was also condemned by the UFWA for appointing a pro-business NLRB chair who voted with management seventy times in seventy-three decisions. In 1976, the UFWA endorsed Carter over Ford, arguing that Carter would sign the repeal of section 14B of the Taft-Hartley Act, which enabled states to enact right-to-work laws, if Congress voted to repeal section 14B.[15] During the Democratic presidential primary in 1980, the UFWA supported Kennedy because he was "the only candidate . . . with a program that would help workers . . . instead of big business."[16] In 1984, claiming that "another four years of Reagan . . . would pose a mortal threat to the labor movement, to American democracy and civil rights, and to the very existence of life on earth," the UFWA convention resolved

---

[12] Ibid., May 1982, pp. 1, 4, 8; September 1982, p. 4; October 1982, pp. 1, 4; November 1982, pp. 1, 7; December 1982, pp. 1, 5; January 1983, p. 3; February 1983, p. 1; March 1983, pp. 1, 3; April 1983, p. 8; October 1983, p. 1; January 1984, p. 1; April 1985, p. 1; telephone interviews with Carl Scarbrough and Nilda Villar on May 26, 1987.

[13] *Proceedings of the Seventeenth Constitutional Convention of the United Furniture Workers of America—AFL-CIO*, Memphis, June 5–9, 1972, pp. 25–26, 50; *Proceedings of the Eighteenth Constitutional Convention of the United Furniture Workers of America—AFL-CIO*, Louisville, KY, June 10–14, 1974, p. 6A; *Proceedings of the Nineteenth Constitutional Convention of the United Furniture Workers of America—AFL-CIO*, Milwaukee, May 17–21, 1976, p. 59; *Proceedings of the Twenty-First Constitutional Convention of the United Furniture Workers of America—AFL-CIO*, Nashville, June 5–6, 1982, pp. 22, 26–27; *Proceedings of the Twenty-Second Constitutional Convention of the United Furniture Workers of America—AFL-CIO*, Chicago, June 25–29, 1984, p. 28; *Furniture Workers Press*, October 1972, p. 3.

[14] *Furniture Workers Press*, July/August/September 1972, pp. 1, 5–8.

[15] Ibid., October, 1972, pp. 1, 7; July/August/September 1976, pp. 1, 3.

[16] Ibid., April 1980, p. 1.

"wholeheartedly" to support Mondale.[17] Conservative political conditions prevailed nonetheless, and the UFWA bemoaned their dampening effect on union organizing during the 1970s and 1980s.

In sum, existing UFWA membership was jeopardized during the 1970s and 1980s by conservative political conditions, recessionary macroeconomic conditions, and increased employer efforts to cut labor costs by avoiding or resisting the union. Membership jeopardization, in turn, drained the UFWA of some of its resources vital to conducting organizing drives.

Union Organizing

In attempting to replenish its membership losses, the UFWA conducted 540 representation elections between 1970 and 1984. The UFWA victory rate in these elections, shown in Table 5.4, was similar to that of earlier periods. The 1970–1984 victory rates in Table 5.4 may be compared with those for the 1950–1960 and 1960–1970 periods in Table 4.2 in Chapter 4. During the 1970–1984 period, the UFWA won 63.1 percent of its representation elections, a victory rate of magnitude similar to those of the earlier periods. The 1970–1984 regional victory rates were also similar to those of the earlier periods. The UFWA was most successful in the East and West and least successful in the South and Midwest. Furthermore, the establishment size differential in UFWA victory rates declined during 1970–1984. Although the UFWA continued to be more successful in small shops than in large shops in the East and West, the gap in victory rates between small- and large-shop elections virtually disappeared in the South and Midwest during the 1970–1984 period.

The pattern of UFWA organizing during the 1970–1984 period differed in two ways from that of the earlier periods, indicating a deceleration in organizing activity. First, the UFWA participated in approximately the same number of elections during the fourteen-year 1970–1984 period as it had during each of the previous ten-year periods. Second, despite the fact that the growth rate of large furniture establishments exceeded that of small ones, the percentage of UFWA elections conducted in shops with one hundred or more workers declined over the post–World War II period, as shown in Table 5.5. The percentage of large-shop elections declined in all regions between the 1950–1960 and 1970–1984 periods. In the South, this decline occurred between the 1950–1960 and 1960–1970 periods and stabilized during the 1970–1984 period. For western elections, which never accounted for more than 17 percent of UFWA representation elections between 1950 and 1984 (see Table 5.4), the percentage

---

[17] *Proceedings,* 1984 UFWA Convention, p. 218.

Table 5.4
Percentage of UFWA Representation Elections Won, by Region and Establishment Size, 1970–1984

Region and Establishment Size[a]	%
East	70.3
	(209)[b]
Less than 100 workers	72.3
	(195)
100 or more workers	42.9
	(14)
Midwest	50.0
	(88)
Less than 100 workers	49.2
	(63)
100 or more workers	52.0
	(25)
South	54.6
	(152)
Less than 100 workers	56.0
	(91)
100 or more workers	52.5
	(61)
West	73.6
	(91)
Less than 100 workers	80.8
	(73)
100 or more workers	44.4
	(18)
Total	63.1
	(540)

Sources: *Proceedings* of the 1970–1984 UFWA constitutional conventions.
[a] Number of workers eligible to vote.
[b] Number of elections in parentheses.

of large-shop elections declined between the first two periods and increased between the latter two periods. During the 1970–1984 period, then, the rate of UFWA participation in representation elections was lower than that of previous periods, as was the percentage of elections it conducted in large shops.

In light of the recessionary macroeconomic conditions that prevailed throughout much of the 1970–1984 period, the deceleration in organizing

Table 5.5
Percentage of UFWA Representation Elections
Held in Shops with 100 or More Workers, by Region, 1950–1984

Region	1950–1960[a]	1960–1970[a]	1970–1984[a]
East	21.1	16.3	6.7
	(261)[b]	(233)	(209)
Midwest	43.5	41.1	28.4
	(124)	(112)	(88)
South	51.9	38.7	40.1
	(135)	(124)	(152)
West	21.2	4.4	19.8
	(66)	(45)	(91)

Sources: *Proceedings* of the 1950–1984 UFWA constitutional conventions.
[a] Time periods begin and end in May or June of the stated year.
[b] Number of elections in parentheses.

activity is not unexpected. Throughout much of the twentieth century, workers have often been most conscious of job security and least inclined to pay union dues and risk employer reprisal for union organizing during recessionary periods of the business cycle. Moreover, to the extent these recessionary macroeconomic conditions, as well as the growing volume of furniture imports, generated plant shutdowns and, consequently, local union closures, the resulting losses in membership and revenues limited UFWA organizing capacity.

Employer union-avoidance behavior, discussed earlier, also took resources away from organizing, as implied by the lengthy and complex effort made by the UFWA during the decertification campaign at Indiana Desk and the growing number of decertification elections. Similarly, geographical capital mobility into low-wage, non-union areas generated plant shutdowns, local union closures, and membership and revenue losses. Also, non-union employers continued their union-prevention efforts by raising wages, as they had done during the 1950s and 1960s (see Chapter 4), closing the wage differential between union and non-union workers, as shown in Table 5.6. Between 1968 and 1986, this wage differential declined in most regions, and, in the Southeast, the average wage of non-union production workers exceeded that of union workers.

Geographical capital mobility into the low-wage southern states with right-to-work laws also detracted in subtle but strong ways from UFWA organizing capacity. Right-to-work laws outlaw union-shop labor agreements with employers, whereby all workers in the bargaining unit must join the union after a probationary employment period. Rather than organizing new shops, local unions in right-to-work states often conduct "internal" organizing drives after the shop has been unionized and a labor

Table 5.6
Ratio of Non-Union to Union Hourly Wages for Wood Household Furniture (Nonupholstered) Production Workers, by Region, 1968 and 1986

Year	New England	Middle Atlantic	Border States	Southeast	Southwest	Great Lakes	Pacific	All Regions[a]
1968	91.7	95.0	90.5	100.0	107.3	91.9	82.9	85.9
1986	94.9	81.6	n.a.	105.3	—	94.6	83.9	87.2

Sources: U.S. Department of Labor, Bureau of Labor Statistics, *Industry Wage Survey, Wood Household Furniture, Except Upholstered, October 1968*, Bulletin no. 1651 (Washington, DC: Government Printing Office, 1970), Table 1, p. 5; *Industry Wage Survey: Wood Household Furniture, June 1986*, Bulletin no. 2283 (Washington, DC: Government Printing Office, 1987), Table 1, p. 3.
[a]Includes the Middle West and Mountain regions, not shown separately.

agreement has been signed, in order to recruit as union members those employees who had previously failed to join the union. Indeed, weakening union security arrangements was part of the anti-union intent of the 1947 Taft-Hartley Act, which permitted states to enact right-to-work laws.[18]

As the UFWA gained more southern members, then, its resources were partly deployed in internal organizing drives, rather than in organizing campaigns among non-union shops. For example, the UFWA organized the La-Z-Boy plant in Florence, SC, in February 1971, chartering local 276. In October 1972, local 276, having formed a Women's Organizing Committee, conducted an internal organizing drive and increased its membership by 50 percent. In October 1973, International UFWA President Fred Fulford appointed Secretary-Treasurer Carl Scarbrough to conduct internal organizing drives in right-to-work states.[19] According to the *Furniture Workers Press,* the rationale for these organizing drives in shops that lacked union-shop agreements was as follows: "If a plant is only half organized, the boss knows it, and when he deals with workers at the bargaining table he's not very convinced that they have full backing.... So everyone's bargaining strength is reduced and all workers get less from the boss."[20]

To increase local union bargaining strength, then, locals that lacked union-shop agreements utilized local union and International UFWA resources for conducting internal organizing drives. In addition, these locals tended to generate lower financial resources for the International UFWA than the locals with union-shop agreements. In order not to alienate union members in right-to-work states from the union, the International often exonerated these locals, as permitted under the UFWA constitution, from paying in full the constitutionally required monthly "per capita tax" to the International, lest the International cause individual member disaffections and disaffiliations from these local unions over the affordability of union dues. On the average, the UFWA exonerated two or three locals annually from paying in full the per capita tax.[21]

In sum, UFWA organizing activity decelerated during the 1970–1984 period as membership decline, resulting from recessionary macroeconomic conditions, growing furniture imports, and increased employer anti-union behavior, effectively compelled the UFWA to divert some of its resources away from organizing and to deploy them for maintaining existing membership. The UFWA took further efforts to check the decline and cut its operating expenses.

[18] Cornfield, "Declining Union Membership."
[19] *Furniture Workers Press,* February 1971, p. 1; October 1972, p. 11.
[20] Ibid., October 1973, p. 2.
[21] Cornfield, "Decline and Diversification."

Checking Membership Decline and Cutting Operating Expenses

During the 1970s and 1980s, the UFWA continued some of the policies it had initiated in the previous period (1950–1970) for checking membership decline and strengthening its organizing effort. These included local union consolidation; organizing of non-furniture workers; geographical wage standardization, to limit capital mobility to low-wage areas; and coordinated bargaining. The UFWA also took new initiatives, in the form of amending the UFWA constitution, in streamlining its operations. Furthermore, these constitutional amendments, which dealt with the governance of the International, affected the formal accessibility of the UFWA general executive board to aspirants for elective office.

Continuing Earlier Policies

The UFWA continued three of the policies it had initiated in earlier eras. First, in an effort to free the International organizers from servicing local unions and to reduce local union administrative expenses, it promoted the policy of local union mergers it had first initiated at the founding UFWA convention in 1939 (see Chapter 3). During the 1970s and 1980s, some thirty locals participated in fifteen mergers.[22]

Second, the UFWA increasingly diversified the target groups of its organizing campaigns by organizing non-furniture workers. This practice was first started during the formative period (1939–1950). The number of non-furniture worker UFWA members had grown sufficiently by the late 1950s that the UFWA, at its 1958 convention, enlarged its membership eligibility requirements, as provided in the UFWA constitution, to include non-furniture workers. Between 1967 and 1982, the percentage of UFWA locals consisting of workers in shops whose products were not included in the UFWA's official membership jurisdiction increased from 8 percent to 28 percent. These tended to be new locals located in the factory-dense, metropolitan areas of regions with high rates of UFWA membership declines, including the New England, Middle Atlantic, and Great Lakes regions.[23]

Third, in its effort to achieve geographically uniform employment conditions and, thereby, lower the rate of geographical capital mobility, the UFWA practiced the policy of chain plant organizing and coordinated bargaining it had initiated during its formative period and used successfully during the 1950s and 1960s (see Chapter 4). Like the chain plant

---

[22] *Proceedings*, 1974 UFWA Convention, p. 16A; unpublished data from the UFWA archives in Nashville, TN.
[23] Cornfield, "Decline and Diversification."

councils that had been established in earlier periods, those which were established during the 1970s consisted of all UFWA local unions that represented the workers of a single multi-plant, or chain, company. The purpose of the councils was to coordinate collective bargaining among the participating locals, in order to achieve similar employment conditions in all plants of the chain.[24]

Councils were established for the workers at the DeSoto, Little Rock-Oklahoma-Memphis Furniture, and La-Z-Boy companies. The DeSoto Council, established in November 1974, included UFWA local 383 in Canton, MS, local 379 in Union, MS, local 396 in Russellville, AR, and local 281 in Fort Smith, AR. At its founding meeting in Memphis, the DeSoto Council planned to meet biannually and, through coordinated bargaining, to achieve similar insurance, pension, vacation, and holiday benefits; cost of living protection; a $3 per hour minimum wage and common contract expiration dates. Given that all of the DeSoto locals were located in right-to-work states and lacked union-shop agreements, the council encouraged internal organizing drives. The number unionized in the smaller Mississippi plants approached 100 percent, but an internal organizing drive was conducted at the four large DeSoto plants represented by local 281 By March 1976, the membership in DeSoto plants had increased by 20 percent.[25]

The Memphis–Little Rock-Oklahoma Furniture Council was established shortly after the UFWA's 2-to-1 organizing victory at the Memphis Furniture Co., whose one thousand-person workforce was predominantly black, in May 1977. The victory at Memphis Furniture was the culmination of a long organizing campaign that included a mass rally attended by religious leaders and such civil rights and labor activists as Bayard Rustin, head of the A. Philip Randolph Institute, and Congressman Harold Ford in February 1977; and a speech by Coretta King, widow of Dr. Martin Luther King, which was attended by several thousand people in April 1977. The council consisted of UFWA local 282, which represented the Memphis Furniture workers, and Little Rock, AR, local 397 and Guthrie, OK, local 272, which represented workers in the sister Little Rock and Oklahoma Furniture companies. Like the DeSoto Council, union representatives from all three plants attended the bargaining sessions in each plant. Local 282's first contract with Memphis Furniture was signed in March 1978. Among the many gains in this two-year contract were a $.50 per hour wage increase, two additional paid holidays, UFWA insurance coverage, a strong

---

[24] *Proceedings of the First Constitutional Convention of the United Furniture Workers of America—CIO*, Rockford, IL, February 13–17, 1939, p. 175; *Proceedings of the Second Constitutional Convention of the United Furniture Workers of America—CIO*, Chicago, May 19–23, 1941, pp. 89–90.

[25] *Furniture Workers Press,* December 1974, p. 8; April 1976, p. 5.

grievance procedure, seniority rights, and job bidding rights. The coordinated bargaining that occurred in the wake of the Memphis Furniture settlement led to contract gains for locals 272 and 397. Local 272 received its first paid holiday, $.35–$.70 per hour wage increases, a stronger grievance procedure, and job bidding rights. Local 397 secured a $.90 per hour wage increase over the life of the three-year contract, UFWA insurance coverage, two additional paid holidays, and paid jury duty.[26]

The UFWA conducted an organizing campaign among the five non-union La-Z-Boy plants during the 1970s and early 1980s. Local 416 of the UFWA had represented the workers at La-Z-Boy headquarters in Monroe, MI, since 1954. The UFWA established a La-Z-Boy Council after its successful seven-month organizing campaign at the Florence, SC, La-Z-Boy plant in February 1971. During the Florence campaign, the company attempted to thwart the union by offering wage raises, holding fish fries, running captive meetings, and turning over the workforce. With assistance from the AFL-CIO Organizing and Industrial Union departments and the Textile Workers, the UFWA won the Florence election 260 to 173, creating local 276 and gaining its strongest support from black workers, who constituted roughly 60 percent of the workforce. Also, the predominantly white local 416 members sent letters, copies of their paycheck stubs, and photographs to the Florence workers, encouraging them to unionize. By March 1971, International Secretary-Treasurer Carl Scarbrough had begun to coordinate collective bargaining negotiations between the Monroe and Florence workers. In August, the Monroe and Florence workers began what was to become a nine-week strike, and the AFL-CIO Union Label Department declared a nationwide La-Z-Boy boycott. Also, the workers in the non-union La-Z-Boy plant in Neosho, MO, walked off the job shortly thereafter. The Monroe and Florence strikers settled with the company in October, receiving $.45 to $.80 per hour wage increases and other benefits, and the Neosho workers returned to work with a consent election promised by the company. The Monroe and Florence workers pledged to meet regularly to inform themselves of contractual and grievance settlements in their plants. In June 1972, locals 416 and 276, as well as the workers in the non-union Neosho, Newton, MS, and Redlands, CA, La-Z-Boy plants, established the UFWA National La-Z-Boy Workers Council.

The UFWA encountered much company resistance and was unable to organize the remaining non-union plants in the La-Z-Boy chain. The union's organizing drives at La-Z-Boy plants persisted through the early 1980s. However, the company deployed several tactics for preventing unionization. For example, in the Newton, MS, plant, whose workforce was

---

[26] Ibid., February 1977, pp. 1, 5; April 1977, p. 8; May 1977, p. 1; October 1977, p. 5; March 1978, pp. 1, 8.

approximately 60 percent white, the company gave preferential treatment in job assignments to white workers, dividing the workers along racial lines. Although the UFWA filed a suit against the company for civil rights violations and received a $32,500 settlement from it, the UFWA failed to organize the plant. During the organizing campaign at the Redlands, CA, plant in April 1973, the company distributed anti-union literature, attempted to convince the workers that they would never recover the wages lost during a strike, and defeated the union. In January 1978, the NLRB upheld UFWA charges that the company had threatened and illegally discharged workers during the organizing campaigns at the Redlands and Dayton, TN, La-Z-Boy plants. In January 1981, the court ordered the company to reinstate and pay $80,000 in back pay to four Dayton workers whom it had illegally fired for union activity. Encountering persistent company resistance, which included the provision of union-scale wages and benefits to non-union workers, the UFWA was unable to organize the Newton, Redlands, Neosho, and Dayton La-Z-Boy plants. Nonetheless, the La-Z-Boy Council continued to engage in coordinated bargaining throughout the 1970s and 1980s and to include worker representatives from the non-union La-Z-Boy plants at its meetings. In November 1986, the Monroe and Florence workers achieved similar contracts, including wage and fringe benefit increases.[27]

In sum, the UFWA attempted to replenish its membership losses and strengthen its organizing effort by continuing its policies of local union consolidation, membership diversification, and chain plant organizing. The UFWA also amended its constitution to cut the administrative and operating expenses of the International.

Cutting International Expenses

To reduce the expenses of the International, the UFWA amended four of its constitutional provisions that also pertained to membership access to elective GEB positions. These amendments might have lowered the turnover rate of GEB members, but most were short-lived or enacted in the latter part of the 1970–1984 period, after turnover had already occurred. First, the UFWA attempted to reduce the frequency of its conventions, in order to reduce this expense. Given that union conventions provided aspirants to elective office the opportunity to become known among the electorate, the convention meeting frequency might have affected the capacity of opposition leadership to develop. At its 1976 convention, the

---

[27] Ibid., February 1971, pp. 1, 3; March 1971, pp. 4, 5; September 1971, pp. 1, 3, 8; October 1971, pp. 1, 3, 4; May 1972, p. 8; June 1972, pp. 1, 3; May 1973, p. 8; October 1973, p. 7; June 1974, p. 3; May 1976, p. 4; February 1977, p. 4; February 1978, p. 1; December 1978, p. 8; February 1981, pp. 1, 5; November 1986, p. 5; telephone interviews with Carl Scarbrough and Nilda Villar on May 26, 1987.

UFWA made an amendment to substitute quadrennial conventions of the International Union for the biennial conventions that had taken place since the UFWA's founding. The amendment engendered debate on the convention floor and was passed by a roll call vote with 79 percent of the votes. Proponents argued that extending the period between conventions would reduce the expenses of the International Union. Opponents held that the amendment broke with tradition and would keep the membership uninformed about the International. By the time of the 1980 UFWA convention, several GEB members and delegates had expressed their dissatisfaction with quadrennial conventions, and the UFWA reverted to biennial conventions. To reduce International expenses, the 1980 amendment required that every other convention be a short, working convention or "mini-convention" (i.e., no guest speakers, etc.) held in the city of the International headquarters. However, the quadrennial convention was reinstituted unceremoniously at the last UFWA convention in 1984.[28]

The UFWA constitution also provided for one mandatory regional convention per region that was to be attended by local union delegates from the region during the period between International conventions. Nonetheless, local unions often failed to conduct the regional conventions, in part because they complained of the expenses, and in 1974 the UFWA constitution was amended, making the regional conventions noncompulsory. When quadrennial International conventions were substituted for biennial ones in 1976, the UFWA reinstituted mandatory regional conventions to compensate for the lost meeting time that was generated by the shift to quadrennial International conventions. Throughout most of the 1970–1984 period, then, the UFWA retained the same International and regional convention meeting frequency it had previously had.[29]

Second, at its 1976 convention, the UFWA extended the terms of office for all GEB positions from two to four years. This constitutional amendment, which was the first change in the term of office since the UFWA founding, was made in conjunction with the amendment for instituting quadrennial International conventions and, therefore, was debated along with the debate over convention meeting frequency. The roll call vote described earlier also served to enact this constitutional amendment. Unlike the quadrennial convention, the four-year term of office remained intact after 1976.[30] However, the turnover rate of GEB members

---

[28] *Proceedings*, 1976 UFWA Convention, pp. 155–163, 166; *Proceedings*, 1984 UFWA Convention, pp. 110–111; *Proceedings of the Twentieth Constitutional Convention of the United Furniture Workers of America—AFL-CIO*, Nashville, June 16–21, 1980, pp. 237–239.
[29] *Proceedings*, 1974 UFWA Convention, pp. 115–118; *Proceedings*, 1976 UFWA Convention, pp. 155–163, 166.
[30] *Proceedings*, 1976 UFWA Convention, pp. 155–163, 166.

did not change in a consistent pattern after 1976 (see Chapter 1, Table 1.3), suggesting that this amendment had little impact on GEB turnover.

Third, the 1970 UFWA convention amended the constitution to allow salaried International and local union representatives (i.e., organizers) with at least ten years of service, who were local union members but who otherwise did not satisfy the eligibility requirements for elective office (i.e., they had insufficient work experience in the furniture industry or under a UFWA contract), to serve on the GEB. The rationale was to provide an inducement to the representatives not to quit their jobs. In principle, such GEB members could be subjected to the control of the UFWA president, who had the authority to hire and fire them as organizers, thereby inhibiting opposition and perpetuating the incumbent leadership as described by Michels's iron law of oligarchy. However, at its 1972 convention, the UFWA amended its constitution, with no debate, prohibiting these representatives from serving on the GEB.[31]

Fourth, to encourage local union mergers and accommodate the increased number of local unions that, following the UFWA's pro-merger policy (see Chapter 4), had grown, the UFWA amended its constitutional provision for the maximum permissible number of members from a local union who could serve on the GEB. Prior to 1970, the UFWA constitution allowed a local with less than 1,000 members to have no more than one member on the GEB and, for each larger local, no more than two members on the GEB. In 1970, the constitution was amended to allow no more than three members of each local with 3,000 or more members to serve on the GEB. To encourage further local union mergers, the constitution was amended in 1974, permitting a local with less than 1,000 members a maximum of one GEB member; a local with 1,000 to 1,999 members no more than two GEB members; a local with 2,000 to 3,999 members a maximum of three GEB members; and a local with 4,000 or more members a maximum of four GEB members.[32]

By increasing the maximum permissible number of large local union members who could serve on the GEB, these constitutional amendments might have effectively reduced the number of locals in competition with one another for elective offices and, thereby, lowered the turnover rate of GEB members. Indeed, similar fears of large local domination of the GEB were expressed by small local union delegates at the 1974 UFWA convention and at the founding UFWA convention in 1939, when large locals were first permitted to have more members on the GEB than small locals

---

[31] *Proceedings of the Sixteenth Constitutional Convention of the United Furniture Workers of America—AFL-CIO*, New York, May 18–22, 1970, pp. 183–185; *Proceedings*, 1972 UFWA Convention, pp. 166–167.

[32] *Proceedings*, 1970 UFWA Convention, p. 159; *Proceedings*, 1974 UFWA Convention, pp. 129–133.

Table 5.7
Percentage of GEB Members from Local Unions
with 2 or More Members on the GEB, 1968–1984

Year	%
1968	40.0 (25)[a]
1970	28.6 (28)
1972	46.4 (28)
1974	35.7 (28)
1976	25.0 (28)
1980	39.3 (28)
1984	32.1 (28)

Source: *Proceedings* of the 1968–1984 UFWA constitutional conventions.
[a] Total number of GEB members in parentheses. This number omits the president and the secretary-treasurer, whose local unions, according to the UFWA constitution, are excluded from the calculation of the maximum permissible number of GEB members per local union.

(see Chapter 3).[33] However, the large locals failed to capture an increasing share of GEB seats. As shown in Table 5.7, the percentage of GEB members from locals with two or more members on the GEB fluctuated in a nonlinear manner between 1968 and 1984. This may have resulted from unevenness in the growth rates of the large local unions. Some large locals grew by absorbing other locals, such as Sheboygan, WI, local 800; or by conducting successful organizing campaigns, such as Memphis local 282; or by mergers such as New York City local 76B-92-76. These locals tended to increase their shares of GEB positions. Other large locals including Gardner, MA, local 154, Baltimore local 75, and Chicago local 18B lost members, and their shares of GEB seats tended to decline.[34] Therefore, it is unlikely that these constitutional amendments affected the turnover rate of GEB members. Had most of the large locals been able to increase their memberships, these constitutional amendments might have contributed to leadership stabilization on the GEB.

Recessionary macroeconomic conditions, increasing furniture imports, conservative national political conditions, and growing employer

---
[33] *Proceedings*, 1974 UFWA Convention, pp. 129–133.
[34] *Proceedings*, 1970–1984 UFWA conventions.

resistance to unions, then, accelerated the vicious cycle of UFWA local union turnover, generating membership decline during the 1970s and 1980s. In response, the UFWA endeavored to protect its existing membership, strengthen its organizing effort, and reduce the expenses of operating the International. Although the constitutional amendments that were taken as cost-reduction steps pertained to the accessibility of the GEB to aspirants to elective office, they were too temporary or occurred too late to lower the relatively high turnover rate of GEB members during this period. Rather than through its effects on the UFWA governmental structure, membership decline contributed to GEB turnover by compelling the union to incorporate new ethnic minorities and women into leadership positions.

More importantly, ethnic minorities and women, motivated by the civil rights and women's movements, mobilized within the UFWA and gained access to leadership positions during this period. Furthermore, ethnic minorities and women were of strategic importance to the UFWA's organizing effort because their proportions of the furniture industry labor force and UFWA membership had increased and because they were among the most pro-union groups in the industry. Moreover, the emergence of ethnic minorities and women on the GEB was facilitated by the UFWA's ideological tradition, a legacy of beliefs about working class unity that eased the leadership transition sparked by aspiring ethnic and gender membership groups.

The Emergence of Minorities and Women into UFWA Leadership Positions

Minorities and women rose into leadership positions after they came to comprise a significant proportion of wage earners in furniture manufacturing. With increased political strength in the UFWA, the legitimation by top leadership of ethnic and gender integration, and the inspiration of the civil rights movement, minorities and women mobilized for increased participation in UFWA governance.

The Entry of Ethnic Minorities and Women into Furniture Manufacturing

During the 1960s and 1970s, new ethnic minorities and women entered furniture manufacturing at increasing rates, as they did nonagricultural industries generally. The entry of blacks, Hispanics, and women into nonagricultural jobs was stimulated in part by the civil rights and women's movements and the subsequent enactment of civil rights legislation, especially the Civil Rights Act of 1964, which banned discriminatory hiring practices by employers. Also, changes in the previous employment patterns of these groups compelled or motivated them to find new sources of employment. With the mechanization of agriculture in the South and Southwest, blacks and Hispanics left the farms for urban employment in manufacturing and services. As sex roles changed, legitimizing the employment of women, and inflation made the one-breadwinner family economically infeasible, women's labor force participation rates escalated enormously during the 1960s and 1970s.[35]

The entry of ethnic minorities and women coincided with the emergence of a "segmented," or "dual," labor market in the United States. Labor market segmentation resulted from unevenness in the rates of growth, capital-intensification, and unionization among U.S. industries. The primary sector of the labor market prevailed in the core of the economy: the large, capital-intensive, unionized corporations in oligopolistic industries that dealt in international markets. Primary sector jobs were characterized by relatively high wages, career mobility, and job security. In contrast, jobs in the secondary sector, which prevailed in the economic periphery of small, labor-intensive, non-union firms, provided relatively low wages, little career mobility, and high rates of employee turnover.[36]

As ethnic minorities and women entered the nonagricultural economy, they became disproportionately employed in periphery industries and secondary sector jobs. Educational barriers and employer discrimination often prevented ethnic minorities and women from employment in the primary sector. Ethnic minorities tended to be employed in low-wage manufacturing and service jobs. Women also tended to be employed in these jobs, as well as in the office clerical jobs of the core industries.[37]

As a growing, low-wage, periphery industry, furniture manufacturing received many ethnic minorities and women between 1960 and 1986, shown in Table 5.8. Blacks accounted for a growing share of furniture manufacturing employment (column 1). Between 1960 and 1980, the percentage black in furniture manufacturing increased from 7.4 percent to 10.9 percent, slightly higher than that of all U.S. employment and manufacturing employment, and then declined 1 percent by 1986. Similarly, the

---

[35] William Wilson, *The Declining Significance of Race* (Chicago: University of Chicago Press, 1978), pp. 62–121; Vernon Briggs, Jr., Walter Fogel, and Fred Schmidt, *The Chicano Worker* (Austin, TX: University of Texas Press, 1977), p. 18; Daniel Cornfield, "Women in the Automated Office: Computers, Work and Prospects for Unionization," in *Advances in Industrial and Labor Relations*, vol. 4, eds., David Lipsky, Donna Sockell, and David Lewin (Greenwich, CT: JAI Press, 1987).

[36] David Gordon, Richard Edwards, and Michael Reich, *Segmented Work, Divided Workers: The Historical Transformation of Labor in the United States* (Cambridge: Cambridge University Press, 1982).

[37] Ibid., pp. 204–210.

Table 5.8
Percentages of Blacks, Hispanics, and Women in the United States, Manufacturing, and Furniture Manufacturing Workforces, 1960–1986

	(1) Blacks	(2) Hispanics	(3) Women	(4) Employment (thousands)
United States				
1960	9.4	n.a.	32.8	64,639
1970	9.6	3.8	37.8	76,554
1980	9.6	5.6	42.6	97,639
1986	9.9	6.6	44.4	109,597
Manufacturing				
1960	6.6	n.a.	25.1	17,513
1970	9.0	4.0	28.6	19,837
1980	9.9	6.8	31.9	21,915
1986	10.1	7.9	32.1	20,962
Furniture manufacturing				
1960	7.4	n.a.	17.3	377
1970	10.1	6.4	25.9	425
1980	10.9	10.0	30.7	530
1986	9.9	11.4	31.0	650

Sources. U.S. Bureau of the Census, *U.S. Census of Population: 1960,* vol. 1, *Characteristics of Population,* U.S. Summary (Washington, DC: Government Printing Office, 1964), Table 213, pp. 569–570; *Census of Population: 1970,* vol. 1, *Characteristics of Population,* U.S. Summary (Washington, DC: Government Printing Office, 1973), Table 236, p. 80; *1980 Census of Population,* vol. 1, *Characteristics of the Population,* U.S. Summary (Washington, DC: Government Printing Office, 1984), Table 287, p. 372; U.S. Department of Labor, Bureau of Labor Statistics, *Employment and Earnings,* vol. 34, no. 1, January, 1987, Table 28, p. 189.

Hispanic share of furniture manufacturing employment increased to 11.4 percent by 1986, exceeding that of their total employment in the United States and manufacturing in 1970, 1980, and 1986. Between 1960 and 1986, women's share of furniture manufacturing employment increased from 17.3 percent to 31.0 percent, slightly lower than that of manufacturing employment and even lower than that of women's share of all U.S. employment. The relatively low proportion of women in furniture manufacturing may have resulted from occupational sex segregation and, specifically, from the tendency of women to be employed in service and clerical jobs, rather than in factory jobs.[38]

---

[38] Francine Blau and Marianne Ferber, "Occupations and Earnings of Women Workers," in *Working Women: Past, Present, Future,* eds., Karen Koziara, Michael Moskow, and Lucretia Tanner (Washington, DC: Bureau of National Affairs, 1987).

Table 5.9
Percentages of Blacks, Hispanics, and Women in U.S. Furniture Manufacturing, by Region and Regional Shares, 1960–1980

Region[a]/Year	(1) Blacks	(2) Hispanics	(3) Women	(4) Employment (thousands)
East				
1960	6.6	n.a.	17.8	88.8
1970	7.2	4.6	22.8	82.5
1980	8.4	9.6	25.1	75.8
Midwest				
1960	4.8	n.a.	19.8	107.4
1970	5.5	2.4	28.3	104.7
1980	4.7	4.0	31.7	116.0
South				
1960	11.8	n.a.	14.7	122.9
1970	16.5	4.0	27.0	172.3
1980	19.4	5.1	37.9	216.4
West				
1960	3.7	n.a.	16.7	35.9
1970	4.7	33.4	20.9	37.6
1980	3.7	45.8	20.2	61.1

Sources: U.S. Bureau of the Census, *U.S. Census of Population: 1960*, vol. 1, *Characteristics of the Population* (Washington, DC: Government Printing Office, 1963), Table 129 of individual state reports; *Census of Population: 1970*, vol. 1, *Characteristics of the Population* (Washington, DC: Government Printing Office, 1973), Table 184 of individual state reports; *1980 Census of Population*, vol. 1, *Characteristics of the Population* (Washington, DC: Government Printing Office, 1983), Table 228 of individual state reports.

[a] Regions are defined as follows: East = MA, CT, NY, NJ, PA, MD; Midwest = MN, WI, IL, IN, OH, MI, MO, KY; South = VA, NC, SC, GA, FL, TN, AL, MS, AR, TX; West = CA, WA.

The entry rates of ethnic minorities and women into furniture manufacturing varied geographically. New employee groups tended to emerge in the regions with the highest rates of furniture manufacturing employment growth and, in the case of ethnic minorities, in the regions where they had resided historically, as shown in Table 5.9. The regional furniture manufacturing employment data in Table 5.9 are based on the twenty-six states with the largest amounts of furniture manufacturing employment. These states accounted for 94.2 percent of furniture manufacturing employment in 1960, 93.4 percent in 1970, and 88.5 percent in 1980, indicating geographical decentralization of the industry.

Table 5.9 (continued)

	(5) Blacks	(6) Regional Shares[b] of: Hispanics	(7) Women	(8) All
East				
1960	20.9	n.a.	24.2	23.6
1970	13.7	14.1	17.1	19.4
1980	11.0	13.7	11.7	14.3
Midwest				
1960	20.7	n.a.	32.7	28.5
1970	13.4	9.4	26.9	24.6
1980	9.5	8.8	22.7	21.9
South				
1960	51.9	n.a.	27.8	32.6
1970	66.0	25.1	42.3	40.5
1980	72.7	20.8	50.4	40.8
West				
1960	4.8	n.a.	9.2	9.5
1970	4.1	46.2	7.1	8.8
1980	3.9	52.7	7.6	11.5

[b] Percentage of each category of U.S. furniture manufacturing employees accounted for by the region. Regional percentages for a given year do not sum to 100% because the regional statistics are based on 26 states. The total number of black U.S. furniture workers was 27,938, 43,067, and 57,773 in 1960, 1970, and 1980, respectively; of Hispanics, 27,124 and 53,128 in 1970 and 1980, respectively; and of women, 65,138, 109,989, and 162,549, in 1960, 1970, and 1980, respectively.

Of the four regions in Table 5.9, the South had the highest percentage black (column 1) and experienced the greatest increase in the percentage black between 1960 and 1980. By 1980, 19.4 percent of the southern furniture manufacturing workforce was black, while that of each other region did not exceed 10 percent. Furthermore, the South came to have a disproportionately large share of all black furniture manufacturing employees in the United States (column 5). Between 1960 and 1980, the southern share of all black furniture workers in the United States jumped from 51.9 percent to 72.7 percent, even though the South never had more than 41 percent of all U.S. furniture manufacturing employment.

The increasing concentration of black furniture workers in the South is partly attributable to the high growth rate of southern furniture manufacturing (columns 4 and 8). Although, during the post–World War II era, blacks migrated northward to the metropolitan areas of the Middle Atlantic and Great Lakes regions, where furniture manufacturing employment was declining, many remained in the South, migrating from rural to urban areas and seeking factory, rather than agricultural, employment. The urbanization of southern blacks, coupled with the high growth rate of southern furniture manufacturing, led to the increasing concentration of black furniture workers in the South.[39]

Hispanic furniture workers became concentrated in the West, especially in Los Angeles, between 1970 and 1980. Of the four regions, the West had the highest percentage Hispanic, as well as the highest increase in this percentage, in furniture manufacturing. By 1980, 45.8 percent of the western furniture manufacturing workforce was Hispanic, and that of each other region did not exceed 10 percent (Table 5.9, column 2). Moreover, by 1980, the West accounted for 52.7 percent of all Hispanic furniture workers in the United States (column 6).

The concentration of Hispanic furniture workers in the West is related to the immigration and urbanization of Chicanos in the region. Throughout the twentieth century, Mexican workers migrated northward, seeking higher-wage jobs in railroad building, mining, and agriculture. Immigration from Mexico was interrupted only during the Great Depression of the 1930s. Mexican immigration was revived in 1942 with the establishment of the Bracero Program, a labor-contracting arrangement designed to increase the agricultural labor supply, especially in the Southwest. With declining agricultural employment and the dismantling of the Bracero Program in 1964, Chicanos, along with an increasing number of undocumented Mexican immigrants, migrated to urban places such as Los Angeles. As less-educated workers, Chicanos tended to be employed in low-wage service and factory jobs, such as in furniture manufacturing. Given that the western furniture manufacturing industry was growing more rapidly (Table 5.9, columns 4 and 8) than that of other places with high concentrations of Hispanic workers (e.g., Chicago and New York City), Hispanic furniture workers became concentrated in the West.[40]

[39] Wilson, *Declining Significance of Race*, pp. 62–87; Cornfield and Leners, *"Unionization in the Rural South"*; William Vickery, *The Economics of the Negro Migration 1900–1960* (New York: Arno Press, 1977), pp. 14–18; Neil Fligstein, *Going North: Migration of Blacks and Whites from the South, 1900–1950* (New York: Academic Press, 1981); Daniel Johnson and Rex Campbell, *Black Migration in America: A Social Demographic History* (Durham, NC: Duke University Press, 1981), pp. 130–132.

[40] Arthur Corwin, ed., *Immigrants—and Immigrants: Perspectives on Mexican Labor Migration to the United States* (Westport, CT: Greenwood Press, 1978), pp. 38–69, 257–295; George Borjas and Marta Tienda, eds., *Hispanics in the U.S. Economy* (Orlando, FL: Academic Press, 1985), pp. 1–12; Robert Thomas, "Microchips and Macroharvests: Labor-Management Relations in Agriculture," in *Workers, Managers, and Technical Change: Emerging Patterns of Labor Relations*, ed. Daniel Cornfield (New York: Plenum, 1987).

The percentage female in furniture manufacturing employment increased in all regions between 1960 and 1980, with the greatest increases occurring in the South and Midwest (Table 5.9, column 3). By 1980, the percentage female in the South had climbed to 37.9 percent of furniture manufacturing employment, and that in the Midwest had increased to 31.7 percent. Furthermore, women furniture workers tended to concentrate in these regions. The southern share of all U.S. women furniture workers had grown to 50.4 percent by 1980 (column 7). Although the midwestern share declined along with that of the East and West, the Midwest accounted for almost one-fourth of all U.S. women furniture workers in 1980.

The concentration of women furniture workers in the South and Midwest is attributable to both the magnitude and growth rates of furniture manufacturing in these regions. As the two regions with the largest furniture manufacturing workforces, the South and Midwest comprised over 60 percent of U.S. furniture manufacturing employment in 1960 and 1980 (Table 5.9, column 7). Also, furniture manufacturing employment grew rapidly in these areas. The South had the highest growth rates, as discussed (Table 5.9, columns 4 and 8). The data in Table 5.9 mask the relatively high rates of furniture industry growth in the Midwest, especially in nonmetropolitan areas. Between 1959 and 1982, the number of furniture factories with 100 or more employees in the metropolitan areas of the Great Lakes region declined by 22.4 percent, while that of furniture factories with 100 or more employees in the nonmetropolitan areas of the Great Lakes region increased by 31.6 percent.[41] This is consistent with the trend of industry "ruralization," especially in the Midwest, that was identified in Chapter 2. Women furniture workers, then, became concentrated in the South and Midwest.

The entry of minorities and women coincided with changes in production technology and in the occupational structure of furniture manufacturing. Beginning with the introduction of the assembly line during the 1920s, furniture manufacturers have continuously adopted new mass production technologies for assembly, wood cutting, carving and shaping, fabric cutting, painting and finishing, gluing and laminating, and other facets of furniture production. Also, the introduction of new materials including particleboard, prefinished surface laminates and film, plastic materials, and foam rubber has simplified cabinetmaking, cushion construction, and metal furniture production.[42]

Technological change was accompanied by a rise in semi-skilled, operative occupations in furniture manufacturing, as implied by U.S. cen-

---

[41] Cornfield and Leners, "Unionization in the Rural South."
[42] Edwin Henneberger, "Productivity Growth below Average in the Household Furniture Industry," *Monthly Labor Review* 101 (November 1978): 26–27.

sus data. Caution must be used in interpreting these data because the U.S. Bureau of the Census modified its occupational classification system in light of technological and occupational changes in most industries. In 1930, skilled cabinetmakers and upholsterers comprised 49 percent of the furniture production workforce; by 1980, workers employed in the skilled, "precision production, craft, and repair occupations" comprised only 32 percent of the furniture production workforce. The percentage of unskilled laborers also declined, from 18 percent in 1930 to 9 percent of the furniture production workforce in 1980. In contrast, the percentage of furniture production workers employed as semi-skilled factory operatives jumped from 34 percent to 60 percent between 1930 and 1980.

Black furniture production workers seemed to experience an occupational upgrading between 1930 and 1980. In 1930, blacks accounted for only 3 percent of the furniture production workforce, and 51 percent of black furniture workers were employed as unskilled laborers. By 1980, two-thirds of black furniture workers were employed as semi-skilled, factory operatives.

The occupational status of women furniture production workers changed little between 1930 and 1980. Women constituted only 6 percent of the furniture production workforce in 1930, and 70 percent of women furniture workers were employed as semi-skilled factory operatives. By 1980, 75 percent of women furniture workers were employed as semi-skilled factory operatives.

White male furniture production workers, compared with black and women furniture workers, were disproportionately employed in the skilled occupations, although their percentage in these occupations declined with the dissolution of the skilled crafts that accompanied technological change. In 1930, white men comprised 91 percent of the furniture production workforce; 52 percent were employed as either cabinetmakers or upholsterers, and 31 percent were employed as semi-skilled factory operatives. By 1980, the portion of the furniture production workforce that was white and male had declined to 58 percent; the portion of white male furniture workers who were employed in skilled production occupations had dropped to 41 percent; and the portion employed as semi-skilled factory operatives had increased to 51 percent.[43]

The introduction of mass production technology, then, accompanied by declines in the skilled craft and unskilled laborer occupations and the growth of semi-skilled, factory operative occupations, may have served as a

[43] The source of all occupational data in this section is the U.S. Bureau of the Census, *Fifteenth Census of the United States: 1930, Population,* vol. IV, *Occupations by States* (Washington, DC: Government Printing Office, 1933), pp. 25, 27, 29; idem, *1980 Census of Population,* vol. 2, Subject Reports, *Occupation by Industry,* PC80-2-7C (Washington, DC: Government Printing Office, 1984), pp. 50–51.

complementary "pull" force to the "push" forces that promoted the entry of minorities and women into furniture manufacturing. Along with the urbanization of blacks, the declining feasibility of the one-earner family, and the banning of discrimination, the increase in semi-skilled, operative occupations may have contributed to the entry of socially disadvantaged workers, especially minorities and women, into the growing furniture manufacturing industry.

In sum, the entry of new ethnic minorities and women into furniture manufacturing during the 1960s and 1970s was part of the broader process by which an increasingly segmented U.S. labor market absorbed these workers. With the mechanization of southern and southwestern agriculture and the subsequent urbanization of blacks and Hispanics in these regions, these socially disadvantaged workers entered the low-wage industries of the economic periphery. Similarly, as the advent of new sex roles legitimized the employment of women, and inflation challenged the one-breadwinner family, many women entered the economic periphery in low-wage jobs. Blacks, Hispanics, and women, then, entered furniture manufacturing. These groups, in turn, would mobilize and seek leadership positions in the UFWA.

The Ascent of Minorities

Several overlapping forces led to the rise of blacks and Hispanics onto the UFWA GEB during the 1970s and 1980s. With the mechanization of southern and southwestern agriculture, minorities entered the furniture manufacturing industry and the UFWA; the civil rights movement of the 1960s inspired minorities within the UFWA to mobilize and seek leadership positions in the union; the southward redistribution of the industry and UFWA membership, especially through the expansion of chain plant corporations, generated a shift in the axis of power in the UFWA away from the Northeast and toward the South, increasing black political strength in the UFWA, as well as the strategic importance of minority participation for the future growth of the declining union; and the UFWA practice of chain plant organizing, coupled with coordinated collective bargaining, galvanized workers from different regions and of diverse ethnic backgrounds to pursue their common economic interests.

In addition, an ideology of working class unity, that workers of diverse ethnic backgrounds should unite against employers who would otherwise divide them to maintain low wages, was present in the UFWA from its founding and promoted ethnic integration of UFWA leadership. The ideology, passed on to the next generation of UFWA leaders in a process of mentoring by the older generation, was proclaimed and adhered to continuously by the top UFWA leadership. Through the mentoring process, the ideology also developed a younger generation of black and Hispanic civil rights activists in the UFWA who led the mobilization in the late 1960s for minority participation in union governance.

Minority Mobilization

Inspired by the civil rights movement and by the passage of the Civil Rights Act of 1964, black and Hispanic UFWA activists began to mobilize for greater minority participation in the governance of the UFWA during the late 1960s. The mobilization led minorities to increase their representation on the GEB during the 1970s and 1980s. The rise of blacks and Hispanics onto the GEB was partly aided by the geographical redistribution of furniture manufacturing capital and UFWA membership. As the industry moved out of the urban East and Midwest and locals in these regions declined, many white, male GEB members from these regions simultaneously retired. As the industry moved into the South and West, where blacks and Hispanics resided, respectively, the political strength of these ethnic groups grew within the UFWA. Moreover, blacks and Hispanics were able to sustain their growing political influence in the UFWA by having the UFWA constitution modified in ways that promoted their views and entry onto the GEB.

The initial civil rights activity in the UFWA following the Civil Rights Act mainly addressed the eradication of racial discrimination by employers, rather than promoting minority participation in union governance. In October 1964, three months after the passage of the Civil Rights Act, AFL–CIO President George Meany called on each International union to develop an equal opportunity program for its industry and to work for the elimination of job discrimination. At its May 1965 meeting in San Diego, the UFWA GEB established an International Union Equal Opportunity Committee for ensuring that the Civil Rights Act was carried out in furniture manufacturing plants. The committee, appointed by UFWA President Pizer and chaired by International Secretary-Treasurer Fulford, consisted of Southern Vice President Carl Scarbrough and GEB members Joseph Magliacano from Newark, NJ, Charles Kaslly from South Bend, IN, and R. S. Johnson, the only black committee member, from Sumter, SC. Reporting to the 1966 UFWA convention, the committee made ten recommendations, which the convention adopted unanimously. Among the recommendations were the assignment of an International officer to work with the U.S. Equal Employment Opportunity Commission (EEOC) when complaints were filed that involved the UFWA, as well as to help UFWA members file complaints with the EEOC; the establishment of local union civil rights committees for membership education on civil rights; the encouragement of locals to actively support civil rights legislation and to ensure equal employment opportunity for minorities in plants; and the distribution of model nondiscrimination contract clauses to locals. Much of the discussion after the reading of the recommendations decried discriminatory employment practices by employers, emphasized the need to combat such discrimination, and seemed to reassure possible skeptics that whites would not be fired in order to hire minorities.[44]

The UFWA civil rights activism turned toward increasing minority participation in UFWA governance at the 1968 UFWA convention in Memphis, TN, the city of Dr. Martin Luther King's assassination earlier that year. The convention delegates stood for a moment of silence in honor of King, and Pizer began his presidential address by noting the tragedy of King's death. After the appointing of the regular convention committees, R. S. Johnson moved for the appointment of a new Committee on Minority Affairs. The motion passed unanimously. Chaired by Johnson, the nine-person committee consisted of five blacks, one Hispanic, and two whites, all of whom were men, and one native American woman of the Seneca Nation.[45]

The report of the committee to the 1968 UFWA convention, in contrast with that of the Equal Opportunity Committee at the 1966 convention, strongly emphasized the need to eliminate racism both in the nation and in the UFWA, to develop minority union leadership, and to act on, rather than give lip service to, the pro–civil rights resolutions that had been passed at previous UFWA conventions:

> We realize this is something that is not going to be changed overnight. . . . First, we feel that our International Union should see to it that there is a program for developing potential leadership of minority groups within our Union; and by doing this will assure that all ethnic groups will be represented on all levels of leadership within our Union. This is of fundamental importance and can be the driving force for . . . the elimination of racism on the human level, especially within our own Union and in the communities where we function.[46]

After much discussion in support of the committee report, the convention adopted it unanimously.

Minority participation in UFWA governance was expanded at the 1970 UFWA convention, when four regional seats, one for each of the regions, were added to the GEB with the understanding that they would be filled by

---

[44] *Proceedings of the Fourteenth Constitutional Convention of the United Furniture Workers of America—AFL-CIO,* Milwaukee, May 9–13, 1966, pp. 53–54, 219–226.
[45] *Proceedings of the Fifteenth Constitutional Convention of the United Furniture Workers of America—AFL-CIO,* Memphis, May 27–31, 1968, pp. 6, 23, 26, 190; *Furniture Workers Press,* June 1968, pp. 2–5.
[46] *Proceedings,* 1968 UFWA Convention, p. 184.

minorities. In his introductory remarks to the convention, Pizer argued for the necessity of incorporating minorities in union leadership positions, noting that "the leadership of the UFWA must represent the entire spectrum of our members."[47]

Although the proposal for adding four seats to the GEB was made by President Pizer and Secretary-Treasurer Fulford, the impetus behind the proposal came primarily from black and Hispanic activists. Leroy Clark, a black activist from Memphis, TN, local 282, was the prime mover for the proposal. Booker McCollum, a black, and Enio Carrion, a Hispanic, both from New York City local 140, were also instrumental in the effort to increase minority participation.[48]

The proposal for adding four GEB seats met with little opposition in the UFWA. Nonetheless, what differences in sentiment did exist seemed to occur along ethnic and geographical lines. Blacks from the South and urban Northeast and Hispanics tended to be the most ardent proponents of increased minority participation. Jewish leaders from the urban Northeast had historically been the most liberal or left-wing of the white ethnic groups in the UFWA and also encouraged minority participation. The white ethnic groups in the UFWA who had traditionally harbored more conservative political views, those of Northern and Western European descent from the nonmetropolitan areas of the Midwest and South and of Italian descent from the urban Northeast, tended to be uninvolved in promoting minority participation. No group actively opposed the proposal for adding seats to the GEB.[49]

In light of the differences in sentiment on the issue, the black and Hispanic activists deliberately chose to expand the GEB with geographically defined seats, rather than challenge nonminority incumbents in contested elections or define new GEB seats explicitly for minorities. Furthermore, an informal but deeply felt understanding that certain large locals could lay claim to specific GEB seats had developed in the UFWA, especially during the previous period of stability (1950–1970). The largest locals in the regions and districts tended to "claim" the geographically defined seats, and the craft seats were often claimed by the largest locals in the craft. For example, New York City local 76 claimed the upholstery seat; Sheboygan, WI, local 800 held the case goods seat; Gardner, MA, local 154 occupied the juvenile furniture seat; and New York City local 140 claimed the bedding seat. Not wishing to upset this system of local union claims to

---

[47] *Proceedings,* 1970 UFWA Convention, p. 11.
[48] Ibid., p. 153; personal interview with Booker McCollum in New York, NY, on June 14, 1985; personal interview with Enio Carrion in New York, NY, on June 13, 1985; personal interview with Leroy Clark in Memphis, TN, on May 31, 1985; personal interview with Carl Scarbrough in Nashville, TN, on July 1, 1986.
[49] McCollum, Carrion, Leroy Clark, and Scarbrough interviews.

the GEB, and seeking to avoid a fight with nonminority incumbents, the black and Hispanic activists sought to increase minority participation by expanding the GEB with new geographically defined seats. Moreover, in 1970, few of the large UFWA locals, with the exception of some of the southern and western ones, had predominantly black or Hispanic memberships who could elect minority leaders. The strategy of adding seats, then, also resulted from the lack of minority political clout within some of the large locals that laid claim to the GEB.[50]

The 1970 UFWA convention passed the amendment for adding the four regional seats. Two blacks and two Hispanics were elected to the new seats. The black GEB members were Maggie Mae Edwards, the first woman elected to the UFWA GEB, and David Driver. Edwards, from Camden, AR, local 250, filled the southern seat, and Driver, from South Haven, MI, local 439, was elected to the midwestern seat. Enio Carrion, of Puerto Rican descent and from New York City local 140, and Pino Espudo of Mexican descent and from Los Angeles local 1010, were the Hispanic GEB members and were elected to the eastern and western seats, respectively.

Given their desire to avoid confrontation with nonminority incumbents, minorities also attempted to increase their presence on the GEB by filling vacancies created by attrition. With Pizer's retirement at the 1970 convention, Secretary-Treasurer Fulford became president and Southern Vice President Carl Scarbrough, of Memphis, TN, local 282, was elected secretary-treasurer. Leroy Clark was elected southern vice president, thereby becoming the first black International UFWA officer. In 1976, when Western Vice President Fred Stefan of San Francisco local 262 retired, Espudo, the son of migrant farm workers, succeeded him in this position and became the first Hispanic International UFWA officer.[51]

Throughout the 1970s and 1980s, minorities filled GEB seats vacated by the retirement of white male GEB members from the old locals of the East and Midwest, as shown in Table 5.10, which gives the percentage distribution of all members who exited from the GEB between 1970 and 1984 and the reasons for exiting, by region, ethnicity, and gender. Of the fifty-eight GEB members who exited, 56.9 percent were white men from the East and Midwest, and 63.6 percent of these exits were due to retirement and other reasons related to old age. Between 1968 and 1970, the percentage of GEB members who were black or Hispanic jumped from 11.1 percent to 26.7 percent. During the 1970s and 1980s, almost one-third of all GEB members, on the average, were black or Hispanic, a higher proportion than that of any previous period in UFWA history (see Chapter 1, Table 1.4).

[50] Ibid.
[51] *Furniture Workers Press,* November, 1970, p. 4; *Proceedings,* 1970 UFWA Convention, pp. 149–156, 223–225; *Proceedings,* 1976 UFWA Convention, p. 285.

Table 5.10
*Percentage Distribution of GEB Exits
and Percentage of GEB Exits Due to Retirement,
by Region, Race and Ethnicity, and Gender, 1970–1984*

Region, Race and Ethnicity, Gender	Exits	Exits Due to Retirement[a]
East and Midwest, white, men	56.9	63.6
East, black[b]	6.9	100.0
South and Midwest, black, men[c]	15.5	0.0
West, men[d]	13.8	12.5
South and Midwest, women[e]	6.9	25.0
All exits	100.0	46.6
N	58	

Sources: *Proceedings* of the 1968–1984 UFWA constitutional conventions and several personal interviews with UFWA staff and members.
[a] Includes retirements, deaths, and exits due to illness.
[b] Includes 1 woman and 3 men.
[c] Includes 1 midwesterner and 8 southerners.
[d] Includes 2 Hispanics, 2 blacks, and 4 whites.
[e] Includes 2 white midwesterners and 2 black southerners.

The changing ethnic composition of the GEB during the 1970s and 1980s was also related to the geographical redistribution of UFWA membership and local unions. Indeed, less than half (46.6 percent) of the GEB exits in Table 5.10 resulted from retirements. Between 1968 and 1984, the percentage of GEB members from the declining locals in the metropolitan areas of the East and Midwest decreased, while that from the growing locals in the nonmetropolitan areas of the Midwest and South and in the metropolitan West increased (see Chapter 2, Table 2.7). Given that blacks and Hispanics were concentrated in the South and West, respectively, and controlled significant shares of the convention votes within these regions, their rise onto the GEB was partly facilitated by the redistribution of UFWA membership, and hence, convention votes, into these regions. Although the UFWA did not collect precise data on the ethnicity of its membership, the officials whom I interviewed identified the predominantly black and Hispanic locals. In the South, the large (two hundred or more members), predominantly black locals—locals 282 (Memphis), 273 (Sumter, SC), 265 (Henderson, NC), 250 (Camden, AR), 276 (Florence, SC), and 383 (Canton, MS)—controlled, on the average, 47 percent of the southern vote during the 1970s and increased their share of the southern vote to 74 percent by 1984. In contrast, the large, predominantly black and/or Hispanic locals in the East—locals 140 (New York City), 75 (Baltimore), and 75A (Baltimore)—accounted for roughly 25 percent of the eastern vote between 1970 and 1984. In the West, predominantly Hispanic local 1010 in Los Angeles held approximately half of the western votes between 1970 and 1984. During the 1970s and 1980s, then, black and Hispanic GEB members tended to come from the growing regions where they had political strength. Most of the black GEB members came from southern locals, and most of the Hispanic GEB members were from the West (see Chapter 2, Table 2.8).[52]

The emergence of minorities on the GEB during the 1970s and 1980s was also spurred by the organization and continuous mobilization of minorities, especially at UFWA conventions. The 1970 UFWA convention adopted unanimously a constitutional amendment adding a Committee on Minorities to the eight constitutionally required, regular convention committees that were appointed by the president and subject to convention approval. This committee reported on problems of minorities to all of the UFWA conventions after 1970, denouncing all forms of discrimination and calling for cooperation between the labor and civil rights movements. The committee often encouraged minority participation in union governance, especially during the early 1970s, when minorities emerged on the GEB. For example, in its report to the 1974 convention, the committee, denouncing race hatred because it was "used by the employer to divide working people," called on UFWA local unions "to make all leadership units ethnically representative of the Union's membership."[53]

In addition to their formal organization, minorities developed their own caucuses that met at many of the UFWA conventions. Blacks began caucusing in the late 1960s, and the first Latino caucus met at the 1974 convention.[54]

In sum, minorities within the UFWA, inspired in the late 1960s by the civil rights movement, mobilized for, and achieved, participation in union governance. Several factors facilitated minority mobilization. As furniture manufacturing capital and UFWA membership shifted southward and westward out of the metropolitan areas of the East and Midwest, the political strength of blacks and Hispanics, who were concentrated in the South and West, respectively, increased at UFWA conventions. Along with the geographical redistribution of capital and union membership came the retirement of white male GEB members from the East and Midwest whose union careers had been bolstered by the stability of their large, old, amalgamated locals that had dominated the GEB during the 1950s and 1960s. Southern blacks and western Hispanics, then, filled many of the GEB seats vacated by the retirees. Finally, minorities sustained their mobilization by

[52] *Proceedings* of the 1970–1984 UFWA conventions.
[53] *Proceedings*, 1970 UFWA Convention, pp. 148–149. Quotations from *Proceedings*, 1974 UFWA Convention, pp. 94, 96.
[54] McCollum interview; *Furniture Workers Press*, June 1974, p. 5.

caucusing informally at UFWA conventions and modifying the UFWA constitution in order to promote their integration in union governance. The Committee on Minorities became a regular convention committee and an outlet for minority views, and the GEB was expanded to increase minority participation in governance.

The rise of blacks and Hispanics onto the GEB occurred with little resistance from other ethnic groups. Several organizational and ideological conditions promoted ethnic integration in the UFWA.

Ethnic Integration

A set of beliefs, or ideology, about working class unity, upheld by top UFWA leadership from the founding of the union, helped to promote the ethnic integration of UFWA leadership during the 1970s and 1980s. The product of the left-wing founders of the UFWA, many of whom had been Communist party members, this set of beliefs was promoted continuously in the UFWA throughout its entire history, even after the ousting of the Left in 1950 (see Chapter 3). The beliefs are reflected in the preamble to the UFWA constitution adopted at the founding convention in 1939: "This organization will endeavor to unite all workers in our industry regardless of craft, age, sex, nationality, race, creed or political belief."[55]

The ideology consisted of the following tenets: employers will attempt to keep workers' wages low by dividing workers along non–class lines (e.g., by race, ethnicity, sex) and, thereby, weakening worker bargaining strength; all workers, consequently, must unite in one organization to strengthen their bargaining position with employers, minimize wage differences among different groups, and achieve a higher standard of living.

The nine-month strike at the Spring Products Co. in 1938–1939 was an early testimonial to the UFWA founders' adherence to these beliefs. Located in New York City, Spring Products was a large manufacturer of metal furniture springs and, as such, fell into the UFWA membership jurisdiction. Compared with other branches of furniture manufacturing in the 1930s, the spring industry tended to employ less-skilled workers, many of whom were black. The strike began in the summer of 1938 when Samuel Marcus, the company owner, asked for a 15 percent–20 percent wage cut and refused to grant a closed shop contract to the predominantly black, four hundred-person workforce, who belonged to UFWA local 91. Several strikers were arrested after violent confrontations with police, and many labor, community, and civil rights organizations lent their support to the strikers.

In February 1939, during the thirtieth week of the strike, a Committee

---

[55] *Constitution of the United Furniture Workers of America,* adopted at the first constitutional convention, February 13–17, 1939, p. 2.

of the Negro People to Aid the Spring Products Strikers was established to acquaint "the public not only with the conditions of Negro labor in this industry, their wages and other problems, but also to publicize the rights of these workers to organize and bargain collectively." Among the committee members were committee chair Charles A. Collier, Jr., of the New York Urban League; Walter White, NAACP president; Allan Haywood, CIO council president; George Harris, president of the Association of Trade and Commerce, a Harlem businessmen's organization; Bonita Williams of the Harlem Workers Alliance; and Reverend Adam Clayton Powell, Jr., of the Abyssinian Baptist Church. The committee attended NLRB hearings and pressured Mayor La Guardia to intervene and broker a settlement. Local furniture unions honored the strike by refusing to work with Spring Products products, and in March 1939, the CIO called a national boycott against Spring Products.

In April, a mass demonstration, attended by four thousand people, was held near the struck plant, and, shortly thereafter, UFWA Vice President Max Perlow, along with the New York CIO, established a committee to ask Mayor La Guardia to investigate police discrimination against the strikers. The strike ended in May 1939 with the signing of a pact that included preferential rehiring of workers who had been employed prior to the strike, a blanket 5 percent wage increase, a forty-hour week, one week's paid vacation, seniority, and arbitration machinery.[56]

The importance of the strike to the UFWA was revealed not only by the consistent front-page coverage it received in the *Furniture Workers Press*, but also by the UFWA's analysis of the meaning of the strike. As Max Perlow put it, highlighting the ideology of working class unity,

> This strike has many sides. It is singular that today it is still possible for an employer such as Mr. Marcus to carry on such extreme terror and exploitation against 400 Negro workers. It is sad indeed that one man can go unhampered, starve hundreds of workers, and threaten the other locals that are coming to the support of the strikers; that he will ruin the industry and union conditions by using Negro workers against white workers; that he will organize small shops and hire cheap help, and that he will undermine and drag down the wages and conditions of all the workers in the industry.[57]

To the delegates of the founding UFWA convention, which took place in February 1939 during the thirtieth week of the strike, the welfare of the

---

[56] *Furniture Workers Press*, January 21, 1939, p. 1; January 28, 1939, p. 1; February 4, 1939, p. 8; quotation from February 16, 1939, p. 8; February 25, 1939, p. 1; March 4, 1939, p. 1; March 18, 1939, p. 1; April 1, 1939, p. 1; April 8, 1939, pp. 1, 3; April 15, 1939, p. 1; April 29, 1939, p. 1; May 6, 1939, p. 1; May 13, 1939, p. 6; May 20, 1939, p. 1; May 27, 1939, p. 1.
[57] Ibid., April 8, 1939, p. 3.

UFWA, the future integration of blacks into the labor movement, and the incorporation of less-skilled workers into the new movement for industrial unionism were riding on the Spring Products strike. The convention resolved, with a rising unanimous vote, that the Spring Products strikers be "fully supported both morally and financially." The most vocal supporters of the resolution, all of whom were left-of-center, Jewish delegates from New York City, emphasized the importance of the strike. For example, Paul Green, from local 45B, discussed the "tremendous importance of this strike, not only for our International Union as a whole, but the labor movement and in particular to the Negro people as a whole." Alex Sirota of local 140, noting the UFWA's determination to organize southern furniture workers, argued that a successful resolution of the strike would facilitate the organization of southern blacks. Louis Cohen, from local 91, argued that the future organization of blacks in the spring industry depended on the outcome of the strike, especially because "all the employers are watching this particular strike, probably hoping to benefit if we lose the strike." Finally, UFWA President Morris Muster, arguing that the future organization not only of blacks but also of unskilled workers depended on the strike, proclaimed that "we have within our power to do that which is necessary to forever install the UFWA as a power for . . . good."[58]

The Spring Products strike was sufficiently important to the founding UFWA convention delegates that they elected to permit local 91 to designate a black member for the seat representing spring accessories workers on the GEB. Thomas V. Sinclair, secretary-treasurer of local 91 and an organizer in both the spring industry and the Spring Products strike, was selected for the GEB position in October 1939, becoming the first black member of the UFWA GEB.[59] For Sinclair, the Spring Products strike was important to the future unionization of blacks, as he put it in the *Furniture Workers Press:*

> We believe the sacrifice these men [strikers] are making for themselves and for their organization is one of the things which will play a large part in cementing the Negro closer to the trade union groups. . . . It is probably the first time in the history of the labor movement that a group of men from such an underprivileged and discriminated-against minority race has ever stayed out on strike for such a long period of time.[60]

---

[58] First quotation from *Proceedings*, 1939 UFWA Convention, p. 186; second quotation from idem, p. 189; third quotation from idem, p. 187; fourth quotation from idem, p. 191.

[59] Ibid., pp. 267–268; *Furniture Workers Press*, March 18, 1939, p. 8; November 4, 1939, p. 3.

[60] *Furniture Workers Press*, February 4, 1939, p. 8.

The ideology of working class unity, symbolized by and exercised in the Spring Products strike, entered the UFWA from the beginning of its efforts to unite all furniture workers in an industrial union. Indeed, the ideology guided these early efforts and was perpetuated continuously within the UFWA. Several factors helped in this perpetuation, including official proclamations and symbolic acts by UFWA officers, intermingling of UFWA members of different ethnicities at UFWA meetings, and transmittal of the ideology through the mentoring of new generations of UFWA leaders by their predecessors.

Official proclamations. The ideology of working class unity was presented for discussion at every UFWA convention in the reports of the International officers and in resolutions. These reports and resolutions consistently denounced all forms of discrimination and promoted civil rights, civil rights legislation, and the civil rights movement. The following are illustrations of these proclamations:

1. In their report to the 1948 UFWA convention, the UFWA officers stated that

   Our union, along with other unions and progressive organizations, has consistently fought all forms of discrimination against Negroes, Jews, Catholics, and other minority groups at every opportunity. We know that those who preach hate and appeal to prejudice are out to undermine American democracy by stirring up divisions among our people.... We have taken these ... actions because we know that unless we can maintain peace and democracy in our land, our members will lose all they have gained or hoped to gain.[61]

2. At the 1958 UFWA convention, the delegates passed a resolution, emphasizing that

   While the role of government ... is vital to the maintenance of freedom and democracy, we must recognize that labor and other forward-minded groups must work hard to make the principle of equal rights for all Americans a living reality. Therefore, be it RESOLVED that ... we reaffirm our policy of seeking to include in collective bargaining agreements clauses prohibiting discrimination ... [and] our support of the National Association for the Advancement of Colored People and other bona-fide

---

[61] *Proceedings of the Fifth Constitutional Convention of the United Furniture Workers—CIO,* Chicago, June 7–11, 1948, p. 28.

civil rights groups and urge UFWA local unions to cooperate with . . . these . . . groups on the community level.[62]

3. To the 1964 UFWA convention, the UFWA officers stated in their report that

> Born in struggle themselves, unions have a great bond with the Negro community. Long ago we learned that American labor cannot be half slave and half free. As long as there are pockets of the dispossessed, the underprivileged, and the disenfranchised, regardless of race or color or creed, worker will be pitted against worker to the detriment of all. . . . Our International Union has always been in the forefront of the struggle for equal rights. . . . We should . . . render what support we can to the hundreds of local and state movements aimed at achieving greater integration in our society, north as well as south. As trade unionists whose watchword is brotherhood and whose goal is a better life, we can ill afford to remain neutral in this fundamental reshaping of our civilization.[63]

4. In their report to the 1976 UFWA convention, the UFWA officers stated that discrimination against minorities existed because

> a small group found it profitable! That same small group also finds it profitable to exploit all workers—and to fight the trade union movement. The enemies of the so-called minorities are the enemies of all of us. That's why bosses are eager to sow the seeds of discord among workers: If they keep us divided, they can take their best shots at exploiting us . . . for their own higher profits. . . . Our best weapon against the employers' "divide and conquer" tactics is our own unity.[64]

5. At the final UFWA convention in 1984, the UFWA officers lambasted the Reagan administration for trying

> to pit workers against each other—workers of "Eastern and Southern European descent" against black and Hispanic workers—and take our eyes off who it is that profits from discrimination. . . . They [employers] divide us among ourselves, and make it that much harder to fight the company with the unity it takes to win. By fighting for justice and equality for all its members, a union builds the unity to fight cuts and concessions. The UFWA has a long history of such struggles. . . . In these days of

---

[62] *Proceedings of the Tenth Constitutional Convention of the United Furniture Workers of America—AFL-CIO,* New York, May 12–16, 1958, p. 126.

[63] *Proceedings of the Thirteenth Constitutional Convention of the United Furniture Workers of America—AFL-CIO,* New York, May 11–15, 1964, pp. 57–58.

[64] *Proceedings,* 1976 UFWA Convention, p. 72.

takebacks, plant closings and fake bankruptcies, it will take maximum unity to fight back effectively.[65]

The ideology of working class unity, then, was perpetuated by the top UFWA officers and pronounced at UFWA conventions. The official proclamations were supported by the deeds of the UFWA. Throughout UFWA history, the *Furniture Workers Press* reported continuously on pro–civil rights events in which the UFWA participated. For example, in 1940, Thomas Sinclair represented the UFWA at the Third National Negro Congress; in 1951, the UFWA arranged to accept contributions to the United Negro College Fund; in 1963, the UFWA established a UFWA Freedom Fund to help support the struggles of civil rights organizations, arguing in a front-page editorial in the *Furniture Workers Press* that "We can no longer stand on the sidelines and cheer the brave, non-violent demonstrators of the South who have faced police dogs and murder. We must take our place in the front lines and pledge continuing support until full equality has been won"; in 1973, Enio Carrion represented the UFWA at the founding convention of the Labor Council for Latin American Advancement, which would "give Latinos a greater voice within the AFL-CIO"; and, in 1985, a UFWA delegation joined some two thousand people in a march from Selma to Montgomery, Alabama, commemorating the twentieth anniversary of the civil rights march.[66]

The ideology of working class unity was also presented as having practical, growth implications for the UFWA. Early on, it was recognized that racial unity would play a significant role in the UFWA's historic goal to organize the low-wage South. At a meeting of a CIO committee on southern organizing in December 1939, UFWA President Muster pledged cooperation in eliminating racial prejudice among black and white workers.[67] Lawrence Ross, a white UFWA organizer in the South, commenting in 1941 on the prospects for southern organizing, wrote "Present always . . . is the division between Negro and white workers. . . . This old prejudice, nurtured and kept alive, for the sake of maintaining division, by certain powerful interests in the South, can be broken down. . . . But it is still a definite handicap that must be overcome."[68] Racial unity paid off in the successful Thomasville organizing campaign of 1946, as noted by the UFWA officers, when the North Carolina workers voted to join the UFWA (see Chapter 3).

By the early 1950s, it had become apparent to the UFWA that southern blacks joined the UFWA more readily than southern whites. Support-

---

[65] *Proceedings,* 1984 UFWA Convention, pp. 49–50.
[66] *Furniture Workers Press,* April 20, 1940, p. 8; May 4, 1940, p. 8; April 1951, p. 3; first quotation from June 1963, p. 1; second quotation from December 1973, p. 2; March 1985, p. 1.
[67] Ibid., December 30, 1939, p. 1.
[68] Ibid., March 1944, p. 5.

ing a resolution that called for promoting racial unity during southern organizing drives, UFWA President Pizer told the 1952 UFWA convention, referring to competition between the UFWA and AFL unions in the South, that "We went down there [South] and plant by plant we beat them [AFL unions], and you know which plants were easiest to be in, where you had a substantial group of Negro workers. . . . Where they had Negro workers, there was no question. The Negro workers down South know which labor organization is their friend."[69]

During the post–World War II era, the UFWA organizing campaigns in the South tended to be most successful in areas with large proportions of black residents. A statistical analysis of the outcomes of UFWA representation elections in the South between 1950 and 1982, which I have reported elsewhere, shows that the racial composition of the county in which the election was conducted was the only significant correlate of election outcome. The higher the percentage black of county residents, the higher the likelihood of a UFWA election victory.[70]

In sum, the ideology of working class unity was proclaimed continuously by UFWA officials. It led the UFWA to ally with and support the civil rights movement and facilitated the UFWA southern organizing effort.

Ethnic intermingling. In practice, the ideology led to the intermingling of different ethnic groups from different geographical areas at UFWA meetings. The UFWA chain plant organizing strategy and the chain plant councils, which were first established during the late 1950s to coordinate collective bargaining among the geographically separate plants of a single chain company (see Chapter 4), provided an organizational forum for different ethnic groups of workers to design and execute a strategy for pursuing their common economic interests against a common corporate adversary. For example, UFWA members from Nashville, TN, Memphis, TN, and Louisville, KY, over 40 percent of whom were black, attended the November 1960 meeting of the Huttig Sash and Door Council; approximately 15 percent of the conferees at the 1964 NPOMI meeting were black; and, of the UFWA members from Athens, TX, Dallas, TX, and Benton, AR, who attended an August 1965 meeting of the Curtis Mathes Council, about 20 percent were black.[71]

Throughout the 1970s and 1980s, chain plant councils convened, and delegates to UFWA conventions representing different locals of the same chain, who were often of different ethnic backgrounds, met informally to discuss their common economic interests. At the 1970 UFWA convention,

---

[69] *Proceedings of the Seventh Constitutional Convention of the United Furniture Workers of America—CIO,* Grand Rapids, MI, June 9–13, 1952, p. 152.
[70] Daniel Cornfield, "Declining Union Membership," p. 1140.
[71] *Furniture Workers Press,* November 1960, p. 1; September 1965, p. 5.

Italian and Hispanic delegates representing eastern and western plants of the Sealy chain convened; black and white delegates from the Huttig chain convened; and black and white delegates from the Cleveland, Dallas, Birmingham, and Baltimore plants of the Flicker chain met together. In 1971, white workers from Monroe, MI, and black workers from Florence, SC, met jointly at a coordinated bargaining session of the La-Z-Boy chain. At a 1972 meeting of the La-Z-Boy Council, comprising workers from Florence, Monroe, Neosho, MO, Newton, MS, and Los Angeles, about one-fourth of the attendees were black or Hispanic, and a meeting of La-Z-Boy workers at the 1974 UFWA convention was mixed racially. Ethnically mixed meetings of workers from the geographically diverse plants of the Sealy, Eastern Products, and DeSoto chains were also convened at the 1974 convention. At a December 1974 meeting of the DeSoto Council, comprising workers from Canton, MS, Union, MS, Russellville, AR, and Fort Smith, AR, almost one-third of the attendees were black. Racially mixed meetings of workers from the DeSoto, Flicker, Sealy, La-Z-Boy, and Michigan Maple Block chains and a meeting of General Interiors workers, including Hispanics and workers of Northern and Western European descent, were held at the 1976 UFWA convention. In 1980, racially mixed meetings of La-Z-Boy and Weyerhaeuser workers were held at the UFWA convention. At the 1984 UFWA convention, racially mixed meetings were held for workers from the Huttig and La-Z-Boy chains.[72]

Ironically, the emergence of the multi-plant, or chain, company, whose strategy of opening new plants in low-wage, non-union areas often divided workers, effectively provided an organizational rationale and means for the union to unite different ethnic groups in a common economic pursuit.[73] The union's strategies of chain plant organizing and coordinated bargaining, both of which developed from the ideology of working class unity and the subsequent desire to establish geographically uniform wages, united workers from different regions and of diverse ethnic backgrounds.

Passing on the founders' legacy. The ideology of working class unity was also perpetuated by a mentoring process among three generations of top UFWA leaders. The first generation consisted of Max Perlow, Alex Sirota, and Morris Pizer, all left-of-center, Jewish immigrants who were instrumental in the founding of the UFWA and whose biographies are described in Chapter 3. The second generation consisted of Solly Silverman, a Jewish, New York City born, left-of-center activist, and Leroy Clark,

---

[72] Ibid., June 1970, p. 6; April 1971, p. 7; June 1972, p. 1; June 1974, pp. 3, 4; December 1974, p. 8; June 1976, pp. 8–9; June 1980, p. 5; June 1984, p. 4.
[73] Cornfield and Leners, "Unionization in the Rural South."

who became the first black UFWA International officer in 1970. Carl Scarbrough and Lowell Daily, UFWA president and secretary-treasurer, respectively, from 1974 to 1987 (when the UFWA merged into the IUE), constituted the third generation. The intergenerational mentoring process is illustrated by the intertwining biographies of the different generations of UFWA leaders.

The son of Jewish-Rumanian immigrants, Solly Silverman was born in New York City in 1917. At the age of fourteen, he took a job at Empire Dinette, a furniture manufacturer in Astoria, Queens. The next day he sought out the union and found Perlow, Pizer, and Sirota, then leaders of an independent furniture workers union in New York City. Silverman partly attributed his union consciousness and desire to join the union to his parents, both of whom were socialists and valued the labor movement highly. His father, a mattress maker, had been a member of the Socialist party, and his mother, who worked occasionally as a seamstress when she wasn't raising the children, encouraged him to seek out the union.[74]

Silverman became active in the union, and later in the UFWA, becoming associated with the left-wing faction in the UFWA and serving on the UFWA GEB during the union's formative period of the 1940s. He regarded Perlow, Pizer, and Sirota, who were roughly ten to fifteen years his seniors, as his mentors in the labor movement. His experience in the Spring Products strike made a lasting impression on him. A member of UFWA local 76B, Silverman was assigned to be an organizer in the Spring Products strike. For him, the strike showed the importance of involving the community and politicians in a strike, especially during that time of high unemployment when it was difficult to prevent people from working in the plant during the strike, and he was permitted to attend Reverend Adam Clayton Powell's church on Sundays to make strike collections. The strike also showed Silverman that blacks would unionize and not work for low wages. And it was during the Spring Products strike that Silverman found Leroy Clark.[75]

Regarded as "one of the most militant strikers in the long and bitter struggle at Spring Products," Leroy Clark began his union career after the strike. He was born in Panama in 1917 and moved to New York City shortly thereafter. His father was a carpenter and member of a segregated, black AFL-Carpenters local union in New York City. His mother was a laundry worker and homemaker. Neither parent was a union activist.[76]

The Spring Products strike drew Clark into the union. In 1937, he

---

[74] Personal interview with Solly Silverman in West Palm Beach, FL, on September 22, 1986.
[75] Ibid.; *Furniture Workers Press,* February 4, 1939, p. 8.
[76] Quotation from *Furniture Workers Press,* May 4, 1940, p. 8; Leroy Clark interview.

took a job as a machinist apprentice, and then a machine operator, at Spring Products. Clark had been anti-union in light of the inferior treatment blacks had received from the AFL and because the owner had convinced him that a union was unnecessary. His interest in unionism increased during his employment at Spring Products because of poor employment conditions and the dictatorial manner in which the owner managed the plant. Solly Silverman had begun to organize the plant before the strike, leafletting and talking with the workers, while Clark helped to organize a workers' committee. The committee, which the owner encouraged Clark and others to establish, failed to wrest improved employment conditions from the owner. Clark helped to unionize the plant and, arrested during the strike, served fourteen months in the Rikers Island Penitentiary.[77]

His Spring Products job was saved for him under a special arrangement, and Clark returned to the shop upon his release from prison in December 1939. He became active in the governance of UFWA local 91. Clark considered Perlow, Sirota, and Silverman his chief mentors in the labor movement. Silverman had worked with Clark during the strike, and Perlow was especially instrumental in helping to launch Clark's union career. Local 91 consisted of workers from two spring manufacturing shops. Spring Products employed about four hundred workers, most of whom were black, and Kay Manufacturing employed roughly six hundred workers, most of whom were Jewish or Italian. The Kay workers, being in the majority, wanted to elect Kay workers to all of the top local 91 offices, while the Spring Products workers threatened to secede if they were not represented in union offices. As an International UFWA officer, Perlow stepped in to settle the controversy, explaining the importance of working class unity and arguing that the local union offices should be divvied up between the two worker groups. Clark was elected local union treasurer and, in 1941, he was elected full-time, paid organizer for local 91. He had already left his mark on the union when he was drafted into the United States Army in December 1941. A March 1942 *Furniture Workers Press* article, centering on Clark's induction into the army, stated: "Let us assure Brother Clark and the thousands like him that we are with them."[78]

After his return from the service in 1946, Clark took an upholstery apprenticeship that Morris Pizer, then UFWA eastern vice president, helped him secure. Clark was one of the first black apprentices, given that the local union constitution had reserved such apprenticeships for the

---

[77] Leroy Clark interview; *Furniture Workers Press,* February 4, 1939, p. 8; December 23, 1939, p. 7.

[78] Leroy Clark interview; *Furniture Workers Press,* December 23, 1939, p. 7; quotation from March, 1942, p. 8.

sons of union members. He was elected shop steward and, in 1948, recording secretary of UFWA local 76. Clark held several UFWA organizer and factory jobs through the early 1950s. In 1955, UFWA President Pizer hired Clark as an International UFWA organizer and assigned him to the South. Clark served in that position until 1970, when he was elected president of UFWA local 282 in Memphis and UFWA southern vice president. It was during his tenure as southern organizer that Clark met Carl Scarbrough.[79]

The son of white, Southern Baptist parents, Carl Scarbrough was born in 1935 in Henderson, TN, a small town in the western part of the state. Neither his father, a farmer, nor his mother, a homemaker, was involved in the labor movement. He graduated from high school in 1952 and in 1953 moved to Memphis, where he worked as a non-union carpenter in residential construction. In 1955, he took a job installing piano keyboards and regulating pianos at the Ivers and Pond Piano Co., a piano manufacturer in Memphis. Local 282 of the UFWA had just organized the plant before Scarbrough was hired. His employment at the piano company introduced him to the union.[80]

Scarbrough's swift rise through the hierarchy of local union offices was partly attributable to the respect he won from his co-workers. He had helped other employees with their employment issues and was perceived by the workers as someone who was not afraid to confront the employer on these issues. Furthermore, other local union officials encouraged him to run for union office. Also, Scarbrough's wife, a union shop steward in another company that had been organized by the International Union of Electronic Workers, explained to him the workings of the labor movement and motivated him to become involved in the union. He was elected department steward in 1956 and, in 1958, shop chairman, the highest union position in the plant.[81]

In 1963, Scarbrough was elected president of local 282. His election was partly facilitated by the fact that his shop, Ivers and Pond, was the largest in local 282, an amalgamated local, although it did not constitute a majority. Also, he was encouraged to run for office by International UFWA Secretary-Treasurer Fred Fulford, whom he had met at NPOMI meetings and at UFWA conventions, and by Leroy Clark, who, as a southern organizer, had been stationed by Pizer in Memphis since the late 1950s. Scarbrough regarded Clark as one of his chief mentors in the labor movement, and from Clark he learned the value of racial unity among workers. Moreover, Clark, who was attempting to build local 282, saw in Scarbrough

---

[79] Leroy Clark interview.
[80] Scarbrough interview.
[81] Ibid.

someone who was interested in the local and had leadership potential. Adhering to the value of racial unity proved to be important for Scarbrough's ascent in local 282. By 1963, roughly two-thirds of the local 282 membership was black. As the civil rights movement unfolded in the South, local 282 joined with the NAACP and the SCLC in civil rights demonstrations and rallies, addressing the issues of the desegregation of public places and equal employment opportunity. Civil rights organizations often participated in local 282 organizing drives. Through his involvement in these civil rights activities, Scarbrough won the respect of the predominantly black, local 282 membership.[82]

Scarbrough's rise to International UFWA president partly occurred in accordance with a plan he devised with Leroy Clark in 1962. Clark wanted to groom Scarbrough for the position of International UFWA secretary-treasurer. Clark was anticipating Pizer's retirement from the presidency and Secretary-Treasurer Fulford's assumption of that position. Clark also assumed that the strength of the local union and the district would determine who became secretary-treasurer, and that the rapid growth of local 282, which he was building, and the southern region generally would give Scarbrough a chance to become secretary-treasurer. Therefore, he helped Scarbrough to attain leadership positions in the local, the district, and, finally, the region.[83]

At the 1964 UFWA convention, Scarbrough was elected southern vice president, a position that had been held by the predominantly white Fort Smith locals almost continuously since 1939. Scarbrough's election to this position resulted in part from his ability to unite the southern districts and the races. The UFWA southern region consisted of district 5 in the Southeast and district 9 in the Southwest, including Tennessee and Arkansas. As Memphis local 282 grew, and the Fort Smith membership stabilized, local 282 and Scarbrough gained political strength in district 9. Leroy Clark had contacts in the predominantly black locals in district 5—Sumter, SC, Henderson, NC, and Winston-Salem, NC—that dominated district 5 voting strength and came to support Scarbrough. By the time of the 1964 convention, Scarbrough's popularity in the South had spread among the black and most of the white locals. Among blacks, Scarbrough was perceived as a civil rights advocate, while whites perceived him as able in collective bargaining.[84]

The contest for southern vice president occurred within the southern caucus at the 1964 convention. Traditionally, each UFWA region met in caucus at the conventions to determine the GEB candidates from the

---

[82] Ibid.; Leroy Clark interview.
[83] Ibid.
[84] Scarbrough interview.

region, and each regional caucus accepted the other regions' candidate slates, which were submitted to the entire convention for the vote. Thus, contests for office generally occurred within regional caucuses at the convention before the officer elections took place. In 1964, Louie Campbell of Fort Smith local 270, the incumbent southern vice president, was stepping down from his position. He had been voted out of his local union office as business agent and became a full-time, paid, International UFWA organizer. As an International organizer, he was disqualified, under the UFWA constitution, from serving on the GEB. The contest for the southern vice presidency was between Scarbrough and Elmer Bost from local 270. Scarbrough won the vice presidency at the southern caucus with 2,100 of the 3,500 votes cast and went on to be elected by the convention. Within the southern caucus, Bost carried the Fort Smith vote and Scarbrough carried all of the black vote and most of the remaining white vote.[85]

With Pizer's retirement in 1970, Fulford became president and Scarbrough became secretary-treasurer. Since the late 1930s, the northeastern and midwestern urbanites had dominated most of the highest offices in the UFWA, leading to tension with the growing nonmetropolitan membership during the 1940s and 1950s (see Chapters 3 and 4). The retirement of Pizer, a New Yorker, and the election of Fulford, from South Bend, IN, and Scarbrough seemed to indicate a shift in the axis of power in the UFWA from the urban areas of the Northeast and Midwest to the nonmetropolitan Midwest and South, a shift that was commensurate with the geographical redistribution of UFWA membership. Nonetheless, the ideology of working class unity continued with the Fulford-Scarbrough team, as suggested by the thematic continuity in the official proclamations and deeds previously cited. Fulford, whose biography is described in Chapter 3, had been associated with the left wing in the UFWA during the 1930s and 1940s and maintained a progressive political stance, after the 1950 ousting of the Left, during his 1950–1970 tenure as secretary-treasurer with Pizer. Fulford supported Scarbrough, who had participated in organizing drives with him in Indiana and Michigan. Moreover, Scarbrough's progressive stance on civil rights, his being a southerner, and his organizing abilities were deemed relevant to the UFWA's historic mission to organize the South and, particularly, southern blacks. What little opposition Scarbrough received was from some of the old, large locals in Chicago and New York City. And as part of the plan he devised with Scarbrough in 1962, Leroy Clark resigned as International organizer, became full-time president of local 282, and was elected southern vice president, with little or no opposition, in 1970.[86]

[85] Ibid.
[86] Ibid.; Leroy Clark interview.

With the untimely death of Fred Fulford in 1974, Scarbrough assumed the presidency, and Lowell Daily became secretary-treasurer. The Scarbrough-Daily team remained intact through the merger of the UFWA into the International Union of Electronic Workers in 1987. Daily, of Swedish and Irish descent, was born in Scandia, Minnesota, in 1927. His mother was a homemaker, and his father, a factory worker, was an active member of the United Automobile Workers union and had helped organize his plant. After graduating from high school in 1945, Daily held a few jobs and, in 1949, took a factory job with Bemis Manufacturing in Sheboygan Falls, WI. At Bemis, a manufacturer of toilet seats, chair bottoms, and other wood products, Daily became involved in the independent local union, which proved to be ineffective in collective bargaining. In 1950, he was instrumental in having the independent union affiliated with UFWA local 800, an amalgamated local in Sheboygan, WI. Pizer and Fulford approached Daily about becoming a full-time International UFWA organizer, and in 1955 he was hired to organize in the Midwest. In 1958, he was stationed in Grand Rapids, MI, as UFWA district 7 (Michigan) director and served in that position until 1974, when he became secretary-treasurer. As organizer and district director, Daily worked often with Fred Fulford, whom he befriended, and won the respect of Pizer. Despite the paucity of blacks in the Midwest, Daily developed an adherence to the ideology of working class unity. He often observed employers who attempted to keep wages low by pitting one white ethnic group against another, and, as secretary-treasurer, he was a civil rights supporter and promoter of ethnic integration on the GEB. In 1974, Pizer, who as president emeritus continued to exercise considerable influence in the UFWA, became a strong Daily supporter. Daily was the consensus candidate for secretary-treasurer among the top UFWA officers when he was appointed to that position.[87]

Through a mentoring process, then, among three generations of UFWA leaders, the ideology of working class unity was perpetuated among the top UFWA leaders. The mentoring process also generated civil rights activism and minority mobilization within the UFWA. The mobilization of minorities during the late 1960s, just described, and the effort to further integrate the GEB were themselves the outcome of leadership mentoring within the UFWA.

Among the minority activists who brought the civil rights movement into the UFWA were Booker McCollum and Enio Carrion, both from New York City local 140, as discussed. Their mentor, Alex Sirota, one of the first generation of UFWA leaders, continued as an activist in his local, 140, through the 1960s and groomed McCollum and Carrion, as shown by their biographies.

[87] Ibid.; personal interview with Lowell Daily in Nashville, TN, on July 1, 1986.

Booker McCollum was born in Dlo, MS, in 1925. His parents owned and worked a small farm, growing cotton, corn, and potatoes; occasionally did sharecropping; and were not involved in the labor movement. After working on the farm, he enlisted in the United States Navy in 1943, served three years, and returned to Mississippi, where he attempted to farm. As the market for merchandise from small farmers was poor, in 1952 McCollum moved to New York City, where his brother and sister had already established residence. Later that year, he was hired as a general helper by National Sleep, a Brooklyn manufacturer of feathers, feather materials, bedding, and pillows. National Sleep consisted of some forty workers who were predominantly Italian, Jewish, Polish, black, and Hispanic, and it was already organized in UFWA local 140, an amalgamated bedding workers local, when McCollum took the job. By the late 1950s, he had successfully trained on the job to become a frame maker.[88]

McCollum rose through the local 140 hierarchy with the encouragement of Alex Sirota, whom he regarded as one of his chief mentors in the labor movement. He was elected shop chairman in the late 1950s; full-time, local union business agent in 1965; and secretary-treasurer of local 140 in 1976, by which time the local union membership had shifted from being predominantly Jewish to being predominantly black and Hispanic. In 1976, he was also elected to the International UFWA GEB as the at-large representative from the East.[89]

Enio Carrion was born in Ponce, Puerto Rico, in 1935. His father, a fire fighter, and his mother, a tobacco factory worker, were supportive union members but not actively involved in their unions. He moved to New York City at the age of ten and graduated from high school in 1953. In the same year, he took a job as an automatic nailing machine feeder at the Joseph Aronauer Co., a manufacturer of bedding spring products, and, during the next three years, worked his way up the job hierarchy, becoming a set up machine man, repairing the machines. The 250-person Aronauer workforce, which was approximately 60 percent Puerto Rican and 30 percent black, was already affiliated with Upholsterers International Union local 601 when Carrion was hired.[90]

The Aronauer workers became dissatisfied with the UIU, and in 1958 they affiliated with UFWA local 140. Carrion was one of the leaders of the move into the UFWA. Through their friends in local 140, the Aronauer workers had become aware of the greater militancy of local 140, compared with the UIU local, and of its superior wages and fringe benefits. Consequently, the Aronauer workers began an election campaign to affiliate with local 140. The employer, who favored the UIU over local 140, fired

[88] McCollum interview.
[89] Ibid.
[90] Carrion interview.

Carrion in an effort to inhibit the workers from affiliating with local 140. Alex Sirota, president of local 140, hired Carrion as a local union organizer for the duration of the Aronauer campaign. Local 140 won the election, and Sirota hired Carrion as a full-time local union organizer, launching Carrion's union career.[91]

With the encouragement of Alex Sirota, whom Carrion regarded as his chief mentor in the labor movement, Carrion rose through the official hierarchy of local 140. He was elected business agent in 1963, secretary-treasurer in about 1971, and president in 1976. In addition, he served continuously on the International UFWA GEB from 1970 on, alternating between the eastern, at-large representative, and bedding workers GEB positions.[92]

Inspired by the civil rights movement, McCollum and Carrion became civil rights activists, participating in civil rights rallies and demonstrations mainly through their involvement in local 140. Under Sirota's leadership, local 140 participated in numerous civil rights protests around the nation. The local often rented buses, filled them with rank-and-filers, and traveled to demonstrations in such places as Washington, DC, Birmingham, AL, and Memphis, TN. Sirota himself was revered by local union members of all ethnic backgrounds as an early champion of civil rights, long before the civil rights movement, and as the prime mover for the elimination of race differentials in wages in the bedding industry during the late 1930s and 1940s. As a UFWA founder and, hence, one of the originators of the ideology of working class unity in the UFWA, Sirota encouraged the development of minority leadership in local 140 before it was customary to do so. Max Perlow also encouraged civil rights activism and minority participation in local 140. Although he was a member of UFWA local 76B, Perlow was hired by Sirota as local 140 newspaper editor and claims department employee after Perlow lost the secretary-treasurership of the International UFWA with the ousting of the Left in 1950.[93]

The first generation of left-wing UFWA leaders, then, despite their removal from International UFWA office in 1950, continued to wield influence in local 140, participating in the civil rights movement during the 1960s and developing a new generation of black and Hispanic union leaders. This new generation of union leaders, including McCollum and Carrion, became civil rights activists, practiced the ideology of working class unity, and, in the late 1960s, went on to press for greater minority participation in the governance of the International UFWA.[94]

In sum, the three-generation mentoring process not only perpetuated

[91] Ibid.
[92] Ibid.
[93] Ibid.
[94] Ibid.; McCollum interview.

the left-wing founders' ideology of working class unity among later generations of top UFWA leaders, but it also created a new generation of minority union leaders, who as civil rights activists mobilized for greater minority participation in UFWA governance. In this way, the mentoring process helped to realize the ethnic integration of the UFWA GEB during the 1970s and 1980s.

The Emergence of Minorities on the GEB

In conclusion, the civil rights movement of the 1960s ushered in new, minority leaders on the UFWA GEB during the 1970s and 1980s. The emergence of minority union leaders was inspired not only by the civil rights movement, which effectively mobilized blacks and Hispanics within the UFWA, but also by an ideology of working class unity that had been nurtured by the top UFWA leaders since the founding of the union. The ideology was perpetuated through official proclamations by top leaders and the mentoring of new generations of leaders by their predecessors. Moreover, the ideology, transmitted through a mentoring process, helped to develop a generation of minority civil rights activists within the UFWA who led the mobilization for increasing minority participation in UFWA governance.

In subtle, ironic, but powerful ways, the geographical redistribution of furniture manufacturing capital also contributed to the rise of minorities onto the GEB. The southward shift of the industry had two effects on the union. First, it contributed to union membership decline, as employers, in search of cheap labor and growing markets, moved out of the unionized Northeast into the low-wage South. Second, it led to a southward redistribution of UFWA membership, convention votes, and, hence, political strength in the union. This was symbolized by the relocation of International UFWA headquarters from New York City to Nashville, TN, in 1979, making the UFWA the first International union to be located in the South.[95] As the lowest paid workers in the South, blacks not only entered the industry but also unionized readily during the 1960s. The geographical decentralization of the industry, led by the expansion of chain plant companies, and the subsequent chain plant organizing strategy of the UFWA, conjoined workers from different regions and of different ethnic backgrounds in a common effort to advance their economic interests in one union. The ideology of working class unity also served here as an integrating force, as it was the rationale for the chain plant organizing strategy that led to coordinated collective bargaining among diverse worker ethnic groups. As the political strength of southern blacks increased in the UFWA, and as the UFWA simultaneously lost members, minorities gained

---

[95] *Furniture Workers Press,* July/August/September 1979, p. 1.

a strong bargaining chip in their effort to gain access to the GEB. The future growth of the UFWA depended in part on the incorporation of minorities into the leadership. As Pizer put it in his opening remarks to the 1970 UFWA convention, "We . . . need some representation from the new minority workers . . . we have to bring in those minority workers, whether black or white or Latin-American. . . . The leadership must show the full face of the organization. . . . This is not merely a gesture of great progressiveness. It is a gesture of survival."[96]

The Ascent of Women

Women emerged as UFWA leaders after they entered as wage earners into the furniture manufacturing industry. The percentage of women in furniture manufacturing began to increase rapidly in the mid-1960s, and the first woman member of the International UFWA GEB was elected in 1970. The black women activists who began the mobilization of women for increased participation in UFWA governance during the early 1970s were inspired by the civil rights movement. Moreover, the mobilization of minorities in the UFWA, which had begun during the late 1960s, became increasingly intertwined with the mobilization of women, as each broadened their mandates to include support of all workers and of the other's efforts to gain access to leadership positions.

Top UFWA leadership contributed to the development of female leadership. High-ranking UFWA officials, as well as the chief women activists, proclaimed the ideology of working class unity on behalf of women's participation in union governance, demonstrating the congruence between UFWA tradition and the development of women leaders and thereby helping to legitimize women as UFWA leaders. Top leadership also participated actively in the development of women leaders. Several women leaders from the large, amalgamated locals had been mentored as trade union and women activists by International UFWA leaders, and others from small locals were identified by top leadership and encouraged to run for GEB positions.

The geographical redistribution of furniture manufacturing and UFWA membership led to a realignment of political strength within the UFWA that favored women candidates for the GEB. The industry and UFWA membership shifted out of the Northeast and urban Midwest into the South and nonmetropolitan Midwest, the regions in which women furniture workers were concentrated and from which a disproportionately large number of women GEB members emerged as national leaders.

[96] *Proceedings,* 1970 UFWA Convention, pp. 11–12.

Women had been marginally involved in the UFWA prior to the mid-1960s. During the late 1930s and early 1940s, women played a dual role in the UFWA. As workers, a few women served as low-level local union officials, especially in the major metropolitan areas such as New York City, Baltimore, and Pittsburgh, and participated in strikes and organizing drives.[97]

As consumers and wives of union members, women encouraged consumers to buy only union-made goods bearing the union label. Wives of union members often belonged to local union "ladies auxiliaries," as they were called, which assisted strikers, participated in union label campaigns, and held social and recreational events. Ladies auxiliaries were established in metropolitan areas such as New York City and in small furniture towns such as Rockford, IL, Bloomington, IN, and Gardner, MA. The local 76 ladies auxiliary in New York City was established primarily by women union members who recruited the wives of other union members into the auxiliary.[98]

Articles in the *Furniture Workers Press* that analyzed and encouraged women's participation in the workplace and the union seemed to reflect an ambivalence many people felt toward women's dual role in the union. For example, one article carried a story about a ladies auxiliary president who was so actively involved in a strike that she didn't know what she would do with her time when the strike was over. This was followed by a phrase designed to encourage women's participation in ladies auxiliaries: "More women just beginning to discover their own possibilities."[99] Another article, encouraging women who were already involved in ladies auxiliaries, lauded many nineteenth-century women social reformers and concluded with "So if you happen to know people who think belonging to an auxiliary isn't quite as 'nice' as belonging to a bridge club, just remember they may still be thinking in their own way that 'woman's place is in the home.' In other words, you're just about a hundred years ahead of them."[100] Also, a 1939 article entitled "Should Married Women Work?" depicted married women workers as secondary wage earners in the household. Married women tended to work "not because they enjoy sweating in a factory, but because their husband's wages are so low they can't support the family." The article went on to decry discrimination against married women workers, to proclaim the right of married women

---

[97]*Furniture Workers Press,* December 7, 1940, p. 8; April 1941, p. 6; August 1941, p. 8; September 1941, p. 8; November 1941, p. 1.

[98]Ibid., April 1, 1939, p. 8; April 22, 1939, p. 3; April 29, 1939, p. 1; May 6, 1939, pp. 3, 8; May 13, 1939, p. 8; May 20, 1939, p. 3; June 10, 1939, p. 8; September 30, 1939, p. 8; January 1941, p. 7; February 1941, p. 7; April 1941, p. 4.

[99]Ibid., January 28, 1939, p. 4.

[100]Ibid., February 24, 1940, p. 4.

to choose whether or not to work, and to support "decent wages so that married women will have a choice of working or not working."[101]

During World War II, women worked in furniture manufacturing and other mass production industries that had been converted to war-production industries. Statistics on the number of women furniture workers during the war are unavailable. However, the U.S. census showed that women accounted for 9 percent of the furniture and store fixtures manufacturing workforce in 1940 and 16 percent in 1950. According to the U.S. Bureau of Labor Statistics, the percentage female of the wood and upholstered furniture production workforce was 21 percent in 1945; in 1954, the percentage female of the household furniture production workforce was 11 percent.[102] These statistics suggest that women constituted a larger percentage of furniture workers during the war than before and after. Many *Furniture Workers Press* articles of the war years noted the dramatic increase in women furniture workers; supported patriotically the employment of women in occupations that had been mainly staffed by men; espoused day-care centers for the children of working women; reported on the support given by ladies auxiliaries to the soldiers and on a few instances of women workers' participation in union governance; and, proclaiming the ideology of working class unity, denounced sex bias in wages and called for wage equalization between men and women workers.[103]

Throughout the war, the UFWA attempted to eliminate sex differences in wages, an effort prompted in part by the growing number of women workers. As the 1943 report of the International UFWA officers put it, referring to the ideology of working class unity, "The influx of women into industry has . . . raised many problems. But the most insidious practice to which women workers have been subjected is the denial of equal pay for equal work. Apart from the injustice of this to the women workers, every union contract is undermined if we permit women to be paid a lower rate than men on the same job."[104] By the end of the war, the

---

[101] Ibid., June 3, 1939, p. 4.

[102] U.S. Bureau of the Census, *Sixteenth Census of the United States: 1940, Population,* vol. III, *The Labor Force,* Part I, *United States Summary* (Washington, DC: Government Printing Office, 1943), pp. 188–189; idem, *U.S. Census of Population: 1950,* vol. IV, *Special Reports,* Part I, Chapter D, *Industrial Characteristics* (Washington, DC: Government Printing Office, 1955), p. 1D–15; U.S. Bureau of Labor Statistics, *Wage Structure, Wood Furniture, 1945,* Series 2, no. 30 (Washington, DC: U.S. Department of Labor, Bureau of Labor Statistics, 1946), pp. 20–23; idem, *Wage Structure, Household Furniture, 1954,* Report no. 76 (Washington, DC: U.S. Department of Labor, Bureau of Labor Statistics, 1954), p. 8; Philip Foner, *Women and the American Labor Movement: From World War I to the Present* (New York: Free Press, 1980), pp. 336–393.

[103] *Furniture Workers Press,* July 1942, p. 5; December 1942, pp. 7, 9; January 1943, p. 3; February 1943, pp. 2, 7; March 1943, p. 5; May 1943, p. 8; June 1943, p. 5; September 1943, pp. 4, 7; October 1943, pp. 3, 7; December 1943, p. 3; March 1944, p. 7; August 1944, p. 6.

[104] *Proceedings of the Third Constitutional Convention of the United Furniture Workers of America—CIO,* Cleveland, May 17–21, 1943, p. 49.

UFWA had eliminated sex differentials in wages in many of their collective bargaining agreements.[105]

After the war, many women exited from the furniture and other mass production industries. Soldiers returned to their former jobs, which had been reserved for them in the union contracts. The *Furniture Workers Press* remained silent on the issue of women's involvement in the union until the 1970s, when women workers began to mobilize in the UFWA.[106]

The Mobilization of Women

The mobilization of women UFWA members during the 1970s and 1980s was partly inspired by the mobilization of ethnic minorities in the UFWA and, more importantly, by the civil rights movement of the 1960s. The connection between the mobilization of ethnic minorities and that of women derived from the fact that black women UFWA activists, whose union activism had matured during the civil rights movement and who were partly inspired by that movement, led the mobilization of women for increased participation in UFWA governance.

Beginning her tenure on the International UFWA GEB in 1970, Maggie Mae Edwards, a black woman from UFWA local 250 in Camden, AR, was the first woman elected to the GEB. She attributed the addition of the four GEB seats for minorities and her election to one of them in 1970 largely to the civil rights movement, rather than to the women's movement. Edwards herself held strong beliefs about race inequality in the United States.[107] Soon after her election to the GEB in 1970, Edwards proclaimed the ideology of working class unity in racial terms in the *Furniture Workers Press,* stating that employers "try to play white workers against Black workers . . . we have to work together to get a better deal for all. . . . One of the most important problems in the U.S. today . . . is the elimination of racial prejudice."[108]

Edwards's civil rights activism during the 1960s, in addition to her union activism, which had begun in the late 1940s, contributed to her ascent through the hierarchy of union offices. Born in Camden, AR, Edwards graduated from high school soon after World War II, when, at the age of seventeen, she took a "tailing" job (catching materials off a wood cutting machine) in the mill room of the Camden Furniture Co., a manufacturer of wood furniture. After about five years in the plant, Edwards had worked at several jobs in the mill room and the cabinet room. She had

---

[105] *Proceedings of the Fourth Constitutional Convention of the United Furniture Workers of America—CIO,* Detroit, June 3–7, 1946, p. 99.
[106] Foner, *Women and the American Labor Movement,* pp. 336–393; personal interview with Max Perlow in New York City on November 23, 1984.
[107] Personal interview with Maggie Mae Edwards in Camden, AR, on May 29, 1985.
[108] *Furniture Workers Press,* October 1970, p. 4.

become adept at the highly skilled patchwork craft, removing errors in the furniture, and was one of the first women patchworkers in the plant. Her mother, a domestic worker, and her father, who had died during Edwards's early childhood, had not been involved in the labor movement. Edwards's husband, Golden Smith, introduced her to unionism. Smith, who had returned from Chicago, where he had been exposed to unionism, worked at Camden Furniture and was the chief in-plant organizer when, in 1946, the plant was unionized and UFWA local 250 was chartered. Edwards participated in the organizing drive, making house calls and attending planning meetings down by the river. Her popularity among the predominantly black and male three hundred-person workforce stemmed from her outspokenness, and she quickly assumed local union leadership positions. After serving as a shop steward for two years, she was elected local union financial secretary, a position she held from the early 1950s to 1982, when local 250 closed due to plant shutdowns. About 1960, International UFWA President Pizer helped her attain a seat on the executive board of the Arkansas State AFL-CIO. She was also politically active in Camden during the 1960s, serving as the first black ward committeewoman and in voter registration drives after the enactment of the Voting Rights Act of 1965.[109]

By the time of her election to the International GEB in 1970, Edwards had gained a reputation as a dedicated and outspoken trade unionist and civil rights activist. It was these qualities, as well as her being a black woman, that led her chief supporters, including Leroy Clark, Carl Scarbrough, Fred Fulford, and Morris Pizer, to back her candidacy for the GEB seat. She was elected by acclamation to the GEB and served four more terms, until her local union closed.[110]

Women UFWA members began to mobilize for greater participation in union governance in 1972. The first meeting of the UFWA women's caucus occurred at the 1972 UFWA convention. The social composition of the women's caucus partly reflected the geographical concentration of women furniture workers in the South. Of the nineteen women who attended the first women's caucus, twelve were from the South. Half of the southerners were black and the nonsoutherners included five whites from the nonmetropolitan East, one white midwesterner, and one Hispanic from New York City.[111]

Under the chairpersonship of Maggie Mae Edwards, who had first been elected to the GEB at the previous UFWA convention in 1970, the women's caucus called for more women union leaders and training for

[109] Ibid.; Edwards interview.
[110] Leroy Clark, Scarbrough, and Edwards interviews; *Proceedings,* 1970 UFWA Convention, p. 225; *Proceedings* of the 1972–1980 UFWA conventions.
[111] *Furniture Workers Press,* June 1972, p. 6.

union activists including women. The women's caucus resolution, which was adopted unanimously by both the women's caucus and the 1972 UFWA convention,[112] read in part as follows:

> Marking a "first" in our Union, nineteen women Delegates have met during this Convention and constituted themselves as a Women's Caucus. . . . We commend our Union for developing a number of women leaders . . . but we believe there is much room for improvement. . . . Despite the fact that almost twenty percent of the Local Unions had included women in their Delegations—not one woman was invited to Chair a committee. . . . It was further noted that in several UFWA Locals which have a large woman membership, they have failed to develop women leaders; . . . THEREFORE, BE IT RESOLVED: . . . We urge the International and all Local Unions to make special efforts to bring women into leadership roles . . . [and] if the International finds it feasible, we strongly urge training sessions for all UFWA activists—including women.[113]

The mentoring process described earlier proved to be an important catalyst in the formation of the women's caucus. This is evident in the biographies of the two prime movers of the women's caucus, Alzada Clark and Etta Haden. Alzada Clark, a black woman, was born in Lexa, AR. Her mother was a homemaker, and her father, a postal worker, was an active union member. Alzada Clark moved to Memphis and married Leroy Clark, then an International UFWA organizer, in 1952. In 1967, she became a full-time International UFWA organizer, a position she held until her retirement in 1975.[114]

Alzada Clark's interest in promoting women union leaders was developed through her involvement in the labor movement and the civil rights movement. During the mid-1960s, as an employee of the Tennessee Labor Council, she attended a convention of the Women's Activities Division of the AFL-CIO in Washington, DC. Clark was inspired by the speakers, who were women local union leaders from around the nation. As a UFWA organizer, Clark was sent to Canton, MS, in 1967 and soon discovered that women were among the most supportive workers of unionism. Moreover, her involvement in the civil rights movement motivated her to organize women, in an effort to help advance all blacks. The women's movement itself had little impact on Clark's desire to promote women union leaders.[115]

Alzada Clark first broached the idea of organizing women UFWA

---

[112] Ibid.; *Proceedings,* 1972 UFWA Convention, p. 211.
[113] *Proceedings,* 1972 UFWA Convention, pp. 211–212.
[114] Personal interview with Alzada Clark in Memphis, TN, on May 31, 1985, and telephone interview with Alzada Clark on July 21, 1987.
[115] Ibid.

members with *Furniture Workers Press* editor Meryl London, who supported the idea, at the 1970 UFWA convention. Clark went on to convene the first women's caucus at the 1972 UFWA convention. She had encouraged Etta Haden, in whom she saw much leadership potential, to lead the women's caucus by the time of the 1974 UFWA convention, when Haden, a black UFWA activist from Baltimore, was unanimously made women's caucus chair in an uncontested election.[116]

Etta Haden, an outspoken champion of women's rights in the UFWA and for women's participation in union governance, was born in Fayetteville, NC, in 1929 and moved to Baltimore in 1930. She received her high school diploma and, in about 1960, took a factory job at the William T. Burnett Co., a Baltimore manufacturer of polyurethane for furniture, rising through the job hierarchy to become a lead worker. She became active in UFWA local 75, which already represented the Burnett workers when she was hired, and after a few months, she was elected shop steward. With the encouragement and mentoring of Max Weinstock, business agent and head of local 75 for many years, Haden moved up the hierarchy of local union offices and in 1973 was elected president of local 75, whose membership was predominantly black and male. She held this position until her untimely death in 1983. She was first elected to the International UFWA GEB in 1976, taking over the district 4 (Maryland and Pennsylvania) GEB seat from Weinstock, who had served in that capacity since 1956 and had died in 1976.[117]

It was through Weinstock, whom she regarded as her mentor, that Haden encountered the progressive ideological tradition in the UFWA. Max Weinstock, born around 1914, was a Jewish-Polish immigrant who had been associated with the left-wing faction in the UFWA and served briefly on the International UFWA GEB during the late 1940s. Like his progressive counterparts in New York City, Alex Sirota and Max Perlow, Weinstock had promoted the racial integration of the local since the early 1960s, when Haden began to rise through the local union hierarchy.[118]

A civil rights activist, Haden's activism grew out of her perception of racial discrimination during the early years of her life. After she took the job at Burnett, her union activism was directed at gaining improvements for all working people, and it was through the labor movement, especially with the Coalition of Labor Union Women, that she came to champion

---

[116] Ibid.

[117] Personal interviews in Baltimore with Ken Williams on June 9, 1985, and Bernice Merritt on June 10, 1985; personal interview with Earl Kiehl in York, PA, on June 10, 1985; *Furniture Workers Press,* December 1980, p. 4.

[118] *Furniture Workers Press,* December 1980, p. 4; Kiehl interview; *Proceedings of the Fifth Constitutional Convention of the United Furniture Workers of America—CIO,* Chicago, June 7–11, 1948, p. 267.

women's rights.[119] Moreover, she believed in the ideology of working class unity. As she put it at the 1980 UFWA convention,

> companies like nothing better than to divide us by using White against minorities, the young against the old, the men against the women. For some who think they can divide us and have us fight against each other, we must unite and fight against them . . . discrimination against women on the job not only hurts women, but also lowers the rates in the shop for men.[120]

Under Haden's leadership, the UFWA women's caucus continued to press for women's participation in union governance, passing resolutions at most of the UFWA conventions after 1972. The post-1972 women's caucus resolutions reflected a broadening of the women's caucus purview. While the resolutions consistently called for increased women's participation in union governance, the 1974 and 1980 resolutions also called on women UFWA members to become involved in the Coalition of Labor Union Women, a labor movement-wide organization that was established in 1974 and had goals similar to those of the UFWA women's caucus. In 1980, the focus of the women's caucus expanded to include support for increased organizing drives conducted by and among women. The 1982 women's caucus resolution went further, calling for voter registration drives, affirmative action for both women and minorities, community daycare services, and extension of "our democratic institutions and the civil rights and liberties of all workers."[121]

Women's participation in UFWA governance increased at the local and International levels of the UFWA during the 1970s and 1980s. The *Furniture Workers Press* reported regularly on the elections of women to local union offices.[122] At the 1974 UFWA convention, the women's caucus proudly announced the names of all eleven women local union presidents, who accounted for roughly 11 percent of all 101 UFWA locals. Seven of the eleven women presidents were from the nonmetropolitan

---

[119] Ken Williams interview; *Furniture Workers Press,* December 1980, p. 4; June 1983, p. 1.
[120] *Proceedings,* 1980 UFWA Convention, p. 192.
[121] *Proceedings,* 1974 UFWA Convention, pp. 167–169; *Proceedings,* 1976 UFWA Convention, pp. 265–267; *Proceedings,* 1980 UFWA Convention, pp. 191–194; quotation from *Proceedings,* 1982 UFWA Convention, pp. 105–106.
[122] *Furniture Workers Press,* March 1974, p. 7; March 1975, p. 3; April 1975, p. 1; June 1975, p. 5; December 1976, p. 2; February 1977, p. 2; March 1977, p. 3; April 1977, p. 2; January 1978, p. 3; May 1978, p. 2; March 1979, p. 5; April 1979, p. 2; December 1979, pp. 2, 4; January 1980, pp. 1, 2, 5; February 1980, p. 2; April 1980, p. 2; May 1980, p. 2; September 1980, p. 2; November 1980, p. 2; December 1980, p. 2; June 1981, p. 2; November 1981, pp. 3, 5; June 1982, p. 6; March 1985, p. 2; March 1986, p. 2; September–October 1986, p. 3; December 1986, p. 2.

areas of either the South or the Midwest, where most women furniture workers in the United States were concentrated.[123]

Women's attendance as local union delegates at UFWA conventions also increased. The percentage female among UFWA convention delegates averaged 1.2 percent between 1939 and 1948; 5.4 percent during the 1950s; and 8.2 percent in the 1960s. Between 1970 and 1984, the percentage of women delegates jumped from 12.4 percent to 23.3 percent of all convention delegates. Women also expanded their presence on the International UFWA GEB during this period, as shown in Chapter 1 (see Table 1.4). Between 1970 and 1984, the percentage female of GEB members increased from 3.3 percent to 16.7 percent.[124]

In sum, the initial mobilization of women in the UFWA was sparked largely by the civil rights movement and the mobilization of minorities. Minority mobilization led to the development of black women UFWA activists who became the chief leaders of the mobilization of women. The mobilization of women sharpened their gender consciousness as growing numbers of women, white and black, participated in union governance, allying with the Coalition of Labor Union Women in the national mobilization of women in the labor movement. Given that the chief activists believed in the ideology of working class unity, and that this ideology contributed to, as well as formed part of, the context in which the mobilization of women occurred, the demands of the UFWA women's caucus broadened further by the early 1980s to encompass the political, social, and economic interests of all workers.

Gender Integration

Between 1970 and 1984, a total of ten women served on the International GEB. No more than five women served on the GEB at any one time.

The geographical distribution of women furniture workers, that is, their concentration in the South and Midwest, was reflected in the geographical and ethnic characteristics of the ten women GEB members. Four were black southerners, and four were white midwesterners. The others were a black woman from the East Coast and a Hispanic woman from Los Angeles.

The geographical origins of the ten women GEB members suggest that their locations in areas whose political strength was increasing in the UFWA facilitated their rise onto the GEB, just as it did in the case of minority mobilization. The shifting axis of power in the UFWA from the Northeast toward the South and nonmetropolitan Midwest, the areas into which furniture manufacturing itself was moving, seemed to favor

---

[123] *Proceedings,* 1974 UFWA Convention, p. 168.
[124] *Proceedings* of the 1939–1984 UFWA conventions.

women in these areas. Four of the five black women GEB members were southerners, and three of the five white women GEB members were from nonmetropolitan areas in the Midwest.

The social characteristics of the ten women corresponded more closely to the ethnic composition than to the gender composition of their locals. Six of the women were from predominantly male locals; two were from a mixed gender local; and two were from a predominantly female local. Ethnically speaking, all of the black women were from predominantly black locals; the Hispanic woman was from a predominantly Hispanic local; three of the other whites were from predominantly white locals; and one white, non-Hispanic woman was from a predominantly black and Hispanic local.[125]

Apart from the efforts of the women's caucus to increase women's participation in union governance, other factors promoted gender integration on the GEB. These were official proclamations by the top leadership in support of women's participation, support from minority activists, and concerted efforts by national UFWA leaders to develop female leadership.

Official proclamations. In their report to each UFWA convention between 1970 and 1984, the top International UFWA officers espoused women's rights and the development of women leaders in the UFWA.[126] The chief rationale for this stance was the ideology of working class unity. As in the official proclamations that supported minority rights and minority participation in union governance, the proclamations on developing women leaders were often cast in terms of unifying women and men workers, lest employers divide all workers through sex discrimination and undermine workers' wages.

Illustrative of this stance is the 1976 officers' report. After condemning the "assignment of second-class citizenship to women," the officers wrote

> Our best weapon against the employers' "divide and conquer" tactics is our own unity. . . . And all of us in [the] UFWA must work to extend and expand the democratic practices which have characterized our organization. . . . Let us train ourselves to accept the right of each special group to develop its own program; to accept that group's leadership in a struggle around their own special needs. Let us give all out support to the wom-

---

[125] Data on the ethnic and gender composition of the ten women GEB members' local unions are from various personal interviews I conducted with nine of the women and other informants.

[126] *Proceedings,* 1970 UFWA Convention, p. 45; *Proceedings,* 1972 UFWA Convention, p. 36; *Proceedings,* 1974 UFWA Convention, pp. 17A–18A; *Proceedings,* 1976 UFWA Convention, pp. 72–73; *Proceedings,* 1980 UFWA Convention, pp. 35, 59–62, 69–70, 214; *Proceedings,* 1982 UFWA Convention, p. 34; *Proceedings,* 1984 UFWA Convention, pp. 48–50.

en's organizations who are campaigning for the Equal Rights Amendment—which has the endorsement of the Coalition of Labor Union Women and the AFL-CIO.[127]

The officers put it even more explicitly in their 1974 report:

> In many of our local unions, there are hidden talents among our women members. Many of them have never developed those talents because their brothers had an older union tradition and they talk louder! But it's time to uncover those hidden talents. . . . We call upon our local leaders to make this a special project: Encourage our women members to take their place on UFWA boards and councils.[128]

Nor were the officers averse to allying the UFWA with a political coalition of women's and other progressive organizations. As they stated in their report to the 1980 UFWA convention, "We have to battle to reverse the trend toward eating away at our inadequate share of the wealth we produce. . . . To win this fight, we will need the active participation of all our allies—in labor, women's organizations, senior citizen groups, civil rights organizations and others."[129]

The 1980 UFWA convention approved of the officers' stance on women's participation in unions. At each UFWA convention, a Committee on Officers' Report was appointed to report its review of the officers' report at the convention. The 1980 committee report, which was approved by the convention,[130] supported the officers' efforts to increase women's participation in the union: "Far too long, the role of women workers has been ignored. We recognize that vast, vital role they can play to achieve success in the field of organized labor, and we wholeheartedly encourage your continued efforts in this area."[131]

Throughout the 1970s and 1980s, then, top UFWA leadership encouraged women's participation in union governance. The encouragement, which was partly manifested in official proclamations, was presented in terms of the ideology of working class unity and, therefore, was deemed to be consistent with UFWA tradition.

Minority support of women. Women's participation in union governance was also supported by the minority activists within the UFWA. The mobilization of women became increasingly intertwined with the mobili-

---

[127] *Proceedings,* 1976 UFWA Convention, pp. 72–73.
[128] *Proceedings,* 1974 UFWA Convention, pp. 17A–18A.
[129] *Proceedings,* 1980 UFWA Convention, pp. 69–70.
[130] Ibid., p. 215.
[131] Ibid., p. 214.

zation of minorities in the UFWA. Just as the women's caucus convention resolutions broadened in support of all workers' rights, so the resolutions of the Committee on Minority Affairs increasingly championed the rights of both minorities and women. The increased support of women's rights in the Committee on Minority Affairs resolutions accompanied an increase in women's participation on the committee. The number of women members of the nine-person committee increased from two to four between the 1970 and 1984 UFWA conventions, with a peak number of six women committee members at the 1974 convention.[132]

The fusing of the women's and minority mobilizations also occurred because both groups came to perceive of each other as socially disadvantaged groups. The report of the 1970 Committee on Minority Affairs addressed exclusively the rights and needs of ethnic minorities, calling for ethnically representative, International UFWA leadership, as discussed earlier. The committee continued its emphasis on minority rights and the development of minority UFWA leadership, but it expanded its mission to include championing women's rights in the mid-1970s and early 1980s. The turning point of the Committee on Minority Affairs occurred at the 1974 UFWA convention, which was the next convention after the 1972 convention, at which the founding of the women's caucus had taken place. The report of the 1974 Committee on Minority Affairs included a resolution on women workers, which was presented by Committee Secretary Maggie Mae Edwards and which called for support of the Equal Rights Amendment, UFWA efforts to create employment opportunities for women workers, and increased participation of women in UFWA governance.[133] According to Committee Chair Enio Carrion, the committee's rationale for including the report on women workers in its report was as follows: "We thought it would be right and proper to have a resolution on . . . full equality for women's rights, because we felt that women are a minority within themselves, and there are certain rights and privileges that we males have that our . . . sisters don't have."[134]

All of the subsequent reports of the Committee on Minority Affairs included a political agenda that combined the rights and needs of both women and minorities. As the 1984 report of the committee put it,

> In every area of life, black, Latino, Asian and other minority groups have been hit hardest by the Reagan cuts [in social welfare programs]. . . .

---

[132] *Proceedings*, 1970 UFWA Convention, pp. 208–211; *Proceedings*, 1972 UFWA Convention, pp. 228–232; *Proceedings*, 1974 UFWA Convention, pp. 92–96; *Proceedings*, 1976 UFWA Convention, pp. 262–264; *Proceedings*, 1980 UFWA Convention, pp. 205–206; *Proceedings*, 1982 UFWA Convention, pp. 112–113; *Proceedings*, 1984 UFWA Convention, pp. 169–170.

[133] *Proceedings*, 1974 UFWA Convention, p. 93.

[134] Ibid., p. 92.

Women have also been primary victims of this administration. Inequality in hiring, pay and promotion continues to plague women workers—with black and Latina women the most underpaid. . . . At this moment in history, we believe that the most effective blow we can strike for full equality is to remove Ronald Reagan from the White House—and all the Reaganites from the U.S. Senate and Congress, and from every state house and legislature. . . . The Committee on Minorities calls upon every delegate to this convention to reaffirm the UFWA's traditional commitment to full and equal rights for all Americans . . . [and] to encourage full participation in union affairs by minority and women members.[135]

What was said in words was also expressed in actions. The support by minority activists for women's participation in UFWA governance is evidenced in the union career of Vernice Sanders, a black woman from Leland, MS, local 382 who was first elected to the GEB in 1984.

The daughter of cotton sharecroppers, Vernice Sanders was born in Crenshaw, MS, in 1935. Since the age of three or four, she had worked in the fields with her parents, who had not been involved in the labor movement. In 1954, she quit school before finishing eleventh grade, in order to work. Soon thereafter, Sanders moved to Leland, MS, where her uncle lived, and held a series of jobs. In 1967, she was hired as an upholsterer by the Dillingham Co., a manufacturer of case goods and upholstered household furniture. The company trained Sanders, who was the first black woman worker to be employed in the plant. She worked in upholstery for twelve years, transferred to the case goods finishing department (spraying and sanding on an assembly line) and then to the rough mill (preparing wood for furniture parts), and returned to upholstery in 1985.[136]

Sanders became active in her local union when she received an unexpectedly low pay increase. Local 382 of the UFWA had already been established by the Dillingham workers when Sanders was first hired. Joining the union was optional under the open shop contract (the Mississippi right-to-work law prohibited union shop contracts), and Sanders joined with the encouragement of her co-workers. Disappointed with the low wages in a recently negotiated contract, Sanders and others left the union. In December 1969, just after Christmas, the workers struck the plant for higher wages. After the strike was settled, Sanders became embittered toward management over the low wage increase. Alzada Clark, the International UFWA representative who was servicing local 382, heard about Sanders's attitude toward management and encouraged her to join the union. Sanders joined and rose quickly through the hierarchy of local union offices. Regarded as outspoken by the predominantly black and male, one

[135] *Proceedings*, 1984 UFWA Convention, pp. 169–170.
[136] Personal interview with Vernice Sanders in Leland, MS, on May 30, 1985.

hundred-person workforce, Sanders was elected local union recording secretary in 1973 and local union president in 1975, a position she continued to hold without opposition.[137]

Vernice Sanders's involvement in the civil rights movement, participating in demonstrations with freedom riders and with minority activists within the labor movement, inspired her to participate in union governance. Especially inspiring was the march in which she participated in 1968, after the assassination of Martin Luther King, Jr., when several hundred workers in the area walked off the job and marched in the rain for two days, what she remembered as her proudest day. She equated civil rights struggles with struggles in the workplace and became a minority activist within the labor movement. During the early 1970s, she became involved in the A. Philip Randolph Institute (APRI), a national, black trade unionists' organization whose leaders inspired Sanders to participate in her union. Her involvement in APRI resulted from her involvement in local labor organizations. She represented local 382 at the central labor council in nearby Greenville, MS. The Greenville central labor council, along with her local, elected Sanders a delegate to the Mississippi State AFL-CIO, and, by participating in the activities of the latter organization, she was introduced to APRI. In 1982, with the encouragement of APRI, she was elected to the board of the Mississippi State AFL-CIO.[138]

Minority activists in the UFWA encouraged Sanders to run for an open position on the International UFWA GEB in 1984. When Maggie Mae Edwards retired, Booker McCollum, Enio Carrion, and Ken Williams, a black leader from Baltimore local 75A, approached Sanders at the convention and asked her to run for the office vacated by Edwards. Sanders, who had not thought about running for a GEB position before the convention, received the support of other southern and national UFWA leaders and was elected the southern at-large representative on the GEB.[139]

In sum, the mobilization of minorities within the UFWA, and the civil rights movement generally, contributed to the gender integration of the GEB. Minority activists supported minority candidates of both genders. Furthermore, with the mobilization of women under way, minority activists increasingly perceived of women workers as an exploited minority in the United States, throwing their support behind gender integration of UFWA leadership positions. The mobilizations of minorities and women became increasingly intertwined as each group reinforced the other's effort to attain leadership positions on the GEB.

---

[137] Ibid.
[138] Ibid.; *Furniture Workers Press,* November 1981, p. 3.
[139] Sanders interview.

Top leadership support of women leaders. Top International UFWA leaders often participated directly in the development of female leadership in the union. Their participation consisted of establishing and conducting leadership training programs, mentoring new leaders, and recognizing outspoken leaders whom they encouraged to serve on the GEB.

The expression of top leadership support of women GEB candidates typically occurred in one of two ways, depending on the size of the candidate's local union. First, women GEB candidates from the large, urban, amalgamated locals were mentored by, or worked closely with, an International UFWA GEB member from the candidate's local. Almost all of the men who had served in the highest-ranking International UFWA offices were from these locals, and they often helped develop the union careers of these women GEB members, first in the local union and then in the International UFWA.

Second, women GEB candidates from the small, typically one-shop, local unions in nonmetropolitan areas were recognized by top UFWA leaders after they had begun to rise through the office hierarchy of their local unions with the support of their co-workers. These women were recognized as being among the most outspoken and dedicated trade unionists and, in some cases, civil rights activists in their districts and regions by the top leadership, who consequently supported their GEB candidacies.

A disproportionately large number of women GEB members came from small locals and, as a result, received the second type of support from the top UFWA leadership. As discussed in Chapter 2 (see Table 2.1), a large majority of all UFWA GEB members came from amalgamated locals with at least five hundred members located in major cities or furniture manufacturing towns. In contrast, five of the ten women GEB members were from small locals in nonmetropolitan areas. The women GEB members from small locals were Maggie Mae Edwards from Camden, AR, local 250; Vernice Sanders from Leland, MS, local 382; June Vayer from Monroe, MI, local 416; and Sharon Bolden and Helen Dalberg, both from Janesville, WI, local 801. The five women GEB members from the large, urban, amalgamated locals, who had worked closely with International UFWA leaders during much of their union careers, were Etta Haden from Baltimore local 75; Adeline Williams and Ida Leachman, both from Memphis local 282; Cynthia Requejo from Los Angeles local 1010; and Andrea Stack from Chicago local 18B.

The preponderance of women GEB members who were from small, nonmetropolitan locals is partly attributable to the timing of both the mobilization of women in the UFWA and the geographical redistribution of the furniture manufacturing industry. The mobilization of women coincided with the shift of the industry into the nonmetropolitan areas of the South and Midwest (see Chapter 2). Moreover, industry geographical redistribution contributed to membership declines in the once dominant, urban, amalgamated locals. The subsequent geographical realignment of political strength within the UFWA reduced the number of GEB seats that the large eastern and midwestern urban locals could claim, opening up the GEB to the smaller nonmetropolitan locals in the South and Midwest, the regions in which most women furniture workers were concentrated.

The type of top leadership support the ten women members received, then, was shaped in part by the coincidence of the UFWA mobilization of women and the industry geographical redistribution. The five women from the small, nonmetropolitan southern and midwestern locals were recognized by top leadership as being among the most outspoken labor leaders after they had gained the support of their co-workers on the shop floor and had risen to high local union offices. The five women from the large, urban, amalgamated locals, in contrast, had worked closely with an International UFWA leader during much of their local union careers, gaining support from both rank-and-file co-workers and top leadership.

Throughout the 1970s and 1980s, the International UFWA conducted union officer training programs in which many women participated. Top UFWA leaders often instructed groups of workers that were mixed by gender.[140] For example, a *Furniture Workers Press* article on a two-day, steward training seminar, which was conducted in Jackson, MS, in 1977 by the International UFWA for Mississippi and Arkansas activists from four UFWA locals, included a photo of Secretary-Treasurer Lowell Daily speaking to a predominantly black and mixed gender audience. Daily participated in a 1977 steward training seminar in Cookeville, TN, with a predominantly white group of members of both genders from three recently organized shops. Similarly, Daily conducted such seminars in Tennessee in October 1980 and in Los Angeles in June 1983.[141]

The International UFWA also trained women leaders by participating in a U.S. Department of Labor National Job Training and Counseling Program (NJTCP). Established in July 1978 with a U.S. Department of Labor grant, the UFWA NJTCP was "designed to train new entrants into the industry, with major emphasis on veterans, minority workers and women, as well as to assist [UFWA] members to learn new skills and upgrade their job levels."[142] Moreover, by providing on-the-job training for program

---

[140] *Furniture Workers Press,* January 1972, p. 1; June 1976, p. 12; July/August/September 1976, p. 12; March 1977, p. 4; July/August/September 1977, p. 2; May 1978, p. 4; February 1980, pp. 2, 4; September 1981, p. 4; April 1982, p. 3; January 1985, p. 3.

[141] Ibid., March 1977, p. 4; July/August/September 1977, p. 2; November 1980, p. 5; June 1983, p. 5.

[142] *Proceedings,* 1980 UFWA Convention, p. 59.

participants, the NJTCP would increase the supply of skilled workers for employers, who participated in the program through the local unions. By June 1980, over 500 workers had participated in NJTCP. Almost 400 had received diplomas, of whom 35 percent were women, 37 percent were black, and 31 percent were Hispanic. By April 1982, when the NJTCP grant expired, 1,085 workers had participated, and almost 900 had graduated from the program.[143]

During the life of the NJTCP, the UFWA held conferences on the role of women in the furniture industry and the UFWA and on industry conditions. For example, at a June 1979 conference held at the Highlander Research Center in New Market, TN, local leaders studied ways of disseminating information on health and safety and economic conditions to trainees; and, in 1980, conferences designed to encourage women to take nontraditional roles were held in Memphis and Baltimore.[144]

More unique was Memphis local 282's organizing school. Established in December 1978, the school offered a six-month program with Saturday training sessions on organizing for local 282 activists and shop stewards. The school was established by Willie Rudd, a black activist from local 282 who was president of the local and International UFWA southern vice president.[145]

Born in northern Mississippi in 1944, Rudd was reared by his mother, a factory worker, and his father, a butcher, in Memphis, TN. His father, an active member of the Meatcutters union, exposed him to unionism at an early age. As a child, Rudd was taken by his father to union meetings, where he developed strong feelings about the central role of unions in supporting workers and solving work problems. His father often attributed the food on the table at home to the union.[146]

After graduating from high school in 1961, Rudd took a job as a laborer at Memphis Broom and Brush, a broom manufacturer; became a broommaker; and, in 1962, took a job as a supplier in the upholstery division of National Bedding and Furniture, a Memphis manufacturer of upholstered, household furniture. In six months, he became an upholsterer, a job he held for the next eleven years.[147]

Rudd rose quickly through the hierarchy of offices in Memphis local 282, an amalgamated local that had just organized National Bedding and Furniture before Rudd's arrival in the shop. Regarded as outspoken by his

---

[143] Ibid., p. 60; *Proceedings,* 1982 UFWA Convention, p. 35; *Furniture Workers Press,* July/August/September, 1978, p. 8; May 1979, p. 5; July/August/September 1979, p. 3; October 1979, p. 3; December 1979, p. 2; March 1980, p. 4; June 1980, p. 6.

[144] *Proceedings,* 1980 UFWA Convention, p. 60; *Furniture Workers Press,* July/August/September 1979, p. 3; October 1979, p. 3; November 1980, p. 2.

[145] *Furniture Workers Press,* January 1979, p. 1.

[146] Personal interview with Willie Rudd in Memphis, TN, on August 5, 1985.

[147] Ibid.

fellow workers, Rudd was elected department steward in 1963. He soon began an internal organizing drive among the four hundred predominantly black and female workers in the plant, only one-third of whom were union members (union-shop contracts were outlawed by the Tennessee right-to-work law). Having mobilized the other stewards in the drive, Rudd helped to bring 90 percent of the plant workers into the union by 1965, when the workers struck the plant for pay and fringe benefit improvements. Rudd was active in the strike and on the picket line and, in 1965, was elected chief steward of the plant and a member of the local 282 executive board. In the same year, local 282 President Carl Scarbrough initiated and solicited volunteers for a local union organizing drive among non-union shops in Memphis. Rudd volunteered and worked closely with Scarbrough and Leroy Clark in organizing drives and as a shop steward for the next five years. In 1970, when Scarbrough was elected International secretary-treasurer and Leroy Clark was elected local 282 president, Rudd, with their encouragement, was elected vice president of local 282. Upon Clark's retirement, Rudd was elected president of local 282 in 1975, a position he has since held.[148]

After becoming a local union officer, Rudd was elected to the International UFWA GEB. With the support of Scarbrough and Clark, Rudd was first elected to the GEB in 1972 to the seat for piano and musical instrument workers (local 282 represented several piano workers), a position he held for four years. In 1976, Rudd succeeded Clark in the International UFWA office of southern vice president, becoming the second black top-ranking International UFWA officer in the union's history.[149]

Rudd helped two black women, Ida Leachman and Adeline Williams, become elected to the International UFWA GEB. Leachman, a graduate of the local 282 organizing school, was born in Holly Springs, MS, in 1929. The daughter of a bird dog trainer and a houseworker, neither of whom had been involved in the labor movement, Leachman graduated from high school in Memphis, where she subsequently had a series of factory and laundry cleaning jobs. In 1969, she took a sewing machine operator job at United Uniform Manufacturing Co., where she worked for ten years before she became a full-time UFWA representative.[150]

Leachman became active in local 282 during her tenure at United Uniform. Local 282 had attempted unsuccessfully to organize United Uniform when she was first hired and resumed its organizing campaign in 1977. Leachman, who had developed pro-union feelings during her early adolescence, actively participated in the campaign, and the union won

---

[148] Ibid.
[149] Ibid.
[150] Personal interview with Ida Leachman in Memphis, TN, on May 31, 1985.

representation in December 1978. Considered strong, outgoing, and outspoken by her co-workers, Leachman was elected department steward in 1979. Soon thereafter, she attended steward classes taught by local 282, the International UFWA, and the Memphis labor council. She also attended the local 282 organizing school and was instructed by Willie Rudd, whom she regarded as her chief mentor and supporter in the union. Just before her graduation, the International UFWA informed Rudd of an opening for a black woman International representative who was needed for an organizing campaign in Ft. Worth, TX. Rudd announced the opening to the class, and Leachman was hired. Upon completion of the campaign, she returned to Memphis, and, in 1980, was hired by local 282 as a representative, servicing shops in Memphis and the southern region. In 1983, the incumbent vice president of local 282 decided not to seek reelection, and Rudd asked Leachman, who had not considered being a local union officer, if she would be interested in running for the office. She was elected vice president, a position she has since held. About one week before the 1984 International UFWA convention, Rudd informed her of a vacancy in the GEB seat for bedding workers and asked her to run for the position. Ida Leachman was elected to the GEB in 1984.[151]

Rudd was also involved in the union career of Adeline Williams. The daughter of farmers who had not been involved in the labor movement, Williams was born in 1933 in Oakland, TN, about thirty miles from Memphis. After graduating from high school, she held a few jobs as a domestic worker and a beauty salon manicurist in Memphis. In 1966, she took a job as a spring roll machine operator at the Aeolian Piano Co., a piano manufacturer in Memphis. She worked several jobs in the plant, including cutting and building butts, punching spring rails, and making base dampers, until the plant closed in March 1985.[152]

Local 282 already represented the Aeolian workers when Williams was hired. In 1967, with the strong encouragement of her co-workers, she was elected department steward, a position she held for the next eighteen years, until the plant closed. As a steward, Williams met monthly with the local 282 officers, including Willie Rudd. In 1979, Rudd, who admired Williams's union activism, asked her to serve out the term of the piano workers' representative seat on the International UFWA GEB, which had been held by local 282 and vacated by the incumbent. Williams agreed to serve, and at the next UFWA convention in 1980, she was elected to that GEB position and served the four-year term.[153]

The union career of Andrea Stack, a woman of Polish descent from

[151] Ibid.
[152] Personal interview with Adeline Williams in Memphis, TN, on August 6, 1985.
[153] Ibid.; Rudd interview.

Chicago local 18B, also exemplifies the impact of mentoring by top leaders on the development of women union leaders. Stack was born in Hinsdale, IL, in 1946. The daughter of a factory worker and a homemaker, neither of whom had been involved in the labor movement, she completed three years of high school and then worked as a waitress. In 1965, she took an assembly line job at the Illinois Molding Co., a Chicago manufacturer of pictures, picture frames, and curios. After working at all stations on the assembly line, Stack transferred to the office in 1969 and performed general clerical tasks. In 1976, dissatisfied with her pay, she resigned from Illinois Molding and took a job as a bank teller, but she discovered that the teller salary was lower than what she had been making.[154]

Stack's career in the UFWA began in 1977 when Sam Sloan, business manager of Chicago local 18B, hired her as the local union office secretary. Sloan, whose biography is described in Chapter 3, helped found UFWA local 18B in 1940, was elected periodically to the International UFWA GEB during the 1940s, served almost continuously as International UFWA vice president of the Midwest between 1950 and 1970, and simultaneously headed local 18B through the 1980s. Stack had known Sloan from her job at Illinois Molding, whose predominantly black, Hispanic, and female workers were already represented by amalgamated local 18B when she was hired. Having had little experience with unionism before her Illinois Molding job, Stack developed pro-union feelings and learned about the union by conversing with her steward and reading the union insurance booklet during her tenure at Illinois Molding. She often attended union meetings, but, despite her desire to become a steward, she was prevented from attaining the position by the incumbent, a tough white woman who threatened challengers. Stack had befriended Sloan when he visited the Illinois Molding office, during which time he often asked her if she was interested in taking the local union office secretarial job when the current office secretary retired. In 1977, after thirty-five years of service, the office secretary retired, and Stack, whom Sloan sought out, resigned from the bank to take the local union office secretarial job. Once Stack was hired as office secretary, Sloan frequently discussed labor history with her. In 1981, the financial secretary of local 18B retired, and Sloan, whom Stack regarded as her chief mentor in the labor movement, asked her to run for the position. In an uncontested election, she became financial secretary, a full-time job in the local, whose membership was predominantly black and Hispanic and male. At the 1984 UFWA convention, UFWA President Carl Scarbrough, whom Stack had met at earlier conventions, asked her if she would run for the GEB seat representing curtain, drapery, venetian blinds, and furniture cover workers. Local 18B had not been represented on the

---

[154] Personal interview with Andrea Stack in Cicero, IL, on July 3, 1985.

GEB since 1974 because of an earlier falling out between local 18B and the International UFWA over the conduct of an organizing campaign. In 1984, Scarbrough told Stack that he would like local 18B to be represented on the GEB. With Sloan's support, Stack ran for the position and was elected to the GEB.[155]

The biographies of three white women GEB members, June Vayer, Sharon Bolden, and Helen Dalberg, all of whom were from small locals in nonmetropolitan, midwestern towns, illustrate the process by which top leadership identified women leaders from locals in which members would have been unlikely to experience a close working relationship with an International UFWA mentor. The daughter of farmers who had been uninvolved in the labor movement, June Vayer was born in 1917 in LaGrange, IN. She graduated from high school and, in 1935, took a job at Woodall's in Monroe, MI, an automobile parts manufacturer, sewing automobile sun visors. During World War II, when the plant was converted to war production, she worked as a spot welding press operator, making fighter plane parts, and attended beauty school at nights. In 1945, she resigned from Woodall's to help create jobs for the returning soldiers and opened up a beauty shop, which she owned for the next eighteen years. In 1963, she sold the beauty shop in order to spend more time with her twelve-year-old daughter. Her husband had a stroke in the following year, and she took a sewing machine operator job at the La-Z-Boy Co., a manufacturer of upholstered reclining chairs. She held the same job until her retirement in 1983.[156]

With the initial encouragement of her husband, a shop steward in the United Automobile Workers union who had urged her to use her union to solve work problems, Vayer was elected department steward in 1964 in UFWA local 416. The one-shop local had already been established when Vayer was hired. Over two-thirds of the plant workforce were recent white migrants from Tennessee and, of the 550 workers, over one-fourth were women. Vayer felt that the women workers in the sewing department were treated unfairly by the supervisors, in comparison with the treatment men workers received, and that the local union officers, older men who had founded the local union but did not understand women's issues, neglected the grievances filed against the company by women workers. Vayer, perceived as trustworthy and outspoken by the predominantly female workforce in the sewing department, defeated her male opponent by a large margin in the election for department steward.[157]

In 1965, as the local union had been dominated by men, the male

---

[155] Ibid.; personal interview with Sam Sloan in Cicero, IL, on December 23, 1985.
[156] Personal interview with June Vayer in Monroe, MI, on July 30, 1985.
[157] Ibid.

union members who attended the union meeting at which officer elections were to be conducted thought it was funny and laughed when Vayer was nominated to run for a position on the shop committee. However, every woman worker in the plant turned out for the election, and Vayer was elected, becoming the first woman shop committee member in the local union. Vayer encouraged other women to run for union office, promoted women candidates, and continued to be reelected annually to the shop committee, negotiating contracts and handling grievances, until 1978. She ran unsuccessfully for local union president in 1976 but was elected president in 1978, a position she held until her retirement.[158]

In 1974, June Vayer was elected to the International UFWA GEB. Vayer and Barbara Blair, also a member of local 416, were elected by the local as the two delegates it was permitted to send to the 1974 International UFWA convention. The women workers in local 416 wanted women convention delegates who could represent women's issues at the convention and engender recognition of women workers in the International. Prior to the early 1970s, when the local was dominated by men, the women members felt that it wasn't their place to serve as convention delegates. By 1974, once Vayer and other women workers felt strong within themselves and that they were just as capable as men of serving as convention delegates, they developed a desire to present women's problems at the convention to the men, whom they regarded as uninformed about such problems.[159]

Vayer and Blair attended the 1974 UFWA convention as trade unionists, rather than as women. At the time, Vayer objected to "women's liberation" because she wanted to preserve, as she put it, her femininity: she wanted to be treated equally as a worker, but otherwise as a woman.[160]

At the convention, UFWA President Scarbrough asked Vayer and Blair if either of them would serve on the International UFWA GEB. Scarbrough knew Vayer from his visits to local 416 and from attending meetings of the UFWA district 7 (Michigan) executive board, of which Vayer was a member. The Monroe, MI, La-Z-Boy plant had had troubled labor relations, and Scarbrough, who was often summoned to Monroe on such occasions, came to know Vayer as an outspoken trade unionist. Moreover, Scarbrough, responding to the women's caucus, wanted a district 7 woman on the GEB. District 7, and its executive board, had become dissatisfied with the quality of International UFWA servicing and organizing in the district, and Scarbrough extended the offer of GEB representation to district 7 in reconciliation. At first, Vayer and Blair declined the offer because they feared serving on the GEB and felt they lacked sufficient knowledge. They

---

[158] Ibid.
[159] Ibid.
[160] Ibid.

stayed up all night discussing the matter. Vayer and Blair, who was single, decided that serving on the GEB would further the cause for which they attended the convention and that a married woman would command more respect than a single woman from the men GEB members. Moreover, they felt that they could always solicit Scarbrough's assistance if they needed help. The next day, they informed Scarbrough that Vayer would run for the GEB position. Among Vayer's strongest supporters were Scarbrough and Secretary-Treasurer Lowell Daily, whose previous position had been district director and who knew Vayer; Etta Haden; district 7 leaders; the International UFWA executive committee; and several predominantly black southern and eastern locals, some of whose support for Vayer had been mobilized by Alzada Clark. Furthermore, Vayer was known among New Yorkers because of the visibility local 416 had received when it went out on strike to support the organizing campaign at the Florence, SC, La-Z-Boy plant in 1970–1971, described earlier. June Vayer was subsequently elected to the GEB, becoming the second woman GEB member in the UFWA, and served ten years before her retirement.[161]

Sharon Bolden, from Janesville, WI, local 801, was elected to the International UFWA GEB in 1976. The daughter of a farmer and a bartender, both of whom had only minimal involvement in the labor movement, Bolden was born in LaFarge, WI, in 1941. She held several factory and clerical jobs after graduating from high school. In 1962, she took a job folding doors at the Hough Shade Co., a manufacturer of accordion doors in Janesville, WI. She was working at a "class 7" job when, in 1969, she applied for a higher-status, "class 4" job as a chipboard laminating machine operator. At the time, women were beginning to be employed in what had been regarded as men's jobs, and the company denied her the job on the grounds that she was unqualified. A self-proclaimed rebel, Bolden had often performed heavy manual farm work when she was growing up and, having decided she could do the job, took her grievance to arbitration. The arbitrator awarded her the job with back pay, and Bolden became the first woman in the plant to hold a "class 4" job. By 1971, she had been promoted to a "class 2" job and worked a series of jobs in the receiving, paint, shipping, and other departments until she resigned from Hough in 1980 for a higher-paying, General Motors job.[162]

Bolden became an active member of UFWA local 801, a one-shop local that had already been organized at Hough when Bolden was hired. Her feelings about "women's liberation" were similar to those expressed by June Vayer. Regarded as outspoken by her co-workers, about half of whom were also from farming backgrounds, she was elected department

---

[161] Ibid.; Alzada Clark interview.
[162] Personal interview with Sharon Bolden in Footville, WI, on August 4, 1985.

steward in 1973 and president of the all white, predominantly female, one hundred fifty-person local in 1974. She remained president until her resignation from the company.[163]

In 1976, she was elected to the district 8 (Wisconsin and Illinois) seat on the International UFWA GEB. The district 8 seat had been held by Rockford, IL, local 707 since 1952. Local 707 membership had declined by the time of the 1976 UFWA convention, and it consequently lost its claim to the seat. Local 707 was merged into Sheboygan, WI, local 800 about five weeks after the 1976 convention.[164] Although Chicago local 18B was the largest district 8 local, it had fallen from the graces of the International, as discussed earlier, and was out of the running for the seat. Local 800, the second largest local in district 8, already claimed the one GEB seat that the UFWA constitution allowed it to have. Moreover, a long-standing personal feud between Sam Sloan and local 800 led local 800 to prevent local 18B from representing district 8 on the GEB. Local 800 threw its weight behind local 801, the only remaining local in the district, and Bolden was elected to the GEB. She served in this capacity until the 1980 UFWA convention, by which time Helen Dalberg had succeeded her in the presidency of local 801.[165]

The daughter of farmers who had no involvement in the labor movement, Helen Dalberg was born in Darlington, WI, in 1953. After graduating from high school, she held a few factory and waitress jobs and, around 1971, took a job as an assembler at Hough, where Sharon Bolden was already employed. A few months later, she transferred to the door-building department, where she worked for ten years and became a lead person. In 1982, she returned to assembly work and has continued to work at this job.[166]

Dalberg's activism in local 801 was originally inspired by her husband and Sharon Bolden. Her husband had been employed at Hough and had served as a steward and officer in local 801. Also, Dalberg had befriended Bolden and admired her union activism, and Bolden encouraged her to become involved in the union. Through her union activism, Dalberg, who had little or no experience with the union, developed a deep interest in improving work and employment conditions and became more self-assured about her ability to speak out on behalf of the workers. She became known in the plant, not only through union Christmas parties, but also because her job in the door-building department afforded her much freedom of physical movement and required her to work with others, in

---

[163] Ibid.
[164] Archives of the International UFWA, Nashville, TN.
[165] Bolden interview; personal interview with Harold Kober in Sheboygan, WI, on August 2, 1985.
[166] Personal interview with Helen Dalberg in Janesville, WI, on August 3, 1985.

comparison with other jobs in the plant. She was elected a member of the negotiating committee in 1976, a local union trustee in 1977, and department steward in 1978.[167]

In 1980, Dalberg was elected president of local 801. The workforce had been declining since the late 1970s, and, in 1980, Hough filed for a Chapter 11 bankruptcy. Workers increasingly feared the loss of their jobs, and tension developed among the local union officers. A controversy about how to govern the local union ensued, and Bolden resigned from the presidency late in her term in January 1980. Dalberg was elected president for the interim, elected president at the next regular officer election in April 1980, and reelected to this office in subsequent elections.[168]

At the 1980 International UFWA convention in June, Robert Sebera, International UFWA vice president of the Midwest, encouraged Dalberg to run for the district 8 GEB seat, which had been vacated by Bolden's resignation. By that time, local 801 had come to "claim" this GEB seat. Despite this, Dalberg felt inexperienced and initially hesitated to run for the seat. However, with Sebera's encouragement, she ran successfully for the position and was reelected to that GEB seat at the 1984 convention.[169]

Despite their support of women GEB members, top UFWA leaders did not consistently support women GEB candidates. This is illustrated by the contest between Cynthia Requejo and Fred Perez for the International UFWA office of vice president of the West. A vacancy occurred in this office in May 1982 when incumbent Pino Espudo, who had held the office since 1976, resigned from his post. Espudo, also business manager of Los Angeles local 1010, was exposed for embezzlement and left the UFWA after making restitution. The local was placed in trusteeship in May 1982 by the International UFWA until officer elections could be conducted, and Requejo was elected local 1010 business manager in July 1982.[170]

It was now the responsibility of the International UFWA GEB to select a western vice president who would serve for the duration of the term (the next election would occur at the 1984 UFWA convention). The GEB began to mobilize support for candidates from the western region, which consisted of the large, amalgamated Los Angeles and San Francisco locals and a small local in Portland, OR. Cynthia Requejo and Fred Perez, secretary-treasurer of San Francisco local 262, emerged as the contenders for the western vice presidency. Many of the Requejo supporters on the GEB wanted to elect a woman vice president (no woman had ever been elected

[167] Ibid.
[168] Ibid.; Bolden interview.
[169] Dalberg interview.
[170] Scarbrough interview; personal interview with Cynthia Requejo in Huntington Park, CA, on July 18, 1985.

a vice president or higher officer in the International UFWA) and felt she was qualified for the position. Many of the Perez supporters felt that he was qualified to serve because he had more labor movement experience than Requejo.[171]

Cynthia Requejo, of Portuguese and Mexican descent, was born in San Diego, CA, in 1949. The daughter of a homemaker and a restaurant chef, who was a member of the Hotel and Restaurant Employees Union, Requejo completed eight years of school, taking her first full-time job in 1966. She held a series of factory and food service jobs until 1976, when she was hired to work in the cabinet room of the Ken Craft Co., a manufacturer of recreational vehicles in Cucamonga, CA. Her first job at Ken Craft was paneling the furniture for recreational vehicles, a job typically held by women. She aspired to a promotion to framer, a job usually held by men, which entailed the building of cabinets. Her supervisor initially informed her that it was a job for a man and that she needed to be able to read a blueprint. After studying a blueprint overnight, she convinced her supervisor that she could perform the job and became a framer, a job she held until 1979, when she became a full-time International UFWA representative.[172]

Regarded as outspoken by her co-workers, Requejo ascended the office hierarchy in amalgamated local 1010, which already represented the Ken Craft workers when she was hired. At the time, a majority of the predominantly Hispanic (especially Mexican and Salvadoran), male, two hundred fifty-person Ken Craft workforce were undocumented, non-English-speaking immigrants, many of whom were from rural backgrounds and had little or no schooling. Being bilingual and a U.S. citizen, Requejo was not intimidated by the supervisors and could articulate worker needs to management. Moreover, the workers were dissatisfied with the shop stewards, most of whom were non-English-speaking, had been promoted to lead positions that brought them closer to management, and, consequently, were neglecting worker grievances. In 1977, at a heated union meeting at which worker complaints about union negligence were aired, Requejo was elected chief steward in an uncontested election. She remained chief steward in the plant until January 1979, when Pino Espudo and Helen Hernandez, the local 1010 business agent who serviced the Ken Craft shop, offered her a job as an International UFWA representative. In 1979, Requejo was elected recording secretary of local 1010, whose eleven hundred members were predominantly Hispanic and male. She went on to uncover Espudo's embezzlement activities, file charges against him with

---

[171] Personal interview with Peter Manzo in New York City on June 13, 1985; personal interview with Fred Perez in San Leandro, CA, on July 15, 1985; Scarbrough, Kober, Requejo, Rudd, Dalberg, and Adeline Williams interviews.

[172] Requejo interview.

the International UFWA, and become elected business manager of local 1010 in July 1982.[173]

Fred Perez, of Mexican descent and the son of a coal miner and farmer and a homemaker, was born in Pittsburgh, Oklahoma, in 1936. In 1947, his family moved to California, where his father and brothers were hired in shops that were organized by the Machinists union. Perez took his first full-time job in the mattress division of the Simmons Co., a San Francisco bed manufacturer, in 1955. After having several jobs in the mattress division, he was drafted into the army in 1959, where he received his high school diploma, and returned to Simmons in 1962. He was trained by the company as an upholsterer, the highest-paying job in the plant, and stayed at that job until 1977, when he took office as full-time secretary-treasurer of San Francisco local 262.[174]

Perez became active in local 262, which had been organized at Simmons during the 1930s, and soon rose through its hierarchy of offices. His initial exposure to unionism occurred at home in the late 1940s and early 1950s when his father and brothers would discuss the activities of their union at the dinner table. By the time he was hired at Simmons, Perez was aware of unionism. During the mid-1960s, he helped organize a credit union for local 262. The workers were receiving loans from their coworkers who acted as "loan sharks," charging them a 50 percent interest rate. The local union officials, however, expressed no support for the credit union, much to Perez's anger. Instead, the Simmons company went on to establish a credit union for its employees, and Perez was elected credit union president about 1966. He was already known by the workers because he was outspoken at union meetings. His reputation as a worker's advocate spread among the Simmons workers during the time he was involved in the credit union. Workers often sought out his assistance not only on financial matters, but also on work-related problems generally. He increasingly perceived the local union officials as neglecting worker grievances, especially those of the non-English-speaking Hispanic, Chinese, and Japanese workers, who accounted for roughly one-third of the three hundred seventy-five-person Simmons workforce and who were unable to communicate with the local union leadership. In addition, Perez felt that, under the leadership of Business Manager Fred Stefan, whose biography is described in Chapter 3, local 262 was run autocratically and members were intimidated by the aggressive and coercive leadership style. He perceived that workers feared speaking out at local union meetings, lest they lose their jobs, and were kept uninformed about the financial status of the local union. Accordingly, Perez ran for local union president, a non-full-

[173] Ibid.
[174] Perez interview.

time position, in 1969 and defeated his opponent by a close margin, regarded as a major upset of the incumbent leadership. Subsequently, he was elected to two more terms as president, notwithstanding that he had been the only local union executive board member who was not allied with Stefan, who retired from the union in 1978. In 1976, Perez was elected by a close margin to the full-time position of local union secretary-treasurer, a position he has since held. By that time, the ethnic composition of predominantly male, nine hundred-person, amalgamated local 262, in which the Simmons plant was the largest of the represented shops, comprised a growing proportion of black and Hispanic workers, who accounted for almost half of the membership.[175]

In 1979, Perez was elected to the International UFWA GEB to fill the at-large western representative seat. The position had been vacated when the incumbent's local union folded, and Perez was elected by the GEB to serve for the duration of the term. At the next regular officer election in 1980, Perez was elected to this seat by the International UFWA convention. The 1982 vacancy in the western vice presidency occurred in the middle of Perez's four-year term on the GEB.[176]

The International UFWA GEB became split over the two candidates for vice president of the West. The split occurred largely along geographical lines, with most of the regions and districts backing the candidate whom their highest-ranking leader was supporting. The high-ranking Requejo supporters included UFWA President Scarbrough, Secretary-Treasurer Daily, and Vice Presidents Rudd and Sebera. Accordingly, the southern GEB members and the GEB members from Michigan (district 7), where Daily had served as district director before his election as secretary-treasurer, constituted the majority of the votes for Requejo. Eastern Vice President Peter Manzo, from New York City local 76B-92-76, the largest local in the UFWA, mobilized most of the eastern GEB votes for Perez. Also, Sheboygan, WI, local 800, the third largest local in the UFWA, committed itself early in the campaign to Perez and lined up the Wisconsin (district 8) GEB votes accordingly. Local 800 leaders had met Perez at previous UFWA conventions through Fred Stefan, a German immigrant with whom they felt a special ethnic bond by virtue of the preponderance of people of German descent in the Sheboygan area. Requejo was relatively unknown to local 800. The majority of votes for Perez were from the East and district 8. Furthermore, the GEB vote did not break down along racial and gender lines. The black GEB members were split geographically over the two candidates, as were the women GEB members.[177]

[175] Ibid.
[176] Ibid.
[177] Kober, Manzo, Scarbrough, Rudd, Perez, and Requejo interviews.

The GEB voted 14 to 13 for Fred Perez, who was reelected western vice president at the next regular officer election by the 1984 UFWA convention. In 1982, Cynthia Requejo was elected to fill the at-large western representative GEB seat that was now vacated by Perez, and she was reelected to this seat at the 1984 UFWA convention.[178]

To summarize, top UFWA leadership tended to be supportive of women GEB candidates and to participate directly in the development of female leadership. Women leaders from the large, amalgamated locals were mentored by International UFWA leaders. Women leaders from the small locals had already risen through the office hierarchies of their locals when top UFWA leaders identified them as dedicated trade unionists and pushed their candidacies for the GEB.

The Emergence of Women on the GEB

Forces similar to those which facilitated ethnic integration also facilitated gender integration on the GEB. As more women entered the industry and the UFWA, the geographical redistribution of the industry and UFWA membership southward and into the nonmetropolitan Midwest, those regions in which women furniture workers were concentrated, led to a realignment of political strength within the UFWA that favored women GEB candidates.

Furthermore, women used their political strength by mobilizing in a women's caucus to promote the gender integration of the GEB. The mobilization of women was inspired in no small way by the civil rights movement and the mentoring of women UFWA activists by International UFWA leaders, which resulted in the strong influence of black women on the initial mobilization. Moreover, with the recognition of women workers as another disadvantaged minority, the mobilization of minorities became increasingly intertwined with the mobilization of women.

The ideology of working class unity constituted a part of the institutional context within which the mobilization of women occurred and which served to promote gender integration on the GEB. Top UFWA leaders, as well as women's activists, espoused the ideology as UFWA tradition, legitimizing and stimulating gender integration in the GEB, and participated actively in the development of women leaders.

Although I have emphasized the forces which promoted women, as a social group, into leadership positions, a final note on the domestic arrangements that facilitated their ascent as individuals is relevant. Past research has indicated that nonmarried women are more active union members than married women, implying that married women's household responsibilities detract from the time they might otherwise allocate to

[178] Manzo, Perez, and Requejo interviews.

union activism.[179] In contrast, eight of the ten women UFWA GEB members were married during most or all of their years as union activists, and one was married during her first fifteen years as an activist, until her husband died. All nine of the women GEB members whom I was able to interview claimed that their families were supportive of their union activism. Moreover, each of the ten women GEB members had child care arrangements that allowed her to become an active trade unionist. Two of the women GEB members had no children; three achieved their highest local union office by the time their children had become old enough to care for themselves; three had husbands or other relatives who performed a significant share of child care responsibilities; and two had children in a wide age range, some of whom could care for themselves and others who were cared for by the older children or other relatives.[180] This suggests that the supportiveness of a woman's family members, and their willingness to participate in household activities, have a greater impact than her marital status per se on her ability to become a labor leader.

The Ethnic and Gender Integration of UFWA Leadership

The ethnic and gender integration of the UFWA GEB during the 1970s and 1980s, following the 1950–1970 period of UFWA stability in which little leadership turnover took place, was closely connected to the civil rights movement of the 1960s, the geographical redistribution of furniture manufacturing and UFWA membership, and the subsequent decline in UFWA membership. Inspired by the civil rights movement, black, Hispanic, and women activists mobilized for increased participation in UFWA governance, each group supporting the others and perceiving one another as socially disadvantaged minorities.

Their efforts at attaining national leadership positions were aided by the realignment of UFWA political strength into the regions where they tended to reside, a realignment that resulted from the geographical redistribution of furniture manufacturers who resisted the union by relocating in low-wage, non-union areas and in areas with growing markets. Ironically, the advent of the large, corporate, multi-locational furniture manufacturer, coupled with the UFWA chain plant organizing strategy, effectively drew together workers from different regions and of diverse ethnic backgrounds in a common effort to improve their economic livelihoods.

---

[179] Barbara Wertheimer and Anne Nelson, *Trade Union Women: A Study of Their Participation in New York City Locals* (New York: Praeger, 1975), p. 151.

[180] Data on the domestic arrangements of the ten women GEB members are from the personal interviews I conducted with nine of the women and other informants.

Black, Hispanic, and women's political strength in the UFWA also increased because their share of UFWA membership increased. Their increasing membership shares, in turn, resulted from agricultural mechanization, which compelled many southern blacks and southwestern Hispanics to find jobs in such low-wage industries as furniture manufacturing; the declining feasibility of the one-earner family, which compelled many women to find low-wage jobs; and the proliferation of semi-skilled, operative occupations in furniture factories that accompanied changes in furniture production technology and generated many low-wage jobs that employed socially disadvantaged minority and women workers.

The ethnic and gender integration of the GEB was also facilitated by the ideology of working class unity, harbored since the UFWA founding by left-wing activists in the 1930s and passed down to later generations of top-ranking UFWA leaders, as well as to minority and women UFWA activists, by their older mentors in the UFWA. The ideology, proclaimed continuously by top-ranking UFWA leaders, legitimized minorities and women as leaders, engendered the mobilization of minorities and women in the UFWA, and motivated top leaders to develop minority and women International UFWA leaders. The ideology also formed the basis of the rationale for promoting minority and women leaders. In their fight against growing employer resistance to the UFWA and declining membership, the UFWA leadership deemed the new minority and women workers of strategic importance to the revitalization of the union. Minority and women union leaders would bolster UFWA organizing drives, strengthening the union in the face of growing employer resistance to the UFWA.

In two respects, this most recent process of leadership change in the UFWA resembled that which had occurred during the UFWA's 1939–1950 formative period (see Chapter 3). In both periods, the rise of new social groups into UFWA leadership positions accompanied a realignment of UFWA political strength resulting from a geographical redistribution of the furniture manufacturing industry and UFWA membership. During the formative period, the spreading of the industry and UFWA membership into the nonmetropolitan Midwest and South, and out of the urban Northeast and Midwest, facilitated the rise of native-born leaders from the Midwest and South who were of Northern and Western European descent onto a GEB that had been predominantly comprised of immigrant Jewish and Italian leaders from the urban Northeast.

Second, in both periods, the emerging leadership groups acquired the status of being strategically important to further growth of the UFWA. During the formative period, especially the Cold-War era when political conditions jeopardized severely left-wing unions such as the UFWA, non-left leaders emerged from the more conservative Midwest and South, replacing the Left in order to accommodate the UFWA to the changing political environment. Given that these regions were mainly composed of native-born workers of Northern and Western European descent, the shift in the political stance of UFWA leadership necessarily accelerated the change in GEB ethnic composition that occurred during the formative period.

Despite the ousting of the Left, the ideology of working class unity continued to be believed and practiced in the UFWA and facilitated the ethnic and gender integration of the GEB during the 1970s and 1980s. In turn, the social diversity of UFWA leadership contributed to the merging of the UFWA into the International Union of Electronic, Electrical, Technical, Salaried and Machine Workers in January 1987. Both International unions were looking for merger partners to strengthen their organizing efforts and reverse their membership declines. The IUE membership, which was approximately ten times the magnitude of the UFWA membership, had declined as domestic electronics manufacturing dwindled in the face of foreign electronics imports. In December 1984, IUE President William Bywater spoke with UFWA President Carl Scarbrough about the possibility of merging and met with the UFWA executive committee at the 1985 AFL–CIO convention in Anaheim, CA.[181]

A self-proclaimed socialist, Bywater's political views would ultimately play a part in the merging of the two unions. Born in Trenton, NJ, in 1920, Bywater was raised in New York City, graduated from high school, and, after working at one factory job, took a factory job with Ford Instrument in 1941. A manufacturer of fire control instruments for navy anti-aircraft guns, Ford Instrument had been organized by the United Electrical Workers (UE) since 1937. Bywater became involved in his local union and was elected local union president in 1949, the year in which the UE was expelled from the CIO on the grounds of Communist domination (and in which the UFWA was slated for expulsion from the CIO on identical grounds—see Chapter 3). Soon after, the CIO established the IUE as the CIO union with the former UE jurisdiction, and many UE locals transferred their affiliation to the IUE. Bywater, who wanted his local to remain in the UE and opposed the split from it, was elected local union president despite the fact that his local voted to affiliate with the IUE. Subsequently, Bywater climbed the IUE office hierarchy and was elected IUE secretary-treasurer in 1980. With the death of IUE President David Fitzmaurice in November 1982, Bywater assumed the presidency and was elected to that position in 1984. Bywater's predecessors had kept the issue of anti-Communism alive in the IUE, red-baiting opponents of incumbent IUE officers, until he assumed the presidency in 1982. Anti-Communism

---

[181] Personal interview with William Bywater in Washington, DC, on December 2, 1986.

ceased being an issue in the IUE, and Bywater now wanted to push the IUE political stance further to the left.[182]

In seeking a merger partner, Bywater wanted to merge not only with a smaller union, but also with a union that held progressive political views. He admired the UFWA's progressive political stance, as well as its racially integrated membership. Bywater felt that by increasing the number of minority members, whom he perceived as having progressive political views, the IUE would more readily modify its political stance in the way he envisioned.[183]

The ideology of working class unity, then, contributed to the merging of the UFWA into the IUE. Moreover, given that the ethnically integrated UFWA executive committee now assumed positions on the IUE executive board in accordance with the merger agreement,[184] the ideology effectively served to promote ethnic minorities into leadership positions and to integrate further the IUE executive board. For both unions, the ideology united workers of diverse social backgrounds to bring new members into the labor movement.

---

[182] Ibid.
[183] Ibid.
[184] *Furniture Workers Press,* August 1986, p. 3.

6
Status Conflict and Leadership Change in the Labor Movement

The case of the UFWA suggests that leadership is dynamic and that new groups, distinguished by their social backgrounds, rise periodically into leadership positions. In contrast to Michels's iron law, leadership is no more likely to degenerate into oligarchy than it is to change. The labor movement, including the UFWA, continuously experienced alternating periods of leadership change and leadership stability. Whereas Michels would seem to have been vindicated by the stabilization of U.S. union leadership during the 1950s and 1960s, his iron law is inconsistent with the great insurgencies of non-skilled factory workers, which gave birth to industrial unionism during the 1930s and 1940s, and of black, Hispanic, and women workers, beginning in the late 1960s, who have begun to ascend the hierarchy of union offices during the 1970s and 1980s.

Both insurgencies consisted of a conflict between high- and low-wage workers, that is, between workers of divergent social statuses. During the 1930s and 1940s, skilled craft workers were in conflict with the new workforce of non-skilled factory workers that had accompanied the rise of mass production manufacturing; during the 1970s and 1980s, high-wage, white, male workers were in conflict with low-wage, black, Hispanic, and women workers, who had migrated from their agricultural backgrounds or from full-time homemaking into the factory or office.

Furthermore, these status conflicts within the labor movement, which were expressed as demands by the emerging lower status group for greater representation in union leadership, occurred when the labor movement began to incorporate as members the new social groups of workers whom employers had recently identified and hired as non-union, low-wage workers. The ongoing search by employers for cheaper, non-union labor tended to jeopardize union membership growth and generate these status conflicts within unions, as unions succeeded in organizing the new workers and, consequently, union memberships underwent internal political realignments. With realignment, new social groups rose into union leadership positions, especially if they were of strategic importance in enhancing the capacity of unions to recruit from the new pool of potential union members.

Periodic status conflict and leadership change in the labor movement also suggest that institutional and attitudinal bases of social stratification within the working class are more malleable than is often implied by theories of working class stratification. These theories posit that unevenness in growth among firms and industries, as well as persistent racism, ethnocentrism, and sexism, have limited the mobility of socially disadvantaged groups into higher-status jobs. However, in focusing on the forces that stratify and occupationally segregate workers of diverse social statuses, theories of working class stratification deemphasize not only the process by which workers of diverse social statuses conjoin periodically in labor unions but also the forces that facilitate the entry of lower-status groups into union leadership positions. By periodically incorporating workers of diverse social statuses into the ranks of membership and leadership positions, unions may serve as a political medium by which status-divergent workers challenge the forces that otherwise stratify and segregate them.

The recurring pattern of status conflict and union leadership change argues for a more dynamic theory of leadership change than Michels's iron law. It also argues for a more fluid view of working class stratification, which, in contrast with prevailing theories, explains how workers periodically challenge the forces of stratification and segregation. After reviewing the research traditions that have emerged as alternatives to the iron law, and those pertaining to working class stratification, I derive a status conflict theory of leadership change from the UFWA case.

The Iron Law of Oligarchy: How Ironclad?

Robert Michels's iron law of oligarchy, and Max Weber's related thesis on the inevitable bureaucratization of organizations, held that formally democratic organizations would necessarily degenerate into oligarchies. As organizations grew and became more complex, they would develop hierarchical authority structures, separating the elected from the electorate. Elected leaders, in the Weber-Michels forecast, would seek to remain in office by appointing staffs, choosing successors, and controlling the means of communication with an increasingly apathetic, but reverent, membership, from which no opposition would emerge.[1]

The iron law consists of two arguments. The first is the emergence of structural hierarchy that accompanies increased complexity and organizational growth, an argument few have disputed.[2] The second, and the more controversial, argument is that leadership stabilizes. This second argument, as discussed in Chapter 1, is based on psychological reductionism. That is, Michels's argument assumes that it is in the nature of the electorate to follow apathetically and revere its leaders, and it is in the nature of leaders to seek and secure power. Such reductionism, as a constant, negates the possibility of leadership change, as well as any causal variables pertaining to organizational change that could realize leadership change. It is the implicit denial of leadership change in the iron law that has prompted scholars to question the gloomy Weber-Michels forecast.

A more fluid and dynamic image of leadership emerged alongside the iron law of oligarchy. From this perspective, oligarchization was but one phase of a broader process of leadership change in democratic organizations. Among the prominent examples of this tradition are Muste's depiction of labor union structure oscillating between being like a "town meeting" and being like an "army" during different periods of the business cycle; Gouldner's "iron law of democracy," in which an organization experienced an ongoing cycle of alternating periods of democracy and oligarchy; Zald and Ash's thesis that the likelihood of factionalism's occurring within a social-movement organization depended on whether the organization had become "becalmed," the extent of membership heterogeneity, the ideological predisposition of the organization to question authority, and the exclusivity of its membership criteria; and Benson's portrait of the labor union as a self-democratizing organization that periodically summoned its democratic ideals to restore internal democracy.[3]

---

[1] Robert Michels, *Political Parties* (1911; reprint, New York: Free Press, 1962); Max Weber, "Bureaucracy," in *From Max Weber: Essays in Sociology*, eds., H. H. Gerth and C. Wright Mills (New York: Oxford University Press, 1946), pp. 196–244.

[2] However, on the noninevitability of hierarchization, see Joyce Rothschild and Alan Witt, *The Cooperative Workplace: Potentials and Dilemmas of Organizational Democracy and Participation* (New York: Cambridge University Press, 1986).

[3] A. J. Muste, "Factional Fights in Trade Unions," in *American Labor Dynamics*, ed., J. B. S. Hardman (New York: Harcourt Brace and Co., 1928), pp. 332–348; Alvin Gouldner, "Metaphysical Pathos and the Theory of Bureaucracy," *American Political Science Review* 49 (June 1955): 496–507; Mayer Zald and Roberta Ash, "Social Movement Organizations: Growth, Decay and Change," *Social Forces* 44 (March 1966): 327–340; Herman Benson, "The Fight for Union Democracy," in *Unions in Transition*, ed., Seymour Martin Lipset (San Francisco: Institute for Contemporary Studies, 1986), pp. 323–370.

Treating leadership as a variable, that is, as subject to change and stability, two research traditions have developed out of this dynamic and fluid alternative to the iron law, as described in Chapter 1. First, the "structuralist" tradition assumed that the degree of leadership change or stability depended on the likelihood of electoral opposition and competition, which, in turn, depended on organization structure. Based on his study of the two-party system within the International Typographical Union (ITU), Lipset argued that the institutionalization of parties allowed for electoral competition and leadership turnover in the ITU, and that the ITU two-party system itself was facilitated by the strong craft identity of the printers and their high and homogeneous status, which lowered the stakes of electoral defeat for incumbents. Edelstein and Warner have argued further that organizational, structural features other than political parties, such as the number of hierarchical levels, the automatic succession to vacant offices, and the percentage of appointed officers, affect the degree of electoral opposition in unions.[4]

The structuralist tradition has two shortcomings. First, it attempts to explain leadership change with structure, conceived of as a static variable. Although structure may account for the conditions conducive to leadership change in an organization, it does not explain the kinds of issues and cleavages that generate leadership change nor the types of external political, social, and economic conditions, which vary during the history of an organization and may promote or inhibit factionalism and leadership change.

Second, the structuralist tradition assumes that structure is static. However, as the UFWA case suggests, factions may succeed in altering the rules of governance to meet their needs or the changing needs of the organization. For example, the mobilization of blacks and Hispanics in the UFWA during the late 1960s led the convention delegates in 1970 to add four seats to the national executive board, in order to increase minority participation in governance. As a tool of the membership, organizational structure itself may be changed by the same groups who seek to ascend it.

Resource mobilization theory is the second tradition that has emerged as a dynamic alternative to the iron law. According to this theory, social movements, and social movement organizations specifically, arise as the requisite resources for mobilization (e.g., leadership, organization, money, labor) become available in society. The theory was developed as an alternative to grievance- and deprivation-based, social movement theo-

---

[4] Seymour Martin Lipset, Martin Trow, and James Coleman, *Union Democracy* (New York: Free Press, 1956); J. David Edelstein and Malcolm Warner, *Comparative Union Democracy* (New Brunswick, NJ: Transaction, 1979).

ries because these could not explain the absence of mobilization among some aggrieved groups. According to Zald and McCarthy, chief proponents of resource mobilization theory, a level of discontent sufficient for mobilization exists constantly in society, but aggrieved groups must control relevant resources to engage in collective action.[5]

For resource mobilization theory, oligarchization is a specific phase of an ongoing, organizational process of resource mobilization. Oligarchization, claimed Zald and Ash, occurs when the movement is becalmed, that is, when it has achieved a secure position in society but has stabilized. Under these conditions, membership apathy increases and leadership becomes complacent. According to Zald and Berger, the likelihood of "bureaucratic insurgency" is higher in organizations that depend on a morally and ideologically committed professional staff, who effectively serve as a reference for evaluating the organization, than in other organizations.[6] Several empirical studies of union insurgencies, which I reviewed in Chapter 1, have taken a resource mobilization perspective. Among the resources that facilitate union insurgency, according to these studies, are caucus formation, a strong link between members and leaders, and direct membership participation in the movement.[7]

Compared to the structuralist tradition, resource mobilization theory treats the organization as a social process, rather than as a static institution, and, therefore, is more helpful in determining the historical conditions under which leadership change is most likely to occur. It also highlights factors, such as organizational ideology, that may predispose one organization more than another toward factionalism and leadership change.

Resource mobilization theory, however, is not without its limitations. Given its deemphasis on grievances and factors that motivate mobilization, the theory is limited in its ability to explain which issues may divide a social movement organization and the social lines (e.g., ethnicity, gender) along which such division is likely to occur.

Despite the processual orientation of resource mobilization theory and the casting of the Weber-Michels thesis in terms of organizational

---

[5] John McCarthy and Mayer Zald, "Resource Mobilization and Social Movements: A Partial Theory," in *Social Movements in an Organizational Society: Collected Essays*, eds., Mayer Zald and John McCarthy (New Brunswick, NJ: Transaction, 1987), pp. 15–42. Also, see Craig Jenkins, *The Politics of Insurgency: The Farm Worker Movement in the 1960s* (New York: Columbia University Press, 1985), pp. 1–27.

[6] Zald and Ash, "Social Movement Organizations"; Mayer Zald and Michael Berger, "Social Movements in Organizations: Coup d'Etat, Bureaucratic Insurgency, and Mass Movement," *American Journal of Sociology* 83 (January 1978): 823–861.

[7] See, for example, John Hemingway, *Conflict and Democracy* (Oxford: Clarendon Press, 1978); Philip Nyden, "Democratizing Organizations: A Case Study of a Union Reform Movement," *American Journal of Sociology* 90 (May 1985): 1179–1203; Russell Schutt, *Organization in a Changing Environment: Unionization of Welfare Employees* (Albany, NY: State University of New York Press, 1986).

change, much of the empirical, resource-mobilization research on union insurgency has failed to compare leadership change during the diverse periods of growth, stability, and decline in the history of an organization. Instead, these studies have examined closely the insurgencies during short historical periods, but without relating them adequately to the changing historical conditions that may periodically strengthen or weaken the whole organization, generate divisive issues within the organization, and prompt leadership change. Moreover, by neglecting the periods of leadership stability, these studies cannot highlight the conditions conducive to leadership change. Their experimental design reduces the capacity of the research to modify or propose an alternative to the iron law because the iron law, as a thesis about the consequences of organizational growth, demands empirical criticism that derives from a comparative analysis of leadership change during the diverse periods of an organization's history.

The theory of leadership change that is developed next builds on the structuralist and resource-mobilization traditions and is an attempt to address their shortcomings. Derived as it is from the analysis of leadership change during the growth, stability, and decline periods of UFWA history, the theory emphasizes the changing historical conditions that affect the timing of leadership change, as well as the factors that effectively draw the lines along which factionalism occurs.

Status Conflict and Union Leadership Change

The social diversity of the U.S. working class, hopelessly divided along such status lines as ethnicity, gender, skill level, and income, has been offered as an answer to Werner Sombart's question, "Why is there no socialism in the United States?" According to this view, U.S. workers have been unable to develop their own political organization for advancing their class interests because they are disunited by invidious status differences. Some writers, moreover, have argued that employers have promoted these status differences among workers, by pitting one group against another, to prevent the development of worker organization.[8]

Theories of working class stratification state that several institutional and attitudinal forces serve to stratify U.S. workers and to segregate them occupationally. Segmentation theory holds that unevenness in growth among firms and industries has created a dual economy that consists of a core of large corporate firms in oligopolistic industries that maintain a high-wage primary labor market and a periphery of small businesses that maintain a low-wage secondary labor market. Low education, racism, and

---

[8]For a review of this research, see William Form, *Divided We Stand: Working-Class Stratification in America* (Urbana, IL: University of Illinois Press, 1985).

sexism consign a disproportionately large number of minorities and women, according to segmentation theory, to inferior jobs in the secondary labor market. Similarly, others argue that persistent racism and sexism effectively segregate minorities and women in low-status occupations. Moreover, some writers claim that the labor movement has reinforced these patterns of stratification and social segregation by refusing to recruit and admit minorities and women and by neglecting those minority and women workers who have unionized. In an unusually dynamic analysis of stratification process, Wilson argued that the post–World War II growth of the black underclass is largely attributable to the geographical redistribution of non-skilled manufacturing jobs away from areas with large black populations and the restructuring of the economy from goods-producing industries to service industries that require higher educational credentials than those possessed by many blacks.[9]

Notwithstanding the persistence of social stratification and segregation among U.S. workers, theories of working class stratification implicitly treat workers as passive objects of institutional and attitudinal forces that stratify and segregate them and, consequently, neglect those forces which may compel, and facilitate the efforts of, workers of diverse social statuses to integrate themselves. Indeed, as I argue later, the rise of new social groups into union leadership positions constitutes part of a worker effort to achieve such social integration and thereby challenge invidious status differences that jeopardize their economic interests.

If socialism has yet to be realized in the United States, a labor movement that unites some of the disparate segments of the working class has been developed. The emergence of the labor movement has depended on the reconciliation of, and has been jeopardized by, status conflict among U.S. workers. Among the many instances of such conflict were the rift between skilled and non-skilled workers during the 1930s, leading to the split between AFL and CIO unions, respectively, and to their reunification in 1955; and racial and gender barriers to craft union membership that were made illegal by the Civil Rights Act of 1964, paving the way for the establishment of the Coalition of Black Trade Unionists in 1973 and the Coalition of Labor Union Women in 1974, which have promoted the interests of their constituencies in the labor movement. Labor unions in the United States, then, embody many of the social cleavages that have occurred within the U.S. working class.

[9] See, for example, Form, *Divided We Stand;* William Julius Wilson, *The Truly Disadvantaged: The Inner City, the Underclass, and Public Policy* (Chicago: University of Chicago Press, 1987); Heidi Hartmann, "Capitalism, Patriarchy, and Job Segregation by Sex," in *Women and the Workplace,* eds., Martha Blaxall and Barbara Reagan (Chicago: University of Chicago Press, 1976), pp. 137–169; Herbert Hill, *Black Labor and the American Legal System,* vol. I (Washington, DC: Bureau of National Affairs, 1977); David Gordon, Richard Edwards, and Michael Reich, *Segmented Work, Divided Workers* (Cambridge: Cambridge University Press, 1982).

Union leadership change, that is, the changing social composition of elected union leaders taken as a group, may be seen as the recurring effort of a union to unite a membership that had become diversified, stratified, and factionalized. Periodic shifts in the ethnic and gender traits of the leadership of a union, for example, may constitute an effort to reunite a membership divided along ethnic and gender lines. This implies that the social characteristics of a union leadership group may not necessarily mirror those of the membership and that union leadership change accelerates when factionalism divides the union.

Factionalism, as suggested by the tradition of research on insurgency movements within unions, seems to occur in cycles. The UFWA case implies, as discussed later, that this cycle is associated with escalating and deescalating conflict between unions and employers. As adversaries, unions and employers pursue divergent interests, the former attempting to improve worker livelihoods, and the latter endeavoring to minimize labor costs in production. The union strategy for accomplishing its goal is to organize as many workers as possible, whereas the employer strategy is to employ the least expensive workforce. Employers typically relocate their operations in non-union, low-wage geographical areas or attempt to reduce labor costs by introducing labor-saving production technology. Class conflict often takes the form of unions attempting to organize the lower-wage workforces recently created and identified by employers. As captive organizations (see Chapter 2), unions follow the geographical movements of capital by extending their organizing drives into non-union, low-wage areas. As they succeed in unionizing these workforces, employers identify new, lower-wage, non-union workforces, continuing the adversarial cycle. Consequently, union memberships periodically become socially diversified, especially if worker social backgrounds vary geographically and by skill level, and economically stratified, as lower-wage new recruits join forces with the higher-wage union members. Factionalism among these social strata within the union may erupt when conflict with employers jeopardizes the growth of the union and undermines union bargaining strength vis-à-vis employers.

The status conflict theory of union leadership change, induced from the UFWA case, conceives of union leadership change as the result of the periodic diversification, stratification, and factionalization of union membership brought on by the adversarial cycle between union and employers. New leadership groups emerge from the lower, recently recruited, social strata of the union membership when union growth is jeopardized. It is these emerging groups that often lead the organizing drives of the union into the pool of non-union potential union members and revive union growth.

A theory of union leadership change ought to address two issues about changes in the social composition of elected leadership. The first is the *timing* of leadership change: the conditions that promote leadership change, as well as leadership stabilization, during different periods in the history of the organization. The second issue concerns *which membership groups* are likely to emerge into leadership positions in periods of leadership change.

To analyze these issues, I will compare the relevant conditions in the three periods of UFWA history. First, the UFWA's formative period, lasting from 1932 to 1950, corresponds to the formative period of the industrial union movement, spearheaded by the Committee for Industrial Organization. With the advent of mass production; the subsequent proliferation of semi-skilled, factory-operative jobs; and the enactment of the Wagner Act in 1935, which facilitated unionization, industrial unionism arose as an alternative form to the craft unionism of skilled craft workers that had prevailed under the banner of the American Federation of Labor since the late nineteenth century. Rather than organizing workers along craft lines, and limiting union membership to skilled craft workers, the movement for industrial unionism sought to organize all workers, regardless of craft and skill level, along industry lines.[10] The establishment of the CIO-affiliated UFWA in 1937 occurred in an era when industrial unionism began to spread among the workers in the mass production industries.

The effort to realize industrial unionism in furniture manufacturing reflects the split between craft and industrial unionism. Moreover, the specific pattern of furniture worker affiliation with labor federations was replicated by workers in other industries, including the needle trades, coal mining, the maritime industry, and metal working, whose early unionization efforts were partly stimulated by the Communist party.[11] In 1932, left-wing union activists in furniture manufacturing in New York City established the Furniture Workers Industrial Union, the first effort at establishing a furniture industrial union in an industry in which the AFL-affiliated Carpenters and Upholsterers craft unions had organized the skilled workers. The FWIU was affiliated with the Trade Union Unity League, a Communist party labor federation that had been established in 1928 as an alternative in industrial unionism to the AFL. In 1935, the Communist party altered its union organizing strategy in favor of working within, rather than in competition with, the AFL and dissolved the TUUL. The FWIU merged into the Upholsterers union with the expectation that the Upholsterers would practice industrial unionism, leave the AFL, and affiliate with the CIO. As the Upholsterers failed to affiliate with the CIO,

---

[10] Daniel Cornfield, ed., *Workers, Managers, and Technological Change: Emerging Patterns of Labor Relations* (New York: Plenum, 1987), pp. 8–24, 331–353.

[11] Bert Cochran, *Labor and Communism: The Conflict That Shaped American Unions* (Princeton, NJ: Princeton University Press, 1977), pp. 43–81.

the former FWIU activists left in 1937 and chartered the UFWA with the CIO. From the late 1930s through the late 1940s, the growth of the UFWA, and of unionism generally in the mass production industries, was stimulated by several factors including the increased union organizing efforts of the CIO and the AFL, which began to organize non-skilled workers; the pro-labor political conditions under the Roosevelt administration; and the growth of mass production industries during World War II.

The UFWA's formative period ended in 1950, after a severe, three-year membership decline. A Communist-led union, the UFWA encountered much employer resistance to its organizing drives and membership raids by non-Communist unions, as did other Communist-led unions, during this period of heightened, Cold-War anti-communism. The raids and resistance to the UFWA ceased in 1950 when the UFWA ousted its left-wing leadership.

Second, during the UFWA's period of stability, lasting from 1950 to 1970, UFWA membership, and that of the U.S. labor movement generally, stabilized, and unions achieved several collective bargaining gains. Among them were periodic wage increases, cost-of-living wage adjustments, and employer-provided, supplementary unemployment benefits and health and life insurance. Variously termed the "Golden Age" of collective bargaining and the institutionalization of a labor-management "accord," this era was characterized by the growth of U.S. manufacturing both domestically and internationally.[12]

The terms given to this era, however, inadequately portray the depth of employer opposition to the labor movement that had resurfaced after World War II. The cornerstone of postwar employer opposition was the Taft-Hartley Act of 1947, enacted over Truman's veto during the Cold War. Branded the "slave labor act" by organized labor, the Taft-Hartley Act undermined two chief union security arrangements that unions had negotiated with employers through collective bargaining. First, it outlawed the closed shop contract, whereby employment was conditional on union membership. Second, the act allowed states to enact right-to-work laws, which outlawed the union-shop contract, whereby union membership was mandatory after a probationary employment period.[13]

The act itself was a victory for the anti-union, employer-led, open

---

[12] Richard Edwards and Michael Podgursky, "The Unraveling Accord: American Unions in Crisis," in *Unions in Crisis and Beyond: Perspectives from Six Countries*, eds., Richard Edwards, Paolo Garonna, and Franz Tödtling (Dover, MA: Auburn House, 1986), pp. 14–60; Jack Stieber, Robert McKersie, and D. Quinn Mills, eds., *U.S. Industrial Relations 1950–1980: A Critical Assessment* (Madison, WI: Industrial Relations Research Association, 1981), p. iv.

[13] Christopher Tomlins, *The State and the Unions* (New York: Cambridge University Press, 1985), pp. 282–316.

shop (i.e., no union security contractual arrangements) movement, which had lain dormant for some fifteen years prior to the passage of Taft-Hartley. Under the leadership of the National Association of Manufacturers (NAM), the open shop movement emerged during the 1920s in opposition to the labor movement which had grown under the favorable political conditions of World War I. Labor union membership declined until the early 1930s, when the Great Depression and the birth of the industrial union movement restimulated labor movement growth. In an effort to halt the surge in labor movement growth of the 1930s and World War II years, the NAM led the effort to enact Taft-Hartley.[14]

The act contributed to the stabilization of U.S. labor union membership during the 1950s and 1960s. Although U.S. manufacturing prospered during this era, union membership as a percentage of the labor force stabilized in part because manufacturers increasingly relocated or established branch operations in the southern states, which accounted for most of the right-to-work laws that had been enacted in the United States, and in other non-union areas in the United States and the Third World. Furniture manufacturing and the UFWA were no exceptions. The industry and UFWA membership increasingly shifted southward out of the unionized Great Lakes, Middle Atlantic, and New England regions.[15]

Third, the UFWA's period of decline, lasting from 1970 to 1987, corresponds to the period in U.S. labor history when U.S. union membership, as a percentage of the U.S. labor force, suffered its longest sustained decline. Several forces contributed to the absolute decline in UFWA membership and the relative decline of the U.S. labor movement, including the continuing geographical redistribution of manufacturing; the growing employer resistance to unions in the conservative political climate under a predominantly Republican chain of U.S. presidents; the internationalization of markets, decline of U.S. manufacturing dominance in the world market, and increasing foreign imports to the U.S.; and the recessionary macroeconomic conditions of the mid-1970s and early 1980s. The UFWA's period of decline ended in 1987 when it merged with the International Union of Electronic Workers, becoming the Furniture Workers Division of the IUE. This merger was one of many union mergers that occurred among distressed unions in the United States during this era.[16]

---

[14] Cornfield, *Workers, Managers, and Technological Change*, pp. 8–24, 331–353.

[15] Daniel Cornfield, "Declining Union Membership in the Post–World War II Era: The United Furniture Workers of America, 1939–1982," *American Journal of Sociology* 91 (March 1986): 1112–1153.

[16] Ibid; Edwards and Podgursky, "The Unraveling Accord"; Gary Chaison, "Union Growth and Union Mergers," *Industrial Relations* 20 (Winter 1981): 98–107.

The Timing of Leadership Change

The UFWA case suggests that the timing of leadership change depends on the presence of conditions that promote factionalism in the union. These conditions are the jeopardization of organizational growth and membership diversification and stratification. In terms of the history of a union, leadership change is more likely to occur during periods in which organizational growth is in jeopardy and membership has become diversified and stratified than in periods characterized by the opposite conditions. This is implied by a comparison of these conditions in the three periods of UFWA history.

The rate of UFWA leadership change was higher during the formative period and the period of decline than in the intervening period of stability. The formative period and the period of decline share three traits that distinguish them from the period of stability and suggest why the level of factionalism and rate of leadership change during them exceeded that during the period of stability. First, membership became diversified and stratified in the formative and decline periods. During the formative period, the UFWA extended its organizing drives out of New York City, especially into nonmetropolitan areas, following the geographical movement of furniture manufacturers into the non-union South and Midwest. The geographical expansion of its recruitment effort led to ethnic diversification of the membership and, consequently, a realignment of political strength among convention voting blocs. Emerging alongside the once dominant, immigrant Jewish and Italian voting bloc from the urban Northeast was a voting bloc consisting of native-born members of Northern and Western European descent from the small furniture towns of the Midwest, South, and New England.

During the period of decline of the 1970s and 1980s, the UFWA emphasized the South in its organizing drives, as it had in previous periods, and made significant inroads among southern blacks. With continuous capital flight out of the urban Northeast and into the nonmetropolitan South and Midwest after World War II, the relative strength of the urban Northeast UFWA voting bloc declined, while that of the nonmetropolitan South and Midwest increased during the period of decline. These two growth regions housed most of the black and women workers who had begun to enter the U.S. furniture manufacturing industry and the UFWA during the late 1960s. Membership of the UFWA was also diversified along with the changing ethnic composition of the furniture manufacturing labor force in the urban Northeast and West Coast. During the 1960s, blacks and Hispanics began to succeed white workers of European descent in the urban Northeast, and Hispanics began to succeed other whites of diverse ethnic backgrounds on the West Coast, especially in Los Angeles. The changing ethnic composition of furniture production workers and UFWA membership was partly attributable to the mechanization of southern and southwestern agriculture and the subsequent migration of less skilled black and Hispanic workers to urban areas. Also, changing furniture production technology led to the proliferation of non-skilled production occupations that were often filled by ethnic minority workers, while the civil rights movement and legislation eroded discriminatory barriers to minority employment. These forces also stimulated the entry of women into the industry during the 1960s, along with changes in gender roles and the declining economic feasibility of the single-earner household.

In addition to its changing ethnic and gender composition, UFWA membership became increasingly stratified during the formative period and the period of decline. Increased social stratification resulted from the continuous efforts of furniture manufacturers to employ cheaper labor. During the formative and decline periods, UFWA organizing drives followed the geographical movements of manufacturers into lower-wage, non-union areas. These were mainly the nonmetropolitan areas of the South and Midwest. Moreover, as manufacturers adopted new production technology, simplifying the occupational structure and skill requirements, the UFWA incorporated new members with less skills and lower wages than the earlier generation of craft workers in the urban Northeast. This was especially the case during the period of decline, when many blacks and women left their poor, agricultural backgrounds for their first experience with unionized factory work in the South and nonmetropolitan Midwest. The emerging membership groups, while experiencing upward social mobility from their agricultural backgrounds, nonetheless entered a union whose existing membership had even higher wages by virtue of the longer duration of unionization in these other regions.

In contrast, little or no membership diversification occurred during the period of stability of the 1950s and 1960s. The UFWA replenished its membership losses, which resulted from the geographical redistribution of the industry, without a realignment of political strength among convention voting blocs. Nor did the ethnic and gender composition of the industry labor force shift dramatically during most of this era.

The second distinguishing feature of the formative and decline periods was that national political and historical events fashioned a group consciousness among the emerging voting blocs in the UFWA. Moreover, this group consciousness led these emerging, upwardly mobile groups to demand representation and participation in the governance of the UFWA from the established, higher-wage groups that dominated leadership positions.

During the formative period, the group consciousness of the emerging voting bloc of native-born members of Northern and Western European descent, mainly from the nonmetropolitan Midwest, was partly shaped by the UFWA governmental structure; their political attitudes, which differed from those harbored in the urban Northeast; and the anti-communism prevailing in national politics, especially during the late 1940s. The regional dimension of the UFWA governmental structure effectively served to carve out the ethnic voting blocs that occurred along geographical lines and were expressed as such by UFWA convention delegates. Compared with the Jewish and Italian voting bloc of the urban Northeast, the emerging bloc from the nonmetropolitan Midwest held more conservative political attitudes and was more sympathetic to the national current of anti-communism. Throughout most of the formative period, the two voting blocs disagreed with one another. Moreover, the emerging voting bloc from the nonmetropolitan Midwest demanded more representation in UFWA governance.

During the period of decline, the civil rights movement fashioned a group consciousness in the emerging black and Hispanic voting bloc, which was present in all regions except the nonmetropolitan Midwest and strongest in the South. The civil rights movement, along with the women's movement, also created a group consciousness in the women's voting bloc, whose strength was concentrated in the South and nonmetropolitan Midwest and cut across ethnic lines. Minorities and women mobilized explicitly for the purpose of gaining more participation in UFWA governance, and each group supported the effort of the other group.

The period of stability, characterized as it was by stability of membership and the distribution of political strength among convention voting blocs, lacked mobilization by any voting bloc for increased representation in governance. Also, no national political events transpired that shaped group consciousness in any membership constituency within the UFWA.

The third distinguishing feature of the formative and decline periods was that organizational growth was jeopardized by a combination of some or all of the following conditions: increased class conflict, inter-union rivalry, and adverse macroeconomic conditions. During the formative period, all of these factors jeopardized UFWA growth. Increased class conflict was symbolized by the passage in 1947 of the Taft Hartley Act, which was designed by an employer-led group to halt the growth of the labor movement, as discussed. Furthermore, the act required unions to sign affidavits verifying that their officers were not Communists, lest they lose the legal backing of the National Labor Relations Board, especially in organizing drives. As a noncomplying, Communist-led union, the UFWA suffered membership losses and organizing difficulties until it signed the affidavit in 1949 and ousted its left-wing officers in 1950.

The UFWA experienced two types of inter-union rivalry in organizing campaigns during the formative period. First, its rivalry with the Upholsterers was part of the broader rivalry between CIO and AFL unions that accompanied the birth of industrial unionism. Second, the UFWA was rivaled and raided by AFL and CIO non-Communist unions until it signed the Taft-Hartley, non-Communist affidavit and ousted its left-wing leaders.

Finally, recessionary, macroeconomic conditions led to unemployment and UFWA membership losses during the late 1940s. Between 1947 and 1950, UFWA membership decreased by over ten thousand members, a decline of about 25 percent of the 1947 membership.

During the period of decline of the 1970s and 1980s, UFWA membership was jeopardized by increased class conflict and recessionary macroeconomic conditions. Increased class conflict took various forms, including employer relocation in non-union areas of the United States and in the Third World; aggressive union decertification campaigns led by employers; and increased employer resistance to union organizing campaigns. The UFWA also suffered sharp membership declines during the recessions of the mid-1970s and early 1980s. Between 1970 and 1985, UFWA membership declined by over ten thousand members, a decline of 37 percent of the 1970 membership.

During the period of stability, in contrast, UFWA membership was not jeopardized by any hostile forces. Class conflict was limited to the geographical redistribution of capital into non-union areas and the union preemption strategy of non-union employers who provided workers with union-scale wages and benefits. The UFWA experienced little employer resistance to organizing campaigns and few decertification elections and recouped its losses. With the AFL-CIO merger in 1955, inter-union rivalry declined among most U.S. unions. Also, the recessions of this era were milder than those that occurred in the other periods.

In sum, jeopardization of organizational growth, following, as well as coinciding with, membership diversification and stratification, distinguished the UFWA's formative and decline periods from its period of stability. Under these conditions, factionalism mounted between the higher-status membership groups already established in leadership positions and the lower-status, upwardly mobile groups rising in the union with a group consciousness fashioned by national political events. The factionalism centered on the sharing of union leadership by the established and emerging membership groups.

Emerging Leadership Groups

The outcome of such factionalism, as suggested by the UFWA case, depends on the perceived importance of the emerging group in restoring organizational growth. Specifically, the emerging membership group is likely to increase its presence in leadership positions if incumbent leadership of the established membership group perceives the emerging group as being of strategic importance to the revitalization of the union.

In the UFWA, the established groups eventually supported the incorporation of rising groups in leadership positions because they believed the new leadership would facilitate organizing drives in what was a growing pool of potential members with social backgrounds similar or identical to those of the emerging membership groups. During the formative period, the issue of maintaining the UFWA's CIO affiliation during the late 1940s hinged on the presence of Communist UFWA leaders. The established faction from the urban Northeast, which consisted of Communist and non-Communist members, resisted taking an anti-Communist stance until the UFWA was slated in 1949 for expulsion from the CIO on the grounds of Communist domination unless it removed its left-wing officers. At this point, the established faction split on the issue, with a majority of the established group siding with the more conservative, emerging group from the nonmetropolitan Midwest. The pro-CIO forces from the urban Northeast and nonmetropolitan Midwest and the anti-CIO left wing campaigned heavily against one another before the 1950 UFWA convention. The pro-CIO forces were united in their belief that Communist leadership was an organizational liability and ousted the left-wing officers in contested elections at the 1950 UFWA convention. The ousting of the Left accelerated the changing ethnic composition of national UFWA leadership. The percentage of Jewish leaders from the urban Northeast, who were disproportionately represented in the Left, declined, while that of the more conservative members of Northern and Western European descent from the nonmetropolitan Midwest increased in national leadership positions.

During the period of decline, incumbent leadership believed that the incorporation of blacks, Hispanics, and women in leadership positions would revitalize the UFWA. Incumbent, white, male leadership, for the most part, responded sympathetically to the growing demands of ethnic minorities and women for increased participation in union governance. Top, white, male leaders proclaimed the necessity of including minorities and women in leadership and actively promoted the incorporation of these groups in national leadership positions.

In both the formative and decline periods, support from incumbent leadership was important for the realization of increased participation by the emerging groups, because the emerging groups comprised only a minority of the convention votes. At most, emerging groups, at the start of their ascent, dominated the votes of one or two regional blocs within the UFWA. To increase their presence in leadership positions, emerging groups had to coalesce with some, if not all, of the established groups. Perceived by incumbent leadership as vital to organizational rejuvenation during periods when union growth was jeopardized, the emerging groups gained sufficient political strength through coalition to increase their presence in national leadership positions.

The UFWA case also implies that a universalistic ideological tradition in the organization may facilitate the incorporation of emerging membership groups, whose social characteristics differ from those of the established membership groups, in leadership positions. A universalistic ideology, one that eschews invidious differences among socially disparate membership groups and promotes the commonality of all membership groups, may serve as a rationale in the arguments made by both the emerging groups and the incumbent leadership before any skeptics as to why emerging groups should be incorporated in leadership positions.

The UFWA's ideology of working class unity, functioning much like the craft identity in the International Typographical Union identified by Lipset, promoted a common class interest among all members and condemned any status divisions (e.g., ethnic, gender) that employers would use to divide the workers and weaken the union. Unlike many of the AFL craft unions extant at the time of the UFWA founding that barred minorities and women from membership, the UFWA, along with CIO unions generally and especially Communist-led unions, barred no one from membership and fashioned its growth strategy and organizational structure on the basis of uniting workers of diverse social backgrounds in one organization. This ideology remained alive in the UFWA, even after the ousting of the Left in 1950, through a mentoring process between older and younger generations of national UFWA leaders. Moreover, most of the left-wing leaders remained in the UFWA, working in local unions rather than in national union offices, and participated actively, along with incumbent national UFWA leaders, in passing on the ideology to the new generations of UFWA leaders. A deeply felt set of beliefs, the ideology was invoked by incumbent leaders to justify the inclusion of emerging groups in leadership during both the formative and decline periods.

A Status Conflict Theory of Union Leadership Change

As a social movement organization dedicated to improving workers' standard of living, the labor union exists in a continuously adversarial relationship with employers, who attempt to control, if not reduce, labor costs of production. Union leadership change, in the status conflict theory that follows, is affected by union-employer conflict in this adversarial process of wealth distribution. Union-employer conflict is central to leadership change because it contributes to the extent and type of membership diversification and stratification in the union, the potential for union growth, and, hence, the conditions that generate factionalism in the union.

Union-employer conflict affects the timing of factionalism. Union membership diversifies to the extent to which employers, seeking to avoid unions, relocate in lower-wage, non-union geographical areas that comprise workers whose social backgrounds differ from those of the unionized workers. As the union follows the movement of employers into the industrializing geographical areas, its membership becomes diversified, depending on the social traits of the workforce in the industrializing areas, and economically stratified. As the union makes recruitment inroads into the industrializing geographical areas, employers resist the union further, jeopardizing its growth. Factionalism breaks out between the higher-status, established membership groups and the lower-status, upwardly mobile, emerging membership groups, over which group(s) will control the union and restore its growth. *The first hypothesis, then, is that leadership change is more likely to occur during periods in the history of the union when its adversaries cause its membership to become diversified and stratified; jeopardize organizational growth; and, consequently, generate factionalism within the union, than in periods when the level of union-employer conflict is minimal.*

Assuming that the emerging membership group controls only a minority of political strength (e.g., convention votes) in the union, it will have to coalesce with at least part of the established membership group to increase its presence in leadership positions. The emerging membership group may be perceived by the established membership group as being of strategic importance to the continued growth of the union, especially if the social characteristics of the emerging group mirror those of a large or growing pool of *potential* members. Under these conditions, incumbent leaders, or some of them, from the established group may support an increase in the presence of the emerging group in leadership positions because they perceive the emerging group as having the capacity to restore union growth. *The second hypothesis, then, is that the emerging membership group is more likely to increase its presence in leadership positions during a period of factionalism if it is perceived by incumbent leaders as being of strategic importance to the renewal of union growth, and if it is consequently supported by incumbents, than in the absence of incumbent support.*

The ease with which an emerging membership group can coalesce with an established membership group may also depend on the level of tolerance each group has toward the other and, generally, toward groups whose social backgrounds differ from its own. The degree of universalism in the ideological tradition of the union, that is, the degree to which the ideology promotes commonality among membership groups, rather than drawing invidious distinctions among them, may affect the level of mutual tolerance, if not affinity, between the established and emerging membership groups. Therefore, *the third and final hypothesis is that the greater the degree of universalism in the ideological tradition of the union, the easier it will be for the emerging membership group to coalesce with an established membership group, and the greater will be the increase in the presence of the emerging group in leadership positions.*

The status conflict theory of leadership change may also apply to formally democratic, social movement organizations other than labor unions. It is the "becalmed" social movement organization, according to Zald and Ash, that is most likely to exhibit the Weber-Michels pattern of oligarchization.[17] This implies that non-becalmed social movement organizations, that is, those expanding or contracting, may be most prone to experiencing membership diversification and factionalized leadership change.

Both the expanding and the contracting social movement organizations may develop a diversified membership by identifying and recruiting different groups from new social environments. In the case of the expanding organization, new membership groups may become incorporated by the organization. For the contracting organization that has saturated its traditional potential membership pool, recruitment from new pools of potential members may be a necessary step for reviving the organization. Factionalism among status-divergent, established and emerging membership groups may erupt into leadership change, especially if organizational growth becomes jeopardized by hostile, counter-movement forces or rival social movement organizations.

The chances of an emerging membership group's coalescing with established membership groups and increasing its presence in leadership positions, assuming the emerging group controls only a minority of votes in the social movement organization, are likely to depend on its perceived importance for maintaining organizational growth or reviving the organization. Indeed, organization members who control vital organizational resources, according to resource-dependence organization theory, are likely to yield the most power in the organization.[18] In the social movement organization whose growth is in jeopardy, the chief relevant resource is new members. Moreover, for factions in formally democratic organizations, new members are a political resource insofar as they constitute a bloc of mobilizable votes. The relevance of an emerging membership group to, and the likelihood of its being perceived by established membership groups as important for, organizational revival or growth

---

[17] Zald and Ash, "Social Movement Organizations."
[18] Jeffrey Pfeffer and Gerald Salancik, *The External Control of Organizations: A Resource Dependence Perspective* (New York: Harper & Row, 1978).

may depend on the similarity between its socioeconomic status and that of the *potential* membership pool, as well as on the dissimilarity between the socioeconomic statuses of the established membership group(s) and the *potential* membership pool. Assuming that socioeconomically similar groups feel greater mutual affinity than do dissimilar groups, as Jackman and Jackman have shown,[19] an emerging membership group whose socioeconomic status differs little from that of the potential membership pool will be more able than an established membership group, whose socioeconomic status differs greatly from that of the potential membership pool, to attract new members to the social movement organization. Under these conditions, the emerging group is likely to be perceived by the established group(s) as being of strategic importance for continued organizational growth. This suggests that *the greater the similarity between the socioeconomic statuses of an emerging membership group and the potential membership pool, and the greater the dissimilarity between the socioeconomic statuses of the established membership group(s) and the potential membership pool, the greater is the likelihood of the emerging group's being perceived by the established group as important for continued organizational growth, of coalescing with the established group(s), and of assuming leadership positions.*

A corollary of this argument is that status conflict may affect how a social movement organization, whose growth is in jeopardy, identifies new pools of potential members. To avoid factionalism based on status conflict and, therefore, to retain their leadership positions, established membership groups may attempt to identify potential membership pools whose socioeconomic statuses are similar to their own. However, this strategy will be infeasible in the absence of such potential members. Moreover, this recruitment strategy is likely to be rarer in social movement organizations whose ideologies are sufficiently universalistic to eschew the drawing of invidious status differences among members and potential members, than in organizations with less universalistic, more status-conscious, exclusionary, or elitist ideologies. The status-conscious social movement organization, if it restricts its recruitment efforts to a shrinking pool of potential members with socioeconomic statuses similar to those of incumbent leadership, may trade off organizational growth for leadership stability; the ideologically universalistic social movement organization, if it recruits from a potential membership pool whose socioeconomic status diverges from that of the incumbents, may trade off leadership stability for organizational growth.

---

[19] Mary Jackman and Robert Jackman, *Class Awareness in the United States* (Berkeley: University of California Press, 1983).

Status Conflict, Union Leadership Change, and Worker Unity

Status conflict and leadership change are no more likely than the oligarchization of union leadership. The emergence of new social groups in leadership positions and oligarchization are alternating leadership patterns characterizing a social movement whose conflict with employers ebbs and flows. Union leadership is as stable as the relationship between unions and employers. The forecast of inevitable oligarchy in Michels's iron law rested on the assumption that the mobilization of insurgent membership groups would not materialize. Similarly, theories of working class stratification tend to present a static view of the socioeconomic characteristics of workers, emphasizing the persistence of stratification and social segregation and neglecting the forces that compel workers of diverse social statuses to integrate themselves in unions. However, the UFWA case suggests that new social groups emerge into leadership positions when union-employer conflict jeopardizes union growth and compels the union to recruit from a new pool of potential members, generating a political realignment within the union; and that oligarchization is likely to occur when stability in the union-employer relationship effectively perpetuates the political alignments among membership groups within the union.

Leadership change, that is, the rise of new social groups into union office, is a consequence of status conflict among workers, a conflict exacerbated by an intensification of union employer conflict. Leadership change is a recurring effort of the union to resolve its own status conflicts by increasing the representation of a lower-status, emerging membership group in positions of union leadership. Moreover, the union's resolution of status conflict and, therefore, leadership change recurs for the greater purpose of reviving the union in the face of intensified employer opposition.

Leadership change and union-employer conflict, then, appear to exist in a cyclical relationship, the occurrence of one seeming to generate the other. As employers identify and hire lower-status, non-union workers, in order to weaken and to escape from their relationship with unions, unions extend their organizing drives into the ranks of these new workers, creating a realignment among competing membership groups of divergent social statuses within unions. As unions incorporate the new workers into their fold and emerging membership groups enter union office, employers search for a new group of non-union workers.

The cyclical pattern of labor union leadership is likely to persist as long as employers continue to identify and employ new sources of non-union labor and unions succeed in incorporating the new workers into the labor movement. Union leadership in the United States has not degenerated into oligarchy, contrary to what Michels might have predicted, because new social groups of workers have periodically entered the labor movement and struggled with some success to ascend the hierarchy of union offices.

Blacks, Hispanics, and women have come to comprise a greater share of labor leaders during the 1970s and 1980s. The trend in gender composition is easier to document than the trend in ethnicity because only the gender surveys were taken at different times. The surveys taken by LeGrande, the Coalition of Labor Union Women, and Baden show that the share of women leaders increased in several unions during this period.[20] The 1978–1979 survey of ethnic characteristics of labor leaders in major unions by the U.S. Commission on Civil Rights is the only survey on the subject. Although blacks and Hispanics were underrepresented in leadership positions, it is likely that the percentage was higher than that of the late 1960s, when black trade unionists first mobilized for greater access to union office.[21] Foner claimed that, following the Black Power movement, which occurred in several unions during the late 1960s, "events since 1968 have demonstrated that sections of the long-entrenched white labor leadership will make concessions to the black membership when their domination is threatened or the union faces dislocation. By sheer numerical strength, black power in the unions has already brought more blacks into policy-making positions on both international and local levels."[22] Moreover, Kochan, Aronowitz, and Form all argued that unorganized minorities and women are among the workers who are potentially most receptive to unionization.[23]

---

[20] Linda LeGrande, "Women in Labor Organizations: Their Ranks Are Increasing," *Monthly Labor Review* 101 (August 1978): 8–14; Coalition of Labor Union Women, *Absent from the Agenda: A Report on the Role of Women in American Unions* (Washington, DC: Coalition of Labor Union Women, 1980); Naomi Baden, "Developing an Agenda: Expanding the Role of Women in Unions," *Labor Studies Journal* 10 (Winter 1986): 229–249.

[21] U.S. Commission on Civil Rights, *Nonreferral Unions and Equal Employment Opportunity* (Washington, DC: Government Printing Office, 1982). Also see Philip Nyden, "Evolution of Black Political Influence in American Trade Unions," *Journal of Black Studies* 13 (June 1983): 379–398; Russell Schutt, "Craft Unions and Minorities: Determinants of Change in Admission Practices," *Social Problems* 34 (October 1987): 388–402; U.S. Commission on Civil Rights, *The Challenge Ahead: Equal Opportunity in Referral Unions* (Washington, DC: Government Printing Office, 1976); Scott Greer, *Last Man In: Racial Access to Union Power* (Glencoe, IL: Free Press, 1959); Michele Hoyman and Lamont Stallworth, "Participation in Local Unions: A Comparison of Black and White Members," *Industrial and Labor Relations Review* 40 (April 1987): 323–335.

[22] Philip Foner, *Organized Labor and the Black Worker 1619–1981* (New York: International Publishers, 1982), p. 423.

[23] Form, *Divided We Stand*, pp. 261–262; Thomas Kochan, "How American Workers View Labor Unions," *Monthly Labor Review* 102 (April 1979): 23–31; Stanley Aronowitz, *Working Class Hero: A New Strategy for Labor* (New York: Pilgrim Press, 1983), pp. 141–150.

The UFWA case suggests that unionized workers of diverse social statuses may integrate themselves periodically, abandoning divisive status conflict in order to protect their union and economic interests. The integration of emerging lower-status membership groups into union leadership positions is most likely to occur in those periods in the history of a union when the jeopardization of union membership growth combines with increased social heterogeneity and stratification of the existing union membership. Under these conditions, emerging lower-status membership groups, if their social characteristics mirror those of the potential membership pool, may hold the key to future successes in union organizing campaigns; subsequently align themselves with some of the higher-status membership groups who perceive the lower-status groups as being of strategic importance to the revival of the union; and struggle successfully against entrenched higher-status groups for access to union leadership positions. When their capacity for self-organization is impaired by such forces as increased employer hostility toward their union, workers of diverse social statuses may become integrated into union leadership positions in order to strengthen their union and improve the economic livelihood of the whole membership. In this respect, the labor movement may harbor the potential for unifying workers of diverse social statuses and achieving a greater degree of social integration.

Subject Index

Boldface numbers refer to tables.

activism, 155, 232; UFWA civil rights, 187, 207, 212
activists, 205, 224; black, 155, 186, 188, 189, 238; black women, 155, 209, 212–213, 217; civil rights, 207–208; FWIU, 252; Hispanic, 155, 186, 188, 189, 238; left-wing union, 251; minority, 208, 221, 222, 239; training sessions for UFWA, 214; women, 209, 223, 237–239
administrative structure, 86
advisory committee, to GEB, 140
affidavits: non-Communist, 20, 105, 256–257
affiliation: certificates of, 75; CIO, 18, 74–83, 258; with district councils, 142; of furniture workers with labor federation, 251; with UFWA, 82, 95, 96, 101, 206–207; of UIU with CIO, 78, 83
AFL-CIO Dishonor Roll of Labor Law Violators, 162, 163
aggrieved groups, 17
agriculture: mechanization of, 178, 185, 239

Alabama, 142
alliances, shifting, 145, 152, 153
amalgamated local unions, 33–35, 46–50, 52, 55–56, 123, 224; large, 94, 223, 233; of New York City, 88, survival of, 58. *See also* GEB members; votes; specific issues
amalgamation, 141, 143; of locals, 67, 90–92, 94–97, 99
anti-Communism, 66, 103, 118, 240, 252, 256, 258
anti-unionism, 66, 118, 164, 169, 252
apprenticeships, 8, 201
Arkansas, 111, 122, 203, 224; delegates, 93; joint councils, 142; UFWA membership, **98**, 99, **161**
Asians, 8, 56, 220
assembly line, 183
Athens, TX, 145, 198
Austell, GA, 97
autonomy, 105; within CIO, 115; UIU, 77, 78, 80

Baltimore, 46, 55, 111, 176, 199; conference in, 225; vote, 190; women officials in, 210

bargaining strength, 169, 250
Batesville, IN, 99
becalmed social movement organizations, 261
bedding industry, 207
benefits, 22, 74, 130, 171; unemployment, 252; welfare, 8, 130; for workers, 9, 74, 162. *See also* fringe benefits
Benton, AR, 145, 198
biographies: of FWIU founders, 69–70; of IUE leaders, 240–241; of local union leaders, 96–97, 235; of top UFWA leaders, 200–202, 205–206, 225–226; of UFWA leaders, 96, 116, 121–122; of UIU leaders, 94–95; of women leaders, 212–216, 221, 226–234
Birmingham, AL, 144, 199, 207
Black Power movement, 264
blacks, 112, 220, 249, 255; denial of union membership to, 6, 7, 8; on executive board seats, 4; in furniture manufacturing, **179–181**, 181, 184; increases in numbers of, 58; in leadership positions, 6, 258, 264; mobilization of, 208, 246; in nonagricultural jobs, 177–178; political influence of, 186, 191, 239; rise of, onto GEB, 185, 186, 192; siding with Left, 111; southern, 27, 118, 188, 191, 197, 204, 254; succession of, 52, 56, 254; unionization of, 194, 200, 208; urbanization of, 182, 185. *See also* discrimination; GEB members; UFWA members; specific issues
black women, 3, 155, 217, 221, 237; southern, 213. *See also* activists
black workers, 2, 6, 172, 193; conflict of, with white workers, 243; in furniture industry, 27, 236; migration of, 255; southern, 198; spring, 118; in training programs, 225
Bloomington, IN, 210
board representativeness, 86, 92, 146, 152; principle of, 87
Border States, **132, 134, 136, 137, 156–157, 161**, 170
Boston, 72, **84**
boycotts, 172, 193
Bracero Program, 182

branch plants, non-union, 138
Britain, 104
Buffalo, NY, 144
bureaucracy, 3, 13, 15, 16, 247

California, 56, 117
Camden, AR, 190
campaigns, 145, 258; decertification, 162, 163, 257; organizing, 129, 170, 172, 197; pro-CIO, 115
candidates, 203, 233, 236; left-wing, 115; minority, 222; presidential, endorsement of, 164–165; women, for GEB, 209, 223, 233, 237
Canton, MS, 171, 190, 199, 214
capital, 135, 138, 178; geographical movements of, 167, 250, 254; redistribution of, 186, 191, 208
casual labor, 31–32, 33
Catholics, 195
caucuses, 191–192, 203–204; black, 191; women's, 213–217, 218, 220, 237
centralization: in International UFWA, 140; strategies for, 139; of UFWA, 123, 124, 140, 145, 153
chain plant organizing, UFWA, 143–144, 170, 185, 198, 199, 208; strategy, 238
chain plants, 133, 135, 138–139, 145, 171; expansion of, 185, 208; La-Z-Boy, non-union, 172–173; organizing drives in, 153. *See also* councils
charter: local union, 139; rate, 158
Chelsea, MA, 144
Chicago, 47, 49, **84**, 94; foreign-born members in, 55; Hispanic workers in, 182; International UFWA headquarters in, 107; large locals in, 176, 204
Chicanos, 182
Cincinnati, OH, 92
CIO: formation of, 1, 20, 45, 66; policy, **108**, 110–112, 114–116, 118
civil rights, 4, 186–187, 195, 197; issues, 111, 116; legislation, 177; protests, 207; women's involvement in, 214. *See also* activism; activists
Civil Rights Act of 1964, 6, 7, 178, 186, 249

SUBJECT INDEX **269**

civil rights movement, 191, 205, 212; contributions of, 12, 27, 185, 222, 238; contributions of, for minorities, 177, 186, 208, 256; contributions of, for women, 177, 217, 237; participation in, 155, 207; in the South, 203
class conflict, 6, 250, 256, 257
Cleveland, OH: convention in, 74–75; delegates from, 199; large locals in, 47, 49, 94; locals, 55, 95, 99, 140, 144
closed shop contracts, 21, 32, 152
Cold War, 66, 106, 109, 112, 116, 154; era, 239, 252; leadership change during, 102–103; politics, 93
collective bargaining, 8, 22, 85, 129, 195; coordination of, 171, 185, 208; gains, 252; negotiations, 172
Columbus, OH, 140, 144
Communism, 103–104, 110, 112–114
Communist party, 67, 72, 104, 114, 122, 251; leaders in, 20; members, 103
Communists, 27, 103, 192, 252, 256, 258
competing groups, 17
conferences: CIO, 75–76; furniture unity, 76–82, 84, 85, 92; on the role of women, 225
consolidation, 139, 140, 153; local union, 170; of UFWA operations, 145
construction, 10, 13
contract gains, 171–172
contracts, 131, 143; with chain plants, 138
convention committees, 85
conventions, 173–174; AFL, 75–76, 78; AFL-CIO, 129, 240; attendance of, by locals, 36, 37, 38, CIO, 103, 104, 110, 114; frequency of, 173–174. *See also* UFWA conventions
Cookeville, TN, 224
coordinated bargaining, 143, 144, 145, 170, 199
corporations: large, 5, 8–9; multi-unit, 135, **138**, 138, 159; non-union, 130
cost-reduction efforts, 157, 259
councils: chain plant, 144, 170–171, 198; district, 142–143; establishment of, 171
craft unionism, 1, 7–9, 12, 31, 32, 67; conflict between industrial and, 66, 75, 251; traditional, 65

craft unions, 5, 9, 10, 68; AFL, 8, 259; local, 31; patriarchal, 6
credit union, 235

Dallas, TX, 145, 198, 199
Dayton, TN, 173
debates, 86–91, 110–111; on constitutional provisions, 92
decline, period of, UFWA, 22, 155, 253, 256–257; GEB members during, 24, **25**, **26**; leadership during, 254, 258; local union closures during, 158
delay-and-frustrate tactics, 133
delegates, 36, 174, 199; to first UFWA convention, 83–91; local union, 45–46, 83, 146; political attitudes of, 118; UFWA, to CIO, 115; UIU, 76; women, 217, 230
democracy, 15, 16, 245
democratic government, debate on principles of, 86, 88
Democrats, 164
demonstrations, 203, 207. *See also* insurgencies
Denver, CO, **84**
discrimination, 7, 92, 187, 191; banning of, 185, 186, 195; against minorities, 116, 195–196; police, 193; against women, 210, 216
disputes, 129
domestic arrangements, 237–238, 238*n*
Dutch GEB members, 56

East: convention votes in, 50, **51**, 52, **61**, 83, **84**, **108**, 109–111; delegates from, 83; elections won by UFWA in, **126**, 126, 165, **166**; GEB exits from, 189, **190**; GEB members in, **53**, 55, 117, 118; GEB seats in, 189; large locals in, 146, 147, 150; locals in, 38, 43–50, **49**, 138, 151; minorities and women in furniture manufacturing in, **180–181**, 183; organizing drives in, 102, 118; roll call votes results in, **148**, 150, **151**, 152; shift away from, 186, 191; stable voting blocs in, 58; tensions in metropolitan, 106; UFWA membership in, **125**, 159, **161**, 213; UFWA representation elections in, **167**; urban, 66, 118; women furniture workers in, 217

elections, 9, 32, 230; closeness of, 14, 15; contested, 121, 258; decertification, 162, 163, 167, 257; GEB, 24, 115, 236; multi-union, 128; officer, 109, 113, 115; representation, UFWA, 125–130, 133, 166, **167**, 198; of women, 216, 230–233. *See also* votes; voting
election victory rates, UFWA, **126**, 126, 129–130, 133, 165, **166**, 198
employees, 163, 181. *See also* workers
employer resistance: and membership losses, 133; strategies, 133, 153; to UFWA, 162, 239; to unionization, 30, 40, 124, 140, 145, 156, 164, 253; to union organizing campaigns, 257; to union organizing drives, 129–133, 139, 252
employers, 3, 29–30, 133; conflict between unions and, 250, 259–260, 263; discriminatory employment practices by, 187; non-union, 22, 40, 124, 130, 257; racial discrimination by, 186; relationships with, 2, 8, 263; relocation of, 124, 257, 260
employment, 21, 32, 220; agricultural, 182; changes in patterns of, 178; in furniture manufacturing, 22, **138**, 159, 178–183; growth, 183; improving conditions of, 93–94, 100, 171; in manufacturing, 178, **179**
English GEB members, 55, 56
equal opportunity program, 186–187
equal pay, 211
equal rights, 196, 197, 220, 221
Equal Rights Amendment, 219, 220
ethnic composition on GEB, 102, 117, 190, 240
ethnic groups, 177, 187; emergence of new, 59; of European descent, 188; on GEB, 117–118; residence of, 106; succession of, on GEB, 34, 50, 52–60, 66, 118–119, 153; white, 188
ethnic integration, 156, 177, 192, 205; of GEB, 156, 205, 208, 238–240; of UFWA, 157, 192–198, 238–241; of UFWA leadership, 185, 192
ethnic intermingling, 198
ethnicity, 52, 58, 106, 264
European descent, 55–58, 117–118, 188; members of, 258; native-born of, 8, 55–56, 254–256. *See also* UFWA leaders; workers
European GEB members, 24, 25, **26**, **53–54**, 55–58, 66, 102, 103, 112; increases in numbers of, 58, 112; proportions of, 117–118
Europeans, 106; Eastern, 55, 117, 196; Southern, 196. *See also* immigrants
executive board: CIO, 104–105; new seats on national, 246; positions, 15; UIU, 82
executive committee of International UFWA, 231
exits from GEB, 189, **190**, 191
expenses, 157, 169, 170; of International UFWA, 157, 173–175, 177; UFWA, **98**
expulsion from CIO, 104, 110, 258

factionalism, 15–16, 109, 110, 121, 246, 260; avoidance of, 262; conditions promoting, 254, 259; outcome of, 157; within a social-movement organization, 245, 250, 261; timing of, 260
fascism, 105, 122
financial resources of International UFWA, 169
Florence, SC, 169, 172, 173, 190, 199, 231
formative period, UFWA, 37–38, 65–66, 251; disagreement of voting blocs in, 256; end of, 119, 121, 252; GEB members in, **25**, **26**, 102; interunion rivalry in, 127; leadership in, 118–119, 153–154, 239, 254, 258; membership in, 20, 124–125; organizing campaigns in, 170; representative seats in, 24
Fort Smith, AR, 56, 83, 106, 199, 203; locals, 43, **44**, 50, 56, **84**, 94, 171; single-shop locals, 45, 48; votes, 111, 204
Fort Worth, TX, 227
Fostoria, OH, 144
founders' legacy, 199–208
founding UFWA convention (1939), 1, 30, 83–87, 193; GEB members elected at, 118; local unions at, 45, 50, 175; policies adopted at, 41–43,

SUBJECT INDEX 271

140, 143, 170, 192; scope of, 83, 84, 85; tensions at, 106; UFWA membership at, **125**
frame makers, 91
free riders, 130
French-Canadian GEB members, 55
fringe benefits, 22, 32–33, **134–135**; coverage for, 131; employer-provided, 33, 37, 40; gaining new, 100, 171–172; won by striking, 193
funding, 92, 117
furniture factories, 37–38, 40–42, 50, 58
furniture industrial union, 65–66, 77, 89
furniture manufacturing, **19, 21**, 21, 22, 159, 238; economic conditions in, 20; ethnic minorities and women in, 177–178, **179**, 180, **180–181**; geographical redistribution of, 135, 138, 238; ruralization of, 41–43; and unionization, 38; women in, 179, 209; wood household, **132, 134–135, 136, 137**
furniture manufacturing industry, 21, 34, 38, 146, 158; geographical decentralization of, 124, 140–142, 159, 208; geographical redistribution of, 156, 209, 224, 237, 239; growth of, 41, 183; low-wage, 156; New York, 68, 72, 74; problems facing, 97; redistribution of, 124, 139; southward shift of, 50, 124, 208; wood, 57
furniture manufacturing towns, 43, **44**, 123
furniture workers, 22, 65, 68, 69, 184; affiliation of, with labor federations, 251; black, 156, 181, 184; demoralization of, 77; ethnic composition of, 254–255; fringe benefits for wood household, **134–135**; Hispanic, 156, 182; Mexican, 182; non-skilled, 118, 184; organization of, 71, 78; picketing, 72; UFWA membership of, **19, 21**, 21; unionized wood household, **136, 156–157**, 157; wages, 133, **137, 160–161**, 162; white male, 184; women, 156–157, 183, 184, 211, 217; wood, 118
Furniture Workers Press, **52**, 83, 102n, 104n, 105n, 106n, 110n, 111n, 112n, 113n, 114n, 115, 115n, 116n, 117, 117n, 122n, 128n, 129, 129n, 130n, 131n, 142n, 143n, 144n, 145n, 160n, 163n, 164n, 169, 169n, 171n, 187n, 189n, 193, 193n, 194, 194n, 197, 197n, 198n, 200n, 201, 201n, 208n, 210, 210n, 211, 211n, 212, 212n, 213n, 215, 215n, 216, 216n, 222n, 224, 224n, 225n, 241n

Gardner, MA, 25, 43, **44**, 95, 99, 144; GEB seats in, 188; ladies auxiliaries in, 210; large locals in, 46, 55, 94, 176; organization of, 72; organizing drives in, 92
GEB, 23–27, 42, 86, 104, 105, 170, 236; composition of, 86, 117; exits, 189, **190**, 190; geographic-ethnic shift in, 102–103; leaders, 48, 56, 189, 226
GEB members, 25, **25**, 27, 87; from amalgamated locals, 34, **35**, 35; Asian, 56; black, 24, **26**, **53–54**, 55, 56, 189–192, 194, 236; election of, 92; ethnic and racial distribution of, 24, **26**, 48, **49**, 50, **51**; immigrant, 112; left-wing, 112, 115; maximum number of, 175; new, 24, 38–39, **39, 59**; percentage of, 34, **35**, 35, 175, **176**; reelection of, 121; terms served by, 122; turnover rate of, 158, 174–177; white male, 186, 189, 191. *See also* specific GEB members; specific issues
GEB members, women, **26**, 27, 217, 218, 231, 233, 236, 238; black, 58, 218; ethnic characteristics of, 57–58; International, 209, 215; origins of, 217–218, 224; social characteristics of, 218; white, 58, 218, 229
GEB membership, 38, 105, 208
GEB positions, 122, 146, 176, 209; elective, 173; terms of office for, 24, 174; for women, 231
GEB seats, 87–88, 106, 113, 115, 176, 232; competition for, 38; election to, 92, 236, 237; geographically defined, 188–189; at International, 236; for local unions, 36, 39; for minorities, 212; new, 187–189; reduction of, 224

gender groups, 59, 177; succession of, on GEB, 34, 50, 57–58, 59, 60
gender integration, 156, 177; on GEB, 156, 217–218, 222, 237–240; of UFWA, 157, 238–241
General Executive Board. *See* GEB
geographical decentralization, 124, 140–142, 145, 180
Georgia, 142
German GEB members, 55, 56, 236
Germany, 92
Gettysburg, PA, 99
governance, UFWA, 83, 157, 177, 256; of International, 170, 207; minority participation in, 186, 191–192, 207–208, 238, 246, 256, 258; participation in, 255; women's participation in, 209, 211, 212, 216–219, 221, 238, 256, 258
Grand Rapids, MI, 25, 43, **44**, 99, 205; locals in, 47, 113; organization of, 72; organizing drives in, 92
Granville, NY, 143
Great Depression, 9, 32, 68, 253
Great Lakes regions, 25, 41, 42, 170, 182–183, 253; convention votes, **84**; furniture workers in, **135**, **136**, **157**; raids in, 106; wages in, **132**, **137**, **160**, **168**; women workers in, 27, 57
Greenville, MS, 222
group consciousness, 255–256
group insurance coverage, 131. *See also* benefits; fringe benefits
growth, 178, 248, 250, 260, 263; barriers to, 21–22; of black underclass, 249; jeopardization of union, 256, 257, 260; organizational, 254, 256, 257, 261–262; policies, 157; rates of locals, 150–151; strategy of UFWA, 83, 94; of UFWA, 93–97, 99, 102, 117–119, 209, 252, 256; of U.S. manufacturing, 252. *See also* labor movement
Guthrie, OK, 171

Hagerstown, MD, 99
headquarters, relocation of International UFWA, 107, **108**, 208
hegemonic despotism, 33
Henderson, NC, 48, 50, 111, 116, 190, 203

Hickory, NC, 97
higher status groups, 257, 260, 265
High Point, NC, 43, **44**, 144
Hispanic GEB members, **26**, **54**, 55, 56, 58, 189–192
Hispanics, 188, 206, 214, 234, 254, 256; in furniture manufacturing, **179–181**, 179, 182; in leadership positions, 258, 264; mobilization of, 208, 246; in nonagricultural jobs, 177–178; political influence of, 186, 191, 239; rise of, onto GEB, 185, 186, 192; urbanization of, 185; West Coast, 118, 191. *See also* activists
Hispanic women, 58, 213, 217, 218
Hispanic workers, 2, 196, 235–236; migration of, 243, 255; participation of, in training programs, 225
Houston, TX, 144
Huntington, WV, 111

ideological tradition, 260–261
Illinois, 142; elected GEB members from, 92, 93, 232; raids in, **107**; UFWA membership in, **98**, 99
immigrants, 69, 106, 118; European, 8, 24, 69; from Mexico, 182; undocumented, 234
imports, 160, 162, 164, 253; furniture, 156, 159, 167; value of, 159
income: International UFWA, 97, **98**; stratification, 145–146, 152–153
incumbents, 258–259, 260; GEB, 23, 24, **25**, 189; left-wing, 115
Indiana, 43, 92, 93, 97, 142; membership gains in, **98**, 99; organizing drives in, 204; raids in, 105, **107**
Indiana Occupational Safety and Health Act, 163
industrializing areas, 260
industrial unionism, 7–10, 12, 31, 73, 83; conflict between craft and, 66, 75, 251; emergence of, 8, 243, 251, 257; in furniture industry, 65–68, 90, 102, 118; movement, 1, 194, 253; realization of, 93, 94; and UIU, 75
initiation fees, 88–89
insurgencies, 2, 16, 18, 243, 247–248, 250
integration: of blacks, 194; of lower-

SUBJECT INDEX **273**

status groups, 265; social, 4, 249, 265. *See also* ethnic integration; gender integration
International Union Equal Opportunity Committee, 186
International Union staff, 146–147
inter-union transfers, 129
intimidating tactics, 133
Ionia, MI, 47, 56
Irish GEB members, 55, 56
iron law of democracy (Gouldner), 245
iron law of oligarchy (Michels), 13–16, 27, 60, 122–123, 175, 263; alternatives to, 30, 59, 246, 248; arguments of, 245; criticism of, 17, 243–248; definition of, 15; implications for, 34; psychological reductionism of, 154
Italian GEB members, 55, 56, 58, 117–118; distribution of, 24, **26**, 52, **53**
Italians, 56, 106, 188, 199, 254, 256
Italy, 92

Jackson, MS, 224
Jamestown, NY, **44**, 46, 55, 72, 99
Jamestown-Buffalo, 142
Jasper, IN, 99
Jewish GEB members, 102, 103; decline of, 112, 117–118; distribution of, 24, **26**, 52, **53**, 55, 56, 58; from urban East, 66
Jewish leaders, 188, 258
Jewish UFWA members, 106, 206
Jews, 69, 195. *See also* voters
job: discrimination, 186; referral, 32; security, 9, 167
jobless pay, 160
jobs, 6, 65, 177–179, 231, 249; low-wage, 182, 239
joint boards, 143
joint councils, 141–143, 147, **148–149**
juvenile furniture trade, 74, 87, 93

Keene, NH, 92
Kentucky, 142

laborers. *See* workers
labor market segmentation, 178
labor movement, 2, 191, 249, 265; employer opposition to, 252; growth of, 93, 118–119, 253, 256; historical background of, 6–12; integration of blacks into, 194; reasons for decline of, 253; women and minorities in, 2, 4, 7, 9–11, 13
ladies auxiliaries, 210–211
Lancaster, PA, 72
Landrum-Griffin Act of 1959, 17
Latinos, 191, 197, 220–221
leaders, 2–3; black, 207; craft union, 68; ethnic characteristics of labor, 264; GEB International, 228; Hispanic, 207; incumbent, 260; Italian, 239; Jewish, 188, 239; left-wing, 102–103, 111, 119, 208, 257, 259; national, 29–30, 33, 34–40; native-born, of European descent, 239–240; new groups of, 30, 207, 264; non-left, 239; top, International UFWA, 223. *See also* UFWA leaders; women leaders
leadership, 243, 250; cyclical pattern of labor union, 263–264; elected, 13, 28, 251; emergence of new groups of, 2, 239, 250, 258–259; GEB, 40, 153; incumbent, 258–259; left-wing, 116, 117, 252; minority union, 187; patterns, 48–49; sharing of, 257; stability, 60, 153, 246, 262; stabilization, 13, 24, 123, 243, 245; top, 223–224, trends, 18; turnover, 24, 59, 122. *See also* UFWA leadership
leadership change, 2–4, 15, 30, 60, 112, 245–246, 248; during Cold War, 102–103; and continuity, 27–28; in labor movement, 243–244; likelihood of, 260–261; national, 40; process of, 18; timing of, 251, 254; in UFWA, 23–27, 30, 34, 60, 102–103, 239, 254
leadership positions: attainment of national, 238; new groups in, 14, 28, 177, 251, 260–262, 265. *See also* blacks; Hispanics; minorities; women
leadership stabilization, 153
leadership succession, 30, 34; of ethnic groups, 118–119
Left, 66, 111, 114, 128; defeat of, 103, 112–113, 115–118; influence of, on GEB, 109, 110, 112–115; ousting of, 121, 192, 240, 258, 259; replacement of, 239

274 SUBJECT INDEX

left wing, 115, 251; anti-CIO, 258. *See also* GEB members; leaders; officers
Little Rock, AR, 171
"Little Steel" formula, 102
local union: autonomy, 31, 88–89, 92; claims, to GEB, 188–189; cohorts, 36–38, 43, 46–50, 52, 55; dynamics, 30, 40–58; functions, 31; membership changes, **151**, 152; membership growth trends, 146, 151; role of, 32; size, 34–40, 43, 45, 46, 58, 59; structure, 31–33, 34–40; turnover, 123–124, 139, 140, 145, 153, 177; voting strength, 45, 46, 47. *See also* offices
local union closures, 38, 123, 153; rates, 139; reasons for, 159, 167; UFWA, 36, 123, 158
local unions, 29–30, 36, 152, 190; black and Hispanic, 190–191; comparison of large and small, 36, 37, 88, 139, 147, 152, 175; with delegations at UFWA conventions, **37**; distribution of convention votes among, 45–46, 50; establishment of joint councils of, 141; fates of, 58, 59–60; at founding UFWA convention, 83, **84**, 85; in furniture towns, 43, **44**; geographical division among, 147; increase of, 175; large, 38, 47–48, 146, 150, 175, 188–189; membership change in 19 large, 150, **151**; membership of New York City UIU, **74**, 74–75; in metropolitan areas, 43, **44**; new, 30, 37–38, 39, 158, 170; old, 39, 158; redistribution of, 40; ruralization of, 42–43, 46, 48, 50; share of GEB seats for large, 176; single-shop, 33, 35, 45–48, 58, 123, 141; small, 124, 142, 158, 223, 237; with 250 or more members, **45**, 45; UFWA, 40, 45, 47, 138, 144, 171. *See also* amalgamated unions; growth; specific issues
Logan, OH, 144
Los Angeles, 72; amalgamated locals in, 46, 56, 233; Hispanic furniture workers in, 25, 182, 254; Hispanic locals, 58, 191; La-Z-Boy plant, 199; locals, 43, **84**, 99, 111, 116, 117, 144; training seminars, 224
Louisiana, **98**, 99
Louisville, KY, 198

lower-status groups, 244, 257, 260, 263, 265

majority proposals, 87–88
manufacturing, 10, 12–13, **179**, 179, 253. *See also* furniture manufacturing
Marion, SC, 144
markets: dual labor, 178; internal labor, 32; internationalization of, 253
Marshall Plan, 103, 104
Martinsville, VA, 99
Maryland, **98**, 99, 142, 215
mass production, 31; industries, 20, 22, 32, 74–75, 77, 79, 251–252; manufacturing, 8, 243; technologies, 9, 65, 183, 184
meetings: captive audience, 124; CIO, 197; GEB, 142, 144, 186; NPOMI, 198, 202; racially and ethnically mixed, 199
membership. *See* union membership
membership groups, 260; dissimilarities between emerging and established, 260–261; emerging, 257–262; insurgent, 263
membership stabilization, 123, 140, 153, 253
Memphis, TN, **44**, 171, 198, 225; black UFWA members in, 106, 190; CIO office, 111; demonstrations in, 207; locals, 48, 50, 99, 144; organizing campaigns in, 176; strike in, 162
men: serving on GEB, 24; white, 2, 3, 8, 12, 186, 189, 243, 258
mentoring, 199–200, 205, 207–208, 259; importance of, 156; of new generations of UFWA leaders, 195; of women, 209, 214, 215, 223, 228, 237
mentors, 201–202, 206, 207, 227, 239; International UFWA, 229
mergers: AFL-CIO, 10, 21, 127, 257; local unions, 140, 170, 175, 176; UFWA, 200, 205; UFWA into IUE, 157, 200, 205, 240–241, 253; unions, 31, 253
metropolitan areas, 43, **44**, 48, 109, 124; ethnic succession in, 52, 56; furniture industry in, 183; gender succession in, 58; new locals in, 170; voting behavior in, 152; wages in, 134

Mexican GEB members, 56
Mexicans, 234
Mexico, 145, 182
Michigan, 43, 97–99, 230–231, 236; GEB members from, 236; organizing drives in, 204; raids in, 105, **107**
Middle Atlantic regions, 41, 42; black workers in, 27, 182; convention votes in, **84**; furniture workers in, **134**, **136**, **137**, **156–157**; non-furniture workers in, 170; shift southward from, 3, 253; wages in, 100, **132**, **137**, **160**, **168**; women workers in, 57
Midwest, 66, 156; convention votes in, 50, **51**, 55, **62**, 83, **84**, **108**, 109–111; delegates from, 83; distribution of UFWA membership, **125**; elections won by UFWA in, **126**, 126, 165, **166**; ethnic groups from, 188, 256; GEB exits from, 189, **190**, 190; GEB members, 53, 112, 117, 118; GEB seats in, 189; International staff members in, 146; locals, 38, 43–50, 123, 138, 151, 156–157; nonmetropolitan, 57, 58, 107, 112, 255, 258; organizing drives in, 92, 102, 112, 118; raids in, 113; relocation to, 217, 224, 237, 239, 254; roll call votes in, 147, **148–149**, 150, **151**, 152; rural, 58, 106; shift away from, 3, 40, 186, 191, 204, 209; small locals in, 88, 146–147; tensions in, 106; UFWA membership in, 159, **161**; UFWA representation elections in, **167**; women furniture workers in, **180–181**, 183, 217
migration, 21, 182
Milwaukee, **84**
mini-conventions, 174
mining, 10, 13
minorities, 7, 9, 177; ascent of, 155, 157, 185–191; entry rates of ethnic, 180; on GEB, 155, 157, 177, 185, 186–192, 208–209; in leadership positions, 3–4, 177, 185, 187–188, 241; in low-status occupations, 249; mobility of, 59, 256; organization of, 191; rights of, 220; unorganized, 264. *See also* discrimination; labor movement; specific issues

minority: access to labor movement, 6; caucuses, 191; mobilization, 2, 186, 191, 205, 212, 217, 220, 222, 237, 239; participation, 188–189, 221; proposals, 87–88; support of women, 219–222; union members, 3, 6, 13. *See also* governance; workers
Mississippi, 224; River, 106, 159, **161**
Monroe, MI, 172, 199, 229, 230
Montgomery, AL, 197
musical instruments industry, 160

Nashville, TN, 198, 208
National Unity Conference of Unions in the Furniture, Bedding and Allied Trades, 82
Negroes. *See* blacks
Neosho, MO, 172, 173, 199
Newark, NJ, 140, 176
New Deal, 92; social welfare programs, 80
New England, 25, 41, 92, 142; convention votes in, **84**; ethnic groups in, 106; furniture workers in, 131, **134**, **136**, **137**, **156–157**; locals, 97; non-furniture workers in, 170; organizing drives in, 92; raids in, **107**; shift away from, 253; strikes in, 102; UFWA membership in, 42, **98**, 99; wages in, **132**, **137**, **160**, **168**; women workers in, 57
new groups, 58, 60
New Jersey, 72, **98**, 99
New Market, TN, 225
New Orleans, 97
Newton, MS, 172, 173, 199
New York, **107**, 142; upstate, 93, **98**, 99
New York City, 43, 93, 251; ethnic composition of, 52, 55; furniture trade unionism in, 67–68, 72; FWIU membership in, 70; GEB seats in, 188; Hispanic workers in, 182; International UFWA headquarters, 107, 208; large locals, 46, 83, 88, 97, 111, 204; locals, 74, **84**, 90, 96, 116, 144; mergers of locals in, 176; organizing drives in, 25, 92, 102, 106, 118, 254; strikes in, 102; UFWA membership in, **98**, 99; vote, 190; women officials in, 210

non-Left, 109, 110, 113, 114, 115
nonmetropolitan areas, 56, 109; furniture industry in, 183; gender succession in, 58; joint councils in, 142; non-union plants in, 138; relocation to, 124, 145, 224; succession of GEB members from, 52; wages in, 134
No-Raiding Pact (AFL-CIO), 127
North, 30, 40, 146
North Carolina, 106, 142, 197
Northeast, 106, 254–256, 258; ethnic groups from, 188; shift away from, 40, 156, 185, 204, 208, 209, 217, 239

occupations, 12; non-skilled, 255; semi-skilled, 184–185, 239; skilled, 184
office: contests for, 204; electoral competition for, 13–14, 246
officers: assignment of International, 186; first black and Hispanic International UFWA, 189; gender traits of, 3; International UFWA, 129, 140, 207, 211, 215, 218, 226; left-wing, 20, 66, 256, 258; national union, 3, 14; non-Left, 103; reports and resolutions of International, 195; women, 3–4, 215, 234. *See also* elections; training programs
offices: highest ranking, 223; local union, 216, 230; UFWA, 204
official proclamations, 195, 218–219
Ohio, **98**, 99, **107**
Oklahoma, 93, **98**, 99, 142, 171
oligarchization, 247, 261, 263
oligarchy, 13–14, 17, 18, 264. *See also* iron law of oligarchy
one-earner families, 178, 185, 239, 255
open shop movement, 32, 252–253
organizational structure, 59, 246
organizations, 244–248; democratic, 13, 244, 245, 261; social movement, 245, 250, 261–262
organizers: appointment of, 140, 141; female International UFWA, 214; International, on GEB, 146, 147, 152, 215; local union, 175; paid International UFWA, 122, 146, **148–149**, 175, 204, 205; servicing activities of International, 143, 170
organizing: campaigns, 129, 170, 172, 197; union, 165; of unorganized, 93–94, 112
organizing activity, UFWA, 40–43, 58, 129, 133, 170, 173; deceleration in, 165–167, 169; war, 97
organizing drives, 87, 124, 143, 239, 250, 255; CIO, 77, 95, 102; conducted by women, 216; CUF, 128–129; employer resistance in, 129–130, 139; extension of, 25, 50, 106, 112, 118, 254, 263; financing, 145–146, 152–153; internal, 167, 169; International UFWA, 145–146, 147, 152; at La-Z-Boy plants, 172; obstruction of, 123; regional, 140; southern, 102, 254; timing of, 48; UIU, 73, 79

Pacific Coast, **98**, 99; furniture workers, **135**, **136**, **157**; locals, 97; wages, **132**, **137**, **160**, **168**
patriarchy, 6
Pennsylvania, **98**, 99, **107**, 142, 215
pension coverage, 131. *See also* benefits; fringe benefits
Philadelphia, 43, **84**
piano manufacturing, 92, 96, 145, 160
picketing, 72, 101, 163
Pittsburgh, **84**, 210
plant relocation, 133–134
plant shutdowns, 33–34, 36, 38, 123, 134, 139, 153
political beliefs, 106
Political Parties (Michels), 13
Portland, OR, 57, 233
predominant status, 129
prejudice, 197, 212
presidents: of GEB, 87, 92, 113, 146; of locals, 204, 216, 235–236; offices of, 116; of UFWA, 140–141, 175, 191, 202, 204, 205; of UIU International, 75; women, 216
pressures on UFWA, 66
psychological reductionism, 59
Puerto Ricans, 206

racial unity, 101, 197–198, 202–203
racism, 6, 7, 187
raids, 109, 112; UFWA, 21, 129; on UFWA, 105, 106, 113, 129, 154, 252;

UFWA membership loss from, **107**, 110; UIU, 105, 106, **107**, 129; United Automobile Workers, 106, **107**
reaction, fight against, 115
realignment, political, 244
rebates, 142, 143
recruitment, 9–11, 70, 254
Redlands, CA, 172, 173
reforms, 16, 140–141
regional division in UFWA, 106–110
relationships: AFL-CIO, 127; UFWA-CIO, 104–106, 114, 117; UIU-UFWA, 109. *See also* employers
reports: majority, 87–88; on women's rights, 218–221
representation on the GEB, 66, 123, 154, 175, **176**, 176
representatives, 87–88; International UFWA, **148–149**, 227, 234
research traditions, 15
resolutions, 114, 117; on human freedoms, 116; left-wing, 110; of local 76, 91; pro-CIO, 110–111, 116; women's caucus, 216, 220
resource mobilization, 248; theory, 17, 246–247
retirement, **190**, 190, 191
revenues, loss in, 167
revitalization of UFWA, 157
right-to-work laws, 40, 124, 130, 167, 169; enactment of, 21, 252, 253
Rikers Island Penitentiary, 201
rivalry: with AFL, 99; between CIO and AFL unions, 257; inter-union, 125, 127–129, 153; types of inter-union, 256–257
Roanoke, VA, **84**, 111
Rockford, IL, **44**, **84**, 144, 232; convention in, 83, 88, 106; ladies auxiliaries, 210
runaway plants, 133, 135, 139
rural areas, 58
ruralization, 41–43, 135, 183. *See also* local unions
Russellville, AR, 171, 199

Salvadorans, 234
San Diego, CA, 186
San Francisco, 25; amalgamated locals, 46, 56, 233; locals, 43, **84**, 96, 99, 144, 235–236

Scandinavian GEB members, 55
seats: branch, 93; district, 92–93. *See also* GEB seats
secretary treasurers: of GEB, 87, 92, 109, 113, 203; offices of, 116, 117; of UFWA, 204–207
security arrangements, 124, 153, 169, 252–253
segmentation theory, 248–249
segregation, 7, 27, 59, 244; occupational, 4–6, 12, 248; reasons for, 5; social, 27, 249
Selma, AL, 197
seniority, 9, 32
service industries, 11, 12
servicing, 141, 142, 143, 146–147, 170
Seventh Congress of the Communist International, 73
Sheboygan, WI, **44**; amalgamated locals, 47, 55, 99, 176, 188
shops: large, 125, 126, 129, 130, 133, 165, 166; non-union, 169; runaway, 129; small, 124, 125, 126, 165
Sixth World Congress of the Communist International, 67
socialism, 2, 67, 248, 249
South: capital mobility to, 30; chain companies in, 138; civil rights movement in, 203; delegates from, 83; demonstrators of, 197; distribution of GEB members in, **49**, **51**, **54**, 56, 57; elections won by UFWA in, **126**, 126, 165, **166**; ethnic groups in, 106, 188; furniture manufacturing in, 38, 41, 72; GEB exits from, **190**, 190; GEB members from, 66, 118, 236; group consciousness in, 256; locals in, 38, **44**, **45**, 45–50, 151, 157; mechanization of agriculture in, 178; membership dues in, 89; minorities and women in furniture manufacturing in, 156, **180–181**, 181–182, 183, 217; nonmetropolitan areas of, 255; organization of, 42; organizing drives in, 92, 102, 118, 124, 129, 153; per capita tax increases in, 150; raids in, **107**; representation elections in, 167, 198; right-to-work laws in, 40, 124, 159, 167; roll call votes in, 147, **149**, 150, **151**, 152; small locals in, 88, 123; stable voting blocs in, 58;

South—*Continued*
  succession of local union cohorts in, 58; UFWA convention votes in, **63**, **84**, **108**, 109–111; UFWA membership in, 97, **125**, 159, **161**; women workers in, 156, **183**, 213, 217. *See also* southward shifts
South Carolina, 106, 142
Southeast, 41, **98**, 99, 203; furniture workers in, **134**, **136**, **156**; UFWA membership gains in, 97, 99; wages in, 100, **132**, **137**, **161**, 167, **168**; women workers in, 57
South Korea, 162
southward shifts, 40, 217, 237; of furniture factories, 58, 150; of furniture industry, 124, 134, 135, 146, 156, 185, 186, 208, 237, 239, 254; into nonmetropolitan areas, 204, 224; of UFWA membership, 191, 209, 253; of UFWA organizing operations, 25
Southwest, 41, 182, 203; furniture workers in, **135**, **136**, **157**; wages in, **132**, **137**, **161**, **168**; women workers in, 57
spring accessories, 87
Springfield, OH, 140
stability, 21, 60. *See also* leadership
stability, period of, UFWA, 121–123, 158, 188, 238; GEB members in, 24, **25**, **26**; leadership in, 153, 254; membership in, 20–22, 125, 252
status conflict, 2–3, 27–28, 263, 265; in labor movement, 243–244; theory, 250, 259–262; and union leadership change, 244, 248, 250; among workers, 2, 249
stewards, 225, 228, 229, 232
stratification, 4–5, 244, 249, 250; membership, 254, 255, 257; social, 2, 27, 249, 255. *See also* income; working class stratification
strikes, 74, 102, 231; at Dillingham Co., 221; general, 71, 74; at Indiana Desk Co., 162–164; at La-Z-Boy, 172; at Newport Parlor Frame Corp., 71; participation of women in, 210; at Springs Products Co., 192–195, 200; at Thomasville Chair Co., 101
structuralist tradition, 246

Sumter, SC, 48, 50, 99, 111, 203; vote, 190
surveys, 3, 57, 100, 138, 159*n*, 264
suspension: of local 45-B, 82; of Perlow, 82

Taft-Hartley Act of 1947, 22, 93, 103, 115, 130, 153; anti-union intent of, 169; compliance with, 20, **108**, 109–110; constraints imposed by, 21; contributions of, 32, 33, 40, 124, 252–253; jeopardization of UFWA membership by, 112; passage of, 103, 256–257; repeal of, 106, 110, 116; section 9h of, 105, 109; section 14B of, 164
Taiwan, 162
tariffs, 164; to prevent layoffs, 160
tax: institution of, 142; per capita, 89, 147, **148–149**, 150, **151**, 151; per capita, to International UFWA, 169
technological change, 5, 156, 183–184, 239, 255
Tennessee, 112, 142, 203, 224, 226; migrants from, 229; western, **98**, 99
tension, between UIU and AFL, 78
terms of office, 174
Texas, **161**
Third National Negro Congress, 197
third party, 104
Third World, 12, 253, 257
Thomasville, NC, **44**, 48, 111, 197
tolerance, 260–261
training, 32; programs, for officers, 224–225
transportation, 10, 13
Truman Doctrine, 104
turnover. *See* leadership; local union

UFWA: case, 33, 34, 254, 259, 263, 264; Communist domination of, 114; establishment of, 18, 45, 48, 52, 251; history of, 18–19, 197, 251–253, 254; internal administration of, 152. *See also* decline, period of; formative period; stability, period of; specific issues

UFWA constitution, 83, 84, 86, 122, 174, 192; amendments to, 36, 157–158, 170, 173–177, 186, 191; committee, 89; provisions of, 90
UFWA conventions, **108**, 122, 154, **161**, 191–192, 197; Committee on Officers' Report at, 219; local union delegates at, 217; meeting frequency of, 24, 173–174; of 1941, 42, 46, 94, 96–97; of 1943, 107, 113; of 1946, 103, 107, 109, 112–114, 128; of 1948, 36, 103, 104, 107, 114, 118, 195; of 1950, 21, 103, 107, 111, 112, 114–118, **125**, 258; of 1952, 140, 198; of 1953, Eastern regional, 144; of 1954, 146; of 1956, 127, 128; of 1958, 36, 141, 142, 144, 147, 170, 195; of 1960, 142, 143, 144, 147, 150; of 1962, 129; of 1964, 129, 147, 196, 203; of 1966, 143, 186, 187; of 1968, 37, 147, 187; of 1970, **125**, 140, 143, 175, 187, 189, 191, 198, 209, 215; of 1972, 175, 213, 214, 215; of 1974, 175, 191, 199, 215, 216, 220, 230; of 1976, 37, 173, 174, 196, 199, 232; of 1980, 174, 216, 219, 227, 232, 233; of 1984, 30, 50, 164, 174, 196, 199, 227, 228, 233, 237; roll call vote results at, 107, **108**, 109, **148–149**, 150, **151**; vote distribution at, 45–46, 48, 50, **61–63**. *See also* founding UFWA convention
UFWA districts, 92–93, **98**, 99; district 1, 97; district 3, 97; district 4, 215; district 5, 97, 111, 203; district 7, 97, 205, 230–231, 236; district 8, 232, 233, 236; district 9, 111, 203; district 10, 97
UFWA Freedom Fund, 197
UFWA leaders, 154, 185; Communist, 258; first generation of, 199, 205; minority, 156; native-born, of European descent, 239; second generation of, 199–200; top, 199–202, 205–206, 208, 225–226, 237, 239, 258; women, 156, 209, 212, 213–218
UFWA leadership, 27–28, 59, 240–241; emerging groups, 177, 237, 258–259; ethnic integration of, 185, 192–195, 238; incorporation of minorities into, 209; International, 220; positions, 27, 112, 185, 222; top, 192, 223–224, 229. *See also* leadership change
UFWA members, 42, 100, 131, 170; black, 106, 198; Hispanic, 25
UFWA membership, **98**, 118, 154, 252, 254–255; change, 27, **98**; decline in, 156–157, 169–170, 177, 238, 240, 257; decline, reasons for, 22, 157, 253; distribution of, **125**, **161**; efforts to replenish, 139–140; expansion of, 99, 239; gains, 20, 21, 94–97; impact of chains on, 135; jeopardization of, 112, 154, 158–160, 162–165, 257; in locals, **35**, 35; losses, 20, **21**, 133, 134, 153, 158, 167, 257; losses, due to raids, 105, 106, **107**; redistribution of, 42, 124–125, 153, 156, 159, 185–186, 190–191, 209; replenishing of losses of, 173; southward redistribution of, 208; stabilization of, 122–125, 133, 139, 145, 154; trends in, **19**, 20–23
UFWA-UIU GEBs joint venture, 128–129
UIU Journal, 113n
underclass, black, 249
unemployment, 71, 252, 257
unfair labor practices, 163
Union, MS, 171, 199
union: admission, sexually restrictive, 7; captivity, 31, 33, 58; decline, reasons for, 12; membership dues, 88–89, 152, 167; offices, 2, 3, 4; preemption strategy, 130, 131; revitalization of, 155; role of, 259; structure, 15
unionism, 7, 12, 67, 118. *See also* craft unionism; industrial unionism
unionization, 11, 38, 85, 178; CIO, 84–85; discouraging, 130; reasons for, 131; resistance to, 30, 40, 124. *See also* blacks
union members, 3, 12, 250; black, 3, 12, 206; local, 50; pools of potential, 260–262. *See also* GEB members; UFWA members
union membership, 7, 10–12, 254, 255; changes, **151**, 151–152; decline, 12, 177, 208, 253; factionalization of, 250; groups, 257; jeopardization of

union membership—*Continued*
  growth of, 244, 254; local, 20, 33; stabilization, 123–125. *See also* UFWA membership
unions: AFL, 10, 95, 101, 103, 106, 128, 257, 259; CIO 10, 75, 76, 79–80, 101, 103, 105, 106, 257, 259; company, 32; competition between UFWA and AFL, 198; conflict between employers and, 250; International, 144, 186; labor, 249; left-wing, 239; national, 31; non-furniture, 128; role of, 6; Russian trade, 104; split of CIO and AFL, 249. *See also* craft unions; employers
union-shop agreements, 167, 169
United Negro College Fund, 197
unity negotiations, AFL-CIO, 76–78
upholsterers, 73, 91, 93
U.S. census, 211
U.S. Congress, 130
USSR, 103, 104
U.S. Supreme Court, 32, 117
U.S.–USSR relations, 66, 119

value added, **138**, 159
Vermont locals, 143
vice presidents, 92, 146, 204; of GEB, 113, 114; of office of International UFWA, 233; of UFWA, 140, 203–204; western, 233, 236–237; women, 233–234
Virginia, 142
voters: black, 256; Jewish, 254, 256
votes, 14, 258, 261; allocation of convention, 58; distribution of convention, 45–48, 50, **51**, 60, **61–63**, 190–191; distribution of, at founding UFWA convention, 83, **84**; GEB, 236–238; roll call, 116, 174; roll call, results, 107, **108**, 146–147, **148–149**, 150, **151**; shares of, 55; southern, 190; western, 191. *See also* elections
voting, 82, 190–191; behavior, 150–152; constituencies, 30, 34, 59–60; results, **108**, 109–111
voting blocs, 57, 59, 254–256, 258, 261; geographical-ethnic, 145–146, 152–154; group consciousness among, 255–256; stable, 48, 50, 52, 58
Voting Rights Act of 1965, 213

wage: differential, 131, **132**, 167, **168**, 207; disparity, 5, 134; equalization, 211; freezes, 32–33; gap, North-South, 100, 101; increases, 68, 71, 74, 171–172, 252; rates, hourly, 100, 102, 131, **132**; reductions, 72, 162; standardization, 41, 92, 170
wages, 9, 100–101, 140, 221; declining furniture worker, 133; geographically uniform, 199; production worker, 159, 159n, 162; raising, 100, 102, 130; sex differences in, 211–212; union-scale, 40
Wagner Act of 1935, 9, 11, 20, 32, 73, 251
war-production work, 97
Washington, DC, 76, 107, 207
welfare, 8, 22. *See also* benefits
West: delegates from, 83; elections won by UFWA in, **126**, 126, 165, **166**; GEB exits from, **190**, 190; GEB members from, **51**, **54**, 118, 191; locals, **44**, **45**, 45–50, 138, 151; minorities and women in furniture manufacturing in, **180–181**, 182, 183; relocation to, 124, 134, 156, 159, 186; roll call votes in, 147, **149**, 150, **151**, 152; stable voting blocs in, 58; succession of Hispanics in, 56; UFWA convention votes in, **61**, **84**, **108**, 109–111; UFWA membership, **125**, **161**; UFWA representation elections, **167**; vice presidency candidates in, 236; votes in, 190–191
West Coast, 41, 42, 93, 254; metropolitan areas of, 56; organizing drives on, 92; raids on, **107**; UFWA growth on, 25; women workers on, 57
West Virginia, 142
westward shifts, 40
whites, 187, 197, 199, 213, 218, 224, 254. *See also* men; women; workers
Winston-Salem, NC, 203
Wisconsin, **98**, 99, 232, 233, 236

women: admission of, 7, 8; dual role of, in UFWA, 210; emergence of, on GEB, 155, 157, 177, 209, 237–238; employment opportunities for, 220; entry of, into labor movement, 9, 255; entry rates for, 180; in furniture manufacturing, 177, **179–181**, 179–185, 255; hostility toward, 5–6; increase in numbers of, 58; Latino, 221; in leadership positions, 3–4, 177, 185, 209, 258–259, 264; in low-status occupations, 249; married, 210, 237–238; members of Committee on Minority Affairs, 220; minority support of, 219–222; mobility of, 59; mobilization of, 2, 209, 213, 219–224, 237, 256; mobilization of, in UFWA, 212, 217, 224, 239; nonmarried, 237; participation of, 219–221; serving on GEB, 24, 155, 157, 177; serving on International GEB, 216, 217, 222, 230–232; support of, by top leaders, 223–224; union members, 3, 12, 13, 58, 217, 229; white, 3, 58, 217, 229. *See also* black women; workers, women; specific issues and organizations
women leaders, 209, 213–214, 226–232, 239; development of, 237; share of, 264; training, 224. *See also* candidates; women
women's liberation, 230, 231
women's movement, 12, 177, 214, 256; contributions of, 27
woodworkers, 70, 73, 91
workers, 1, 9–12, 31, 95, 243–244; Chinese and Japanese, 235; craft, 243, 251, 255; foreign-born, 55; Italian and Jewish, 25, 118, 201; low-wage, 243–244, 250; mattress, 71; meetings of, 199; minority, 10, 12, 155–156, 209, 255; native-born, of European descent, 118, 240; non-furniture, 170; non-skilled, 8, 10, 11, 184, 194, 243, 252; non-union, 2–3, 5, 27, 102, 130, 244, 250, 260, 263; from North Carolina, 197; organization of, 81; piano, 87, 145, 226–227; salaries of, 101; semi-skilled, 184; skilled, 8, 225, 243, 251; spring, 118, 192–194; status differences among, 248, 249; unification of, 265; unionized, 23, 38, 265; white, 6, 173, 243, 254. *See also* black workers; furniture workers; specific issues
workers, women, 219–220, 230; emergence of, 6, 156, 243; married, 210; in Midwest, 57, 237; mobilization of, 2, 212, 222; training programs for, 225; unionization of, 10, 12
working class organization, 59–60
working class stratification, 7; theories of, 27, 30, 59, 60, 244, 248–249; theories of, description of, 4–5; view of theories of, 263
working class unity, ideology of, 177, 204, 216; contributions of, 155, 185, 199, 217, 241, 259; originators of, 207–208; perpetuation of, 195, 197, 205; proclamation of, 198, 211, 212, 218–219; promotion of integration by, 192, 193, 237, 239–240
working conditions, 41, 69, 71
working hours, 41, 72
workplace control, 32
work week: length of, 68, 71; reduction, 71
World War I, 32, 68, 253
World War II, 22, 40, 252; fringe benefits achieved during, 100; labor movement growth during, 103, 119, 253; union membership growth during, 10, 97; wage freezes during, 32–33; war-production industries in, 7, 20; women in furniture manufacturing during, 211–212

Name Index

Boldface numbers refer to tables.

Adams Engineering Corporation, 144
Aeolian Piano Co., 145, 227
Allegretti, Nick, 113, 114
American Civil Liberties Union, 72, 163
American Furniture Co., 94
American Seating Co., 105
Anderson, Victor, 85, 88
Apostle, Richard, 5n
Aronauer, Joseph Co., 206–207
Aronowitz, Stanley, 264, 264n
Ash, Roberta, 16, 16n, 245, 245n, 247, 247n, 260n, 261

Backman, Axel, 95
Baden, Naomi, 4, 4n, 264, 264n
Bambrick, James, 7n
Bandler, Richard, 91, 93
Barbash, Jack, 31n
Baxter, Charley, 95
Bemis Manufacturing, 205
Benson, Herman, 16, 16n, 17, 17n, 245, 245n

Berger, Michael, 16, 16n, 247, 247n
Berger, Suzanne, 5n
Bernstein, Irving, 10n, 75n
Billings, Warren, 80
Bingham, Alfred, 72
Binnall, Thomas, 95, 96, 115
Blair, Barbara, 230–231
Blattner, Nicholas, 94–95, 113
Blau, Francine, 179n
Bluestone, Barry, 30n
Bolden, Sharon, 223, 229, 231, 231n, 232, 232n, 233, 233n
Bonacich, Edna, 6, 6n
Borjas, George, 182n
Bost, Elmer, 204
Breakfast Room Furniture Manufacturers' and Assemblers' Association, 74
Briggs, Vernon, 8n
Briggs, Vernon, Jr., 178n
Brophy, John, 76, 76n, 79, 80, 81, 82, 82n, 85
Brown, Leon, 95
Brown, Robert, 111
Bucher, George, 76n, 80, 85, 87, 93, 113, 128
Buckner, Floyd, 122
Burawoy, Michael, 33, 33n

283

Bureau of Labor Statistics, 3, 23, 57, 100, 100*n*, **132**, **134**, 134*n*, **136**, **137**, **156**, 159*n*, **160**, **168**, **179**, 211, 211*n*
Burnett, William T. Co., 215
Bywater, William, 240, 240*n*, 241

Camden Furniture Co., 212–213
Campbell, Louie, 122, 204
Campbell, Rex, 182*n*
Carrion, Enio, 188, 188*n*, 189, 197, 205–207, 220, 222
Carson, Walter, 122
Carter, Jimmy, 164
Cerofeci, James, 96–97, 97*n*
Child, John, 15, 15*n*
Clairmont, Don, 5*n*
Clark, Alzada, 214–215, 221, 231, 231*n*
Clark, Leroy, 112*n*, 188, 188*n*, 189, 199–204, 213, 213*n*, 214, 226
Clark, Paul, 17*n*
Cloward, Richard, 13*n*
Coalition of Black Trade Unionists, 2, 4, 12, 249
Coalition of Labor Union Women, 2, 3, 4, 4*n*, 12, 249, 264, 264*n*
Cochran, Bert, 67*n*, 104*n*, 251*n*
Cohen, Louis, 87, 194
Coleman, James, 14, 14*n*, 246*n*
Collier, Charles A., Jr., 193
Comfort Springs Co., 81
Command Investigations Bureau (CIB), 163
Committee of 6, 82, 83
Committee of 7, 80, 81, 82
Committee on Constitution, 86
Committee on Local Unions, 90, 91
Committee on Minorities, 191, 192, 221
Committee on Minority Affairs, 187, 220
Committee of the Negro People to Aid the Spring Products Strikers, 192–193
Committee to Preserve American Color Television, 160
Cook, Alice, 4*n*, 15, 15*n*
Cornfield, Daniel, 5*n*, 6*n*, 9*n*, 10*n*, 11*n*, 12*n*, 22*n*, 29*n*, 31*n*, 32*n*, 33*n*, 34*n*, 36*n*, 38*n*, 41*n*, 42*n*, 127*n*, 130*n*, 133*n*, 135*n*, 158*n*, 159*n*, 169*n*, 170*n*, 178*n*, 182*n*, 183*n*, 198*n*, 199*n*, 251*n*, 253*n*

Corwin, Arthur, 182*n*
Costello, Emil, 76*n*, 80, 81
Crow, Jim, 110–112, 116
Curtis Mathes Co., 145, 198
Custer, Howard, 93

Daily, Lowell, 200, 205, 205*n*, 224, 231, 236
Dalberg, Helen, 223, 229, 232–233, 234*n*
Daniels, Arlene Kaplan, 4*n*
DeCicco, Michael, 121–122
Dedrick, 163
DeSoto Council, 171, 199
Dewey, Thomas E., 103
Dickenson, Mary, 17*n*
Dillingham Co., 221
Dornbecker Co., 96
Douthitt, Frank, 109, 113
Driver, David, 189

Eagle Chair Co., 70
Eastern Products, 199
Edelstein, J. David, 14, 14*n*, 15, 59, 59*n*, 246, 246*n*
Edwards, Maggie Mae, 189, 212–213, 220, 222, 223
Edwards, Richard, 5*n*, 178*n*, 249*n*, 252*n*, 253*n*
EEOC. *See* U.S. Equal Employment Opportunity Commission
Emerson, Bert, 85
Empire Dinette, 200
Englander Co., 144
Equal Opportunity Committee, 187
Espudo, Pino, 189, 233, 234
Etzioni-Halevy, Eva, 13*n*

Failla, Victor, 93, 94–95
Favorito, Vince, 95
Fay, George, 82*n*
Ferber, Marianne, 179*n*
Finch, Doak, 101
Fink, Gary, 3, 3*n*, 69*n*
Fitzmaurice, David, 240
Flicker, 199
Fligstein, Neil, 182*n*
Fogel, Walter, 178*n*

NAME INDEX

Foner, Philip, 4n, 6n, 7n, 12n, 211n, 212n, 264, 264n
Ford, Gerald, 164
Ford, Harold, 171
Ford Instrument, 240
Form, William, 2n, 3n, 5, 5n, 248n, 249n, 264, 264n
Fort Smith Table Co., 122
Foster, William Z., 67, 67n, 73n
Franklin, Charles, 8n, 9n
Friedman, Samuel, 17, 17n
Fulford, Fred, 93, 116, 117, 121, 141, 146, 169, 186, 188, 189, 202–205, 213

Galenson, Walter, 67n
Gardner Upholstered Furniture Co., 95
General Box Co., 144
General Interiors, 199
General Motors, 231
Germer, Adolph, 85
Gifford, Courtney, 13n
Gilbert, Louis, 92
Gilbert, William, 85n, 114n, 146, 147n
Glad, Louis, 95
Glocker, Theodore, 31n
Gordon, David, 5n, 178n, 249n
Gould, William, 6n
Gouldner, Alvin, 16, 16n, 245, 245n
Great Northern Chair Co., 94–95
Green, Paul, 85, 87, 93, 194
Green, William, 72
Greer, Scott, 264n

Haas, George, 7n
Haden, Etta, 214, 215–216, 223, 231
Hague, Frank, 72
Hannula, Toivo, 95
Harris, Abram, 8n, 9n
Harris, George, 193
Harris Hub, 94
Harrison, Bennett, 30n
Hartmann, Heidi, 5–6, 6n, 249n
Hatch, 75
Hawkins, 163
Hauserman, E.F. Co., 95
Haywood, Allan, 104n, 193
Hedstrom Union, 95
Hemingway, John, 17, 17n, 59, 59n, 247n

Henneberger, Edwin, 183n
Herberg, Will, 13n
Hernandez, Helen, 234
Heywood Wakefield Co., 144
Hicks, Orlandis, 111
Highlander Research Center, 225
Hill, Herbert, 6, 6n, 249n
Hillman, Sidney, 76
Hochstadt, Jack, 71, 92, 95, 115
Hoffmann, Sal, 75–82, 82n, 128
Hough Shade Co., 231, 232, 233
Hounshell, David, 66n
Howe, Irving, 16, 16n
Hoyman, Michele, 4, 4n, 6n, 264n
Hutcheson, William, 70, 78–79
Huttig Sash and Door Co., 144, 198, 199

Illinois Molding Co., 228
Indiana Desk Co., 162, 163, 167
Ivers and Pond Piano Co., 202

Jackman, Mary, 262, 262n
Jackman, Robert, 262, 262n
Jacoby, Sanford, 9n
Jasper City Council, 163
Johnson, Daniel, 182n
Johnson, Herbert, 93
Johnson, R.S., 186, 187
Johnson, Rudolph, 111
Junius Parlor Frame, 71, 72

Kampelman, Max, 67n, 104n, 110n, 115n
Kaslly, Charles, 87, 186
Kay Manufacturing Corp., 144, 201
Ken Craft Co., 234
Kennedy, John F., 164
Kessler-Harris, Alice, 6n, 7n
Kiehl, Earl, 215n
King, Coretta, 171
King, Martin Luther, Jr., 187, 222
Kiss, Joe, 69
Klehr, Harvey, 67n
Kober, Harold, 232n, 234n, 236n
Kobyleski, John, 95n
Kochan, Thomas, 131n, 264, 264n
Kopland, Sylvia, 13n

La Guardia, Fiorello, 193
Lamont, Corliss, 72
La-Z-Boy, 169, 171–173, 199, 229–231
La-Z-Boy Council, 172, 173, 199
Leach, George, 94
Leachman, Ida, 223, 226–227
LeGrande, Linda, $4n$, 264, $264n$
Lehrer, Susan, $8n$
Lembke, Jerry, $17n$
Leners, Mark, $41n$, $135n$, $159n$, $182n$, $183n$, $199n$
Leonard, William, 95
Lester, Richard, $13n$
Lewis, John L., 76, $76n$, 81, $81n$, 89
Lichtenstein, Nelson, $102n$
Lipset, Seymour Martin, $2n$, 14, $14n$, 246, $246n$, 259
London, Meryl, 215
Lorwin, Val, $4n$
Loveridge, Ray, $15n$

McAdory, Mildred, 112, 117
McCafferty, Frank, 95
McCarthy, John, 17, $17n$, 247, $247n$
McCollum, Booker, 188, $188n$, $191n$, 205–207, 222
McCormick, Neil, 146
McDowell, Arthur, $73n$, $76n$
McGee, Willie, 117
McGovern, George, 164
McKersie, Robert, $252n$
Magliacano, Joseph, $114n$, 186
Manista, Robert, $95n$
Manufacturers Association of Grand Rapids, 99
Manzo, Peter, $234n$, 236, $236n$, $237n$
Marcus, Philip, $13n$, $15n$
Marcus, Samuel, 192, 193
Markham, A.L., 88, 93
Marsh, Ernest, 85, 92, 100, 115, 116, 117
Marshall, George, 103, 104
Marshall, Ray, $6n$, $7n$, $10n$
Martin, Roderick, $17n$
Matthaei, Julie, $6n$
Maujer Parlor Frame Co., 72
Meany, George, 129, 186
Memphis Broom and Brush, 225
Memphis Furniture Co., 171–172

Merritt, Bernice, $215n$
Michels, Robert, 13, $13n$, 16, 17, 30, 59, $59n$, 122–124, 154, 175, 243–245, $245n$, 247, 261, 263, 264
Michigan Maple Block, 199
Milkman, Ruth, $4n$, 7, $7n$
Miller, Morris, 113, 114
Miller Parlor Frame Co., 72
Mills, D. Quinn, $252n$
Mondale, Walter, 165
Mooney, Tom, 80
Moran, Austin, $90n$
Murray, Philip, 101, 117
Muste, A.J., 15, $15n$, 245, $245n$
Muster, Morris, 1, 42, 43, 76–78, 80–85, 92, 93, 97, 100, 109, 113, 114, 128, 194, 197

National Association for the Advancement of Colored People (NAACP), 195, 203
National Association of Manufacturers (NAM), 20, 32, 103, 124, 253
National Bedding and Furniture, 225
National Education Association, 4
National Labor Relations Board. See NLRB
National Sleep, 206
National War Labor Board, 102
National Winter Piano Council, 145
Needleman, Ruth, $7n$
Nelson, Anne, $238n$
Newport Parlor Frame Corp., 70–72
Nixon, Richard, 164
NJTCP. See U.S. Department of Labor National Job Training and Counseling Program
NLRB, 9, 11, 20, 22, 32, 85, 103, 105, 163, 164, 173, 193, 256
Northrup, Herbert, $8n$
Nyden, Philip, $6n$, 17, $17n$, $247n$, $264n$

Officers Advisory Council, 113, 114, 119
Osberg, Lars, $5n$

Perez, Fred, 233–237
Perlow, Goldie, 72

Perlow, Max, 68n, 69–71, 71n, 72n, 73n, 74n, 75–80, 82, 82n, 83, 85, 87, 88, 90–92, 97, **108**, 109–111, 113–116, 193, 199–201, 207, 215
Perry, Grace, 96n
Persily, Joseph, 76n, 80, 85, 93
Pfeffer, Jeffrey, 261n
Pierson, Frank, 16, 16n
Piore, Michael, 5n
Piven, Frances, 13n
Pizer, Morris, 69, 71, 75, 76, 78, 80, 82, 83, 85, 88, 89, 91, 93, 97, 100, 104, 105, 110–111, 113–117, 119, 121, 129, 130, 141, 142, 186–189, 198–205, 209, 213
Podgursky, Michael, 252n, 253n
Potofsky, Jacob, 114
Powell, Adam Clayton, Jr., 193, 200
Pratt & Reed, 96
Proudman, Joseph, 76n, 80, 93

Raevsky, Sam, 79
Ramsdell, L.B. Co., 95
Randolph, A. Philip Institute (APRI), 222
Reagan, Ronald, 164, 220–221
Reagan administration, 196
Reich, Michael, 5n, 178n, 249n
Requejo, Cynthia, 223, 233–234, 236–237
Reskin, Barbara, 6n
Roosevelt administration, 9, 252
Ross, Lawrence, 197
Rota, Alfred, 76, 80
Rothschild, Joyce, 245n
Rudd, Willie, 225–227, 227n, 236, 236n
Rustin, Bayard, 171

St. Jean, Rosie, 96n
Salancik, Gerald, 261n
Sanders, Vernice, 221–223
Saposs, David, 67n, 104n
Sayles, Leonard, 29n
Scarbrough, Carl, 122, 164n, 169, 172, 173n, 186, 188n, 189, 200, 202–205, 213, 213n, 226, 228–231, 233n, 234n, 236n, 240
Schmidt, Fred, 178n
Schutt, Russell, 6n, 17, 17n, 247n, 264n

SCLC. *See* Southern Christian Leadership Conference
Sealy, 199
Sebera, Robert, 233, 236
Seidman, Joel, 13n
Sheflin, Neil, 7n, 10n
Siebert, O.W. Co., 95
Silverman, Solly, 69n, 85n, 114n, 122n, 199–201
Simmons Co., 96, 235–236
Sinclair, Thomas V., 194, 197
Sirota, Alex, 69, 70, 70n, 75, 76, 80, 82, 83, 85, 89–91, 93, 114, 194, 199–201, 205–207, 215
Sloan, Sam, 85n, 93n, 94, 94n, 113n, 115, 115n, 116n, 121, 228–229, 229n, 232
Smith, Golden, 213
Sombart, Werner, 2, 2n, 248
South Bend Toy Manufacturing Co., 116
Southern Christian Leadership Conference, 203
Southern Furniture Show, 162
Spears, Davis, 92
Spero, Sterling, 8n, 9n
Spring Products Co., 192–195, 200, 201
Stack, Andrea, 223, 227–229
Stallworth, Lamont, 4, 4n, 6n, 264n
Stefan, Fred, 96, 96n, 121, 189, 235–236
Steinway Co., 96
Stewart, George, 92
Stieber, Jack, 25n
Story & Clark, 96
Strauss, George, 29n
Sundin, Edward, 95
Sutton, Elmer "Mule," 90n

Tanner, Lucretia, 7n
Tattam, William, 17n
Taylor, Lubert, 96
Teunis, Fredric, 87
Thomas, Robert, 182n
Thomasville Chair Co., 101
Thomasville Furniture Industries, 162
Thomasville Strikers' Relief Committee, 101
Thompson, James, 33, 33n
Tienda, Marta, 182n

Tomlins, Christopher, 103n, 252n
Trojan-Dante Luggage Co., 162
Trow, Martin, 14, 14n, 246n
Troy, Leo, 7n, 10n
Truman, Harry, 103, 104, 117, 252
Tulin, Justine Wise, 72

Ulman, Lloyd, 31n
Un-American Activities Committee, 116
United Uniform Manufacturing Co., 226
U.S. Bureau of the Census, **138**, 159n, **179**, **180**, 184, 184n, 211n
U.S. Commission on Civil Rights, 3, 3n, 6n, 264, 264n
U.S. Department of Labor, 3n, 7n, 11n, **19**, 23n, 57n, 102n, **132**, **134**, 134n, **136**, **137**, **156**, **160**, **168**, **179**; Wage and Hour Division of, 100, 100n
U.S. Department of Labor National Job Training and Counseling Program (NJTCP), 224–225
U.S. Equal Employment Opportunity Commission (EEOC), 186
U.S. Senate Committee of the Judiciary, 73n
U.S. Tariff Commission, 160

Vayer, June, 223, 229–231
Vickery, William, 182n
Villar, Nilda, 164n, 173n

Wage and Hour Administration Board, 85

Wallace, Henry, 103, 104
Ward's Furniture Co., 48, 90
Warman, Oscar, 163
Warner, Malcolm, 14, 14n, 15, 15n, 246, 246n
War Production Board: Furniture Industry Advisory Panel of, 97
Webb, Beatrice, 13, 13n
Webb, Sidney, 13, 13n
Weber, Max, 244–245, 245n, 247, 261
Weinstock, Max, 215
Wertheimer, Barbara, 7n, 238n
Weyerhaeuser, 199
White, Walter, 193
Widick, B.J., 16, 16n
Williams, Adeline, 223, 226, 227, 227n, 234n
Williams, Bonita, 193
Williams, Ken, 215n, 216n, 222
Wilson, William Julius, 178n, 182, 249, 249n
Winter Piano Co., 145
Witt, Alan, 245n
Woodall, 229
Wood & Brooks Co., 144
Wright, Fielding, 117
WROK, 86
Wysocki, Eugene, 95n, 99n

Zahl, Julius, 95n
Zald, Mayer, 16, 16n, 17, 17n, 245, 245n, 247, 247n, 260n, 261
Zide, Abraham, 52n, 67n, 68n, 69, 69n, 70, 70n, 72n, 73n, **74**, 74n, 75n, 76n, 114n, 116n

Index of Unions

Boldface numbers refer to tables.

AFL, 1, 8, 10, 52, 65–67, 70–75, 77–81, 92, 115, 201, 251–252. *See also* Subject Index: unions; specific issues
AFL–CIO, 4, 10, 18, 163, 219; Mississippi State, 222; Union Label Department, 172. *See also* Subject Index: mergers; unity negotiations; specific issues
AFL–CIO Organizing and Industrial Union, 172
Allied Industrial Workers, 145
Amalgamated Clothing Workers, 70, 101
American Federation of Labor. *See* AFL
American Federation of Labor—Congress of Industrial Organizations. *See* AFL–CIO
American Nurses Association, 4
Automobile Workers. *See* United Automobile Workers

Barbers and Beauty Culturists, 101
Boilermakers, 94

Cabinet Section of FWIU, 69, 71, 73
Carpenters, 20, 23, 45, 65, 67, 68, 70, 71, 73, 75, 78, 84, 85, 92–93, 95, 99, 127, **128,** 251
Chefs, Cooks, and Pastry Cooks, 101
Cigar Workers, 101
CIO, 10, 48, 52, 74–85, 89, 90, 92, 103–106, 110–118, 128, 240, 251–252, 258; Industrial Council, 133; New York, 193. *See also* Subject Index: conventions; unionization; unions; specific issues
CIO Steel Workers, 96
Coalition of Labor Union Women, 215–217, 219
Committee for Industrial Organization. *See* CIO
Committee for the Unification of the Trade Unions, 73
Communications Workers, 11
Confederated Upholsterers and Furniture Workers of America. *See* CUF
Congress of Industrial Organizations. *See* CIO
CUF, 128–129; Articles of Confederation, 129

289

Food and Commercial Workers, 11
Furniture Council, 68, 70
Furniture Workers Division of IUE, 157, 253
Furniture Workers Industrial Union (FWIU), 18, 66, 67–74, 115, 121, 251–252

Government Employees, 11

Hotel Employees, 11
Hotel and Restaurant Employees Union, 234

Independent Union of Piano Workers, 144
Industrial Workers of the World, 94
International GEB, 233
International Typographical Union (ITU), 14, 246, 259
International UFWA, 23, 88, 89, 97, 99, 101, 107, 143, 150, 229, 232n. *See also* Subject Index: specific issues
International Union, 23n, 88–89, 142, 174, 187, 194, 196. *See also* Subject Index: specific issues
International Union of Electronic, Electrical, Salaried, Machine and Furniture Workers, **18**
International Union of Electronic, Electrical, Technical, Salaried and Machine Workers. *See* IUE
International Union of Electronic Workers, 202, 205, 253
IUE, 18, 157, 200, 240–241; Furniture Workers, Division of, 253
IWA, **107**

Labor Council for Latin American Advancement, 197
Letter Carriers, 11
Lithographers, 101
local 18 (UIU), 94
local 18B, Chicago (UFWA), 55, 94, 95, 176, 228–229, 232
local 34, Jamestown, NY (UFWA), 99
local 36, Granville, NY (UFWA), 143

local 37 (UFWA), 113
local 44 (UIU, retail upholsterers), 68, **74**
local 45-B, New York City (UIU), 82, 85
local 75, Baltimore (UFWA), 55, 111, 176, 190, 215
local 75A, Baltimore (UFWA), 190
local 76, New York City (UIU or UFWA), 55, 68, 71, 73, **74,** 74, 83, 90, 91, 94, 111, 121, 144, 176, 188, 210
local 76B, New York City (UIU or UFWA) (furniture woodworking), 73, **74,** 74, 83, 90, 91, 94, 122, 140, 176
local 91 (UFWA), 192, 194, 201
local 92, Newark, NJ (UFWA), 140, 176
local 102, New York City (piano industry) (UFWA), 96, 97, 99, 144
local 103, Buffalo, NY (UFWA), 144
local 108 (UIU, retail mattress), 68, 71, **74**
local 136B, Boston (UFWA), 111
local 136B, Chelsea, MA (UFWA), 144
local 140, New York City (UIU or UFWA), 55, 73, **74,** 74, 83, 111, 116, 188, 190, 205–207
local 154, Gardner, MA (UFWA), 55, 95, 96, 99, 144, 176, 188
local 155, South Bend, IN (UFWA), 93
local 250, Camden, AR (UFWA), 190, 213
local 262, San Francisco (UFWA), 56, 96, 99, 144, 235–236
local 265, Henderson, NC (UFWA), 112, 116, 190
local 270, Fort Smith, AR (UFWA), 90
local 272, Guthrie, OK (UFWA), 171, 172
local 273, Sumter, SC (UFWA), 56, 99, 116, 190
local 276, Florence, SC (UFWA), 169, 172, 190
local 281, Fort Smith, AR (Ward's Furniture Co.) (UFWA), 90, 171
local 282, Memphis, TN (UFWA), 56, 99, 111, 144, 162, 171, 176, 190, 202–203, 225, 227
local 284, Martinsville, VA (UFWA), 99
local 286 (UFWA), 101
local 290, Logan, OH (UFWA), 144
local 305, Batesville, IN (UFWA), 99

INDEX OF UNIONS **291**

local 331, Jasper, IN (UFWA), 99
local 334 (UFWA), 162
local 335, Tell City, IN (UFWA), 99
local 379, Union, MS (UFWA), 171
local 382 (UFWA), 221, 222
local 383, Canton, MS (UFWA), 171, **190**
local 384, Birmingham, AL (UFWA), 144
local 386, Marion, SC (UFWA), 144
local 396, Russellville, AR (UFWA), 171
local 397, Little Rock, AR (UFWA), 171, 172
local 415, Grand Rapids, MI (UFWA), 56, 99, 113
local 416, Monroe, MI (UFWA), 172, 229, 230, 231
local 420, Ionia, MI (UFWA), 56
local 450, Cleveland, OH (UFWA), 55, 95, 99, 140, 144
local 451, Columbus, OH (UFWA), 140, 144
local 452, Fostoria, OH (UFWA), 144
local 453, Springfield, OH (UFWA), 140
local 466, Gettysburg, PA (UFWA), 99
local 472, Hagerstown, MD (UFWA), 99
local 496, Bloomington, IN (UFWA), 85
local 569, New York City (Carpenters), 68
local 576, Los Angeles (UFWA), 56, 85, 96, 99, 116, 117
local 707, Rockford, IL (UFWA), 144, 232
local 800, Sheboygan, WI (UFWA), 55, 99, 176, 188, 205, 232, 236
local 801 (UFWA), 231–233
local 1010, Los Angeles (UFWA), 56, 117, 144, 191, 233, 234–235
local 1057, New York City (Carpenters), 68, 70
local 1090, Portland, OR (UFWA), 56, 96
local 1204 (Carpenters), 68
local 1608, Chicago (UFWA), 94–95
local 2035, New York City (Carpenters), 68

Machinists, 144, 145, 235
Marine Cooks and Stewards, 101
Mattress Section of FWIU, 69, 70, 73
Memphis-Little Rock-Oklahoma Furniture Council, 171
Metal Bed Section of FWIU, 69, 73

National Maritime Union, 101
National Piano, Organ and Musical Instruments Council (NPOMI), 145, 160, 198, 202
New York Woodcarvers Association, 68

Painters, 73
Papermakers and Paperworkers, 144
Paperworkers, 105
PATCO, 164
Piano Workers Organizing Committee, 96
Postal Workers, 11

Restaurant Employees, 11
Retail, Wholesale Department Store Employees Union, 144

Service Employees, 11
Shoe Workers, 101
State, County and Municipal Employees, 4, 11
Steel Workers, 4, 144
Steel Workers Organizing Committee, 85

Teachers, 4, 11
Tennessee Labor Council, 214
Textile Workers, 141, 172
Trade Union Educational League. *See* TUEL
Trade Union Unity League. *See* TUUL
TUEL, 67, 69, 70
TUUL, 18, 66, 67, 69, 72–73, 115, 251

UAW, 4, 16, 20, 85, 99, 105, 106, **107**, 144, 205, 229
UBC. *See* Carpenters
UE. *See* United Electrical Workers

UFWA, 1, 2, 15, 18–19, 33, 45, 48, 59, 86, 197, 251–254. *See also* Subject Index; International UFWA; UFWA conventions; UFWA leadership; UFWA membership; specific issues
UFWA National La-Z-Boy Workers Council, 172
UFWA Rank and File Committee for CIO, 115
UIU, 18, 20, 21, 23, 45, 47, 72–80, 82, 85, 88, 93, 95, 113, 128, 206. *See also* Subject Index: autonomy; local unions; raids; specific issues
UMW. *See* United Mine Workers of America
United Automobile Workers. *See* UAW
United Electrical Workers, 101, 104, 240
United Farm Equipment Workers, 104
United Furniture and Allied Trade Workers' Union, 95
United Furniture Workers of America. *See* UFWA
United Hebrew Trades, 70
United Mine Workers of America, 20, 89–90
Upholsterers, 65, 66, 67, 84, 127, **128**, 251, 256–257
Upholsterers International Union. *See* UIU
Upholstery Section of FWIU, 69, 73

Vermont-Granville Joint Board, 143

Women's Activities Division of AFL–CIO, 214
Women's Organizing Committee, 169
Woodcarvers Association, 72
Woodworkers, 20, 105, 144